EXPERIMENTS WITH POWER

CLASS 200 | NEW STUDIES IN RELIGION

EDITED BY Kathryn Lofton AND John Lardas Modern

EXPERIMENTS WITH POWER

Obeah and the Remaking of
Religion in Trinidad

J. BRENT CROSSON

The University of Chicago Press
Chicago and London

The University of Chicago Press, Chicago 60637
The University of Chicago Press, Ltd., London
© 2020 by The University of Chicago
Published 2020
Printed in the United States of America

29 28 27 26 25 24 23 22 21 20   1 2 3 4 5

ISBN-13: 978-0-226-70064-9 (cloth)
ISBN-13: 978-0-226-70548-4 (paper)
ISBN-13: 978-0-226-70551-4 (e-book)
DOI: https://doi.org/10.7208/chicago/9780226705514.001.0001

Library of Congress Cataloging-in-Publication Data

Names: Crosson, J. Brent (Jonathan Brent), author.
Title: Experiments with power : Obeah and the remaking of religion in Trinidad /
    J. Brent Crosson.
Other titles: Class 200, new studies in religion.
Description: Chicago ; London : The University of Chicago Press, 2020. | Series:
    Class 200, new studies in religion | Includes bibliographical references and
    index.
Identifiers: LCCN 2019052057 | ISBN 9780226700649 (cloth) | ISBN 9780226705484
    (paperback) | ISBN 9780226705514 (ebook)
Subjects: LCSH: Obeah (Cult)—Trinidad and Tobago—Trinidad. | Trinidadians—
    Religion. | Religion and sociology—Trinidad and Tobago—Trinidad. |
    Justice—Religious aspects.
Classification: LCC BL2532.O23 C76 2020 | DDC 299.6/7—dc23
LC record available at https://lccn.loc.gov/2019052057

⊚ This paper meets the requirements of ANSI/NISO Z39.48-1992
(Permanence of Paper).

For Dalila
And for Vita, whose spirit brought us together

―――――――――

CONTENTS

PREFACE

In many ways, I did not want to write a book about obeah. After all, the long-standing criminalization of obeah had marked "Rio Moro," a pseudonym for the place in rural southern Trinidad where I have spent a good part of the past fifteen years, as a backward place of superstition. And backward was not the direction that those whom I have come to love wanted to go. The first time I arrived for a long-term stay, Papoy, the man who has become a second father to me, told me to set down my backpack and then declared that we were going to his garden. "Forward ever, backward never!" he exclaimed, quoting Maurice Bishop, the Grenadian revolutionary leader who was tragically killed in a series of events that ended with the US invasion of Grenada in 1983. Moving forward, however, meant taking off our shoes. With his cutlass (machete) in hand, Papoy scaled the impossibly steep slopes of his garden, which had become a slippery mud paste in the rainy season. Following his lead, I took off my shoes to get a better grip. Later, he told me that he had let me stay by him only because I had been willing to move forward barefoot.

While many Trinidadians might see Papoy, a barefoot, dreadlocked Rastafarian who was extremely poor by Trinidadian standards, as a vestige of the past, he was resolutely forward looking. Papoy saw small-scale farming as the future, not the oil and gas that drove Trinidad's economy. Like many Rastas, his attitude toward obeah was derisive, often echoing colonial views of the practice as backward superstition. Nevertheless, he claimed to be fully capable of practicing it. If a couple came to him with marital strife, he told me, he had a foolproof spiritual "experiment" to treat their problems. He would give them some holy water and instruct them in its use. Every time they began to quarrel, they would have to put some of the holy water in their mouths and keep it there for five minutes. In this way, Papoy

FIGURE 0.1. Papoy and his grandson watching the helicopters land. Photograph by the author, 2010.

avowed sarcastically, they could vanquish the negative spiritual forces that their neighbors had sent to destroy their relationship.

When I started long-term field research, I thus perceived obeah as something that people in Rio Moro—who were often stigmatized as backward and superstitious in the national imagination—wanted to distance themselves from, whether through humor, disavowal, or outright condemnation. I wanted to focus on the questions of justice, police brutality, and socioeconomic inequality that I saw as more pressing concerns for my lower-class interlocutors in Trinidad. Even as national newspapers fixated on the alleged role of obeah (or "witchcraft," as they also called it) in episodes of "demonic possession" at the local secondary school, the area's lack of piped water service and the military occupation of Papoy's village went largely unreported. Police and military helicopters used the community's only playing field as a landing pad, from there flying into the hills where people farmed to burn swaths of cultivation and carrying back large containers filled with marijuana. "They chop the best [marijuana]" for their own uses, it was explained to me, "and they burn the rest." The media frenzy around the alleged obeah in Rio Moro served only to reinforce the rural area's marginalization, implicitly authorizing state violence against a "backward" region.

It was the force of the dead, however, that changed the attitudes of both Papoy and me toward obeah. Like many stigmatized terms for African-identified religious practices, "obeah" is associated with the powers of the dead, or *jumbies* (the Kongo-inspired Trinidadian word for spirits of the dead). When the police killed two young women and one young man in Rio Moro, the talk of obeah and the powers of the dead permeated the community's calls for justice. This tragedy opened up for me a new way of seeing obeah as a technology of justice-making, and it began a yearslong process in which I interviewed and accompanied "spiritual workers" in Rio Moro. Spiritual workers involved in responses to this police violence spoke about their work not as frivolous superstition but as "science" or "experiments." Using the very terms that epitomized forward-looking progress in narratives of modernization, spiritual workers placed obeah resolutely within present and ongoing concerns of justice.

For Papoy, his own change in attitude came with the death of his wife, Vita. In the wake that took place on each night following her death (as was customary) and was accompanied by drumming, he danced with Vita's spirit. While this was happening, I was inside working on the eulogy that I had been charged with writing, but the shouts that accompanied a crescendo in the drumming in the predawn hours called my attention. I saw Papoy bent at the waist dancing with his arms folded across his chest, and I felt what was happening before anyone told me that he was dancing with Vita. As dawn broke, the drummers and the grave diggers piled into the back of a pickup truck, beating the drums all the way to the cemetery. As we took turns digging her grave with a single shovel, my friend Ratty turned to me and said, "I don't believe what the preacher and them say. When you dead, you doesn't go away to some other place. You does stay right here on earth." After all, Ratty was here at the grave site, he told me, because Vita had entered his dreams that morning to wake him up.

Papoy always told me that, when it came to religion, he did not believe until he "experimented." As Vita continued to visit him and to make things happen for him, he told me that he was turning from the Protestant Christianity of his youth and the Bible-based Rastafarianism of his recent years toward "an African way of being." Rather than a recognized religion, this "way of being" was defined by the very thing that had stigmatized obeah as a malevolent practice—the active presence of the dead in the world of the living. This book is thus animated by the dead, in particular by the spirits of Vita and one of the victims of the police shootings (known as Arlena in these pages). In many ways, I am still not sure of all that obeah means. But I know what obeah has done, and if obeah can signify living with the powers of the dead as both afflictions and allies, then this work is a result of obeah.

FIGURE 0.2. Ratty (the corner-store mural behind him depicts a Rastafarian version of the Last Supper, with Haile Selassie I replacing Jesus). Photograph by Olivia Fern, 2011.

Of course, it is not simply the dead but also the living that have made this work possible in countless and unquantifiable ways. I owe a great debt to my partner Dalila Jazmin Loiacomo and to my family (Susan, Bruce, and Courtney, most especially), for all of their support in the difficult process of writing. In Trinidad, Papoy, Vita, and their daughter, Giselle, became a second family to me. It is hard to fathom how much has resulted from our relationship. Papoy married my partner and me in Trinidad. Giselle now runs the sustainable farming program we all cofounded, hosting both local and international groups on the farm. As I write this, she is being interviewed on national television in Trinidad for her efforts in providing an example of an alternative livelihood there. Roofs, retaining walls, burials, and farm tools have been ongoing collaborative projects that have kept us connected across the distance between Texas and Trinidad. Giselle's two wonderful sons—Jahshell and Daniel—were continual inspirations during field research and the many subsequent visits. Jahshell is the only adolescent I know who drives tractors and large trucks, working on his own as a produce vendor in the closest city's vegetable market. Giselle's husband, Ancil, is also a friend and, as a master mechanic, was a great help in times of need.

Ratty was my liming partner for field research, and I learned about dreams, fishing, and Shango through conversations underneath his tamarind tree. Ratty's sister told me about her Apache true self and her spiritual work across the Nations. Mariella, Lisette, and Mother Jackie were all kind enough to share their time and spiritual wisdom with me in conversations that usually lasted hours. Preacher showed me the ropes of graveyard spiritual work, Philip spoke God's truth if I gave him puncheon, and Roland told me all about Mother Cornhusk and silk cotton trees. Clarence Forde's son, Remy Forde, was kind enough to explain the depths of Trinidad's Kabbalah to me. Eniola and Burton philosophized on African religion over beastly cold Stags during my sojourns in the North. All of those spiritual workers who wish to remain unnamed were absolutely essential to the making of this book. Finally, I owe an incredible debt of gratitude to Olivia Fern, who took many of the photographs in this book. A brilliant photographer and artist in Trinidad, Olivia was kind enough to accompany me to Papoy and Vita's community and put up with the many hardships of field research.

There are too many academic colleagues who have aided in this project to name here, and the following list must remain partial. Certainly, this work would not have been possible without the support and friendship of the incredible community of Caribbeanist scholars who have shared the better parts of academic work with me. In Trinidad, Alexander Rocklin shared rotis, Hosay celebrations, and archival research sessions. My Fulbright colleagues, most especially the photographer Gigi Gatewood (whose photographs also appear in this book), were road warriors and collaborators. At Caribbean studies conferences, Kyrah Daniels, Louis Römer, Rachel Cantave, Ryan Jobson, Omar Ramadan-Santiago, Stephanie Jackson, and Sabia McCoy-Torres have all been invaluable companions, conversation partners, and liming allies. I owe a special thanks to the Institute for Gender and Development Studies at the University of the West Indies (UWI) in Trinidad for being kind enough to host me and make my research possible there. In particular, Gabrielle Hosein has been an incredible conversation partner at UWI. Daurius Figueira, Maarit Forde, Patricia Mohammed, Rhoda Reddock, and Brinsley Samaroo were all kind enough to meet with me at UWI. In Santa Cruz, Mark D. Anderson, Donald Brenneis, and Mayanthi Fernando have been immensely helpful. In New York, Aisha Khan was an excellent mentor. Deborah Thomas was kind enough to read a very early version of one of this book's chapters. Leniqueca Welcome offered invaluable feedback. At the University of Texas–Austin, fellow Trinidadianist Lyndon Gill has been a lifeline. In Austin, the Departments of Religious Studies and Anthropology have been extremely supportive and intellectually engaging environments. At UT-Austin, Chad Seales has been a crucial conversation partner. Both the Warfield Center for African and African American Studies and the Teresa Lozano Long Institute for Latin American Studies at UT-Austin have been amazing sources of dialogue and support for my research.

This work has been supported by the Fulbright Institute for International Education, the Mellon Foundation, the American Council of Learned Societies, the Ruth Landes Memorial Research Fund, the University of California–Santa Cruz Department of Anthropology, the University of Texas College of Liberal Arts, the Warfield Center for African and African American Studies, and the Teresa Lozano Long Institute for Latin American Studies. A generous subvention grant from the Office of the President at the University of Texas at Austin has helped defray the cost of publication. The editorial staff at the University of Chicago Press, in particular Kyle Wagner, have also been extremely helpful guides in this process. Finally, parts of chapter 1 were published in the *Journal of Africana Religions*, and smaller portions of chapter 5 and the epilogue were published in the journals *Ethnos* and *Method and Theory in the Study of Religion*.

INTRODUCTION

Well, you see, when you make an offering to the powers, make a guard [talisman], draw a seal, or fix [spiritually protect] a house . . . you are performing an experiment. You are producing some kind of result. Some people call it wanga, some people say obeah. But I call spiritual work experiments.

MARIELLA GRANGER, spiritual worker, Rio Moro, Trinidad, 2011

AN EXPERIMENT WITH POWER

In late 2011, the nation of Trinidad and Tobago was in the midst of a state of emergency that would last 108 days.[1] I had been conducting fieldwork in a region of southern Trinidad that the government had designated as one of the "crime hot spots" subject to a nighttime curfew under the government's emergency policing powers. When darkness began to fall and the streets emptied, I stayed inside the house of the family I lived with and often joined them in watching Trinidad's most popular television program at the time—*Crime Watch*. A kind of vigilante call-in program with a taste for "bacchanal" (drama) and graphic images of violence, *Crime Watch* captured the imagination of a country preoccupied with the sharp surge in murder statistics that had marked Trinidad's entry into the twenty-first century. Although many people pointed out that the government had political motivations for calling the state of emergency (which effectively outlawed any form of public protest), official and popular justifications cast it as a chance to redeem a nation plagued by what government officials had called "marauding groups of thugs," "demons," or "a very obvious moral and spiritual malaise" (see Dhalai 2011; Ramsaran 2013).[2] On the evening following the declaration of the state of emergency, we tuned into *Crime Watch* and saw the police and military load black men from a public housing project into the beds of police pickup trucks as the show's host and local residents looked on in consternation. In total, more than seven thousand people would be rounded up during the 108-day duration of the state of emergency, with the overwhelming majority of them black men from lower-class neighborhoods who were later released for lack of evidence of criminal wrongdoing (see Achong 2018; Ramsaran 2013; Wilson 2018).

It was in the middle of the state of emergency's moral crusade against "thugs" and "demons" that the controversial host of *Crime Watch*, Ian Alleyne, provided some unexpected news that hit close to home. He reported that six of the seven police officers who had recently shot and killed two young women and one young man at my field site had been arrested for murder. Under conditions of martial law, when the normal impunity of the police seemed even greater, this turn of events was unexpected.[3] The police had cast the three young people as violent criminals who were worthy of extermination, and in the fervent anticrime milieu of Trinidad, it seemed that such rhetoric of lower-class black criminality would be used to justify this set of police killings, as it had justified many other fatal uses of police force on the island and across the Americas. In light of the marked improbability of these arrests, Alleyne declared that it must have been "obeah" that caused the police to be charged with first-degree murder. "Obeah" is a complex and hard-to-define term that has contested West African etymologies.[4] Essentially, it is a popular word for the use of what "spiritual workers" call "powers" to solve specific problems, and my field site was known in the national imagination as the epicenter of obeah and African-identified religious practices on the island. In a state of martial law that had rendered protests illegal, the host asserted that obeah still had the power to afflict certain police and force their confessions. In this instance at least, African-identified rites had seemingly trumped the state of emergency's suspension of lower-class black persons' rights.[5]

My field research in Trinidad was marked by this fraught conjunction of obeah with moral and legal crusades against African-identified persons and practices. In 2010, when I arrived for my long-term research, Rio Moro was in the midst of an episode of "mass demonic possessions" and Pentecostal/charismatic "spiritual warfare" that pitted born-again Christian crusaders against the perceived violence and atavism of obeah (see chapters 1 and 6). Indeed, obeah was popularly associated with harm and immoral-ity, and my field site's reputation for obeah produced ambivalent responses among residents. Initially, I envisioned my project as showing that obeah was a religion. Since I thought that religion (at least in its proper forms) was exclusive of harm, I anticipated that this move would morally vindicate obeah from these ambivalent popular associations. Like other scholars and cultural activists, I conceived of these associations as the product of obeah's long-standing colonial and postcolonial denigration and criminalization. Obeah was a crime in Trinidad until 2000 and remains a crime in much of the anglophone Caribbean.[6]

Yet in the aftermath of the horrific police shootings at my field site and in the midst of the state of emergency, the moral terms of obeah's connection to harm seemed to be inverted. The potential violence of obeah was a force that could afflict wrongdoers and force confessions when a racist and classist criminal justice system failed to take action. "If [state] justice does not take its course," as a family member of the slain victims told me a few days after the police shootings, "obeah will." This talk of obeah's afflicting force as an alternative source of justice produced some confusion for me and my project of redeeming obeah from harm, and I wanted to know more about how spiritual workers involved in the rites to redress police violence felt about this work. A few days after hearing the news of the officers' arrests, I thus made my way to the house of a spiritual worker named Bishop Kerron Dawes (Bishop being his title within the Caribbean's Spiritual Baptist tradition).[7] Dawes had been the "spiritual father" of Arlena, one of the female victims of the police shootings, and residents in Rio Moro told me that he was involved in the "obeah" that was seeking justice for the deaths.[8]

I found Dawes in the living room of his board house on stilts, kneeling in front of a large tapestry of the elephant-headed Hindu power known as Ganesh, lighting *deyas*—the candles set in a small clay dish that are perhaps the most iconic symbol of Hinduism in Trinidad. Next to his altar to Ganesh sat an altar to the African-inspired Orisha deity known as Ogun in Trinidad and many other parts of West Africa and the Americas.[9] In the opposite corner, a banquet table with formal place settings was laid out for the powers of the Afro-esoteric practice called the Trinidadian Kabbalah, with the room's remaining corner reserved for an altar to the "Chinese powers" and to the Virgin Mary. In a single room, Dawes had managed to encapsulate the diverse "sides and paths" of grassroots African religion in Trinidad, which encompassed the traditions of the island's diverse laboring populations (McNeal 2011). After emancipation and the legal end of the transatlantic slave trade, indentured laborers were shipped to Trinidad in

FIGURE 0.3. Detail of an altar in a grassroots Orisha shrine in Trinidad. Jesus joins the South Asian saint Sai Baba of Shirdi, an Egyptian pharaoh, the Hindu god Shiva, and a blue background tapestry for the "Chinese powers" in a shrine devoted to the West African Orishas. In the foreground, the clay dishes of *deyas* sit on a *taria* plate, a popular implement in both Spiritual Baptist and Hindu rites. Photograph by Olivia Fern, 2011.

the late nineteenth and early twentieth centuries, with the largest number arriving from India.[10] Today, in terms of census categories, persons claiming descent from either Africa or India each account for roughly 35 percent to 40 percent of the population (with the remainder falling into the census categories Mixed; Mixed [African and Indian]; White; Chinese; Amerindian; Syrian, Lebanese, or Arab; and Other). Like many other African-identified spiritual workers, Dawes incorporated the traditions of Trinidad's diverse populations into his resolutely African religious practices. As I stood on the threshold of Bishop Dawes's living room, I wondered how the "obeah" that Dawes had allegedly performed in response to Arlena's death fit into this complex mosaic of traditions.

After Dawes finished lighting the *deyas*, he rose from Ganesh's altar and invited me to sit. I began our conversation by mentioning the news of the arrests and the rumors of obeah surrounding them. I asked whether obeah was indeed the "religious tradition" he had used to seek justice for these deaths. After bowing his head for a few seconds, Dawes looked at me and began to answer. "It's not a 'tradition,'" he told me, unsettling the terms in which I had just framed his spiritual work (and my hoped-for vindication of obeah). "It's, uh, what is the correct word?" he asked rhetorically, pausing to search for an elusive alternate term. "Some people might see what I do as evil, but that child was murdered and the police officers thought to themselves they could get off scot free. No, that's not justice! In these cases there are specific things you can do, but it's not a tradition. . . . It's an experiment with power. It's what they does call 'high science.'"

As other spiritual workers in Trinidad had done over the decade of my field research there, Dawes unsettled common assumptions about what constitutes a religious tradition when he described his work. In the face of pernicious associations with "evil" and "black magic," I came to my conversation with Dawes and my research in Trinidad wanting to defend obeah as a religious tradition. Yet Kerron Dawes's words (and those of other spiritual workers) seemed to reverse the terms of this redemptive project. Rather than making obeah into a religion, they made me ask how spiritual work challenged the hegemonic limits of the category of religion itself. They often did so by using terms associated with "science" rather than "religion" or "tradition" in Western understandings. Against accusations of "evil" based in the assumed moral and racial limits of religion, they asserted the right to experiment with power.

When other academics ask me what I do, I often tell them that I study obeah—a criminalized religious practice in the Caribbean. The reactions to this description inevitably raise similar presuppositions to those I brought to my conversation with Dawes. Obeah must look like what most people think of as religion—a system of beliefs with a well-defined constituency of avowed adherents, shared ethical injunctions, a distinctive pantheon or prophet, and public places of worship. Obeah might thus find its place among the mosaic of traditions in Bishop Dawes's living room or in a world religions textbook. Yet grassroots, African-identified spiritual workers do not usually identify publicly as practitioners of obeah, even though they often adopted the term to describe their problem-solving practices in private conversations with me. They considered themselves followers of one or more of the three principal "paths" of African religion that spanned Dawes's living room: Orisha, the Caribbean Spiritual Baptist faith, or the Trinidadian Kabbalah (with potential Hindu or Chinese "sides" to these paths) (see McNeal 2011). There was no designated obeah altar in this complex array of traditions, even as all of these altars could raise accusations of obeah in the anglophone Caribbean.[11] Nor were there temples, organizations, or churches of obeah, and (as I detail in chapter 3) obeah challenges the common idea that religion is a practice of making individuals into the subjects of an ethical

tradition, a notion that has been central to scholarly critiques of the category
of religion itself.[12] Instead, spiritual workers insisted on other things. Obeah
is associated with harm as well as healing. Obeah more often signals hidden power rather than public displays of its practice, and—as Bishop Dawes
himself suggested—obeah is also more like what most people conceive of as
science or experimentation than a religious tradition.

At first it seemed simple enough to explain away each of these points
of contrast between obeah and regnant ideas of religion as the result of
colonialism and obeah's criminalization. First, obeah's association with
harm could simply be a result of widespread colonial representations of
sub-Saharan African religious practices as diabolical black magic or witchcraft. Indeed, such representations were often the basis for European assertions that the West and Central Africans who were enslaved in the Americas
did not innately possess religion, moral reason, or civilization. Within this
moral and racial hierarchy, obeah became a harmful superstition, warrant-
ing state policing rather than the liberal tolerance granted to religious matters of conscience. Second, the idea that obeah involves hidden power rather
than public confessions of faith could be attributed to the criminalization
of obeah and the need to hide its practice from the police (see, e.g., Castor 2017, 60). Finally, the notion that obeah is science might be interpreted
as an attempt to garner legitimacy for it, camouflaging stigmatized African practices in authoritative Western garb. Instead of the Catholic saints
who scholars and practitioners have read as cloaking West African deities
with "religion" in the Americas, it was "science" that cloaked obeah with
legitimacy in this interpretation (see Herskovits and Herskovits 1947; Hogg
1961; Littlewood 1993). Extending this narrative of masking, one could read
obeah as pretended science, echoing the long-standing scholarly idea that
non-Western "magic" is simply "false science"—an amoral pursuit of mastery over nature that fails to achieve the understanding of Western science
or the ethical values of religion (see Frazer 1922; Tambiah 1990; Tylor 1871).

Certainly there is much to be said for the story of obeah's exile from
hegemonic ideas of religion. The idea that enslaved sub-Saharan Africans
did not possess religion (and thus did not possess innate moral capacities
in the absence of either white governance or the right kind of Christianity)
has set the limits of moral citizenship and legal rights in modern nation-
states (e.g., P. Johnson 2011; S. Johnson 2004; Sehat 2011; Weisenfeld 2007).
Yet by using language associated with science, spiritual workers were not
simply vying for legitimacy in the face of these exclusions. Nor was their
talk of obeah's power to harm simply a reflection of colonial representations

of African practices as negative foils for religion proper, moral subjectivity, and modern Western science. Indeed, I began to understand that obeah *was* about cultivating an ethics of justice (but this cultivation, as we shall see, was not virtuous in the ways that ideas of religious ethics or liberal ideals of law often assume). I came to recognize that spiritual workers were elaborating an alternate theory of the relationships among religious practice, experimentation, justice, and power. This theory redrew the moral and racial limits of the category of religion. I then realized that my original project of legitimizing obeah as a religious tradition was simply reinscribing those limits, revaluing obeah under the racial terms that separated religion from obeah in the first place. Rather than searching spiritual workers' descriptions for colonial discourse or legitimizing motives, maybe it was time to take my interlocutors at their word and consider religious practice an experiment with power.

RELIGION'S SHADOWS

My own research project thus changed significantly as a result of spiritual workers' theorization of their practices. Initially, I felt that documenting obeah as a religious tradition—in the ways that this category is legible in most modern nation-states—was the best bet for revaluing obeah and decriminalizing it across the region. Obeah, however, remains illegal in much of the anglophone Caribbean, and strong efforts to decriminalize it under constitutional protections of "religious freedom" or "conscience" in Jamaica or Antigua and Barbuda have been stalled by local claims that obeah is not religion but harmful "witchcraft" or "black magic" (Crosson 2018).[13]

As Diana Paton (2009) has argued, these difficulties in recognizing obeah as a religion (and decriminalizing it in parts of the Caribbean where it remains illegal) stem from the fact that obeah was defined as what was not religion. Religion has been the very epitome of social cohesion, shared tradition, moral value, and communal identity in many scholarly and popular representations, but obeah has represented the exclusions that make this idea of religion possible. Making religion across divergent colonial settings, in other words, meant excluding a wide variety of religious practices described as superstition, magic, witchcraft, or obeah. These words all bear different, though often overlapping valences (e.g., Evans-Pritchard 1937; cf. West 2007), but they all show how the separation of secular power and religion was enacted through the exclusion of "superstitions" from both sides of

the secular-religious binary (Crosson 2018; Josephson-Storm 2018). Instead
of joining a host of recent studies that focus on the dialectic of religion and
the secular, *Experiments with Power* shows how the race-based exclusion of
African-identified practices from both sides of this dialectic was a foundational act in the making of religion and secularism as modern "universals"
(see Long 1986).

[handwritten margin note: excluded from both sides religion × secular]

This exclusion of obeah from the category of religion was often framed
in terms of pervasive (if contradictory) attempts in the global project of
Western modernity to separate religion from power. In this reckoning, tolerable or true religion is distinct from both "secular" power (i.e., politics,
science, labor discipline, or law) and "supernatural" power (i.e., superstition, magic, or witchcraft) (Asad 1993; Cavanaugh 1995; Josephson-Storm
2018; Rocklin 2019). Initially, the institutional authority and ritualism of
the Catholic Church was the target of Reformation invectives against the
improper mixing of power and religion (Orsi 2006). Over the course of
the Enlightenment and the eighteenth century, the center of gravity for
such European invectives shifted to sub-Saharan Africa (Johnson 2011).
Coinciding with the explosion of transatlantic slavery, such denunciations
separated Enlightenment ideals of religion from African (not-)religion.[14]
Amoral, interested in power, wed to materiality, and potentially violent,
African "fetishism," "obeah," "witchcraft," or "black magic" became the
prime counterexamples that the best-known Enlightenment thinkers, including Hobbes, Bodin, Locke, Brosses, Hume, and Kant, used to define
proper religion as a domain of moral reason, voluntary assent, and conscience (see Buck-Morss 2000; Latour 2010; Johnson 2011, 2014a, 2014b).

Just as these Enlightenment ideas of African (not-)religion were con-
gealing, obeah was first criminalized as an organizing force in the largest
slave rebellion of the eighteenth-century British Caribbean — Tacky's Rebellion or the Coromantee War of 1760.[15] As anti-obeah laws spread across the
post-emancipation Caribbean in the nineteenth century, this criminalized
practice came to be defined as what religion-as-conscience was not supposed
to be: an "assumption of supernatural power" that aimed to harm or take
advantage of others for monetary gain (e.g., *Laws of Trinidad and Tobago*
1884). Because tolerable religion remained supposedly separate from the
realms of juridical power and labor, obeah's assumption of power to make
money (or to enact punitive justice) was criminalized in post-Emancipation
colonial laws as fraud or vagrancy (Paton 2012). The idea that obeah and
other African-identified practices were based on the assumption of power
was a foil that sanctified Western liberal theories of religion (and state

power) through what Paul C. Johnson (2011, 398) has called a "labor of the negative."

Obeah played a central role in this immense post-Reformation labor of separating religion from the assumption of power. Yet, paradoxically, this work of religion-making has continually undergirded violent projects of state power, helping determine who does not possess proper religion or moral discipline and is therefore in need of governance, punishment, or reform. The colonial persecution of obeah and the 2011 state of emergency's professed exorcism of lower-class black "thugs" and "demons" are but two examples of the violence authorized by the moral and racial limits of religion. Many middle-class Trinidadians, irrespective of racial or religious affiliation, justified their desires for increasingly harsh action against criminalized domestic populations—even summary execution—with well-worn invectives against the lack of moral discipline that lower-class blackness allegedly epitomized.[16] Echoing British colonial discourses on the limits of civilization and respectability, these invectives were often justified through allegations of New World Africans' loss (or lack) of their own religion (see also Fanon [1952] 1986; Forde 2018; Hall 2002; Welcome 2018; Wilson 1973). These moral-racial discourses, of course, are far from particular to Trinidad or the Caribbean. Notions that black persons are somehow "demonic" or that African-identified religion is really diabolical witchcraft have also played key roles in justifications for contemporary police shootings in the United States, imperial incursions in the Caribbean, and violence against African-inspired religions in Brazil.[17]

The criminalization of obeah thus reveals a broader contradiction between a definition of religion that transcends power and the ways that this definition has authorized state violence and policing. Just as Mayanthi Fernando (2014) has argued that the violent contradictions of liberal secularism (between stated aims of tolerance and continuing exclusions) are deferred by projecting this violence onto religious and racial others, these contradictions of religion-making have been continually displaced onto African (not-)religion. Such acts of deferral mean that we cannot pursue these contradictions through idealized recuperations of "good," "liberal," or "lived" religion. Echoing Talal Asad's (2003) insistence that secularism be pursued through its "shadows," Experiments with Power argues that religion must also be pursued through what it excludes rather than through its recognized representations.

Because the limits of religion continue to be entangled with political contestations and state violence, the deferral of problems with power to

African religions remains a popular trope in contemporary worlds. Dawes and other spiritual workers repeatedly told me that others saw what they did as "evil." The identification of evil with African (not-)religion has been a key part of Western modernity's moral and racial discourse, particularly in popular representations of obeah and "voodoo" for American, British, French, and West African audiences.[18] Like the anti-African invectives of European Enlightenment gentlemen, these contemporary representations draw a good part of their force from pervasive Western distinctions between religion proper (as devotional or expressive) and magic (as an instrumental assumption of power).

Yet rather than embrace the amoral image of "black magic," my inter-locutors elaborated alternate ethical conceptions rooted in the redistribu-tion of networks of power. The proper emic term for this redistribution of power is "spiritual work," and my interlocutors self-identified as "spiritual workers." For grassroots practitioners, all three principal paths of African religion in Trinidad could involve spiritual work—transformative interven-tions of healing, harm, protection, and justice-making that might happen in a one-on-one consultation, a hidden act, or a collective ceremony of spirit manifestation.[19] Instead of using the word "magic," the grassroots spiritual workers I knew were more likely to describe these interventions as "experi-ments" or "science" that employed "powers" to solve specific problems. I came to see how this talk of experiments signaled not a thin veneer of Euro-pean legitimacy but an alternate theorization of religious practice that dif-fered from the moral and racial economy of the magic-religion divide. The pages that follow redescribe religion using this language of science, power, work, and experimentation. The aim of *Experiments with Power*, therefore, is not simply to lay bare the racial limits of the category of religion as a moral foundation for state violence but also to draw on the theories of spiritual workers to go beyond those limits.

OBEAH, LIBERALISM, JUSTICE

Over the past three centuries, illumination of the contours of religion has cast long shadows, ostensibly separating matters of conscience from as-sumptions of power. From eighteenth-century slave rebellions to contempo-rary responses to police brutality, many state officials and Caribbean people have not recognized obeah as religion because it is associated with the use of power to enact retributive justice. In response to resonant invectives against "religious violence" and Islam in the twenty-first century, scholars have often defended religious practice as a matter of piety and ethical subject making whose relationship to violence is baseless, incidental, or reformatory.[20] Throughout the course of modernity, however, assumptions of more-than-human power have undergirded the authority of governments, criminal justice systems, political candidates, and state-sanctioned forms of religion. Certainly, racism goes a long way to explain which assumptions of supernatural power are superstitions and which are patriotic or legally recognized. Yet racial and religious distinctions also work to insulate modern Western ideals of religious or political "freedom" from the coercive power that is integral to such ideals. Throughout this book, I use the term "liberal" as shorthand for these fraught ideals of freedom. I propose that (what gets called) obeah provides the basis for a critique of these ideals, offering ontologically divergent sensibilities of power, religious practice, and justice.

The liberal tradition has its roots in the antisuperstition project of the Western European Enlightenment that first led to the criminalization of obeah, but it is a project of reform that is defined by universal aspirations. Its sacred object is the (prototypically white male) individual, whose agency, conscience, rights, or economic freedoms are defined in opposition to coercive power (whether of centralized religious institutions, governments, or superstitious beliefs). Because the individual must be separable from coercive power, force is rationalized and subjected to the "rule of law," in which law is supposed to protect individual rights and treat all citizens equally. In this idealized view, both law and religion are purified of authoritarian power, with dictatorial rule, superstition, or religious extremism being the property of others whom the liberal West (and its postcolonial proxies) must civilize.

For spiritual workers, these liberal ideals of secular law and religion often oversimplified the ways that spiritual, political, and interpersonal power worked.[21] Because many of my interlocutors did not believe that state law or democratic politics were simply rational systems based in consent (as liberal ideals of governance would insist), obeah was a vital critical discourse about the contradictory and occluded workings of power in their midst. If power functioned as liberal ideals of the rule of law and democracy said it should, then state law and its representatives would work to curb extralegal violence and the police would not have assassinated Bishop Dawes's unarmed spiritual daughter. As I explain in greater detail in chapter 1, while the police claimed to be acting in accord with these ideals during this assassination — by killing dangerous "thugs" who threatened citizen life — others alleged that an organized crime network had paid the police unit to kill the owner of the car that Dawes's spiritual daughter had borrowed to go buy barbecue. Was the death of Dawes's spiritual daughter and her two friends a reflection of the rule of law or of the less-than-transparent relations of power that often contradicted the law's injunctions? Could state law be trusted to punish its own representatives, or was it necessary to engage in hidden power to make justice through obeah?

Power in liberal nation-states and their colonies has thus functioned through violent exclusions, but limited forms of inclusion have also been a part of this power (see Fernando 2014, 19). In what Povinelli (2002, 2011) calls "late liberal" multicultural states, these inclusions of marginalized groups happen through a politics of visibility (rather than substantive rights). The visibility of minoritarian groups (in national holidays, street names, or cultural centers) is privileged as a sign of state tolerance, even as visibility to the state implies the regulation and remaking of difference into commensurable forms. In Trinidad and Tobago, since the late twentieth century, forms of multicultural recognition have partially fractured Afro-creole Christian hegemony in the national culture and political leadership of the postcolonial state. In the 1990s, as the first Hindu political leaders rose to national power, the stigmatized African religions of Spiritual Baptism and Orisha were given small grants of land, forms of legal recognition, and a national holiday (Castor 2013, 2017).[22] This first period of national government led by the so-called Hindu or Indian party also saw the decriminalization of obeah in Trinidad and Tobago (in the year 2000). Yet even as the government (partially) recognized two stigmatized African-identified religions, it has been much harder to make obeah into the kind of religious or cultural tradition that can become a political constituency (and thus an object of state patronage). Indeed, the government rationale for decriminalizing obeah was not that it was an autonomous religious tradition worthy of a land grant or a holiday, but that its criminalization threatened the freedom of the two state-recognized African faiths.[23] Certainly, this contrasting attitude toward obeah reflected the enduring stigmas that the term carried, but it also revealed the radically different orientation to power that (what gets called) obeah implies. While the multicultural state's recognition of religious minorities involves a politics of visibility, obeah signals a politics of hidden power. More than an expressive identity claim, this power addresses the very concerns of justice, rights, and physical protection that state law is supposed to secure in liberal theories of governance.

For Bishop Dawes, a language of hidden power and experimentation, which diverged from liberal ideals of both secular law and religion, was required to express spiritual responses to injustice. Yet precisely because obeah played a crucial role in my interlocutors' articulations of (in)justice, obeah was not unequivocally avowed or morally univalent—an insight that chapters 1–3 explore more fully in order to rethink religion, violence, and ethics. The spiritual workers I know both disavowed obeah as an abuse of power and saw their own work as obeah, depending on the context. Because obeah expresses the hidden reality of power—a reality that produces unjust violence as well as avenues for justice-making—it cannot be unequivocal.

Obeah thus takes us away from "religion" as a matter of moral community, individual conscience, mutually exclusive identities, or ethical subject making. In order to theorize (or generalize) about their practices, spiritual workers used terms that have often played the opposites of religion in Western modernity. Yet rather than reproducing the morally dualistic language of (not-)religion that colonialism bequeathed them, spiritual workers theorized with words that also seemed to defy the racial circumscriptions of black magic, witchcraft, or superstition. In different ways, science, experimentation, and work provided a language to talk about religious practice and the ambivalence of power beyond the moral-racial limits of "religion." This book focuses on that alternate language as a way to retheorize the intertwined categories of religion, race, and justice.

SPIRITUAL WORK, MATERIAL REPERTOIRES, AND AFRICAN RELIGIONS IN TRINIDAD

Between 2006 and 2017, I conducted research with spiritual workers in a region of rural southern Trinidad that I call Rio Moro. Bucking stereotypes of the Caribbean beach destination, Trinidad is an island popularly known as an industrialized, urban society with a developed middle class; it economically depends on oil and gas rather than tourism. In many ways, Rio Moro conformed to neither of these contrasting images of the Caribbean and Trinidad (even as its subsoil was an important source of oil and gas rents for the nation). It possessed no tourist infrastructure but was also marginalized from the more urban-centric image of Trinidad. As I detail, this region was doubly detached from national visions of development by its location in "deep south" Trinidad, far from northern centers of economic and political power, and by its association with obeah.

My longest continuous stint of research with spiritual workers in this region of "deep south" Trinidad took place for twenty months between 2010 and 2012. My interlocutors tended to be lower-class "grassroots" practitioners of African religions. The spiritual workers I knew often reflected a broader grassroots, experimental tendency to pursue all three of the principal traditions of African religion in Trinidad (Orisha, Spiritual Baptism, and the Trinidadian Kabbalah) to varying degrees. It was important to make distinctions between these traditions, for they reflected kinds of power that were good for solving different kinds of problems while also suggesting different kinds of Africas. Orisha (formerly known as Shango) is a religion of spirit manifestation, devotion, and divination inspired in good part by Yoruba indentured laborers who arrived in Trinidad shortly after the British Empire outlawed slavery in 1834 (Trotman 2007). Spiritual Baptism is an Afro-Caribbean Christian movement originating in Trinidad and/or St. Vincent (depending on contested origin stories) whose practices are characterized by rituals of blindfolded spiritual travel (known as "mourning") and religious cosmopolitanism (Duncan 2008; Stephens 1999; Zane 1999). The Trinidadian Kabbalah (also sometimes known as Circle Work) is a practice of spirit manifestation and spirit travel that draws heavily on written and oral knowledge about ancient Egypt, the secrets of Moses and Solomon, and an idiosyncratic array of spiritual "entities" that can manifest in humans.[24]

My grassroots interlocutors who followed all three of these strands of African religion called this orientation "the threefold path." This multisided path did not simply join together religious traditions that are sometimes treated as separable—namely, Yoruba-inspired "traditional religion" (Orisha), autochthonous Afro-Caribbean Christianity (Spiritual Baptism), and esotericism (Kabbalah)—but also joined together different images of Africa and Africanness. Inspired by Stewart and Hucks's (2013) call for scholarship to pay attention to a "proliferation of Africas" rather than an Africa that is "bounded and calcified," I follow my interlocutors' Rasta-inspired biblical interpretation in conceiving of Africa as a "house that contains many mansions" (John 14:2, KJV). In Rastafarian usage, "mansions" refer to the different paths or organizational forms of Rasta living. These mansions are parts of a single house, but they cannot be reduced to a unitary whole (forming something more like an "assemblage" than a single totality).[25] Following this metaphor, Africa is a common house and a bounded physical entity (a continent), but this entity contains complexities and differences that exceed the physical and conceptual parameters of a bounded, unitary form. The house of Africa in Trinidad contains the "mansions" of the "Yoruba-centric" tradition of Orisha, the Egypt-centric hermeticism of the Kabbalah, and the notion of an authentic early Christian Church originating in Africa that Spiritual Baptists espouse.

Like mansions, each of these three African paths is complex and internally divided. Spiritual Baptists committed to transnational norms of Protestant Christianity, for example, might eschew the Orisha and Kabbalistic practices that a great number of other Spiritual Baptists embrace (Stephens 1999). Some Yoruba-centric Orisha practitioners committed to transnational standards of "African traditional religion" might strongly dissociate themselves from the Spiritual Baptist elements typically incorporated into grassroots Orisha ceremonies as colonial Christian impositions, while others embrace or themselves possess a Spiritual Baptist foundation for African practice in Trinidad (Castor 2017; Houk 1995; Lum 2000). Work on Orisha in Trinidad has not usually gone into extensive detail regarding Spiritual Baptist practices, but this scholarship has estimated that at least half of Orisha practitioners are also Spiritual Baptists (Houk 1995, 36), and Castor (2017, 32) asserts that most Orisha practitioners are or were Spiritual Baptists. Looking at any one path of African religion in Trinidad provides evidence of all three paths. Even as they partially overlapped for my grassroots interlocutors, the three paths of African religion in Trinidad might be internally divided or differentiated from one another through appeals to proper tradition and orthodoxy. They are mansions with many rooms that inhabit the house of Africa. This house is not simply a physical continent but also a living practice of various philosophical, ethical, and genealogical conceptions distributed across continents (Castor 2017; Edwards 2003; Stewart and Hucks 2013; Olupona and Nyang 1993).

Most work on African religions in Trinidad has focused on the Yoruba-inspired practice of Orisha, reflecting a broader "Yoruba-centric" (Castor 2017) tendency in postcolonial conceptions of authentic "African traditional religion" (see Henry 2003; MacGaffey 2012; Matory 2001; Shaw 1990). Most of these studies, however, note Spiritual Baptist, Kabbalistic, Catholic, and/or Hindu elements as parts of local Orisha practice in Trinidad—elements that have sometimes caused points of conflict with local and transnational Yoruba-centric authorities (see Castor 2017; Henry 2003; Houk 1995; Lum 2000; Mahabir and Maharaj 1989; McNeal 2011; Reddock 1998). In comparison with Orisha, there has been less work devoted to Trinidad's largest African religion, the Spiritual Baptist faith (but see Duncan 2008; Glazier 1983; Henry 2003; Lum 2000; Stephens 1999). Besides the brief descriptions offered in accounts devoted to Orisha, there has been no extended work on the "secretive" Trinidadian Kabbalah, which has been wrongly categorized as European, following the broader tendency to mislabel certain practices as "Western esotericism" when practitioners often conceive of them as African-inspired (Houk 1995; cf. Finley et al. 2014).[26] Spiritual Baptist ritual repertoires hold these three strands of African religion in tense conjunction, offering modalities of spirit travel across different realms of power that grant the possibility of multiple ethno-religious identities. This travel is enacted largely through the Spiritual Baptists' distinctive ritual of "mourning"—an extended period of blindfolding and fasting that incites the spirit to leave the body and travel in a layered, tripartite topography composed of the Depths, the Spiritual Nations, and the Heights.[27] As the chapters of this book unfold, I explain more about how these partially overlapping "paths" of grassroots African religion in Trinidad materialize alternate conceptions of the relationship among religion, race, and ethics by traversing a topography of contrasting spiritual powers.

Instead of isolating one of these strands of the threefold path, thus producing an object that conforms to modern ideas of religions as mutually exclusive confessional entities or Africa as a monolithic source of primordial tradition, I treat African religion in Trinidad as a lived experiment with power. My interlocutors spoke of the forces that scholars might call "deities" as "powers" with different (often-contested) "sides." These sides were associated with the three different "paths" of African religion, as well as with the Spiritual Baptist Nations of India and China, which are prominent destinations for blindfolded mourners traveling in the "Spiritual Lands."[28] Power, as my interlocutors understand it, cannot necessarily be circumscribed within the notion of "one exclusive 'religious' community *against* others," which, as David Scott (1999, 56) argues, was central to the European management of colonial civil society.

As an accusation or practice of working spiritual power, what gets called obeah could include the Hindu, West African–inspired, Catholic, and esoteric traditions on display in Bishop Dawes's living room. Obeah exceeds a model of religions as mutually exclusive communities, each gathered around their distinct sets of beliefs and rituals. This is precisely the reason often behind the popular assertion that obeah is not a religion: each spiritual worker possesses an idiosyncratic repertoire of practices rather than a standardized creed or fixed set of rituals. Yet a closer look at the practice of any of the "world religions" reveals a heterogeneity of material practices and sources of inspiration. Perhaps because it has been (not-)religion for so long, obeah highlights the need for another model of religious categorization. I suggest that the word "repertoire" can help to furnish such a heuristic.

In the performing arts, "repertoire" refers to both a typical stock of performances and the idiosyncratic skills and sensibilities that make different performances possible for particular actors. The stock material practices that spiritual workers generally share (and that are popularly associated with obeah) are the lighting of candles, the performance of "bush baths," the manufacture of guards or *tabej* (i.e., protective talismans), the "fixing" or "dressing" of physical property, the use of spiritually charged oils, and the recitation of prescribed words to achieve certain ends. As with experimental art or theater, spiritual workers can intentionally violate or invert the conventions of these repertoires, emphasizing the contingency of situations of power rather than their scripted nature. This is precisely the kind of experimentation that Bishop Dawes performed when he transgressed the norms of a good burial for his spiritual daughter to bring her killers to justice, as I detail in chapters 2 and 3.

It is important to note that these stock material repertoires run across confessional lines in Trinidad. The most pervasive sign of obeah is the lighting of candles—particularly candles that are not white, though white candles can sometimes also communicate obeah. It is patently obvious, however, that a variety of religious traditions light candles (or *deyas*) in Trinidad, often with the intention of interceding in one's own affairs or someone else's.[29] "Bush baths" refer to spiritual cleansings performed by bathing someone with water in which various types of "bush" (i.e., medicinal herbs) and/or store-bought essences (like red lavender or Florida water) have been steeped. During my field research, Hindus, Spiritual Baptists, and Orisha practitioners performed cleansings that they all referred to as "bush baths." The manufacture of "guards"—talismans in the form of consecrated necklaces, small bundles pinned to the inside of clothing, bracelets, or rings—was another pervasive part of spiritual workers' repertoire. I also witnessed Hindu pundits and Muslim imams manufacture *tabej*, an Arabic-inspired South Asian word that they equated to "guards." Fixing or dressing physical property involves spiritually protecting automobiles, houses, or gardens, and various forms of Christianity, Hinduism, and African religion achieved this protection in different ways. The use of "sweet oil" (usually olive oil) or store-bought spiritual oils was popularly associated with both obeah and African religions more generally. Yet Pentecostal Christians or

FIGURE 0.4. A spiritual worker has prepared to give a client a bush bath, drawing a spiritual "seal" with white talcum powder and filling a bucket with herb-infused water. A white candle was placed inside the center of the large circular seal, and the client was told to straddle the flame. The spiritual worker watched the movement of the flame to diagnose the source of the client's spiritual harm. The client was then bathed inside the circle, using the bucket and a calabash gourd dipper. The seal drawn in talcum powder is unfinished in this photograph. This particular spiritual worker explicitly allowed me to photograph finished seals and practices with clients (as long as their faces were not pictured). However, I have omitted all such photos from this text as a result of personal judgment about their appropriateness. Photograph by the author, 2012.

Muslim imams (often avowedly opposed to any practice identified as obeah) could also use spiritually charged oils to anoint persons or places (see chapter 5). Finally, the ability to use prescribed words to achieve a certain end (what was often referred to as "prayers") was an important part of spiritual work, with phrases drawn from Sanskritic texts, the Koran, the King James Bible (particularly Psalms), and/or popular esoteric books (most especially *The Sixth and Seventh Books of Moses*).

Because all of these practices can be identified with both obeah and (in colonial terms) various forms of recognized religion, these stock repertoires were usually sites of debate in obeah trials, with defendants arguing that they were engaging in practices that were analogous to or a part of recognizable religious traditions (most particularly Christian ones). Other material practices, such as beating spirits out of someone with a *cocoyea* broom or "tying" a man (i.e., submitting a male lover to one's will), were seldom seen in my field research but are important parts of the performance repertoires that have defined popular representations of obeah in theater and song.[30] Still other material practices, particularly those associated with intervening in court cases, were exceedingly common in my field research but are relatively underrepresented in popular tropes of obeah (e.g., Superville 2018).

Again, taking seriously spiritual workers' use of the word "science" affords a revealing vantage point on (what often gets called) obeah. In rejecting the disembodied universalism of popular notions of science and emphasizing performativity, scholars of science studies have argued that a conception of scientific research programs as "repertoires" can provide a more nuanced account of how experimental projects typically knit together divergent paradigms and disciplines (Ankeny and Leonelli 2016). Similarly, I argue that spiritual work articulates contrasting ethical, religious, and racial paradigms within an experimental, pragmatic ethos that privileges the specificities of the problem at hand rather than the reproduction of mutually exclusive traditions. A problem, such as that which Bishop Dawes faced in the police killing of his spiritual daughter, was a network that cut across not simply distinctions between religious "paths," but also those between state law and religious ritual, sacred and secular, living and dead, and human and nonhuman. "Science," for spiritual workers (and many science studies scholars), denoted not a transcendent universalism but a *situated* practice of *partially* articulating divergent epistemic communities, paradigms, and forms of existence to address specific problems.[31]

science studies — repertoires

POWER, SCIENCE, WORK

Spiritual workers' notions of science, power, and work, however, might differ significantly from widespread perceptions of these terms in liberal modernity. In contrast to secular purifications of religion, "power" was not separate from the quintessential objects of religious devotion for my interlocutors. In fact, "powers" was the common term for entities that other frameworks of religion might render as "deities," "spirits," or "saints." The phrase "catching power" in Trinidad thus refers to what scholars have called "spirit possession." Power is spiritual, political, and interpersonal for my interlocutors, encompassing realms often parsed as "religious" and "secular" in modern nation-states (see Castor 2017; Alexander 2005). Dawes's use of "experiments with power" as an alternative to tradition, therefore, played on this slippage between what would, in Western liberal secularism, be opposed as "religious" versus "political" notions of authority and force. Emerging from a more general intimacy between "rights" and "rites" in Trinidad (Khan 2007), this experimental approach to religion retains a dual focus on both devotion to deities and everyday problems of power relations. "Power" is thus a key and capacious term for African-identified spiritual workers, and it is no coincidence that this notion of power seems to collapse a fundamental moral distinction between instrumentality and religious ethics that has undergirded ideals of liberal secularism in the West. As each of the following chapters details in different ways, this idealized purification of religion from secular power has taken shape against the foil of African (not-) religion's supposed instrumentality and amorality. Spiritual workers' conceptions of power, however, obviate this racial division between ethical religion and instrumental magic—an insight pursued throughout *Experiments with Power*.

Just as "power" defies the purification of the religious from the secular, so too does "spiritual work" defy the separation of public and private, religion and market, or spiritual and material (Alexander 2005). Spiritual work is remunerated labor, and most of my interlocutors made a living from the gifts they received for their work—monetary and material gifts that were usually not demanded or quantified but expected. This monetary gift exchange was a key way in which obeah was criminalized as something other than religion after Emancipation in 1834. Undercover police posing as clients often obliged spiritual workers to accept marked bills as payment be-

undercover cops!!

cause this was evidence of obeah as "fraud" in courts of law (Paton 2015).[32] If such practices could become remunerated work rather than religion, then they could become an illegitimate livelihood grouped under the crimes of fraud and vagrancy that have formed the basis for post-Emancipation anti-obeah laws (see Handler and Bilby 2012; Paton 2015).

Rather than fraud, spiritual work reflects different ways of drawing the relationship of labor, religion, and secular power. Both "work" and "experiment," in contrast to Western ideas of religion as an ethical tradition or a matter of belief, are overtly instrumental; one works to get things done and to make a living. In the Trinidadian English/Creole, the word "work" is also far more capacious than in North Atlantic English. "Work" can refer to dance, obeah, religious practice, transformation, or employment, and my interlocutors often referred to the three primary African religious traditions in Trinidad as "work" rather than "religion" (see Winer 2009).[33] In all of these meanings, no kind of work simply happens by faith alone; transformative material labor and embodied action are necessary (see also Brown 2001).

The use of the word "work" in the pages that follow reflects a dialogical process of thinking through (what gets called) obeah with my interlocutors. Early in my field research, I made a preliminary presentation of my work at a cultural arts center in Trinidad, calling obeah "sorcery." In doing so, I was inspired by other scholarly works that translated the Africana practices of their interlocutors into the oft-denigrated terms of (not-)religion — sorcery or black magic (see Chireau 2006; West 2007). One of the audience members, a practitioner of African religions in Trinidad and a close friend, raised his hand to object to my use of the word "sorcery" on the grounds that it carried some heavy (and derogatory) baggage. After considering his feedback, I decided to follow other scholarship in using the word "healing" as a benign and legitimizing term for African-identified practices.[34] Yet both academic colleagues and spiritual workers often insisted that (what gets called) obeah exceeded conventional notions of healing, leading me to abandon this project of lexical redemption. Both moves of translation wedged African-identified religious practices into Western categories rather than focusing on the ways these practices might present understandings that can "recursively" transform a scholar's categories of analysis (Holbraad 2012). Rather than using terms like "sorcery," "witchcraft," or "healing," it is thus an intentional decision to stick with my interlocutors' own terms "work" and "experiment" in the pages that follow.

As with "power" and "work," the word "science" in Caribbean English

sorcery — healing — obeah

both encompasses and exceeds North Atlantic notions of that term. In contrast with a celebratory discourse of "scientism," which has been used to
validate various forms of religion as "scientific" since the late nineteenth
century, science is no less morally ambivalent than obeah for my interlocutors, and this is one of the best reasons for arguing against the idea that science simply provides a positive and legitimating front for "African tradition"
(see chapter 6).[35] Both "science" and "obeah" signal the use of hidden or
esoteric powers at my field site, and the two words have been synonyms for
at least a century in the English/Creoles of the Caribbean (e.g., Herskovits
and Herskovits 1947; Winer 2009). Because power can never be fully transparent, there is always the potential to misuse knowledge or to employ authority for purposes that are different from their exoteric rationales. This
ambivalence requires constant "work" to balance opposing forces, decipher
hidden powers, and redress problems caused by those powers. Rather than
a triumphal discourse of "scientism," which scholars have described as a
Western project of disenchanting the world and rendering it transparent
(see Gottschalk 2012; Stengers 2012), "science" in the Caribbean redescribes
religion as (at least in part) a "healing-harming" (Ochoa 2010b) engagement
with esoteric power.

While my interlocutors' notion of science differs significantly from
many understandings of scientific practice, it is not out of line with scholarly descriptions of science in the twentieth and twenty-first centuries. One
of the best-known figures in contemporary science studies and sociocul-
tural anthropology, for example, describes science not as the observation of
transparent facts but as the heavily mediated accessing of hard-to-perceive,
"invisible" forces (Latour 2010). Indeed, the idea that science is about a
performative (and transformative) engagement with "occult," or hidden,
powers is a contested theme in descriptions of experimental practice that
runs from the seventeenth century through to the present day (e.g., Asprem
2018; Henry 1986; Yates 1964, [1972] 2013). This does not mean that spiritual
workers draw no distinctions between their own practices and what occurs
in university laboratories. Yet there is obviously an important resonance
between science and obeah that spiritual workers employ to theorize about
their practices.

Following spiritual workers' theories of experimentation means, to
some extent, venturing beyond the theoretical and conceptual lexicon of
scholarly studies of religion. This book thus argues that it is necessary to
cross disciplinary boundaries centered on the post-nineteenth-century
opposition of religion and science (Numbers 2010), drawing on science

studies to reframe the study of religion. Yet in marked contrast with the contemporary "cognitive turn" in studies of religion, the aim of this work is *not* to assert that religion could be studied as an objective, universal phenomenon with millennia-old origins in "hardwired" biological predispositions (e.g., Geertz 2013; Tremlin 2010). Rather than arguing for some kind of bio-cognitive basis for religion that would then make it "scientific," "natural," or transhistorical, I draw on critical studies of science that have long questioned the very idea that science simply describes and explains preexisting natural facts. In reality, this bio-cognitive approach to religion reproduces a colonial endeavor, in which Western (usually male) scholars are the scientists who present a disembodied, objective view on natural truths. Instead, I draw on the approaches of feminist science studies, in which experiments are performative interventions that alter or remake relational worlds rather than exercises in presenting a "God's-eye view" of preexisting objects (Barad 2007; Haraway 1991; see also Putnam 1990). In other words, to experiment is to interfere in the world rather than to simply peer at phenomena from a distance (Hacking 1983). As a transformative intervention, experimentation is, therefore, not a morally neutral act (Barad 2007).

This approach to experimentation resonates with recent work on African religions that has used feminist performance theory to understand religious practices as more than simply ritual reproductions of idealized sacred orders and ethical norms. Against pervasive representations of both Africa and religion as sites of tradition that focus on such repetitive rituals, Yolanda Covington-Ward (2016, 8) has called for increased attention in scholarship on religion to "the less often studied moments when everyday interactions veer from their norm, creating ruptures and challenges in struggles for power and authority." The very phrase that my interlocutors often use to refer to their religious practices—"spiritual work"—reflects this focus on the transformation of power relations through embodied, often counternormative labor. *Experiments with Power* retheorizes religion through this experimental framework by making novel connections between studies of scientific experimentation and Africana religions.

The study of religion itself is an experiment. Yet, rather than experiments in a controlled laboratory setting, studies of religion and religious practices are experiments with power in lived worlds that involve questions about the ethical ambivalence of scholarly interventions. Instead of objects that scientists study, religious practitioners are theorists who can alter the ways that scholars themselves theorize (and thus transform) "religion." The words that spiritual workers themselves utilized—"work," "ex-

periment," "science," and "power"—are thus the touchstones in this book's experiments. Following the call of Caribbean anthropologist Michel-Rolph Trouillot (2003), I aim to treat my interlocutors as theorists rather than informants (see also Bonilla 2015; Fernando 2014). In this way, *Experiments with Power* unsettles the relationship between universal theory and provincial practitioner—or between agent of study and object of study—that has characterized many ethnographies of religion. This experiment's object (of transformation rather than study) is not a circumscribed ethno-racial tradition, but the category of religion and attendant discourses of ethics, criminality, and race. Spiritual workers are thus theorists who helped me to see religion in a new light, unsettling assumptions about what is universal and who remains racially circumscribed. While science has long been the exemplar of universalizing pretensions, obeah (and other criminalized forms of African "magic") have often been the epitome of mistaken, racially circumscribed superstitions in Western modernity. In different ways, the chapters of *Experiments with Power* trace the consequences of inverting this race-making assumption about the relationship between universalizing theories and African religious practices.

RIO MORO AND RURAL COSMOPOLITANISM

During the fourteen months that elapsed between the anti-obeah spiritual warfare that marked the start of my longest period of field research and the end of the state of emergency, I lived with a family whom I had known from previous fieldwork in Rio Moro. Formal livelihoods in Rio Moro were scarce, and residents lived against a backdrop of abandoned cacao plantations, which might look to the untrained eye like virgin forest. These lands were largely abandoned in the years following the 1970 Black Power Revolution and the subsequent oil boom, but because the lands were still held by absentee landowners, they were difficult to occupy. As in other parts of the Caribbean, the cultivation of marijuana in the deep forests behind the abandoned plantations had come to fill the vacuum of a postagricultural landscape, gutted by neoliberal trade policies and the Trinidadian petrostate's neglect of the region. Both obeah and rural livelihoods placed Rio Moro and its residents in an often-criminalized position, whether or not they actually cultivated marijuana or engaged in other illicit activities.

Against the potentially negative popular image of Rio Moro as a place

of rural tradition, illicit activity, and African atavism, I have shown elsewhere how Rio Moro was characterized by a "rural cosmopolitan" experience of intensive cultural and linguistic heterogeneity, particularly in the late nineteenth and early twentieth centuries (Crosson 2014). US enslaved persons who joined the British side in the War of 1812, known locally as "Merikins," formed an anglophone contingent in Rio Moro after the British Empire granted them land in the region in return for their service.[36] Over the course of the nineteenth century, these 'Merikins would coexist in Rio Moro with Spanish-speaking Venezuelan cacao laborers and plantation overseers, Yoruba- and Congolese-speaking indentured laborers, Mande-speaking communities of self-liberated West African Muslims ("Mandingos"), Cantonese-speaking Chinese shopkeepers and indentured laborers, Bhojpuri- and Tamil-speaking South Asian indentured laborers, Warao-speaking Amerindians, and (after Emancipation) former enslaved persons from neighboring anglophone islands. These non-Francophone groups in Rio Moro lived amid a population in the nineteenth century that largely spoke French patois, with many slaves and slave owners arriving from other Francophone islands in the Caribbean starting in the late eighteenth century. People were multilingual to some extent, although an African-French patois and then an English/Creole (beginning in the early twentieth century) became the lingua francas of laborers. While represented as peripheral to Trinidad's self-consciously cosmopolitan modernity, a closer look at Rio Moro's history reveals experiences of cosmopolitanism that existed outside the metropolitan and urban centers of colonial and postcolonial power (and were thus largely undocumented).

While an openness to diverse influences is usually associated with urbanity, class status, and formal education in stereotypical ideas of cosmopolitanism, grassroots spiritual workers in Rio Moro seemed to invert the premises of this stereotype. McNeal (2011) notes the marked openness of grassroots African religion to Spiritual Baptist, Hindu, or Kabbalistic influences, and he contrasts this "flexibility" to the "Yoruba-centric" orthodoxy of more educated, middle-class Orisha devotees (who largely took up African religion after Trinidad's 1970 Black Power Revolution) (Castor 2017). In some ways this distinction between grassroots and Yoruba-centric forms of African religion is useful, and my interlocutors tended to be resentful of some of the more overbearing attempts by urban middle- and upper-class Orisha practitioners (and the Nigerian or US African American ritual specialists they helped bring to Trinidad) to purify local traditions in line with a Yoruba-centric notion of authentic practice (see also Henry 2003).

In other ways, however, I found this distinction to conceal a greater diversity of opinions among middle-class cultural reformers, who often praised the authority of local grassroots practitioners and refuted the pervasive myth that New World Africans had lost their traditions or had gotten them mixed up, needing to return to Africa to find an authentic religion. Highly educated cultural reformers could also question whether Yoruba tradition in contemporary Nigeria, or any form of African practice, was really "pure" or "primordial" (e.g., Gibbons, as cited in Hucks 2006). Nevertheless, distinctions of class, as a range of observers have noted (McNeal 2011; Castor 2017; Henry 2003), did make a difference in approaches to African religions and the negotiation of authoritative knowledge about them. I thus sometimes use the terms "Yoruba-centric" and "grassroots" to describe *ideal-type* ends of a class-inflected spectrum of African religion in Trinidad. Rather than necessarily occupying one position on this spectrum, practitioners navigated the contrasting ideas of Africa that the ends of this spectrum yielded in complex ways. For rural cosmopolitan spiritual workers, Africa could represent both a place of primordial racial tradition and an ethos of experimentation that digested disparate influences.[37]

My research with spiritual workers in Rio Moro would not have been possible without my long-term attachment to a respected family there. Like many others in Rio Moro, their history revealed rural cosmopolitan networks, with their genealogies leading back to Barbados, Grenada, Venezuela, and elsewhere. The father of the family I lived with in Rio Moro, a farmer in his late fifties, is known by the pseudonym Papoy in this work. Papoy's father came to Rio Moro from neighboring Barbados in the early twentieth century to labor on the booming cacao plantations, and his mother was a descendant of enslaved people who had belonged to one of the French Creole plantations in Trinidad. Most of Papoy's other siblings (except for his half-Indian brother, Francis) had been fathered by the white(ish) Venezuelan overseer of the local cacao plantation, who had children with a number of different women in Rio Moro. When I started field research, Papoy self-identified as Rastafarian, having left behind the Adventist Christianity he had been raised on fifteen years prior to my stay. This rejection of Adventism and his embrace of a Rasta lifestyle led to a period of extreme poverty, ostracization by many of his former social familiars, and imprisonment—Rastas with dreadlocks were highly targeted by the police in the twentieth-century anglophone Caribbean.[38]

Just before I first met him, Papoy had begun to emerge from this period of material deprivation by clearing the steep hillside surrounding an aban-

FIGURE 0.5. The family. From top left (clockwise): Vita, Papoy, Giselle, Glendon, Olivia. Photograph by the author, 2011.

doned US military base with a cutlass and planting food crops. Papoy lived in a three-room house with his wife, Vita; their twenty-six-year-old son, Glendon; their twenty-eight-year-old daughter, Giselle; and Giselle's nine-year-old son, Jahshell. While they had forgotten the name of the disease that they had been told would kill Glendon before he reached adulthood, it was probably cerebral palsy. Glendon was nonverbal and bedridden, unable to use any of his limbs. Vita, whose family had come to Rio Moro from

FIGURE 0.6. Jahshell wears his grandmother's (Vita's) dreadlocks while his uncle Francis looks on. After her death, the family saved her hair. Photograph by the author, 2015.

the neighboring island of Grenada in the early twentieth century, sold the produce from their garden as well as various dry goods in a small shop in front of their house. I slept in one room of the house, sharing it with Jahshell and Glendon. During the last five months of my fieldwork I lived in an apartment in the urban East-West Corridor of northern Trinidad, conducting research at the University of the West Indies archives while frequently making the two-hour drive back to Rio Moro to stay with Papoy and Vita's family. Since my long-term field research, I have been back to stay in Rio Moro on at least ten different occasions, of periods ranging between ten days and two months, recently for the funeral of Vita. This book is dedicated to her memory.

Taking part in the sociality that centered on Papoy and Vita's farm and their daughter Giselle's sale of food preserves to a widely distributed range of "parlors" (roadside shops) throughout Rio Moro helped me to learn the fabric of everyday life in southern Trinidad. What most people call Rio Moro comprises a rather large area, and I was aided in the latter part of my long-term field research by a particularly fickle piece of machinery, a 1980 Ford Cortina that I acquired from a man named Krishna. The "Fix or Repair Daily" (to use the phrase that "older heads" [elders] in Trinidad often insisted was the esoteric meaning of "Ford") required constant maintenance, and I spent considerable amounts of time standing over the hood of the car with anyone who professed a knowledge of mechanics. The car was something like what having a dog must be like in the United States; it served as a social lubricant that humans talked over, about, and around.

More important than the fickle aid of my Ford was my fictive kinship within Vita and Papoy's household. This relationship gave me a place and an identity in a region whose residents are understandably wary of outsiders (both Trinidadian and foreign). As I spoke with my interlocutors about a subject that people often avoid in public discourse and regard with intense ambivalence, this level of trust was essential. In Rio Moro, my field research involved complex negotiations of my positionality as the only white person in Rio Moro at the time (and an American male at that). My embodied experience of whiteness as a marked category, of course, did not erase the conferral of privilege (or the outright hostility) that my presence could inspire. Elsewhere, I have detailed some of the vicissitudes of this ex-

FIGURE 0.7. The FORD ("Fix or Repair Daily"). Photograph by the author, 2012.

perience and reflected on the ethics of "studying people" (Crosson 2020). Yet I was not the only one studying others in Rio Moro. Like the removal of my shoes that served as a kind of test for Papoy, my actions were silently observed and interpreted. For weeks I slept in a hammock or in the back of the Ford Cortina, until Vita and Papoy felt like they had seen enough of my actions to invite me into their home. Our relationship was never formally quantified — a quantification that would have diminished the lasting obligations that forging a kind of kinship carries. These material and emotional exchanges around burials, new roofs, medical care, or retaining walls are the substance of my relationship with Vita and Papoy's family and of my place in Rio Moro.

Repeated interactions and exchanges over sustained stretches of time also led to deeper levels of trust with spiritual workers. I conducted in-depth informal interviews with seventeen different spiritual workers, who are my principal interlocutors in this book. I recorded multiple interviews with each spiritual worker (interviews that sometimes lasted as long as five hours and left me in awe of my interlocutors' abilities of concentration). I found that multiple interviews were essential to building trust and significantly deepened our conversations. In particular, attitudes toward obeah changed significantly over the course of different interviews, informal conversations, or mundane interactions. Obeah carries a strong negative charge, and especially for lower-class people with already-precarious respectability in Trinidadian society, outright disavowals of the term were commonplace in initial conversations. Among spiritual workers, however, these attitudes usually became more complex with the sedimenting of trust and time (cf. Meudec 2017). This does not mean, however, that obeah went from being a negative to a positive and unequivocally avowed phenomenon. Obeah was still about justice, with the potential for punitive harm, misuse of power, or radical disagreements about just action that this association implied.

I also had unrecorded conversations with a much wider range of African-identified practitioners about their own practices of spiritual work. I sat in on private sessions of spiritual work and attended the collective rituals of spirit manifestation where a wider cross-section of spiritual workers and those seeking help converged. During lulls in ritual activity and in the moments preceding consultations, I had conversations with more than fifty participants in spiritual work and spirit manifestation ceremonies, which I wrote about in daily field notes. In addition, I conducted recorded interviews with Pentecostal pastors, Hindu pundits, school teachers, politicians, psychologists, and police officials to study different facets of this project.

Conversations with Papoy were also incredibly instructive. In many ways he saw his life as an exercise in comparative religion, and he looked for opportunities to reason with me about my research. He had rejected the form of Christianity that had deeply shaped much of his life, embraced a Bible-based Rastafarianism, and ultimately (after experiencing visitations from Vita following her death) had moved toward what he called the "ancestral" or "African" side. A few days after Vita's funeral, he summed up his philosophy of religion to me in this way: "I don't believe and I don't doubt until I experiment." Papoy spoke about belief and doubt as an unfinished, visceral, and lived experiment with a variety of religious traditions that was rooted in both an Afrocentric sensibility and the rural cosmopolitan fabric of Rio Moro. This philosophy of religious practice was very much present among spiritual workers, and Papoy's experimental approach to religion is a guiding principle in this book's critique of moral-racial ideas of Africa (and Rio Moro) as atavistic.

CHAPTER ITINERARY

The three parts of *Experiments with Power* trace different facets of the moral-racial limits of religion and the alternate theories of experimentation, science, or power that my interlocutors proposed. This tripartite organization mirrors the threefold topography of Depths, Spiritual Nations, and Heights that often structured *mourning* travels through the spiritual realm for my interlocutors. Mourners first die a spiritual death in a period of blindfolded seclusion, descending into a realm that Spiritual Baptists and Kabbalah practitioners call "the Depths," before ascending to travel in "the Spiritual Nations" and "the Heights." A series of interludes threads between the book's chapters, following the journeys of Arlena, Bishop Dawes's spiritual daughter, through this spiritual topography of power. The first interlude describes the context of her death at the hands of police and the following vignettes trace her *mourning* journeys in the three spiritual realms, guided by Bishop Dawes. The theoretical concerns of the book's chapters follow her journey. Part 1, "The Depths," focuses on the questions of ethics, religious violence, and experimentation with the unjustly dead that this realm conjures. Part 2, "The Nations," then follows Arlena in traversing the Spiritual Nations of Africa and India, dwelling on how spiritual work and obeah refigure the relationship between racial difference and the category of reli-

gion. Finally, part 3, "The Heights," examines questions of sovereignty, rationality, obeah, and "high science."

Arlena is both a real person and a composite of the different people I
knew who had experienced police violence and/or had undertaken the journey of *mourning*. Throughout this work, the names of persons and places
are pseudonyms. The anonymity of my interlocutors is particularly important because some of the episodes of police violence that I discuss are open
court cases. In Trinidad, it is not unusual for a trial to take seven to ten years
to come to completion. "That is enough time for records to be lost, for witnesses to get killed, for police officers to be retired," as Bishop Dawes himself
reminded me. Justice is still an open question for many of my interlocutors,
and I have done my best to balance the necessity of obscuring or chang-
ing minor identifying details with a faithfulness to the events as they were
recounted to me in the pages that follow.

I have also tried to strike a similar balance in descriptions of spiritual
work. Spiritual workers granted me access to an interaction that is confi-
dential and stigmatized, with the stipulation that I would not photograph
or identify any of the clients. Many (but not all) spiritual workers did not
want their faces to be photographed or their names to be used, requests that
I have respected. They showed me much more than I can detail in these
pages, and the material descriptions of spiritual work that follow also with-
hold certain specificities. This book, therefore, does not purport to com-
prehensively reveal what obeah "really is and how it is done," as various descriptions written by outsiders and avowed practitioners have promised (see
Cassecanarie 1895; see also chapter 6). To my mind, such a promise is ultimately a false one. Even the books of "practical magic" purporting to reveal
"Hindoo," "Kabbalistic," or "Egyptian" secrets, which have formed central
parts of spiritual workers' repertoires for over a century, were not codified
scriptures of obeah for my interlocutors but incomplete (and potentially
dangerous) instruction manuals for experimentation (perhaps something
like the notoriously fallible pictograms for assembling Ikea furniture). It
took embodied intuition, learned experience, and spiritual inspiration to
bring these experimental designs to life (see fig. 6.2). For a long time, therefore, I tried to circumvent the persistent desire to reveal what obeah was,
refusing to give any definition that would codify what it "really" entailed (a
demurral that frustrated readers of my early manuscript to no end). I have
tried to address this frustration by remaining attentive to the material repertoires of spiritual work without treating obeah as an object to be definitively unveiled. Rather than a codified object, (what gets called) obeah is a

lens for reconceptualizing the limits of religion, science, ethics, and justice in the chapters that follow.

The first three chapters of this book, which make up part 1 ("The Depths"), focus on spiritual workers' responses to the police shootings in Rio Moro as the ethnographic basis for rethinking the relationship of religion, violence, experimentation, and ethics. Chapter 1 draws its title from the most popular chant improvised during the protests that followed the police shooting of Bishop Dawes's spiritual daughter and her friends: "The police don't know what obeah does do." As this refrain suggests, obeah intimated a justice-making force that exceeded the limits of state law, and (as with most systems of justice) potential harm was a part of its power. This chapter thus works toward a new interpretation of obeah and spiritual harm to gain a different understanding of the relationship between religious practice and violence more broadly. I reconceptualize religion as a claim about the location of sovereign power, making religious practice inextricable from questions of force, violence, and justice.

Chapter 2 — "Experiments with Justice: On Turning in the Grave" — delves more deeply into the material practices of justice-making that obeah entails to propose an experimental approach to religion. Bishop Dawes described his spiritual work following the police shootings as an "experiment with power" rather than "a tradition" or "a ritual," literally inverting the orientations of "a good burial" for his spiritual daughter by burying her face-down. Spiritual workers, in a variety of contexts, turned persons and objects around, upside down, or inside out to alter entrenched situations of power by contradicting the exoteric norms of a tradition. Refuting the racial trope of Africa as a place of unchanging tradition and modern ideals of law and ritual, this chapter argues for the value of the experimental in rethinking both religion and justice.

Concluding the "The Depths," chapter 3 — "Electrical Ethics: On Turning the Other Cheek" — focuses on spiritual workers' ethical conceptions, which they often articulated using electrical metaphors. Much scholarship has taken up Asad's (1993) critique of the discursive separation of religion from power mainly as a critique of a "Protestant bias" toward immaterial belief, offering an alternate vision of piety as the making of ethical subjects through the embodied practice of a tradition. I argue that both the "Protestant bias" toward immaterial conscience and recent scholarly correctives of piety replay the moral-racial limits of religion. In the midst of the 2011 state of emergency and the aftermath of the Rio Moro police shootings, spiritual workers contrasted their ethics of power and electricity to Jesus's injunction to "turn the other cheek" no matter the context of the blow. Instead of the norms of a tradition or a shared sense of the good, spiritual workers turned toward the moral ambivalence of obeah or science as an ethical framework that could navigate the complex polarities of the contemporary security state.

The next two chapters, forming the second part, "The Nations," look at the implications of the limits of religion for conceptions of racial difference. Chapter 4—"Blood Lines: Race, Sacrifice, and Religion"—argues that attitudes toward animal sacrifice (a practice that many Trinidadians pejoratively refer to as "blood") have defined the moral and racial limits of the modern category of religion. Invectives around race at my field site often attributed sacrificial harm to obeah while defining acceptable forms of Christianity or Hinduism as nonsacrificial (despite evidence to the contrary). The intertwined categories of religion and race, I suggest, work to parse acceptable from unacceptable forms of violence along lines of "blood," as a signifier of both intergenerational obligation and sacrificial religion. Chapter 5, "A Tongue between Nations," starts from spiritual workers' experimentation with difference to retheorize the relationship between race, religion, and secularism. In contrast with the secular transcendence of religious difference, I show how spiritual work is an art of "crossover" that enacts a nontranscendent negotiation of difference for Indian and African Trinidadians.

The final chapter, which comprises part 3 ("The Heights"), looks at how my interlocutors' equation of obeah with science fundamentally alters the debates around rationality that have structured the study of non-Western religions and the constitution of modernity. At first blush, this lexical equivalence of science with obeah seemed like a calculated attempt to garner the authority that science often confers in popular discourse. Yet when my interlocutors named science as the cause of "mass demonic possessions" at Rio Moro's secondary school, I realized that science bore the same associations with potential harm and the misuse of power that obeah could communicate. "Science" at my field site did not simply confer legitimacy and signal a triumphal story of rational disenchantment. Obeah and science presented a political theology of occult—in the sense of "hidden"—powers that unsettled my own presumptions about what it meant to be modern.

I close the interwoven chapters and interludes of *Experiments with Power* with an epilogue that focuses on recent episodes of intolerance toward obeah in North America and the Caribbean. I compare these events with manifestations of anti-Muslim nationalism in the United States, drawing some conclusions about the limits of both religion and tolerance in contemporary worlds. Despite attempts to separate "political Islam" and liberal religion (or instrumental magic and devotional piety), all recognized religions involve questions of justice-making force or authority. I conclude by arguing that while vigorous attempts at portraying Islam or obeah as nonviolent have sought to counteract derogatory Western representations of these practices, such revaluations can end up reproducing the moral-racial exclusions that have made Western liberal ideals of religion possible. *Experiments with Power* suggests that an alternative language for religious practice, inspired by those who were often left out of the category of religion, is necessary to confront such exclusions.

I
THE DEPTHS

FIGURE 1.1. Funeral procession for one of the victims of the police shootings, along the edge of the abandoned cane fields in Rio Moro. Photograph by the author, 2011.

Number Twenty-One Junction

The crossroads where the police opened fire on Arlena and her two friends was known as "Number Twenty-One," because it had been home to the twenty-first and final scale of the now-defunct national sugarcane company in Trinidad. Arlena had been liming (hanging out) at a local bar early on a Friday evening when her friends Jackie and Otis had suggested they go to get food. The nearest open food stall was a ten- to fifteen-minute drive through abandoned cane fields to Number Twenty-One Junction. People used to drive ox carts loaded down with the charred green of cane to the crossroads, but with the company closed, people drove to Number Twenty-One Junction to get barbecue at a food stall that had recently opened there. As neither Arlena nor her two friends had a car, they asked to borrow the automobile of another man who was hanging out at the bar. Unbeknownst to them, organized crime networks had allegedly paid a corrupt police unit to assassinate this man over a business conflict. As the friends climbed into the car and began their journey, they passed a police unit that most likely identified the vehicle as it turned off the main road to pass through the cane fields. Seven officers sped to Number Twenty-One Junction, telling employees to close down the barbecue stall and remain inside as the officers waited for the vehicle's arrival.

Arlena knew the back roads that passed through the cane fields well, as she had grown up in her grandmother's house just off the main road. At sunset, the twisted stalks of cane left to grow wild turned a deeper green in the golden light. As they neared the junction, Arlena would have driven past the public cemetery, where a clearing of white tombstones and the red earth of fresh graves broke the monotony of cane. This was the same cemetery where, more than a week later, Bishop Dawes would lay Arlena, his spiritual daughter, down into one of the red holes, not to rest but to rise and seek justice. This place would have been one of the last things that Arlena saw before driving into a hail of bullets at Number Twenty-One Junction. The seven police waiting for the car made no attempt to stop the vehicle and find out who was inside of it before pulling the trigger of their high-powered automatic weapons.

The car spun to stop in the middle of the crossroads. As on so many other occasions of fatalities at the hands of the police, the officers would claim that they were involved in a shoot-out with dangerous criminals and had returned fire. The three people in the borrowed vehicle were all in their twenties, unarmed and with no criminal records. As autopsies later showed, Arlena did not die in that initial hail of bullets; she was shot in her back by police weapons at point-blank about an hour later. "Something wrong in Trinidad and Tobago," the cousin of one of the three victims told me a week later. "Something wrong. . . . They shooting people wrongfully and everything is exchange of gunfire, but you never hear a police man get shoot. Is a lie. And a lie will always be a lie. But trust me, if you don't pay by the arm of the law, you are going to pay by obeah."

FIGURE 1.2. "What really goes on is that a lot of people because of poverty they is not capable of getting justice in this country. So if they comes to me, I will assist them." Roland Braveboy, spiritual worker, 2011. Photograph by Gigi Gatewood.

1

WHAT OBEAH DOES DO

Religion, Violence, and Law

"The police don't know what obeah does do," protesters in Rio Moro chanted as the towering flames of roadblocks kept police at bay. These words formed the refrain of the most popular chant that protesters improvised during the week of demonstrations that followed the police shootings of Arlena and her two unarmed friends in Rio Moro in 2011. During the protests, the cousin of one of the female victims, a well-known Orisha *mongba* (ritual leader) and Kabbalah operator, lit candles and said prayers in the middle of the crossroads adjacent to the local police station. Protected by the black smoke of burning car tires and a ring of protesters, his performances in the middle of occupied crossroads were intended as a show of force against the authorities. While riot police monitoring the demonstrations were armed with semiautomatic weapons, protesters wanted the police to know that they were armed with obeah.

Although police shootings and protests about them were far from uncommon in Trinidad (see Amnesty International 2012; Samad 2011; Welcome 2018), their deaths represented much more than a problem peculiar to Trinidad. In the days that followed the shootings in Rio Moro, Arlena and her two friends' deaths would echo around the Atlantic in events dominating the international anglophone media that residents of Rio Moro read and watched. The following week, the shooting death of the black British man Mark Duggan in Trinidad's former colonial metropole, sparked the "2011 England riots," in which five persons were killed and three thousand arrested, even as the police involved in the original shooting were eventually acquitted. Just as the flames of these riots were dying down, Trinidad and Tobago declared the beginning of the state of emergency in the name of fighting crime. A few months later in Florida, a self-appointed neighbor-hood patrol, in an act that he would claim was divinely ordained, fatally shot seventeen-year-old Trayvon Martin in Florida, a crime for which he too was eventually acquitted.[1] In the face of this conjunction of racialized criminality, exceptional policing powers, and "law enforcement" impunity—conditions that characterized not simply Trinidad but also the entire Americas and much of the world—those who had loved Arlena and her friends could be expected to have little hope of achieving any kind of redress for her murder.

On the first night of the wake for Arlena—typically an all-night af-fair that continues on every evening until the dead person is interred—the mourners overflowed from the wake and into the street in the early hours of the morning. On each of the nights following these deaths, wakes turned into early morning roadblocks, as mourners placed fallen electrical poles, truck trailers, an exercise bicycle, and broken appliances in the middle of the main road. To these piles of debris protesters added busted car tires that kindled the flames of the roadblocks—towering flames that ensured that police backhoes would not be able to remove the debris until the fires had subsided eight to ten hours later. The brother of one of the victims snatched the exercise bicycle from the heap of the debris before the flames touched it. He began riding the stationary bicycle in the middle of the blocked main road whenever news reporters came around, mocking the foreign chief of police's well-known penchant for distance running and road bicycling in tight spandex (the top cop was a Canadian Mountie the government had imported to clean up the crime situation). The brother told reporters that the chief of Trinidad and Tobago's protective services had better put all that exercise to use and come running to Rio Moro.

Wakes turned into weeklong protests, as family members with little faith in the official coroner's report held off on burial to try to get inde-pendent autopsies. This extended the liminal period of the wake, when the unburied person is still between life and death, and protesters said that they could feel one of the dead women "animating" the roadblocks. As they chanted about obeah in front of police officers monitoring the protests, they invoked a popular association between obeah and the afflicting powers of the unjustly dead. Obeah, Africa, and the threat of affliction were intimately bound up as a site of power at occupied crossroads, and it was this poten-tially harming force that protesters invoked with their chants and perfor-mances of "what obeah does do."[2]

This chapter looks at how these contested performances of obeah can transform commonsense conceptions of the relationship between violence, religion, and law. As the state and the protesters, the law and the dead, or police and obeah vied for sovereignty at asphalt junctions, the efficacy of these performances depended on the investment of flesh and blood with the potential for justice-making force. Without the power of these performances, the dead would likely have remained what police initially painted them to be—violent lower-class criminals worthy of execution.

Initially, the prominent and public role of obeah in the protests surprised me and disconcerted me with respect to my intended research project. In the months preceding the police shootings, the early stages of my long-term fieldwork had been marked by circumspection surrounding obeah. Spiritual workers often diagnosed the source of their clients' afflictions as obeah, distancing themselves from the word as a source of harm. Residents of Rio Moro had also denied that obeah even existed in the region after national media attributed a series of "mass demonic possessions" at the local secondary school to obeah. Obeah's association with harm seemed to make it an object of denial or denigration, as scholars working in other parts of the Caribbean have also noted (e.g., Meudec 2017; Paton 2009; Forde 2012).

I thus started field research in Rio Moro committed to dispelling the association of obeah with harm and presenting it in a more positive light. I saw this association with harm as an artifact of Caribbean people's internalization of colonial stigmas against obeah—a widespread approach in scholarship and cultural activism that I will call the "colonial false consciousness" model. Yet, as I began to realize a few months later, this same association with harming force was the very reason obeah was so important during the protests against the police shootings. As I talked to spiritual workers about the role of obeah in responses to police brutality, I had to reexamine my own attempts to redeem obeah in Rio Moro and the broader assumptions about the relationship between religion and violence that they reflected. Obeah's association with harm was part of its power, and dispelling that association would negate its justice-making force. This force was just as evident in the eighteenth-century slave rebellions that first led to obeah's criminalization as it was in the protests against the police shootings of Arlena and her friends in 2011.

By arguing that obeah cannot be separated from its potential for harm, my goal in this chapter is not to make obeah exceptional or to downplay the negative effects of its association with harm. The purported relationship between obeah and violence has been central to its criminalization from the eighteenth century onward, and it is precisely that association that has made the decriminalization of obeah as a recognized religion so difficult in much of the region today (see Crosson 2015, 2018; Paton 2009). Yet I began to realize that purifying obeah of harm reinscribed the very ideas of good religion (and bad magic) that formed the rationale for obeah's criminalization in the first place.

Instead of making obeah into "good" religion, it is more important to question the idea that religion can be completely separate from harm in the first place. The entanglement of religion and violence is not simply a baseless myth (cf. Cavanaugh 2009); it is the existential shadow against which liberal secular projects of governance and racialization take shape, as I detail in this chapter's opening sections. The idea that good religion (or good governance) can be separated from coercive force is the foundation for the ideals of liberal secularism. Rather than simply leading to a reality in which church and state are separate and political power is a matter of consent, this ideal masks and distorts empirical realities of power. Religious movements, state violence, and security interventions are entangled in contemporary nation-states, whether the United States, Brazil, Haiti, India, Guatemala, or Côte d'Ivoire (e.g., Ghassem-Fachandi 2012; "Luto na Luta" 2017; McAlister 2014; McGovern 2012; O'Neill 2015; Povinelli 2009). Obeah's association with harm is not exceptional among religious practices, but the degree to which such an association has led to obeah's moral condemnation and criminalization reflects the racial foundations of liberal secular norms of religion and state power. Rather than simplistic oppositions between piety and violence or moral religion and instrumental magic, a study of obeah provides a more complex view on the power of law and the moral-racial limits of tolerable religion in modern nation-states.

In this chapter, I begin with an overview of the complex issues surrounding the association between obeah and violence. I show how this association points toward some foundational problems with the relationship between religion and instrumental force in Western modernity. From the initial criminalization of obeah to the contemporary War on Terror, I argue that religion is a race-making project that has revolved around accusations of religious violence. I then move to the core of this chapter's argument, showing how the 2011 protests and my interviews with spiritual workers transformed my understanding of the relationship between religious practice and violence. Rather than simply being an artifact of colonial false consciousness, I started to see obeah's association with harm as a part of its justice-making power. In broader terms, I came to realize how recognized systems of religion and law obviously involved the question of justice-making force. The real question was where the proper locus of this power lay, and obeah provided an answer to this question different from those answers provided by liberal ideals of the rule of law and the rules of religion. Rather than the codified maxims of a legal or a religious tradition, obeah showed how religious practice and justice involved exceptional performances of power.

RELIGION AND VIOLENCE

The long-standing relationship between obeah and harm has proved a key stumbling block for scholarly approaches to the term and for the efforts of cultural activists to garner state recognition for obeah as a legally protected religion.[3] As historian Diana Paton (2009) has convincingly argued, the wide array of literary and scholarly works that seek to demonstrate that obeah is about healing and protection rather than harm run up against popular attitudes in the region that understand obeah "as a dangerous and hostile phenomenon."[4] Paton (2009, 1) goes on to state that such hostility "suggests that arguments that work through demonstrating the inaccuracy of negative views of obeah can only go so far." Certainly, I would not suggest that such attempts to revalue obeah as a positive phenomenon are not crucially important. The actual practices of spiritual workers that get called obeah could be labeled as healing and protection. Yet the spiritual workers I knew also saw their own work as counteracting the harmful obeah of others, and in contexts of problem-solving work, one person's "healing" could easily become another's harm. Obeah always carries this instability of "healing-harming" (Ochoa 2010b) force, and this chapter is an attempt to come to terms with obeah's ambivalence rather than making it into a morally univalent practice of healing. Confronting obeah's association with harm addresses the limits that Paton sees in arguments that attempt to erase such an association as false consciousness.

In my own participation in public debates about obeah's decriminalization elsewhere in the Caribbean, the association with harm has been the basis for a persistent counterargument against those who would insist that obeah is a cultural tradition of healing protected under constitutional provisions for "religious freedom" (Crosson 2018). Independent anglophone Caribbean nations invariably enshrine religious freedom as a central promise in their founding documents, but for many people in the region, obeah's association with harm makes it not-religion (and thus outside of legal pro-

tection). In Jamaica, one of the leading proponents of obeah's decriminalization, the Baptist reverend Devon Dick, has argued for obeah's legalization
by saying that any harm caused by the practice could be dealt with under
existing criminal ordinances. In a rebuttal to this argument published in
Jamaica's leading national newspaper, this very acknowledgment of obeah's
possible harm was turned against Reverend Dick: "I find it paradoxical that
a Christian pastor, the Reverend Devon Dick, could be advocating . . . for
the right to practise obeah in the name of religious liberty, while in the same
breath invoking the caveat, 'providing no one is harmed by these practices.'
I was born and raised in Jamaica and I never heard of anyone going to see
an obeah man to seek blessing for his neighbour. Every mention of a visit
to the obeah man was always out of evil motives, such as to bring harm to
others and to set back their progress" (Grey 2015). Obeah's popular relationship to harm automatically invalidates it as religion according to this common rebuttal.

One way to respond to such rebuttals during debates over obeah's
legalization is to insist that obeah's association with harm is an illusion—a
product of colonial stigmas unwittingly reproduced by Caribbean people.
Yet obeah's power to harm was absolutely central to its role in the protests
that followed the police shootings at Number Twenty-One Junction. Rather
than deny that obeah can imply harm—a denial that, as Paton argues, has
its limits—this chapter questions a more basic premise of the arguments
against obeah's legalization as a religious practice: that any "religion" can be
separated from the exercise of harming force in the first place.

The challenge of including obeah in the category of religion (with its
attendant "freedoms") has been conditioned by the core assumption that
religious practices are about pious devotion, ethical subject making, or
immaterial belief rather than the exercise of force.[5] This attempt at separating religion from juridical force has a long history, with scholars positing
various points of origin, both modern and premodern (e.g., Assmann 2009;
Cavanaugh 1995; Stroumsa 2009). According to a common origin story, this
conception has its roots in the Enlightenment, which produced the very
same ideals of religious liberty that are enshrined in anglophone Caribbean
constitutions. According to this origin story, foundational doctrines of religious tolerance first emerged in the late seventeenth century as a reaction to
the "wars of religion" that marked the Reformation in Europe. The fractur-
ing of the Catholic Church and the specter of "the war of all sects against
all" (Sullivan 1992, qtd. in Guinn 2011, 99) produced the idealized premise of
liberal secularism: the separation of religion from juridical power, political

conflicts, and physical harm.[6] An idealized separation of church and state was supposed to prevent religious violence, but this ideal-type separation required an exclusionary definition of the "truly fundamental part" of religion and the excision of "superstition," "hypocrisy," or any kind of coercive force from tolerable religion (Locke [1689] 1796). Enlightenment gentlemen cast this new idea of a universal core of religion in a nonconformist Protestant image, separating tolerable from intolerable forms of religion. Permissible religion was about moral reason and conscience rather than material practices, and it did not concern itself with civil legal affairs (Crosson 2018; Locke [1689] 1796). By leaving exercises of force to the state, religion could become a domain defined by individual conscience or moral sentiment rather than institutional and disciplinary power (Asad 1993; Cavanaugh 1995).

Yet as rebuttals to obeah's decriminalization make clear, religion is not separate from secular power under liberal democratic regimes of religious liberty. Rather, the separation of harmless religion from harmful or inessential not-religion becomes a key way to legally delimit rights, citizenship, legitimate violence, and "freedom" (Rocklin 2015; Sehat 2011; Sullivan 2005). For the founding Anglo-American Enlightenment architects of liberal religious tolerance, a certain idea of religion was the explicit foundation for membership in the social contract between state and citizen (with those who allegedly lacked this foundation excluded from the republic) (see Crosson 2018; Locke [1689] 1796; Sehat 2011). Alongside Enlightenment rhetoric about "universal" rights, the line between religion and not-religion helped to distinguish the citizens who could enjoy those rights from those that required supervision and disciplining. Paradoxically, the idealized notion of a purely moral religion separate from force ethically enabled the violence of states against nonwhite others whose possession of Christian conscience was supposedly dubious, nascent, or nonexistent. Liberal secularism was founded not on an attempt to minimize or excise religion from public life but on the codification of a specific idea of religion as the moral foundation for the rule of law and citizenship (Sehat 2011).

The criminalization of obeah reflects the ways that ideas about religion—as separate from power—have authorized state force against (not-)religion. In the Caribbean, obeah was criminalized across the region in post-emancipation ordinances that often defined it as the "assumption of supernatural power." Wedding power to the supernatural in inappropriate ways, obeah was legally defined as a fraudulent practice that "pretended" to harm others. Rooted in European images of Africa, but applicable to a variety of subaltern groups, post-emancipation obeah ordinances allowed British colonial officials to separate laborers' exercise of religion from any potential exercise of economic or political power. From obeah's initial crimi-nalization in connection with Tacky's slave rebellion of 1760 to the protests in Rio Moro in 2011, obeah remained bound to the threat of subaltern politi-cal force in the anglophone Caribbean. The category of obeah was thus a key means through which subaltern political organization (and the nonplanta-tion livelihood of spiritual work) could become fanaticism or superstition— assumptions of power that were acts of violence (whether "pretended" or real) rather than proper religion, proper labor, or proper politics. As the rebuttal to Reverend Dick makes clear, arguments for obeah's decriminal-ization under doctrines of religious liberty run into the exclusionary limits of tolerance in the modern nation-state. Contemporary arguments for both obeah's decriminalization and its illegality are similarly premised on the limit of harm. Making obeah into tolerable religion, with the caveat that any harm enacted in its name would still be criminal, depends on the same (impossible) purification of religion from harming force that is the basis for Western secular ideals. Religion must be separated from force even as reli-gion remains entangled with all kinds of violence.

The attempt to prescribe some kind of normative relationship between proper religion and violence is not particular to efforts to decriminalize and revalue obeah (or to keep it illegal). For example, the September 11, 2001, attacks intensified contestations over normative claims about violence and religion, and those claims echoed long-standing invectives against religious violence that featured centrally in debates about obeah's value. In 2002, for example, Pope John Paul II, dismayed by the "religiously motivated" attacks of September 11, convened twelve leaders of "the religions of the world" to agree on a statement about the basic premises of religion. With the unani-mous support of his guests, the pope issued a proclamation that "whoever uses religion to foment violence contradicts religion's deepest and truest in-spiration" (Tagliabue 2002). As anthropologist James Faubion (2003) noted, it would be hard for many to disagree with this definition of religion's "deep-est and truest" core (even as contemporary notions of religion are just as likely to associate it with intractable conflict as with nonviolence). Yet as Faubion also notes, such a proclamation risked assigning a vast number of religious followers to "analytical purgatory" by making the proselytization, political imperatives, or conflicts that accompany religious practice across the world into deviant anomalies. Faubion asserts that the terms scholars

bring to problems of religion and violence come "perilously close" to reproducing the same kind of analytical purgatory.

Following September 11, there was a vast outpouring of work on religion and violence, much of which reproduced the sentiment that religion,
in its "good" forms at least, is an antidote to violence and conflict. While
acknowledging the enactment of violence in the name of religion, these
approaches focused largely on the ways that religion, as the description for
one such post–September 11 scholarly volume reads, can provide "resources
for the overcoming of violence" (Crockett 2006). This trend has continued,
with an edited volume on religion and violence published in 2016 focusing almost entirely on religion's role in "peacemaking" around the world
(Phan and Irvin-Erickson 2016). The one sore thumb that sticks out from
the collection of peaceful religions in Phan and Irvin-Erickson's (2016) volume is "political Islam," which as one of the chapters argues, is responsible
for the conflict in Darfur (Yousif 2016). Nevertheless, such violence can be
read as the fault of the "politicization" of religion rather than of true religiosity, which at its core is devoted to peace and nonviolence. In the face of
"new atheist" or post-9/11 assertions that religion is inherently violent, these
scholarly works uphold a vision of religious practice (at least in its liberal
forms) as tolerant, nonviolent, or democratic (e.g., Armstrong 2015; Kripal
2007; Schmidt 2012; cf. Fessenden 2012).

In contrast, other studies have remained sensitive to the complex relations between religious practices and violence, criticizing the overriding
excision of violence from proper religion in post-Reformation polemics
about "good" and "bad" religion. For example, lawyer-philosopher David
Guinn (2011) notes how analysis of religion and violence in the West has
been overwhelmingly shaped by liberal secularism, with its emphasis on the
legal protection of religious freedom and the separation of church and state
as buffers against religious violence in the aftermath of the Reformation's
so-called wars of religion. As Guinn (2011, 99) argues, however, this liberal
secular codification of proper religion as separate from political power or
the exercise of force is "only one understanding of religion and a narrow
interpretation of religiously associated violence." Nevertheless, this "one
understanding" of good or proper religion, bound to cultural and political
contexts of modern Western liberalism, reigns supreme in most treatments
of religious violence (as well as in those treatments that prescribe a more
ardent secularism to counteract religion's association with violent conflict
in contemporary worlds). This does not mean, as Guinn himself seems to
suggest, that violence and religion are more often intertwined outside of

religious violence

the bounds of the West and liberal nation-states. To my mind, however, it does mean that the (always-unfinished) purification of religion from violence in liberal Western discourse has been accomplished by projecting religious violence outside the boundaries of the West, onto practices of "radical Islam" and "black magic" that supposedly seek to harm others (see also Crosson 2018; Fessenden 2012).

This act of projection was exceedingly evident in colonial attitudes toward African religion, and it continues to help occlude or authorize imperial violence. As a number of scholars have convincingly argued, violent US military interventions in the twenty-first century have often been couched in Christian religious terms of crusade, redemption, tolerance, and/or salvation (Asad 2003, 2007; Fessenden 2012; Povinelli 2008, 2009; Vogler and Markell 2003). Yet unlike the supposed mixture of religion and violence in "voodoo," "obeah," or "political Islam," evangelical Christian religious values somehow manage to redeem the violence of US imperialism as liberating or humanitarian in much US political discourse (Asad 2007; Povinelli 2009).

Such "humanitarian violence" (Atanasoski 2013) is not limited to foreign US military interventions; it is a logic that pervades liberal secularism (Asad 2007). Yet such moralized violence is hardly ever couched as "religious violence." This is partly because of liberal ideals of good religion as inherently nonviolent, and partly because of liberal democratic notions of good politics as based in consent rather than force. Asad (2007), however, draws on Weber's work to insist that the modern nation-state is premised on violent conquests and securitization measures that extend beyond its borders (see also Weber 1948, 71–72). Rather than the religious or cultural beliefs of "radical Islam," it is the economic, clandestine, or martial incursions of liberal secular nation-states (most especially the United States and its allies) and the attempts by less militarily equipped populations to retaliate that condition forms of violence in contemporary worlds. The focus of these accounts is the violence of the secular nation-state, whereas religious practice (or pious Islam at least) is represented primarily as a matter of ethical subject making (e.g., Hirschkind 2006; Jouili 2015; Mahmood 2003a, 2005). In a different set of accounts that work to counteract the Orientalist assumption of Islam's inherent violence, motivations for "political Islam" are to be found in the repercussions of European colonialism, US-led imperialism, and the shortcomings of postcolonial state projects—factors understood as "material" rather than religious.[7] The violence popularly associated with Islam, for these scholars, is less a property of any particular religious tradition or theological orientation than of politics within and between avowedly secular nation-states.

In stark contrast to these emphases on religion's nonviolent essence or modern secularism's violence are a wide variety of works that see religion as the root cause of conflict. Taking most virulent form in the post-9/11 "new atheist" literature, these works present the popular view that religion has been responsible for a wide variety of violent conflicts throughout history, which can be solved only through the allegedly moderating and rational influences of liberal secularism, state law, and/or atheism (see, e.g., Dawkins 2006; Harris 2004, 2007; Hitchens 2007). Nevertheless, the moral valence of this body of work remains the same: associations of religion and violence are inherently bad. Rather than upholding a good core of nonviolent, liberal religion as an antidote to the violence of religious fundamentalism (e.g., Kripal 2007; Schmidt 2012), these new atheist approaches condemn religion wholesale as the cause of violent conflict.

Echoing these condemnations, elisions, or denials of "religious violence," obeah's popular association with harm has been the object of both moral invectives against its practice and attempts to revalue it by explaining away such harm. In this latter explanation, the association with violence is the product of the colonial state's stigmatization and prohibition of obeah, and the overwhelmingly ambivalent attitudes of contemporary persons in the anglophone Caribbean toward the word represent their internalization of colonial discourse. "Although obeah was sometimes used to harm others," as Bilby and Handler (2004, 153) argue in an influential essay, "this negative [colonial] interpretation [of obeah] became so deeply ingrained that many West Indians accept it to varying degrees today." I refer to this approach to obeah's association with harm as the "colonial false consciousness model." As implied or explicitly stated by a number of authors, this model asserts that obeah is not really what many contemporary Caribbean people seem to think it is. Instead, obeah actually represents African-inspired practices of healing and protection, which were positively valued before their colonial denigration (and might reattain this meaning if scholars and cultural activists insist on what Bilby and Handler call obeah's "positive functions" of healing and protection).

In many ways, this is almost certainly the case, and it would be a mistake to underestimate the effects of colonial stigmatization and prohibition on contemporary attitudes. Indeed, the negative terms of colonial representations have often seeped into published representations of obeah, with even recent scholarly works sometimes following the colonial trend of defining obeah as something other than religion (equating it with "witchcraft," "sorcery," or "black magic").[8] Because of these associations, obeah often provoked disavowals and moral condemnations in Rio Moro. A few months before Arlena's death, for example, a series of "mass demonic possessions" closed down the local secondary school, an event that I detail in chapter 6. As the national media and Pentecostal-charismatic Christian spiritual warriors attributed these events to Rio Moro's tradition of obeah and witchcraft, residents countered that obeah had died out in the region. Matthew, a longtime resident of Rio Moro, went so far as to tell me that obeah did not exist in rural Rio Moro, but it did in the minds of urban Trinidadians: "Let me explain this obeah business to you. People from Port of Spain, Central, San Fernando [Trinidad's urban centers] come to Rio Moro to look for obeah. Rio Moro people doesn't go and look for obeah. . . . I personally know these things. . . . Who knows what is obeah really? Who knows more obeah than the people in the Port of Spain area, in Central, and San Fernando?" Reversing the denigrating stigmas of obeah, which placed it at the supposedly backward rural margins of the island, Matthew insisted that urbane Trinidadians "should rephrase themselves when saying that Rio Moro is obeah." While Pentecostal Christian leaders from the island's urban centers were coming to Rio Moro's secondary school to perform "spiritual warfare" against the region's touted obeah, Matthew insisted that they were coming to the wrong place.

Speaking about obeah with people in Rio Moro before the police shootings, then, I often met with disavowal, condemnation, or a temporal quarantining of obeah in a moribund past. These disavowals hinged on obeah's association with harm and a desire to distance one's own religion from the violence that characterized obeah in colonial and postcolonial representations. For many Trinidadian Hindus and Christians, as I show in chapter 4, the disavowal of obeah was a shared discourse that distanced their own recognized religions from the supposed instrumentality and violence of not-religion. These associations of obeah with harm continue to have profound effects, motivating the contemporary episodes of intolerance toward obeah that I detail in this book's epilogue.

The colonial false-consciousness model, therefore, is right to assert that we need to critique negative attitudes toward obeah. Nevertheless, this approach can end up reifying a line between "positive" and "negative" meanings of obeah—a line that recapitulates moral-racial ideas of religion in the West, founded on the (impossible) purification of lived religion from harm. As I show in the following two chapters, the line between "negative" and "positive" attitudes toward obeah is not so clear in practice. In many cases, spiritual workers asserted that the "negative" associations of obeah with harm were "good" for solving particular problems. Moreover, the idea that Caribbean people have simply internalized negative colonial ideas about obeah denies them agency, oversimplifying the lived attitudes of my interlocutors and overlooking the diversity of values that obeah holds within different contexts.[9] Some of the same people who asserted obeah's justice-making power after Arlena's death had, in response to the second-ary school "possessions," told me that obeah did not really exist. What did these contradictory attitudes toward obeah and the contested line between its "positive" and "negative" meanings indicate about the relationship of reli-gion, justice, and violence more broadly?

OBEAH, STATE VIOLENCE, AND
THE RULE OF LAW

When the police shootings at Number Twenty-One Junction happened approximately nine months after the "demonic possessions" at Rio Moro's secondary school, I was thus convinced that attitudes toward obeah in the Caribbean region were overwhelmingly negative. The protests and funerals that followed the shootings, however, highlighted positive avowals of "what obeah does do" in Rio Moro. One of these public avowals punctuated a week of demonstrations, in a dramatic performance of obeah at the same cross-roads where the police had shot Arlena and her two friends. As residents proclaimed the power of obeah, I began to think that obeah's association with violence could be a justice-making force in the many cases where state law failed to protect subaltern persons.

This performance of obeah at Number Twenty-One Junction coincided with the cessation of roadblocks and the visit of a high-profile lawyer to the area. The demonstrations in Rio Moro had attracted significant national media attention, especially after the host of the nation's most popular tele-vision program — Crime Watch — had come all the way from the capital early in the morning to "lead" a protest march a few days after the shootings. Reversing the usual plot of Crime Watch, in which the host supposedly aided police in catching "bandits," the program gave significant airtime to the protests against those the host called "bad police." As demonstrations con-tinued to block the main road with fiery barricades, a high-profile lawyer responded by offering to represent the families of the victims free of charge but on the condition that they stop protesting.[10] The lawyer announced that he would come down to Rio Moro at the end of the week, so instead of roadblocks, the families planned a "peace march" to coincide with his visit that would start at Number Twenty-One Junction and end at the village playing field.

More than one week after the shootings at Number Twenty-One Junction, the lawyer climbed onto the bed of a pickup truck parked at the crossroads. He took up a bullhorn and began to address the crowd of marchers gathered at the junction. He told them that they had retained a lawyer and that the time had thus come for them to stop blocking the roads. "We believe in the rule of law," he told the crowd, "and justice is not in the road but in the halls of justice."

While the lawyer insisted that justice was not in the road, just before he addressed the crowd, the brother of one of the victims had knelt down in the middle of Number Twenty-One Junction, on the asphalt that his sibling's blood had stained. In the spot where the borrowed car had spun to a stop in the middle of the junction, he lit seven candles—four black, one red, one yellow, and one white—affixing them to the asphalt with melted wax. He began to sway from side to side, speaking in an unknown tongue. While most of what he said was unintelligible to those gathered, the names of the seven police officers who had shot up the borrowed car (as well as the names of some of the officers monitoring the protests) were pronounced with surprising clarity. After his prayers ended, my friend Norris remarked that all the officers had left the scene, giving the protesters sole possession of the crossroads. "Must be obeah," Norris explained.

The next day, an account of the lawyer's words to the protesters, entitled "Justice Not in the Road," was accompanied in a national newspaper by a photo of the brother, with his eyes closed and arms raised, kneeling in front of the candles in the middle of the crossroads. This conjunction of word and image brought together two apparently divergent creeds: justice-making obeah "in the road" and a belief that justice was, by definition, "not in the road." In its rhetorical form, the lawyer's address to the protesters was itself reminiscent of a Christian creed. The first words of the Nicene Creed, "We believe in the Father," became "we believe in the rule of law"—a collective statement of shared belief in a sovereign power that resided elsewhere. Yet, the co-incidence of obeah and police killings at Number Twenty-One Junction suggested that law and justice were, in fact, made in the road—in performative assertions of force, whether police brutality, roadblocks, or rites of obeah.

The juxtaposition of obeah and the rule of law at Number Twenty-One Junction showed how "the road" was a key site of the performance of law and power. In many ways, "the road" in Trinidad was something like what liberal political theorists have called "the secular": a public space that all walks of society, at least in theory, could access regardless of differences in class, race, or religion. It is impossible to name all of the Trinidadian carnival songs that have celebrated being "in the road" as the realization of an embodied right to space (even as everyday public space remains highly segregated according to class differences, even—or especially—during the principal carnival Tuesday celebrations in contemporary Trinidad; see Forde 2018). In colonial Trinidad, the public space of the road, like secularism itself, was a heavily regulated spatial regime that used differences of class, race, religion, and gender to exclude and criminalize certain populations (Seales 2013). Rather than the protection of laborers, the regulation of their entry into public space (and of their moral conduct in the private spaces where most spiritual work happened) was the main function of the police and the rule of law in colonial Trinidad.[11] As in the United States, the central crimes used to regulate ex-slaves were infractions of vagrancy and/or moral order offenses, of which obeah was one example (Handler and Bilby 2012; DuBois [1935] 2014; Paton 2015). The punishments for these offences in the British Caribbean after emancipation (for both Indian and African laborers) included imprisonment, hard labor, and public flogging with the cat-o'-nine-tails. While the lawyer asserted that the rule of law would give my subaltern interlocutors justice, it had more often meted out harsh punishments for minor offenses of "vagrancy" (i.e., being in public space rather than on a plantation) in colonial Trinidad.

In contrast with vagrancy and moral order offences, violent crimes (when the victim came from the laboring classes) met with negligible fines and high rates of dismissal in colonial Trinidad (Trotman 1986). As historians have noted, this discrepancy in punishment suggests that vagrancy and moral order offenses, where flogging had become the ideal punishment, were less tolerable to the colonial justice system than violence against lower-class people. "The whip," Trotman (1986, 137–38) writes, "was used liberally for those convicted of practicing Obeah and praedial larceny [theft of crops] or for the unemployed convicted of being incorrigible rogues or vagabonds," but relatively negligible fines without floggings were more frequently administered for violent crimes against the person. Noting the centrality of corporal punishment in the colonial justice system, Brereton (1981, 133) asserts that "the whole machinery of law enforcement was directed against the lower classes" in nineteenth- and early twentieth-century Trinidad. The control of labor, the policing of the bounds of private property, the enforcement of public morality, and the maintenance of borders between religion and superstition were more important in the eyes of the law than violent crimes enacted upon the bodies of laborers. When persons were arrested for the crime of obeah or acts defined as vagrancy, the law itself enacted violence upon the bodies of these "criminals," using the whip as the instrument of justice.

While liberal ideals of the rule of law depict it as a force for curbing or domesticating violence (see Sarat and Kearns 1993), state law in the Caribbean was thus founded on physical violence against lower-class persons. As Diana Paton has argued in the case of Jamaica, abolitionist arguments for (Christian) moral reform transitioned into an emphasis on the need to physically discipline former slaves after emancipation. Thus, by 1865, "at the symbolic level, the ideal punishment was now a flogging inflicted on a male criminal. The island's prisons continued to contain large, and growing, numbers of prisoners, but there was little talk of their moral capacities" (Paton 2004, 147). Genealogies of the law in the post-emancipation Caribbean trouble the shift from coercion to freedom that the break of emancipation has been supposed to signal. "If we recall that public flogging was maintained as a form of criminal punishment in Jamaica for most of the twentieth century," Deborah Thomas (2011, 108) has suggested, we might raise similar questions about the emancipation that political independence promised in the mid-twentieth-century British Caribbean.

As the criminalization of obeah suggests, there has been a persistent link between the regulation of lower-class "vagrancy," ideas about African "superstition," and the regulation of "religion." While Paton argues that the Christian terms of abolitionist reform were largely abandoned for lower-class black populations in the British Caribbean after emancipation, these religious rhetorics continued to arbitrate the entrance of nonwhite populations into respectable society and (eventually) citizenship. In other words, as in much of the Americas, a prerequisite for blacks' entrance into moral subjecthood and political position was the practice of the right kind of Christianity (Sehat 2011; Weisenfeld 2007). At the core of colonial rationales for the violence of the law was the idea that New World Africans did not possess innate moral capacities or "religion." Certainly in the late nineteenth century, religion was "discovered" in some parts of continental Africa, as David

Chidester (1996) has argued. But this begrudging European conferral of "primitive," "native," or "traditional" religion on colonized continental Africans was usually not possible (in colonial understandings) for former slaves in the New World. Even if they once had some kind of native religion (an idea that Europeans would not admit until the latter part of the nineteenth century), they had allegedly lost that religion in the experience of enslavement and the Middle Passage. According to European ideas that conflated religion and ethics, not having religion meant not having moral subjectivity. The violence of the law in the Americas could thus be moralized as a necessary reformative force for populations that were (in the eyes of many white people) not innately moral. The law would thus focus on these populations' containment and disciplining rather than their protection.

As this broad history and the events at Number Twenty-One Junction show, the rule of law has long been an embodied performance of power rather than a system for minimizing violence against lower-class persons. More broadly speaking, in modern states policing is often the point at which liberal ideals of the rule of law, envisioned as a neutral body of codes and procedures, become violently performative. In a resonant way, obeah represented the limits of creedal conceptions of religion, as a codified set of shared beliefs and moral taboos, by showing that religion involved embodied performances in exceptional contexts of force. The protests culminated in this awkward conjunction of two kinds of religion and two kinds of law, juxtaposing the Nicene Creed of the rule of law against the performance of obeah in the road at Number Twenty-One Junction.

Residents seemed caught in between these conceptions of religion and law, illustrating what critics have noted as the double bind of liberal secular governance (Agamben 2005; Schmitt 1985; Yelle 2010). My interlocutors held on to hope that the justice system would punish the police officers, but they also knew that they had to perform a power outside of secular law (and in the middle of the road) for this to be a possibility. In the Americas, after all, law enforcement continues to be an exercise of violence against lower-class black populations. In contrast, the rule of law that the lawyer proclaimed was supposed to subordinate extrajudicial violence to codified procedures. Yet the rule of law continually requires embodied acts of violence and states of emergency that are exceptions to written rules in modern nation-states.[12] In this way, as Michael Lambek (2012) has noted, modern law, as the truth-making technology of the state, produces truth performatively, much as religious rites do. Within this framework, what makes justice is not the access to unmediated truth but the knowledge of transformative procedures that ritual specialists, whether lawyers, spiritual workers, or police officers, embody and perform to contest the moral valence of power. This performative quality means that juridical and spiritual power is an embodied contest rather than simply a rule-governed system, a situation that can yield both oppressive and subversive implications (see also West 2005, 2007).

As the protests came to a close without resolution at Number Twenty-One Junction, I felt caught in a similar double bind with regard to my study of obeah. Was obeah a harmful or ineffectual force that people disavowed, one that was subordinate to the rule of law or the ethical codes of (good) religion, which existed somewhere else besides the road? Or was obeah's harm a justice-making power that was positively embraced in the road, combatting the violent reality of racist and classist criminal law in the Americas? Ultimately, I learned that the answer to neither question was a simple yes or no. Rather than a belief in either obeah or the rule of law as unequivocal forces for justice, residents in Rio Moro saw both realms as potentially ambivalent performances of power. Even as I hoped that the protests might show obeah's association with harm to be inherently protecting and justice-making for subaltern persons, obeah remained as ambivalent as state law for some of those who had lived with and loved the dead at Number Twenty-One Junction.

"BUT OBEAH IS DANGEROUS"

As protesters mobilized the potential violence of obeah as a justice-making force in the aftermath of the police shootings at Number Twenty-One Junction, my own initial intention to denounce the association of obeah with harm was thrown into confusion. Two months after the police shootings, this confusion was further exacerbated by claims that the unprecedented arrests of the officers involved in the shootings were compelled by the harming force of obeah. The forces sent to afflict the officers had, according to my interlocutors, caused one of them to confess. After spending time in the nation's mental hospital, the officer had delivered a confession and entered witness protection, leading to the unexpected arrest of the remaining officers. If obeah had indeed relentlessly afflicted the officers to produce justice, did spiritual workers see this harming power of obeah as restricted to such contexts of extreme abuses of power? Could the harm of obeah thus be positive—a justice-making force in situations of injustice? If it was not possible to separate obeah from violence, then perhaps obeah could still be defended by redeeming the ends to which the harm was put.

After I heard the news of the officers' arrests on the television program *Crime Watch*, I began to ask Papoy such questions. He pushed back against my suggestions that obeah was a force only for resisting abuses of power, a force that had simply worked on the side of the families of those murdered at Number Twenty-One Junction. The police officers, Papoy reminded me, had also hired spiritual workers to protect themselves from criminal accusations and spiritual harm. Papoy also asserted that it was not simply the police but also Arlena's own sister who had been afflicted as a result of her family's justice-seeking obeah, as the vengeance of the dead could rebound to those who sought to wield its power. Arlena's sister had reportedly begged spiritual workers to reverse whatever obeah they had done because it was harming her own family (an episode of spiritual and physical harm that forms the basis for interlude 6). For a better understanding of these complexities of obeah, Papoy suggested that I talk with a spiritual worker named Mother Mariella, who lived about twenty minutes away from Papoy's house by car.

Mother Mariella became a key figure throughout the rest of my fieldwork. As an elder in the Orisha tradition with extensive experience in Kabbalah and Spiritual Baptist practices, she had in-depth knowledge of the threefold path of African religion in Trinidad. Her great grandmother, Ma Diamond, had been the teacher of Trinidad's most infamous spiritual worker and Orisha *mongba* Ebenezer Elliot (Pa Neeza), and Mariella had spent a great deal of time during her own life with Baba Clarence Forde, the then-recently-deceased head of Trinidad and Tobago's national Orisha organization. Other spiritual workers had directed me to her, but I had been unable to find her house, as she lived on an unnamed dirt trace whose location could be described only in terms of landmarks. Papoy described the large mango tree that marked the trace's entrance and told me to watch out for an equally large pothole in the road; it would tell me I had reached my destination.

The next morning I drove the Ford Cortina to the place where the dirt trace on which she was said to live met the main road. As I started driving down the trace, I had to slow to a stop in front of a deep, axle-grinding pothole. Through the Cortina's open window, I asked a woman walking down the trace if she knew where Mother Mariella lived. She pointed me to a board house on stilts farther down the road and continued walking on ahead of the Cortina, whose progress was severely affected by having to slowly navigate an obstacle course of potholes. The woman turned out to be Mariella's daughter-in-law, who lived with her, and she informed Mariella upon reaching her home that an "Indian man" was coming down the road to look for her.

When Mariella saw me she was somewhat surprised to see a white man instead of an Indian man. I was equally surprised because I did not feel that I looked Indian, nor had anyone ever taken me for a descendant of the South Asian indentured laborers who accounted for about 40 percent of Trinidad's population. She had dreamed of an Indian man the night before, she told me. She saw him walking down her trace. He was coming to seek a better understanding of "the African side." "Sometimes the power does communicate with me in that way," she explained. When her daughter-in-law told her an Indian man was walking down the trace, she was prepared to explain a few things to him. Even though I turned out to be a white man, she took the uncanny conjunction of events as a sign and invited me onto her porch.

We sat down and had the first of many hours-long conversations about African religion in Trinidad. Much of what follows in these pages is indebted to her life of experience across Trinidad's three principal "paths" of African religion (Orisha, Kabbalah, and Spiritual Baptism) and to what she called her "experiments" with these traditions to solve clients' problems through spiritual work. While she did most of the talking, toward the end of our first conversation she turned the tables, asking what I was trying to do by studying African religion in Trinidad. I explained that I wanted to counteract long-standing racial biases against African religion that had made obeah into a feared and stigmatized practice. She looked at me for a while. "That is all well and good," she said, "but obeah *is* dangerous."

Like the Pentecostal Christians who had tried to exorcise obeah from Rio Moro's secondary school, for Mariella, obeah was a real and potentially dangerous force at work in the world. Unlike many Caribbean charismatic Christians, however, this danger was not a sign of the need to eradicate obeah through spiritual warfare, thus helping to pave the way for a kingdom of God without fear and death. The potential danger of (what got called) obeah was a part of its power, she told me, and I would do well to get myself some protection if I was undertaking this study.

CONCLUSION

It is almost certainly the case, as scholars have rightly insisted, that negative attitudes toward obeah in the Caribbean and beyond are a product of the continuing effects of colonial stigmatization and prohibition (e.g., Bilby and Handler 2004; Stewart 2005). I still share concerns with these popular negative attitudes toward obeah and the virulent anti-African sentiments that often accompany them. This was the concern that motivated the project I described to Mother Mariella. What her response made me realize, however, is that the circumspection of my interlocutors in Trinidad toward obeah is a part of the word's very power in discourse and practice. In fact, my interlocutors' contrasting disavowal of the term following the school possessions as well as their adoption of it in response to Arlena's murder were both premised on obeah's relation to harm. Drawing on the social theorizing of my interlocutors in Rio Moro, I now assert that in many cases — particularly instances that involve state and interpersonal violence — the harm associated with obeah can become an important tool for spiritual workers who are concerned with counteracting their clients' afflictions. As spiritual workers generally deal with people's most intractable problems, in situations where medical and legal remedies have failed, this proximity to harming force is an integral part of spiritual workers' labor. Although obeah remains a morally stigmatized practice in the anglophone Caribbean, associated with harm in the minds of many, this apparent stigmatization is also integral to the practical power of the term, as the mobilization of obeah in the protests against the police shootings illustrated.

Perhaps more important, the line between healing and harm, protection and injury, or legitimate and illegitimate force is not as clear as the model of colonial false consciousness might imply. Like my interlocutors' divergent appraisals of obeah's value, the delineation of force as harming or healing is often situated and contingent. For the police officers who killed the young women in Rio Moro, the affliction of the dead was a harming force that they counteracted with their own protecting spiritual work; for those who loved the dead, this affliction was a potentially healing and justice-making influence (even as it could turn against them). An ethnographic consideration of obeah thus affords a more complex view on ethics, whether spiritual or political, in which moral polyvalence is inherent in the exercise of force. Such an approach to the ethical conceives of social fields as contested terrain in which the healing-harming ambivalence of certain powers is integral to their efficacy in making justice and injustice (see chapter 3).

An important way to counteract the effects of colonial stigmatization is to focus on the historical construction of obeah, insisting either that colonial lawmaking created obeah as a category or that it transformed an originally positive or neutral term into a negative one. Somewhere in the past, these approaches often imply, we might find a point of origin—in either colonial constructions or venerable homeland traditions—that will reveal the truth of what obeah really is, thus explaining (and explaining away) obeah's persistent associations with forms of harm. These interventions perform important work, yet they may risk subordinating the tactical polyvalence of present uses of obeah to an authorizing past event, obscuring the contingent and shifting entanglements of justice, religion, and harm in lived contexts. Far from denying the connections between contemporary instantiations of obeah and the figures of colonialism, slavery, indenture, and homeland tradition, I advocate for an investigation of the ways these links between past and present are made and unmade in tactical situations of power and law (Scott 1991).

While the law is an authority charged with protection and justice-making in regnant models of liberal governance and the rule of law, state law continues to inflict grave harm on subaltern persons (while often failing to protect them from harm) in modern states. In the face of this contradictory valence of law, one of the principal tasks of spiritual workers I knew was intervention in the criminal justice system to either vindicate clients or incite an often-unresponsive legal system to take action in a matter. Obeah is thus an ideology and practice of justice-making, and, like most forms of law, potential harm is a constitutive feature of its force.[13] In other words, even though colonial stigmatization has most certainly shaped contemporary attitudes, we need not purify obeah of harm to decolonize or revalue the term. In attempting to make obeah a morally univalent practice of healing and protection, one might even enact a particularly Euro-Christian project of moral purification and redemption, discounting Caribbean spiritual workers' own insistence on the danger of obeah as false consciousness. My fieldwork in Rio Moro brought me up against the limits of this redemptive project. Initially, I thought the best way to defend obeah from continuing intolerance was to dispel its associations with danger and harm, making it into (what I thought was) "legitimate" religion. This chapter, however, has been an exercise in ethnographically deconstructing that redemptive project.

Modern law in liberal democracies, as legal scholars Sarat and Kearns

(1993, 2) note, ideally aims to subordinate violence to written norms that draw the line between right and wrong. Scholars have said the same thing about religion. Indeed, the idea that good religion supersedes violence is a major premise of Euro-Christian narratives of moral (and racial) supersession. The story of a Christian God of love supplanting a violent and jealous Hebrew God is a key prop of many stories of Christian distinction. Yet this widespread narrative is contradicted by Jesus's own constant invocations of hellfire and violent punishment or Old Testament invocations of God's mercy and compassion (Lamb 2011). Perhaps this counterfactual narrative has such power because it reflects ideals of religion that emerged from the Enlightenment and were operationalized to justify Christian moral superiority in colonial settings (despite the ever-present reality of colonial violence). Chapter 4 explores this narrative of supersession as the basis for the racial stigmatization of practices of animal sacrifice and obeah. In the present chapter, the argument is that this liberal narrative of religion (and law) superseding violence is a key "analytical fiction" of Western modernity (Trouillot 2003), which has been used to criminalize or denigrate non-European religious practices. It is not "religious violence" that is a myth (Cavanaugh 2009), but the idea of good religion (or law) domesticating violence that remains a tenacious (yet counterempirical) origin story for both modern conceptions of Christianity and liberal nation-states.

Supposedly, liberal democratic theory beheaded the monarch and subordinated sovereign violence to the rule of law, just as Enlightenment thinkers were dispensing with the need for exceptional miracles and divine violence as the basis for (and evidence of) God's sovereignty. Yet law continues to depend on racialized violence in mundane states of exception, and religion continues to involve performances of exceptional power—whether in charismatic healing, spiritual warfare, or acts of divine justice (e.g., Benjamin 1986; McAlister 2014; O'Neill 2015; Yelle 2010). The exceptional powers of obeah and policing at Number Twenty-One Junction showed how both religion and law were more than systems that curbed violence and subordinated exceptional power to ethical codes. They were performances of the disputed location of sovereign power—whether such power was located in god(s), the rule of law, the police, the dead, or obeah. Defined as the power to dispose of life and authoritatively operate outside natural and social laws, sovereignty is rooted in the violence (or the miracle) of states of exception (Yelle 2010). As assertions about the locus of sovereign power, neither religion nor law can escape the violence on which performances of sovereignty are ultimately based.

Nevertheless, as the opening sections of this chapter discussed, religion and state law are so often supposed to be forces for curbing, channeling, or interdicting violence; otherwise, religion becomes fanaticism or witchcraft, and the rule of law becomes autocracy.[14] In contrast, obeah, with its open recognition of the healing and harming power of law or religion, highlights the ambivalence of the rule of law, in which racialized violence is inflicted in the name of order, security, and the moral redemption of society in contemporary Trinidad (and much of the rest of the world). The colonial and postcolonial laws against obeah in the Caribbean promised a similar work of reform, allegedly replacing potentially violent or atavistic superstition with science, law, rational governance, and proper religion. Contemporary Pentecostal-charismatic spiritual warfare against the obeah of Rio Moro (as I detail in chapter 6) also promises a resonant work of reform, in which the sovereign order of both law and God can be realized through the defeat of obeah, demons, or native religion. Modernity, as Seligman and colleagues (2008) rightly note, is a continuous, always-unfinished project of reform in which violence will be redeemed by ethical conceptions of religion or politics. The violence of dictatorships or religious fanaticism is supposedly redeemed by the rule of law and liberal democracy. Yet such performances of redemption are enacted through almost unthinkable acts of violence—a father's sacrifice of his own son for the liberation of humanity, the indiscriminate civilian suffering inflicted by US air strikes and economic sanctions in the name of "freedom," or the mass incarceration of racialized populations to ensure "citizen security."

Rather than making racial distinctions that allow for a separation between legitimate force and uncivilized violence, confronting the link between religion and violence means understanding an inherent tension between the rule and the exception in lived practices. The rule of law and the notion of religions as sets of rules, beliefs, and prescribed rituals reach their limits at exceptional crossroads of violence and (in)justice. This is the crossroads that obeah occupies, suspending or inverting the law through experiments with power. In the next chapter, "On Turning in the Grave," I detail how spiritual workers intentionally violated or reversed religious norms to make justice for their clients. If some of the grossest abuses of power have been exercised in states of exception to the law, then some of the most powerful forms of resistance have also taken exception to religious and legal norms. This is what happened at Number Twenty-One Junction, as performances of exceptional violence and experiments with power both showed the ambivalence of the rule of law and its foundation in harming force.

In the Valley of Dry Bones

Three years before the events at Number Twenty-One Junction, Bishop Dawes laid the blindfolded Arlena down into her "spiritual grave," placing her inside the outlined shape of a coffin, drawn with white chalk on the floor of the mourning room. Arlena was embarking on her first journey of mourning, secluded in a special room reserved for such blindfolded travels in the back of Dawes's Spiritual Baptist church. As her pointer—the person who would guide Arlena on her spiritual journey of mourning—Dawes made sure Arlena's head pointed toward the west when she laid down inside the white chalk outline of a coffin. Such an orientation was not incidental. Corpses were usually laid in their graves with their heads pointing in the direction of the setting sun, and like the sun and the dead, Arlena was going down beneath the horizon into what Bishop Dawes called the "spiritual tomb" to visit "the Valley of Dry Bones." Three days later, if Arlena had not yet "burst the tomb"—or spontaneously rose up from her grave of her own accord singing exuberantly—Bishop Dawes would pick Arlena's body up and turn it so that her head pointed to the east. Like the easterly rising sun, or the "Son of Man" who had risen from the grave after three days, Arlena's spirit would ideally rise from the Depths and begin to travel in a realm that Spiritual Baptists call the Nations, to spiritual locations known as India, Africa, or China.

First, however, Arlena had to go down into the Depths, beginning her journey as all initial mourners did: with her simulated death. Over Arlena's supine, westward-pointing body, Bishop Dawes read from Ezekiel 37:1–10, a key passage for understanding the Depths and this stage of figurative death in mourning. In the King James Version, preferred by Spiritual Baptists, this passage gives a firsthand account of Ezekiel's own journey into the Valley of Dry Bones:

> The hand of the LORD was upon me, and carried me out in the spirit of the LORD, and set me down in the midst of the valley which was full of bones,
> And caused me to pass by them round about: and, behold, there were very many in the open valley; and, lo, they were very dry.

And he said unto me, Son of man, can these bones live? And I answered, O
  Lord God, thou knowest.
Again he said unto me, Prophesy upon these bones, and say unto them, O ye
  dry bones, hear the word of the LORD.
Thus saith the Lord GOD unto these bones; Behold, I will cause breath to
  enter into you, and ye shall live:
And I will lay sinews upon you, and will bring up flesh upon you, and cover
  you with skin, and put breath in you, and ye shall live; and ye shall
  know that I am the LORD.
So I prophesied as I was commanded: and as I prophesied, there was a noise,
  and behold a shaking, and the bones came together, bone to his bone.
And when I beheld, lo, the sinews and the flesh came up upon them, and the
  skin covered them above: but there was no breath in them.
Then said he unto me, Prophesy unto the wind, prophesy, son of man, and
  say to the wind, Thus saith the Lord GOD; Come from the four winds,
  O breath, and breathe upon these slain, that they may live.
So I prophesied as he commanded me, and the breath came into them, and
  they lived, and stood up upon their feet.

When Bishop Dawes finished reading Ezekiel's words, Arlena opened
her "spiritual eyes" even as her "carnal" eyes remained closed behind the
blindfold.[1] She saw skeletons dancing in a dim dry valley, and the music
they danced to was the rhythm their own bleached bones made knocking
together—"clip, clop, clip." Dressed all in black, Ezekiel himself stood at
the head of the skeletal dancing troupe. Followed by the skeletons, Ezekiel
approached Arlena, stopping in front of her. As spirit entities often did during mourning, he posed a question to Arlena that was like a gate through
which she had to pass to progress in her journey.

"What is a man?" Ezekiel asked.

"Dust," Arlena answered, drawing on the description in Genesis of
humans' mortal return to dust when God kicked them out of the garden.

Ezekiel laughed. "And tell me, mortal, have you ever partaken of that
which they call an X-ray?"

Arlena answered in the affirmative.

"And have you ever seen in that X-ray that which they call the soul?"

Arlena had to answer in the negative. She told him that she had seen
something like the skeletons that stood before her, but as she told him this,
she noticed that the skeletons were no longer dancing. They had fallen to
pieces around Ezekiel, a collection of disarticulated bones.

"Breathe upon these bones that they may live!" Ezekiel commanded her, and Arlena began to search through the bones and the dust of the dry valley. Slowly she placed bone to bone, reconstructing entire skeletons. This is where Arlena gained her knowledge about setting broken bones, which she would use to heal neighbors and clients in Rio Moro (see also Forde 2002). As she placed the bones together, she began to recite her "key" — usually a short biblical passage that a pointer gives to a mourner for guidance during difficult trials in the Spiritual Lands. The key that Bishop Dawes had given her for the Depths was a verse from Psalm 139: "The night shineth as the day: the darkness and the light are both alike to thee."

As she said these words, the skeletons began to rise up on shaky legs and move again. "The darkness and the light are both alike," Ezekiel repeated. "And yet they call us who dwell in the Depths evil!" Ezekiel laughed at the irony of his own words as he placed a black band of cloth around Arlena's wrist and spun her around and around. She would bring this black cloth back with her to Trinidad, and she would wear it to church on Sundays to show that she is a woman who had gained knowledge of the Depths. Ezekiel continued to laugh at his own words as he walked away followed by the clip-clopping of the rearticulated skeletons. "It is in death that we know life," Ezekiel said, his voice trailing off as he disappeared into the darkness.

FIGURE 2.1. A Spiritual Baptist pointer baptizes a first-time mourner. Trinidad. Photograph by the author, 2011.

FIGURE 2.2. Bishop Dawes rings his handbell atop Arlena's grave mound. Photograph by the author, 2011.

EXPERIMENTS WITH JUSTICE

On Turning in the Grave

A TURN IN THE GRAVE

When Bishop Dawes laid his spiritual daughter Arlena down into her physical grave in Rio Moro's public cemetery, located amid the abandoned cane fields around Number Twenty-One Junction, he made sure that her head pointed toward the east, in the direction of the rising sun.[1] The family members charged with lowering the coffin into the freshly dug hole using a couple of thick ropes had almost gotten it wrong, as they had Arlena's head pointing west, the usual orientation for those who were going down into the depths of their grave. Even as the coffin was already halfway down, Bishop Dawes began to quarrel with the men who were slowly letting the ropes that supported the casket slip through their hands. He made them haul the casket back up. He then spun his spiritual daughter's coffin around and laid her with her head pointing in the direction of a mourner getting ready to rise from the tomb. At only twenty-one years of age, her life cut short by police bullets, Arlena went down into the grave at a semi-upright angle. Her body was an arrow pointing at the part of the sky where the sun would appear the next morning.

The grave digger circled the hole he had just stood inside, his clothes covered with clay earth, and sang the hymn "Soon Shall We Meet Again." The men who had lowered their loved one into the grave took turns with the grave digger's shovel, scooping the heavy clay soil they had piled at the edges of the grave back into the hole. The first clods of soil made hollow thuds as

they landed on the coffin's top, and then the shovelfuls of earth on earth became softer as the hole filled. As the last clods landed on top of the grave, the
dead woman's brother used the back of his shovel to form the excess earth
into a packed, coffin-sized mound that Bishop Dawes then climbed on top
of. As the setting sun silhouetted his body, he raised his arm into the air and
pointed east, making his arm an arrow that mirrored the orientation of the
casket below him. "No grave can hold this body down," he proclaimed to
those gathered; "we have sent it out to do a work" (fig. 2.3).

   In this burial of Arlena, Bishop Dawes was reversing the order and
orientation of a good burial. Because a spirit was typically thought to stick
around immediately after death in Rio Moro, the material actions of a burial
typically sought to weigh the spirit down and separate it from the world of
the living. When family members lowered Arlena into her grave with her
head pointing west, this orientation was meant to point her spirit in the direction of the setting sun, inciting it to rest. When Dawes flipped her body
around so that it pointed east—the direction that he also pointed toward
with his hand—he might have seemed to be violating mortuary norms.
Some attendees of the funeral even said that Dawes (with the assistance of
other spiritual workers) had violated what, according to scholars, is a cross-
cultural taboo on prostrate burial, inverting the proper orientation of Arlena's corpse by placing it facedown in the coffin. Why were Dawes and other
spiritual workers literally turning over both his spiritual daughter and the
norms of mortuary rituals in the grave?

   I visited Bishop Dawes's house months after the funeral, shortly after
the police involved in the shooting of his spiritual daughter were unex-
pectedly arrested. Confronted by the mosaic of Hindu, Kabbalistic, Christian, Buddhist, and Yoruba traditions on display in his living room altars, I
wanted to know which of these traditions had inspired his justice-seeking
mortuary rites. When Dawes responded that this work was "not a tradition"
but an "experiment with power" or "science," he planted a seed of "epistemic
disconcertment" in me that would root and ramify over my following years
of field research in Trinidad (see Verran 2001). Like many scholars of African diasporic religions, I had assumed that Dawes was engaged in the practice of a tradition (or, as his domestic altars to various West African, Christian, and Hindu powers showed, multiple traditions). As Beliso de Jesús
(2015, 3) has argued, African-inspired religions are quintessentially traditional, in that they are "legitimized only through connections to an authentically experienced past." These contested connections separate inauthentic
"inventions" from authentic tradition (Beliso de Jesús 2015, 55, 193). What I

FIGURE 2.3. "No grave can hold this body down." Bishop Dawes stands atop Arlena's grave mound as the sun sets behind him. Photograph by the author, 2011.

did not know, however, was that my interlocutors would speak about experiments or science, using words that seemed to diametrically oppose tradition in modern economies of race and religion. Alongside the (re)making of an ethical or ethnic past through embodied ritual disciplines, Dawes was engaged in the making of a largely unexpected future through practices that

were "not a tradition." In the face of what he knew to be the normative rituals of justice, which heavily weighted the words of officers over lower-class
black people, he sought to produce an exceptional result. This, he said, was
an experiment with power.

In this chapter, I take this epistemic disconcertment as an occasion for
proposing an alternative "experimental" framework for religious practice
that my interlocutors elaborated. It is not simply African religions that have
been overwhelmingly shaped by a framework of "tradition" in the twentieth and early twenty-first centuries. Following Talal Asad's (1986) influential
polemic for studying Islam as a "discursive tradition," much recent critical
work has sought to approach religious practices as "traditions" (see Anidjar
2009; Anjum 2007; Asad 1986; Beliso de Jesús 2015; Bouzar 2012; Scott 1991).
Asad (1986, 5, 14) argues that traditions "instruct practitioners regarding
the correct form and purpose of a given practice," defining these practices
as correct through their connection to an authoritative past moment when
a practice was instituted. This does not mean that traditions are static, for
ideas about the past (and how to remain faithful to it) change. Nevertheless, the focus of such traditions remains that of defining correct practice
through a (constantly debated) relation to an exemplary past rather than in
altering present relations of power or creating an unexpected future. Rejecting Western modernity's emphasis on breaking with tradition, a number of
recent studies of religion have drawn on this framework of discursive tradition to look at the ways that pious subjects attempt to inhabit rather than
resist norms (e.g., Hirschkind 2006; Jouili 2015; Mahmood 2003a, 2005).
When I asked Dawes which tradition inspired his inversions of mortuary
norms, I drew on these scholarly critiques to frame his justice-seeking practices.

Yet if "traditions" are defined by collective norms and shared rules
that refer to an authoritative past (as any dictionary definition of the word
attests), then where did a frame of tradition leave spiritual workers' practices of violating or reversing norms to create an altered future? Certainly,
anthropologists of Africa have often encountered practices that seemed to
intentionally invert shared mores. These scholars, however, asserted that
such "rituals of reversal" ultimately functioned to underscore the collective
norms that ruled "African traditional societies" (e.g., Gluckman 1953; Spencer 1988; Turner [1969] 2017, 1974). Reflecting a much broader tendency to
define ritual as a functional or expressive mechanism in the service of social
control (cf. Bell [1992] 2009, 197), these approaches to "rituals of reversal"
still placed them within the framework of tradition. In this interpretation,

Bishop Dawes's inversions served to underscore the deviance of his own practices, thus affirming the normal order of a good burial.

This chapter argues something different. The counternormative practices of Dawes and other spiritual workers were meant not to express the collective norms of a tradition, identifying a past moment when these norms were instituted, but to effect future justice. Drawing on theories of "divine violence," this chapter shows how justice cannot be conflated with shared norms but often demands breaking the rules of legal or religious traditions. In the previous chapter, I showed how a political theology of the rule of law, which the well-known lawyer upheld at Number Twenty-One Junction, insisted that compliance with shared rules and procedural norms could secure justice. Rather than blocking roads and working obeah, protesters should "let the law handle it," he said. In a remarkably similar way, the scholarly turn toward tradition has emphasized what Naisargi Dave (2012, 7) has called a "juridical ethics—practices and techniques that work to more deeply inhabit law rather than to undermine it" (see also Ziarek 1995). In this common view, echoed by Shweder (2016), "justice" is equivalent to the impartial application of laws and ethical rules.[2] As some scholars have noted (e.g., Bell [1992] 2009, Yelle 2010), the modern category of religion (and the ideas about ritual that accompany it) has tended to be represented in the terms of this juridical ethics, as codified traditions of ethical norms. I wondered, however, whether such frameworks risked leaving Dawes's practices of intentionally breaking and inverting norms precisely where colonial regimes placed them—as illegal practices outside the bounds of a recognized religious tradition.

Dawes himself unsettled these limits when he asserted that his justice-seeking practices were "experiments," rather than a "tradition," to "ensure that justice is served." Tradition remains an incredibly important framework for Dawes and other spiritual workers, but the framework has exclusionary limits. This chapter follows Dawes and other spiritual workers in suggesting that a focus on justice rather than tradition redefines experimental religious practices as something other than deviant. Like experimental art or divine violence, spiritual workers' experimentation contravened norms to produce a radically contingent state of affairs. Instead of establishing a new form of "correct practice," Dawes and other spiritual workers' inversions of burial norms derived their power from their incorrectness. In this chapter, what my interlocutors call "experiments" refer precisely to the moments in which ritualization departs from the juridical ethics that have dominated both conceptions of ritual and recent scholarly turns toward tradition.

This chapter thus focuses on spiritual workers' practices of turning persons and practices around, over, or inside out to produce a radical change in a particular state of affairs. I show how the application of a certain racialized framework of tradition has led to scholarly and popular misinterpretations of Dawes's counternormative burial practices (and of counternormative spiritual work more generally). I then use my interlocutors' theories of experiments and power to redescribe these practices of overturning, focusing on the "divine violence" (Benjamin 1986) of justice-making ruptures in religious and state law. First, however, I begin with the experiment with power that inaugurated obeah's criminalization in the wake of Tacky's Rebellion in eighteenth-century Jamaica, illustrating the tension between experimentation and tradition in modern race-making projects. In many ways, this chapter is a polemic against these projects, redescribing the opposition between tradition and innovation that has undergirded racialized distinctions in Western modernity. Scholarly debates about the proper conceptualization of African American practices have often revolved around this opposition, emphasizing either the creole inventiveness of New World Africans or the continuities of tradition between Africa and the Americas.[3] I argue that spiritual workers' ethos of experimentation signals something different. Unlike scholarly emphases on creole innovations, this ethos of experimentation is not defined by novelty, and it does not seek to institute new norms of tradition. Experiments with power, such as Dawes's burial practices, are repeatable practices that are defined, in part, by the norms they invert. In contrast to the Herskovitsian search for Africanisms in the New World, the lens of experimentation does not define Africanness in terms of the preserved continuities of discrete practices (although such continuities undoubtedly exist). Rather, inversions, reversals, and experiments in African spiritual work signal an ethos that disrupts this opposition between tradition and innovation in Western modernity.

RITUAL, TRADITION, EXPERIMENTATION

One of the central props of the germinal Enlightenment separation of African tradition from history and modernity was that Africans did not experiment. Instead of open-minded, experimental investigation, they were allegedly preoccupied with ritualistic repetition — a repetition that modeled the mistaken certainties of relatively unchanging tradition (e.g., Brosses

[1760] 1970, Hegel [1837] 1956). Years later, in one of the best-known descriptions of an African society in the twentieth century, *Witchcraft, Oracles, and Magic among the Azande*, the British anthropologist Evans-Pritchard stated that his interlocutors—and their magical practices—were "rational" but that they did not understand "the real causes of things." Their magic and witchcraft were rational but not real because "they are not experimentally inclined" and relied on the rote explanations of tradition rather than empirical testing. "Not being experimentally inclined," Evans-Pritchard (1937) continued, "they do not test the efficacy of their medicines" (qtd. in Otto and Stausberg 2014, 155). Three decades later, in a series of well-known articles, Robin Horton (1967a) echoed Evans-Pritchard's argument in asserting that "African traditional knowledge" was rational—internally consistent and explanatory. Yet, as did Evans-Pritchard, Horton (1967b) argued that this knowledge was limited by Africans' imputed lack of experimentation and reliance on static traditions to explain phenomena. He alleged that Western culture was "open" because it experimented, whereas African cultures were "closed" because they repeated the same ritual traditions rather than engaging in experimentation (Horton 1967b).[4]

This contrast between an experimental, dynamic West and a tradition-bound Africa has not disappeared; it structures both negative images of Africa as atavistic and Romantic ideas of Africa as traditional, more in touch with nature, and inherently magical. When in 2007, the French head of state Nicolas Sarkozy, on a diplomatic visit to Senegal, insisted on Africans' resistance to "progress" and "development," he more bluntly echoed Horton's idea of African traditional societies as closed and relatively static: "The African peasant only knew the eternal renewal of time, marked by the endless repetition of the same gestures and the same words. In this realm of fancy . . . there is neither room for human endeavour nor the idea of progress" (qtd. in Ba 2007).

The gist of the former French president's comments continues to echo through accusations about the "civilizational," "superstitious," or "cultural" causes for diasporic and continental Africans' alleged resistance to development and progress, from the former head of the US Agency for International Development in Haiti to Sarkozy's successor, Emmanuel Macron (see Anyangwe 2017; Ba 2007; Brooks 2010; Harrison 2010; Harrison and Huntington 2000). In these commentaries, Afro-Caribbean religion or a generalized notion of African tradition is the very cause of contemporary poverty and resistance to modern science, development, and progress. In many of these representations, science and the experimental method were more than

practices performed in laboratories. They were what Michel-Rolph Trouillot (2003) has called "North Atlantic universals"—a set of concepts, such
as modernity, development, religion, and national sovereignty, that signal
both universal pretensions and prescriptive moral and political projects.
Because these categories presume universality, they are the terms through
which non-Westerners, as Talal Asad (2003, 14) notes, have been invited to
gauge their own (in)adequacy in both colonial and late liberal projects of
economic, political, and moral reform. As Trouillot emphasizes, the defini-
tional limits of these universals are inherently exclusionary because they are
defined through certain germinal oppositions, including most particularly
the dichotomy of African tradition and modern conceptions of science, development, and experimentation.

These oppositions were very much on display in the "experiments" that
inaugurated the criminalization of obeah. As with the justice-seeking protests in the wake of Arlena's death, obeah entered colonial discourse as an in-
spiring force for resistance to racialized violence, and the first laws to criminalize obeah were written in response to the largest slave rebellion in the
eighteenth-century British Caribbean—Tacky's Rebellion of 1760. Leaders
of this uprising in Jamaica were identified by colonial officials as obeah
practitioners who had administered oaths that bound rebels to secrecy
and had manufactured powders that might bring rebels luck and protection
in battle. After the capture of these leaders, colonial officials were intent on
trumping the imputed power—the obi or obeah—of their captives through
what colonial observers called "experiments" (*Report of the Lords* 1789, 117;
see also Edwards [1793–1801] 1972). Electricity was then the current scientific fascination, and authorities subjected the alleged obeah practitioners
to electrical shocks while projecting images on their bodies with magic lan-
terns (an early technology of image projection). According to the Jamaican
planter and historian Bryan Edwards ([1793–1801] 1972), one of the leaders
of the slave rebellion remarked that "his master's obi exceeded his own" after
receiving particularly powerful shocks in these "experiments."

Obeah's criminalization, then, literally began with an experiment with
power. Yet rather than simply showing that Europeans could experiment
while Africans remained mired in superstition, the colonial accounts of one
of the rebel leader's words seemed to reverse this relationship. Describing the
electrical shocks as the very obeah that colonial authorities condemned, the
captured leader of the rebellion cast Western experimentation in Europe's
image of African ritualism. While North Atlantic universals were based in
the opposition between an experimental Europe and a superstitious Africa,

the experiments that the British performed on the first accused obeah practitioners seemed like something far different from the open-ended experimentation that has been upheld as a Western virtue. Rather than subverting norms and creating novel conditions, the public experiments following
Tacky's Rebellion aimed to affirm the power of colonial law in carefully controlled demonstrations on bound subjects. Through the "repetition of the
same gestures and the same words," to repurpose Sarkozy's phrase, colonial
experiments demonstrated certain truths, hierarchical power relations, or
natural laws. Experiments, like those that followed Tacky's Rebellion, thus
resembled what Horton (1967b) characterized as "closed" rituals—the very
change-resistant, scripted procedures of which Enlightenment Europeans
accused Africans (e.g., Brosses [1760] 1970, Hegel [1837] 1956). As spectacu-
lar displays of scientific discoveries performed authority in colonial settings
(Prakash 1999, 2003) and colonies were envisioned as "laboratories" (Nelson
2003), science experiments played this role of demonstrating the power of
North Atlantic truths. In short, the experiments with power that followed
Tacky's Rebellion evidenced what Dave (2012) calls "juridical ethics" by bol-
stering regnant norms and legal codes in colonial settings.

Certainly, one meaning of the word "experiment" is a demonstration of
a truth or a law under controlled conditions. The experiments with power
that led to obeah's criminalization would seem to echo this definition. The
word "experiment," however, can connote a tentative or novel procedure
that will disrupt norms, provoking an unexpected state of affairs. Experiments in art, theater, film, or (to some extent) laboratory sciences are often
defined by the radical alteration of a normal state to make contingent what
had been taken for granted. What defines a particular work as experimental is not that it is new or unprecedented (innovation can be found across
many forms of "traditional art") but that it is "out of step with the dominant techniques and styles of the moment, preferring the unfamiliar to the
familiar" (Jameson 2010). When Dawes said that his spiritual work was "not
a tradition" but an "experiment with power," he was invoking this counternormative connotation of the experimental. He was making a distinction
between tradition and experimentation that any number of scholars have
made in describing modern science, art, literature, or film (e.g., Feyerabend
1975; Jameson 2010; Nyman 1999). Science, as Thomas Kuhn ([1962] 1996)
famously insisted, involves both the extremely valuable work of "normal
science," which, as Marx and Bornmann (2010, 442) note, confirms the "beliefs, norms, and values shared by members of a group of scientists," and
what Kuhn called the experimental "paradigm shifts" that lead to scientific

revolutions, in which new frameworks supersede disciplinary norms.[5] Science, in short, is both traditional and experimental, and African religion in Trinidad is no different in this respect. Unlike Kuhn's story of dramatic paradigm shifts, however, experimentation and tradition in spiritual work are not successive stages of a progress narrative but modalities that exist in dialectical tension and are good for different situations.

From the experiments with power that helped to inaugurate the criminalization of obeah to those that followed the deaths of Arlena and her friends, what got called obeah has been intertwined with experimentation. While North Atlantic rituals of power might place Western science and African religion on either side of an experimentation-tradition divide, this segregation is what Michel-Rolph Trouillot (2003) called an "analytical fiction" of modernity. Ironically, the eighteenth-century displays of technology that were supposed to demonstrate the power of European experimentation were (in Westerners' own terms) more traditional than experimental—they upheld regnant norms through self-confirming, predictable performances. In contrast, spiritual workers' experiments with power in the wake of Arlena's death inverted the norms of burial traditions to reverse the normal power relations of law in Trinidad. Unlike the opposition between individual innovation and genealogical tradition that structures both Western liberal thought (see Povinelli 2006) and representations of African traditional religion (see Beliso de Jesús 2015), experimentation and tradition were not mutually exclusive modalities for my interlocutors. Even the most radical experimentation needs a normal state—the traditional order of burial, a set of artistic conventions, an accepted scientific paradigm, or a control condition—to be powerful. Experimentation and tradition, in sum, are the generative polarities of a dialectic rather than racialized opposites. As Bishop Dawes's account of his own experiments with power shows, both tradition and experimentation were vital modes of practice for spiritual workers in Trinidad.

FROM LAW-PRESERVING RITUALS
TO EXPERIMENTS WITH POWER

The tradition of North Atlantic modernity conditioned me to expect that Dawes would use other words besides "experiment" to describe his practices. When I asked Bishop Dawes to situate his justice-seeking burial practices, I expected him to frame his work using the words "tradition" or "ritual." While "tradition" has been closely aligned to definitions of religion in modernity, "ritual," as Jonathan Z. Smith (1980, 113) reminds us, also forms "one of the basic building blocks of religion." Smith (1980, 124–25) goes on to note (in language strikingly similar to scientistic discourse about the experiment or the laboratory) that ritual creates "a controlled environment where the vagaries of ordinary life may be displaced." According to dictionary definitions, ritual could imply both a prescribed procedure for a religious rite or a prescribed code of behavior regulating social conduct but both definitions speak of ritual's character as controlled and governing repetition (see Smith 1980, 114). For a long line of theorists, ritual embodies the character of religion as an essentially ordering and meaning-making force, a performance of the sacred that either reaffirms existing social structure or enacts an idealized subjunctive order in contradistinction to the vagaries of the profane world (e.g., Durkheim [1912] 1964; Seligman et al. 2008; Smith 1980; cf. Bell [1992] 2009; Smith 1993, 300–302; Yelle 2010).[6]

While the word "experiment" can express the demonstration of authority and known truth, as it did in the first trials against obeah practitioners, it also connotes the alteration of a baseline condition to produce a novel result. For many of my interlocutors, "experiment" provides a more accurate descriptor than "ritual" for the material practices of spiritual work because it foregrounds improvisation, novel combinations of disparate elements and traditions, or counternormative actions. When Bishop Dawes buried his spiritual daughter facedown and semi-upright, he was performing acts that violated and inverted his own conceptions of proper burial ritual, and it was precisely through this inversion of prescribed order that Dawes hoped to achieve unprecedented effects. Although both science and religion present some ideal of invariance, experimentation aims to intervene in a material assemblage, to introduce a novel element that breaks with a baseline control to produce some effect. Especially in the realm of the arts, experimental methods imply the disruption of convention to produce the unfamiliar, rendering taken-for-granted norms contingent (Jameson 2010). Bishop Dawes situated his work as experiment, rather than ritual or tradition, precisely because he aimed to destabilize the norms of law and burial practice by inverting convention.

When Dawes contradicted me by saying that his work was an experiment, he was not denying the importance of collective norms in religious practice. Like other spiritual workers, Dawes was committed to an array of recognized religious traditions. The idea that there were separable, normative, and racially marked bodies of orthopraxy was on display in Dawes's living room, which contained spatially separate altars to Hindu, Kabbalistic, Yoruba, and Christian traditions (see introduction). These distinct altars instantiated what Trinidadian practitioners of African religions call "paths" (McNeal 2011), or what practitioners of Afro-Cuban religions might call *reglas,* "rules" or "orders."[7] Yet alongside this dynamic mosaic of orders, Dawes asserted that there was a place for the exception as well as the rule in his religious practices.

When I asked Dawes about tradition, he responded by discussing powers that reversed or negated religious and legal orders. These reversals of a corpse's orientation and other burial rites were precisely what made his practices different from a communal tradition. In cases of natural death, he insisted that there were traditions (reflected in his living room altars) that would govern someone's burial. He used the example of Babalorisha Clarence Forde, the then-recently-deceased leader of Trinidad's national Orisha organization, who was also a threefold practitioner: "It have a tradition in the case of Baba Forde, who died the death of God's people, lived a full life, who was in his bed and died. So his funeral would be about jubilation, happiness, thanksgiving, praising God. He was buried under Orisha, [Spiritual] Baptist, and Kabbalah [rites]. But in the case of Arlena . . . she was murdered in cold blood, so the work in her funeral would be much different."

Because Babalorisha Clarence Forde was a threefold practitioner, he was buried under rites that reflected the three principal traditions that shaped his life. Forde's wake featured the singing of Spiritual Baptist hymns inside his compound's Orisha *palais.* When I showed up on the morning of his funeral in 2010, people were lining up to view his corpse on display inside his "tabernacle"—the building in his compound devoted to the Trinidadian Kabbalah. After Kabbalistic rites, Forde's coffin was paraded through the cemetery by the costumed dancers of a Yoruba-centric Orisha shrine's Egungun masquerade troupe.[8] As with Bishop Dawes, Baba Forde's life and death reflected the multiple traditions of African religion in Trinidad.

Yet because the conditions of Arlena's death were "much different," Dawes asserted that the collective traditions might not be appropriate for her funeral. "There are some things we do in the light of day, in public," Bishop Dawes told me, "but it also have what they call the secret parts of spirituality." Because his mortuary practices for Arlena's funeral inverted accepted norms, Dawes realized that his actions might shock the conscience of most and had to remain secret. Rather than conducting a series of public rituals to celebrate a life and join people together, Dawes had to conceal what he had done from many of Arlena's own family and friends: "When we finished dealing with the body, according to what we did, nobody was supposed to see that body. If people would have open the box, there would have been grief, bawling, people wanting to touch her body, crying. So that's why we had the box sealed."[9] Dawes was well aware that his counternormative actions might be seen as negative, evil, or bad, but he insisted, as did other spiritual workers I had met, that bad was good for certain things. As I argued in the previous chapter, (what gets called) obeah is not inherently bad or good for spiritual workers, but it *is* dangerous, powerful, and ultimately based in partially hidden practices rather than revealed and collective traditions. By overturning the norms of revealed traditions in secret practices, spiritual workers could release oppositional, vengeful, or violent forces in exceptional situations of power. As Bishop Dawes went on to tell me:

> Spirituality is a movement, you know; it moves, it shapes us, it makes things happen . . . and everything have its opposite in the spirit [world]. The work we did was to oppose the way law happen in this country . . . to oppose other [spiritual] work the police [had] done. Because them police had pundit [Hindu religious leaders] working for them, you know. And because of what was done, things that were going in their [the police officers'] favor have been reversed. At the end of the day, there must be a balance . . . between darkness and light, good and evil, negative and positive. But without negative, there will be no mystery to it. There will be no opposite. Negative is not good or bad, it just have its purpose. That is what makes spirit beautiful and that is what makes it also a bit dangerous.

Dawes admitted that his spiritual work harnessed "negative" or "opposite" spiritual forces to reverse the luck of the police officers and the typical biases of the criminal justice system, but he insisted that negative force had its place. Its purpose was to oppose, reverse, and overturn an entrenched state of affairs. Rather than the order-affirming repetitions of ritual or tradition, Dawes's experiments were meant to turn over the order of legal and religious ritual by turning over the corpse of his spiritual daughter in its grave.

As Bishop Dawes described and justified his justice-seeking spiritual work in his living room that day, I wondered whether his practices might not form a kind of tradition after all. As he told me how his work was "to oppose the way law happen in this country," I speculated that (what got called) obeah might be a type of system of law. Certainly other spiritual workers had suggested something similar to me, claiming that obeah was a form

of redress when the courts failed black people (see chapter 3). As Mindie
Lazarus-Black (1994a, 1994b) and Diana Paton (2004) have suggested, obeah
represented a subaltern legal system in colonial situations where the courts
failed to protect subaltern populations (and were largely mobilized against
them). As a number of scholars have noted with regard to other religiously
motivated civil rights or anticolonial movements, spiritual work could reflect
the ethical ideals of religious traditions, which would provide a higher moral
law when the systems of state law proved unjust and immoral (see, e.g., Pagnucco 1996).

As our conversation entered its third hour, however, Dawes began to
reject the principles of one of his self-avowed religious traditions, Christianity, and to advocate for actions that seemed to violate the norms of many
religious traditions:

> If you kill somebody I believe you ought to be killed. . . . Jesus said we
> must love one another, but if you kill me, you don't love me. So there were
> certain things we did, yes, to ensure that justice is served. Because the law
> does not protect poor people . . . and just because one is a police officer
> does not give you the rights to go around murdering people. . . . I am a
> very good spiritual judge — not a carnal judge — a *spiritual* judge. In the
> spirit, it is not the law of this land, but justice. And justice is no easy thing.

Bishop Dawes thus spoke of religious commandments — "love thy neighbor" or "thou shalt not kill" — not as laws but as guidelines whose validity
was subject to particular situations. He then distinguished two terms that are
often conflated: "law" and "justice." Walter Benjamin (1986) made a similar
distinction between fixed rules (*Recht*) and context-dependent guidelines
(*Richt*) to show how law (*Recht*) and justice (*Gerechtigkeit*), though seemingly similar, were opposed and incommensurable terms. The notion of law
operative in liberal political theory and in the rule of law represents encoded
procedures and norms that, in theory, are universally applicable to all citizens. Treatments of religions as creeds or confessional communities similarly conceive of religious injunctions as relatively fixed and shared laws.
Benjamin (1986), however, argued that justice could never exist within such
a framework. "Thou shalt not kill" could not be a universal injunction for
Benjamin precisely because justice involved what he called the "divine violence" that violates ethical injunctions and laws.

In a resonant way, Dawes insisted that justice often involves working
outside of laws — whether religious commandments or criminal codes — to

enact spiritual violence. I had thought that justice-seeking spiritual work might represent an alternate system of religious laws and moral commandments, but divine or spiritual violence did not seem to institute a set of higher laws for spiritual workers. Crucially, for both Benjamin and Dawes, divine violence comes not to establish or enforce law but to suspend it. As Bishop Dawes went on to tell me, "If justice is not served within the natural courts, God don't ever let those things go unrewarded. We all pay. So you might feel you get off scot-free. You might be setting down, you're married and somebody else come in your home and make you watch them kill your wife and children." This act of divine violence does not mean that the murder of one's wife and children is ethical; instead, it breaks the law in the name of justice. For both Benjamin and Dawes, this is why religion can never be completely encapsulated by ideas of tradition, ritual, or law. If religion is more than a set of beliefs, rules, ethical injunctions, commandments, and guidelines—if it is ultimately about experimenting with more-than-human power—then religion presupposes a sovereign violence that breaks the law. This is just as true for Bishop Dawes's "obeah" as it is for the human sacrifice that is the basis for modern Christianity, the extralegal violence that founds regimes of state law, and the divine violence that is the hinge of Benjamin's messianic Judaism (see also Derrida 2002; Smith 2014).

As I sat talking to Bishop Dawes about a horrifying act of police violence in the midst of the state of emergency, it was patently clear that states were not different from religions in their entanglement with a sovereign violence that suspends law. For over two months, the government had implemented an exception, suspending civil rights and due procedure to secure what officials touted as the rule of law. Paradoxically, an idealized vision of universal laws aimed at curbing violence had to be implemented with an exceptional force that exceeded legal limits. As a number of scholars have noted, such extralegal violence is always at the foundation of the rule of law in modern nation-states (Benjamin 1986; Derrida 2002; Sarat and Kearns 1993). During the 2011 state of emergency that followed Arlena's death, state representatives repeatedly invoked God (conflating divine power with the nation) as the authority that invested the state with exceptional powers (see Dhalai 2011; Ramsaran 2013, 133). In these contexts, religion was not simply the source of a higher ethical law that curbed and condemned violence; it was a contested claim about the location of the sovereign power to break the law. This was just as true for Dawes's "obeah" as for the political theology that animated the state of emergency.

As our conversation entered its fourth hour, the gold sunlight of the early evening began to turn the abandoned cane fields stretching behind his house a deeper green. Because we were still under curfew, I wanted to get going before it got too late. Bishop Dawes shook his head and commented on how slow the justice system was in Trinidad. "It takes years" for a case to be decided, he reminded me: "Five years, ten years, fifteen years in a case like this. That is enough time for evidence to be lost, for witness to get killed, for police officers to be retired. You get off scot free. You walking down the street, and you killed somebody and you walking free. *God is a god of justice.* You think you escape the law? But you could never escape justice." Indeed, as I write these words, more than seven years after Arlena's death, the jury trial against the officers has yet to begin. A witness to the murders was shot and killed, although police say the incident was unrelated to the case. Five years after the preliminary magistrate hearing, the officers have yet to be indicted (a step that follows magistrate hearings and precedes jury trials), and one of the officers sued the state for the delay, promising to further prolong the case. Meanwhile, news of police misconduct, including kidnappings, shootouts, and wrongful deaths, have continued to make headlines (e.g., "Three Cops Charged" 2018; Rampersad 2018; Seelal 2018b; "James Was Unarmed" 2018). More than seven years after charges were laid against the officers involved in the shootings at Number Twenty-One Junction, Bishop Dawes's warning about the torpor and corruptibility of state legal proceedings has proven far from unwarranted.

Despite the anticipated torpor of state law, Dawes closed our conversation by talking about an inescapable justice—not a punishment that would avenge the meek in the afterlife but a divine violence that made justice outside the law in the here and now. One of the officers had gone mad, he reminded me; the house of another officer had mysteriously been shot up. As I left Dawes's house and began the drive back to Papoy and Vita's, I saw Arlena's brother liming in front of a bar. I pulled over to the side of the road and had a beer with him as the sun was going down. Remembering my conversation with Dawes, I told Arlena's brother that I wondered whether the justice system would really punish the officers involved in her death. He assured me that there was a spiritual justice unfolding:

> Remember, it had plenty lighting of candles [i.e., spiritual work] during the protests. Because they [the spirits of the murdered] [are] not something that gone and leave just so and stay just so. Spirit is a living thing that will never sleep. It will never fall; it will always be there while this case go on, until we get justice. Spirit is a living thing that in the air, that

> moving right through. Plenty moving, and plenty more to move. The law
> is one thing, but spiritual-wise that different. That different. Everybody
> have a spirit, and right now them three deceased they around, you know.
> They around. They ain't rest yet.... It have the arm of the law, but it also
> have the lash of spirit.

Despite the torpor of the law, the spirits of the dead promised to inflict what residents called "spirit lash"—blows that inflict an internal harm commonly attributed to obeah and spirits of the dead.[10] The experiments of Dawes and other spiritual workers were helping to keep the dead around in order to make justice through such lashes.

In accounts of justice-seeking facedown burials in Trinidad and Tobago, corpses were periodically buried facedown with a whip in their hands to arm them for the spirit lashes they were charged with inflicting (see Pearse n.d.; Rocklin 2013a, 2019, 125–26). The law in the anglophone Caribbean was also made with the lash, as public whippings were often the chosen form of punishment for vagrancy charges or obeah well into the twentieth century (see chapter 1). While the state legal apparatus punished people with physical lashes, criminalized obeah could work outside the law to inflict spiritual lashes by inverting the burial norms that typically governed relations with the dead for African Trinidadians (and, until cremation became popular in the latter twentieth century, for Indian Trinidadians). Such "obeah" was not simply opposed to the law; it represented an ideology of justice and power that sought to overturn the normal power relations of law (see Lazarus-Black 1994a, 45). Nor did these spirit lashes represent a "folk" system of law, which the "modern" legal apparatus of the state came to regulate and supplant. Rather, obeah has reflected a centuries-long and constitutive interaction with state law, in which the exercise of legal power has often harmed subaltern peoples, and justice has been made through power rather than objective and transparent procedures. Justice, therefore, has not been made through the normative laws and injunctions of a "discursive tradition" geared toward ethical subject making and ritual orthopraxy (Asad 1986). "Justice," as Walter Benjamin argued, "is not a virtue like other virtues (humility, neighborly love, loyalty, courage), but rather constitutes a new ethical category.... Justice is the ethical side of the struggle. Justice is the power [*Macht*] of virtue and virtue of power [*Macht*]" (qtd. in Khatib 2011). As an experimental ethics of power, obeah existed in this realm of justice. Such an ethics of power, for Benjamin, was about "the great impasse of knowledge extending between law [*Recht*] and justice [*Gerechtigkeit*]."

For spiritual workers in the Caribbean, the disjuncture between law and justice was evident in the very criminalization of their own practices. This disjuncture was also evident in the ways that spiritual work overturned ritual norms and relations of power. Because ritual and religion have so often been interpreted through the lens of a "juridical ethics" (Dave 2012) or a discursive tradition (Asad 1986) that aims to embody norms, spiritual workers more often used the terms "work," "science," and "experiment" to describe their practices. Unlike many scholarly understandings of ritual, "work" and "experiment" signal not simply the importance of repetition but also transformative labor and material interventions that induce an altered state of affairs. These practices were secret and dangerous not simply because they had been criminalized but also because they expressed the esoteric power of inverting or violating ritual orders. This was why Dawes and other spiritual workers called their justice-seeking practices "experiments" and distinguished them from traditions.

PRONE TO SEEK JUSTICE

When Dawes said his work of inverting burial norms was an experiment rather than a tradition, this certainly did not mean that his material practices were inventions without precedent. Dawes acknowledged that other spiritual workers had performed similar burials in cases of untimely death, and the colonial archives featured intermittent reports of facedown burials being discovered when a casket was accidentally opened or in cases of grave robbery (see Day by Day 1901 in Rocklin 2013a; "Items of News" 1909; Pearse n.d.; Rocklin 2013a). These burials thus raise the question of whether such spiritual work was a tradition in Asad's (1986) sense of the word—was it a normative order of practice defined through its connection with a past moment of inception? Scholars have often treated facedown burial in the Caribbean in this way—as a cultural survival that recapitulates a homeland past. Yet such an approach has led to an interpretation that is the opposite of Dawes's stated purpose in burying his spiritual daughter facedown. In 1901, for example, a newspaper article described an accidentally discovered facedown burial as "a peculiar Indian custom" because the name of the corpse in question was South Asian (Day by Day 1901 in Rocklin 2013a). Other accounts, when the corpse was of African descent, read facedown burials as evidence of either creole "superstition" or African tradition (e.g., "Items of News" 1909; Handler 1996; Pearse n.d.).

Beyond the shores of Trinidad, facedown burials have been an enduring puzzle for scholars interested in "deviant burial" (Reynolds 2009). Scholars unanimously agree that prone burial has never been normative in any locale but has been a practice that violates shared taboos. Rather than breaking norms in the name of justice, scholars have interpreted these practices within the framework of a juridical tradition, taking such practices to be evidence of traditional ways of punishing or banishing the corpses of those who had transgressed communal mores.

This is the interpretation given for the prone interment at the earliest-known slave burial site in the Caribbean and Western Hemisphere. Handler (1996, 84) sees this Barbadian prone burial from the late seventeenth or early eighteenth century as "evidence for the perpetuation of African mortuary practices in the New World," citing West African practices of prone burial, which (according to contemporary reports) were used to humiliate those accused of witchcraft, ensuring that their spirit did not return to the world of the living. As Handler (1996, 82) himself recognizes, however, references to prone burial in West African ethnography or ethnohistory are scanty, although all of them allegedly uphold the idea of prone burial as punishment for socially unacceptable persons, usually identified as "witches."

The greatest documented scholarly evidence of prone burial practices comes not from West Africa but from Western Europe (although this might be attributed to a sampling bias) (Reynolds 2009). According to the most exhaustive survey of prone burial practices, completed in 2009, a full third of all facedown burials from around the world have been found in Britain (Arcini 2009). The most recent recorded example was also found in Western Europe, in a grave in Flanders that dates to the First World War (Arcini 2009). While scholars can come to no definitive conclusions, the interpretation generally offered for these practices is the humiliation of socially unacceptable persons, especially "witches," whose spirits were supposedly unwanted in the world of the living (see Reynolds 2009). Thus, scholarly interpretations of prone burial, whether African, Afro-diasporic, or European, have reproduced the general tendency to interpret the practice as punishment for transgressors of social taboos.

In Trinidad, depending on the race of the corpse, observers could read facedown burial as either an African custom or a South Asian tradition that derived from an authenticating ethno-racial past. Even though most

Hindus in Trinidad today practice cremation and consider burial a colonial Christian imposition (see McNeal 2012), Hindus in the Ganges Plain
of northern India, from which most indentured laborers hailed, did practice burial rather than cremation in cases of untimely death (Gottschalk
2003; Parry 2004). They even sometimes buried women who had died in
childbirth facedown, allegedly to prevent the return of the dead woman's
spirit (Sutherland 1991, 145–46). Ethnographic references to facedown burial
appear in the literature on northwestern Ghana (Poppi 2011, 39), coastal
Cameroon (Handler and Lange 1978, 198–99), and Zambia (Walker 2004,
198), but all of these practices, like the cases of South Asian or European
prone burials, are reported as attempts to punish those accused of witchcraft, to castigate violators of social taboos, and/or to prevent from returning the spirit of someone who dies an inauspicious death or who breaks
social norms (cf. Guerts 2002).

In contrast to Bishop Dawes's own account of his justice-seeking, facedown burial practices as experiments, scholarly observers of this rite have
tended to make sense of it through the frameworks of primordial pasts and
juridical ethics. This means that scholars have often interpreted these practices as expressions of ethno-racial origins or attempts to punish transgressors of traditional taboos. When Bishop Dawes told me that his counternormative burial practices represented "an experiment with power" rather than
"a tradition," he refuted such an interpretation. It was patently obvious that
he was not attempting to punish or banish Arlena's spirit for a transgression
of social norms. Rather, Bishop Dawes was transgressing shared taboos to
keep Arlena's spirit around to work for justice.

RITUALS OF REVERSAL OR
EXPERIMENTS WITH POWER?

For anyone familiar with the anthropological literature on African performance, the prominent role of reversal and inversion in African expressive
culture will come as no surprise. There is, of course, a rather extensive literature on rituals of "rebellion" or "reversal" in Africa (e.g., Gluckman 1953;
Spencer 1988; Turner [1969] 2017). Yet scholars have usually presented these
rituals as ultimately operating within the frame of tradition that defined the
continent for anthropologists. Victor Turner (1974, 72), for example, wrote
that the rituals "invert but do not usually subvert the status quo, the struc-

tural form, of society; reversal underlines that chaos is the alternative to cosmos, so they [i.e., "tribal" peoples] had better stick to cosmos, that is, the traditional order of culture." Following this line of reasoning, the carnivalesque inversions of the normal order that have often characterized Trinidadian society for observers ultimately served to reaffirm the traditional order by temporarily negating it. The reversals of Trinidad's storied carnival tradition, in which devils and robbers are celebrated and elite society mocked, were "pressure valves" for social tensions, reaffirming social hierarchy through parody and intensification (see Burton 1997; Eagleton 1981; Hernandez-Ramdwar 2008). In his magisterial work *Afro-Creole*, Richard Burton (1997, 223) went so far as to say that the whole of West Indian society was characterized by this "culture of opposition and inversion." Following the tack of theorists of rituals of reversal in continental Africa, Burton saw such reversals of order as ultimately ineffectual performances, which ended up reinscribing the norms of the traditions they inverted. He thus concluded that this West Indian "rebelliousness" reflected "an inability to effect lasting changes in the structures of power it rebels against" (223).

Trinidad's carnival (and West Indian society) has thus been interpreted within a framework of rituals of reversal that ultimately reinscribe the norms of social order (cf. Alonso 1990). Inverting a corpse and the orientation of a coffin might seem a rather pointed example of performing reversal, yet the aim of these inversions was not to release social pressures and ultimately reaffirm the rules of a "traditional order" (at least as Western social scientists conceived of it). Rather than a structural-functionalist emphasis on ritual's delineation of accepted social roles, ethical norms, and hierarchy, these experiments with power seemed to perform something else.

In contrast to a structural-functionalist approach, Andrew Apter (1991, 213) has suggested that a penchant for the inversion of opposites in West African "gnosis" signals a "method of critical practice that reproduces, revises, and when necessary, changes the order of things" (see also Mudimbe 1985). In this reading, public rituals contain secret knowledge that can oppose and undo these rituals' exoteric aims. At the level of secret meanings, for example, the Yoruba ritual of making a king, which ostensibly aims to suppress witchcraft, also unmakes that king, feeding him to witches (Apter 1991). Hidden meanings reveal the predication of kingship on the embodiment of power's paradoxical nature, showing that the sovereign's ability to uphold laws rests on transgressing them. Secret meanings, as Apter (1991, 223) notes, are ultimately dangerous, showing that the power of authority is ultimately based on its own subversion: "The 'deeper,' paradoxical interpretations of

Yoruba ritual revise and subvert official ideologies not through faulty logic or a perverse sense of play, but because they grasp power ultra vires, opposed to authority, breaking its structures and rules." Rituals and traditions, in other words, contain the power to undo their own exoteric meanings. Although on the surface ritual practices aim to do just what scholars have claimed that they do—bolster a traditional order or punish those who have transgressed taboos—their inversions have the potential to revise and subvert such order.

In contrast, Western notions of tradition (and religion) stress social cohesion and relatively fixed orders, opposing a modernity of individualism, invention, and rejection of traditional norms. Africa, as I noted earlier, entered the modern Western imagination under the sign of atavistic tradition. The "discovery" in the late nineteenth and early twentieth century that sub-Saharan Africa had "religion" occurred through this same category of "native tradition" (Chidester 1996). Yet this inclusion of sub-Saharan African practices into the category of "religion" as "tradition" continued to reflect the exclusions of the allegedly universal "world religions" framework that emerged in the nineteenth century. As Tomoko Masuzawa (2005) has noted, this world religions paradigm was typically divided into Eastern and Western. With the exception of nineteenth-century European racial discourses about "Afro-Asiatic" or "Hamito-Semitic" areas of northern Africa, the rest of Africa was left entirely out of this division of religion into East and West. As Masuzawa also notes, this major dichotomy of East-West was joined by a tertiary realm of "minor," "primitive," "native," or "traditional" religions. Eventually, according to Chidester (1996) at least, such "native religion" was "discovered" by Westerners in sub-Saharan Africa as Europe consolidated its territorial dominion on the continent in the late nineteenth century. Sub-Saharan Africa thus entered the category of "religion" as "minor" native tradition rather than "major" world religion. While the world religions framework had originally limited the realm of venerable tradition to Eastern and Indigenous religion (Masuzawa 2005, 1–5), Africa eventually joined this "world" by being native and traditional.

The implicit preservation of sub-Saharan Africa's exclusion from the "world" of the world religions paradigm was reflected in my own assumption that Dawes was practicing an eminently traditional religion and—in the umbrella term that has come to describe non-Abrahamic religions of sub-Saharan origin—"African traditional religion." The authenticity and integrity of this traditional orientation, scholars have assumed, is opposed to invention (Beliso de Jesús 2015, 3, 55, 159, 177, 193). In contrast to this opposition between tradition and invention, spiritual workers did not understand tradition and experimentation as mutually exclusive modalities; instead, they reflected exoteric and esoteric dimensions of religious practice that were good for different situations of power.

Many scholars have speculated that the secrecy associated with obeah is a result of its criminalization and stigmatization. Hiding from the police, spiritual workers were forced to flee to the bush to perform their rites. The legitimization of obeah, these scholars assert, would involve its public recognition, bringing spiritual work out from the shadows and into the light of day (Castor 2017, 60). Certainly, other forms of African religion have achieved some success in gaining state recognition and the patronage of political parties (see Paton 2009; Castor 2017; Henry 2003). Yet the secrecy of obeah, like its association with harm, cannot simply be reduced to a product of colonial stigmatization or its exclusion from normative Western ideas of religion. Obeah expresses the esoteric side of ritualization, a hidden meaning that reverses and revises a normal state of affairs. Much work in natural science and religion is geared toward the performative confirmation of existing norms, as the first experiments with power on accused obeah practitioners or much "normal science" show. But these practices happen alongside experimental moments in which the norms of a tradition become contingent rather than routine or taken for granted (Feyerabend 1975; Kuhn [1962] 1996). What gets called obeah exists in this exceptional space of overturning, subverting, or suspending norms to open up an entrenched state of affairs to alteration. Such was the work that Bishop Dawes and others performed when, rather than turn the other cheek, they turned over Arlena's corpse.

FIGURE 3.1. Mama Lata with market basket in a grassroots Orisha shrine. Photograph by the author, 2011.

To Balance the Load

Arlena was lying on the earthen floor of the mourning room in the Spiritual Baptist church on Cha Cha Trace in Rio Moro, but when she opened her spiritual eyes she found herself in an immense open-air market in the Nation of Africa. She made her way among a dense proliferation of stalls, each with distinct wares and smells. She remembers passing the odor of burnt meat, lavender, and leather until she came upon an old woman with deeply creased hands in a brown dress, surrounded by a number of covered baskets. Although she could not see the woman's eyes, hidden as they were by a brown shawl wrapped around her head, she heard the woman's voice offering her a choice between her two largest baskets, indicated by her wrinkled hands. One basket held the good—happiness, joy, levity. The other held the bad—pain, suffering, gravity. As in other key moments of her spiritual travels, Arlena was presented with a choice that was also a test, and her ability to move forward in the Nation of Africa was premised upon her choosing the right basket.

Instead of choosing between the baskets, however, Arlena picked up both of them—to "balance the load," as she told the old woman. She heard the woman laugh with approval as she raised her head from the shadows of her shawl to look at her. Arlena saw a dark calabash bowl in the hollow of the shawl where the woman's face should be. Inside the bowl was a flickering light. Arlena would carry the calabash bowl and the light inside of it back to Trinidad. This was how she first came to know Africa and became a "calabash woman," charged with wielding this water-bearing gourd as the ritual implement of Africa during her church's Spiritual Baptist services. When she came back to herself on the floor of the mourning room in Cha Cha Trace, Bishop Dawes told her that the woman she had met was Mama Lata—an Orisha that exists only in Trinidad and whose name is French patois for "Mother Earth." Mama Lata, she came to understand, had shown her that Africa was not simply a place but also an ethos of difficult balance that refused a mutually exclusive choice between good and bad.

ELECTRICAL ETHICS

On Turning the Other Cheek

THE SPIRITUAL CAR BATTERY

"You as a person, you have a good force and a bad force," the spiritual worker Baba Khan said, pointing at me.[1] "A light force and a dark force. So if you pray on the ray of goodness, even though you praying on the ray of goodness, you also building the energy of darkness. You understand?"

My interlocutors in Rio Moro often asked me whether I understood what they were saying. The question "you understand?" is ubiquitous in Trinidadian English/Creole, punctuating conversations, adding emphasis, and making sure the lines of communication were flowing. On this occasion, however, I was not exactly sure that I understood Baba Khan. I had asked him whether he thought obeah was a force for harm, as many alleged, or a practice of healing and protection. When I asked him for further clarification, he invoked a common metaphor that other workers used to talk about spiritual power—electricity: "Well, there's one force. If you go outside to your car battery and you charge your battery, you charge both positive and negative. You understand? The both is always charging. Energy is going to both forces. It's going to the positive force and it's going to the dark force. It's not going separate. . . . And it does happen like that with spiritual power—like what they call obeah. You understand what I'm saying?"

I certainly understood his metaphor, for Baba Khan had helped me jump-start my car on a few different occasions, and we had used my cables to connect the positive and negative poles of our car batteries. In the last days of my longest stint of field research in Trinidad, my Ford Cortina had a mysterious electrical problem. There was nothing wrong with the alternator or battery, so the fault seemed to lie in a hard-to-locate leak in the electrical wiring that was shorting the loop between positive and negative. After sitting all night parked on the street in front of the particular Orisha feast or Kabbalah banquet I was attending, my car battery would invariably be dead. Baba Khan was a frequent attendee at these nocturnal events and I knew that he had a car, so I often asked him to jump-start the Ford Cortina. At one point, Khan had asked me if I knew what would happen if we reversed the polarities of the cables, connecting the negative pole of one battery to the positive pole of the other. I told him that there would be a surge of energy that might even cause the battery casing to crack. "Yeah, real power!" he said.

The criminalization of obeah began with a demonstration of electricity, as colonial authorities tried to display their more powerful "obeah" by administering shocks to the leaders of Tacky's Rebellion who had been convicted of obeah (see chapter 2). Baba Khan's metaphor of the car battery, however, raised some different resonances in thinking about electricity and obeah. Certainly, "power" can refer to the one-way relation of authoritative domination that electricity was ideally supposed to perform on those first accused obeah practitioners. But power, in Khan's reckoning, was not a one-way street. Power was an interplay of ethically contrasting forces. Without this interplay between "good" and "bad," spiritual power could not flow.

In the interlude that prefaces this chapter, Arlena's decision to pick up both "good" and "bad" on her first journey in the Spiritual Nation of Africa presents a similar ethics of tense balance between contrasting forces. In different ways, both Arlena's vision and Khan's metaphor of electricity insist that "bad," "negative," or "darkness" have their place and are essential to an ethics of power and agonistic balance. Similarly, when Bishop Dawes reversed the polarities of a good burial in the funeral of his spiritual daughter, turning her body over in the grave to seek justice, rather than turn the other cheek, he insisted on an alternate ethical framework in which (as he told me) "negative is not bad or good, it just have its purpose." While he was aware that "some people might see what I do as evil," spiritual work that inverted ritual norms was not without its virtues in his estimation. Such reversals, like the crossing of jumper cables, could be useful for generating surges of power that were potent as well as potentially dangerous. Negative, as other spiritual workers often explained, was a necessary part of power, and spiritual force was generated like electricity—through the alternation of negative

FIGURE 3.2. Orisha flags and electrical wires, Trinidad. The bamboo poles of Spiritual Baptist and Orisha flags were often likened to electrical poles, since they brought spiritual current into a practitioner's home. Photograph by Gigi Gatewood, 2011.

and positive polarities. Spiritual workers thus sometimes likened the ritually prepared bamboo flag poles, which marked Spiritual Baptist, Kabbalistic, and/or Orisha houses, to electrical poles because they relayed spiritual "alternating current" into devotees' homes.[2]

    This chapter explores the electrical ethics of spiritual workers to make a turn away from certain tendencies in common conceptions of religion and ethics. The notion that religion, in its most essential form, is a realm of duty ethics, enforcing taboos or inculcating shared moral rules, is a popular idea that has been given various points of origin.[3] In recent studies of religion and culture, a turn away from duty ethics toward virtue ethics has led to an alternate image of religious practices as ethical disciplines that allow pious subjects to embody the virtues of a tradition (Asad 1986; Mahmood 2005; Hirschkind 2006; Jouili 2015). In either estimation, however, religion is primarily devoted to reinforcing shared, normative conceptions of the good. Beyond the bounds of what is usually considered religion, a renewed scholarly interest in ethics has also resulted in what Michael Lambek (2010) and Joel Robbins (2013, 448) have called a turn toward "the good," which encompasses concerns as diverse as "studies of value, morality, imagination, well-being, empathy, care, the gift, hope, time, and change." When presented with

Arlena's choice between good and bad, how do individuals, these scholars ask, struggle with such choices, trying to foster and embody the good?

In the face of this "ethical turn" (Fassin 2014), Arlena's refusal of this choice between good and bad or Baba Khan's metaphor of the spiritual car battery are the guiding images for another approach to ethics in this chapter. These images of appropriate balance, as the basis for both an embodied habitus and self-reflective moral reasoning, are marked as "African" at my field site, but they speak to experiences of ethical contradiction, refusal, and difficult balance that are remarkably mundane. In these experiences, the ethical disciplines and norms of goodness in legal or religious traditions do not necessarily produce virtuous actions (as recent critical work on ethics has recognized).[4] Rather than a turn toward the good, Arlena, Khan, Bishop Dawes, and other spiritual workers posited the ability to carry, contain, or work ethically opposed forces as a virtue. Arlena's vision suggests that virtue can actually begin by refusing the tendency to simply turn toward the good, and spiritual workers' own struggles to bring about justice highlighted the limitations of collective legal and religious norms of goodness. Rather than assuming a hierarchy of values (or multiple competing hierarchies) — an assumption that has structured both value-monist and value-plural conceptions of ethics (Robbins 2007) — my interlocutors often talked about ethical oppositions between bad and good as complementary polarities that were both useful. The spiritual workers I knew thus conceived of good and bad in terms of their spiritual topography of the Heights and the Depths — an ethical topography that differed radically from seemingly similar moral hierarchies of heaven and hell. While often associated with death, demons, and moral counternormativity, the Depths were not necessarily evil; they were a vital profundity that gave lofty ethical ideals and virtues their situated depth. In this reckoning, virtue was not located in an individual choice between bad and good or the embodiment of collective norms, but in the *conduct* of the ethically contrasting polarities that composed lived situations of power.[5]

At first glance, these alternate ethical worlds of electrical polarities or Heights and Depths might seem to recapitulate exceedingly popular representations of practitioners of obeah or "voodoo," which have highlighted their alleged moral ambivalence or their embrace of the negative polarity of power that Baba Khan described.[6] If proper religion has often been conflated with "good" morality and ethics, then images of African-identified practices as "magic," "witchcraft," or "superstition" have been associated with mistaken or amoral assumptions of power. Drawing on Khan's image of

contrary yet inextricable polarities, however, one might say that these seemingly opposed images of good religion and black magic are complementary
poles that have generated power. Certainly, the power to criminally regulate African-identified persons and practices has drawn its authority from
such an opposition. Arguments over ethical conceptions, therefore, are not
simply the province of scholars; they are debates that shaped the criminalization of African-identified practices, exerting long-standing impacts on
the African diaspora. In this chapter, I delve into the continuing ramifi-
cations of this moral contrast between instrumental "magic" and virtuous
"religion" for contemporary spiritual workers who face legal and racial discrimination. How have these ethical conceptions shaped what gets to count
as religion, and how might those who are often excluded from such conceptions offer alternate ethical frameworks?

Despite the power of these ideas, Khan's spiritual car battery and Arlena's ethics of balance do not simply play a negative foil to Western fictions
of good religion. Spiritual workers' theories of balance present an alternate
conception of virtue in which the interplay of contrasting forces is the basis
for an ethics of justice, responsibility, and power. Spiritual workers' conceptions of balance, though inextricable from justice, did not mirror the
Western image of the scales of justice, a metaphor premised precisely on
imbalance—on the tipping of scales that allows for a judgment in favor of
one party in a conflict (see Winslade 1971). Nor is this balance the image of
nondevelopmental harmony—the static traditional society—that preceded
the fall of progress and change in many religious and anthropological narratives (see Fabian 1983; Wolf 1982). This contrast between tradition, as a realm
of clear consensus about a hierarchy of ethical values, and modernity, as a
fragmented realm of conflicting value spheres, has been a key trope in scholarly representations (e.g., MacIntyre 1981; Weber 1948, 323–62; cf. Robbins
2004, 2007). In the ethics of spiritual work, however, balance is not static
harmony; it is extremely difficult, oppositional, dangerous, and never finished. It is an approximation that requires work, movement, and transformation. The aim is not simply choosing the good or embodying the norms
of an ethical tradition, but finding which values (whether bad or good) are
appropriate for divergent situations. In some situations, particularly cases
of injustice, spiritual workers avowed that bad could be particularly good.
One especially acute case of such injustice was Arlena's physical death at
the hands of police, and this chapter focuses on the ethical debates that her
death and other situations of justice-making occasioned.

I begin with an overview of the long-standing scholarly and popular opposition between (a certain idea of) religion, as a realm of ethical training or moral edicts, and African (not-)religion as instrumental magic. Such an opposition most certainly echoes Western secularism's purported purification of "good" religion from the instrumental concerns of power, politics, or profit. Yet the negative and positive polarities of this opposition shape not simply European representations of "good" religion but also the ethical debates within forms of African-identified religion across the African diaspora. The remainder of the chapter focuses on these debates at my field site, where practitioners of African-identified religions argued for or against the value of obeah in the wake of the police shootings at Number Twenty-One Junction. By focusing on debates among practitioners of African-identified religion, I show how traditions or religions are not simply unitary fields of shared norms.[7] Despite practicing African-identified religions, some of Arlena's own family condemned the obeah undertaken in response to her death, insisting that certain biblical injunctions, particularly Jesus's commandment to turn the other cheek, were universal codes of ethical conduct, with the power to suspend such laws reserved for God alone. For others (who also identified as Christians) these religious codes and the codes of state law were not necessarily commensurable with justice. Both police brutality and the spiritual work that responded to it showed how justice and injustice marked instances of sovereign powers that exceeded religious injunctions or state laws. Simply choosing what regnant religious or legal traditions defined as good was not necessarily a virtue in these situations of power.

As spiritual workers insisted on the value of obeah by elaborating ethical frameworks of difficult balance and exceptional power, they showed how both Western conceptions of ethics and characterizations of African-identified practices have often been structured by the racialized division between instrumental magic and moral religion. My hope is that an awareness of the ethical oppositions that continue to underlie ideas about religion might clarify the contours of contemporary intolerance toward obeah within and beyond the Caribbean.[8] While intolerance for various forms of racialized (not-)religion remains a key feature of power in modern nation-states, the terms of this intolerance were far from settled at my field site. Obeah does mark a different ethical orientation toward power, but whether that orientation is simply bad or whether it marks an alternate conception of virtue is an open debate in the region.

THE "PROTESTANT" BIAS AND THE
SPIRITUAL WORK ETHIC

"Religion" has long been a category through which African-identified practices have been excluded from legal rights and conceptions of morality. As
opposed to ethical traditions that devote themselves to the cultivation of
the good, African-identified religious practices, in both explicitly derogatory and more sympathetic representations, are associated with power and
interest.[9] Certainly, this opposition between instrumental power and the
good, though often contradicted by lived experience, is part of broader ideas
about proper religion and ethics in contemporary worlds. Considering this,
it might be worth taking a step back from obeah to consider why instrumental power should be unreflexively opposed to the good and why this opposition continues to crop up in many accounts of religion and ethics.

An influential work on ethics from an anthropologist of religion begins
with this opposition between power and the good: "Ethnographers commonly find that the people they encounter are trying to do what they consider right or good, are being evaluated according to criteria of what is right
and good, or are in some debate about what constitutes the human good.
Yet anthropological theory tends to overlook all this in favor of analyses that
emphasize structure, power, and interest" (Lambek 2010, 1).

Other scholars have similarly insisted that a focus on ethics and the
good can counteract an imputed obsession with power in social theory
(e.g., Ortner 2016; Robbins 2013). These accounts thus implicitly assume
that ethics and the good are opposed to power, force, or instrumental action.
Other accounts have disavowed this tendency to conflate ethics with the
good or have critiqued the lack of attention to instrumental strategies in relation to ethical imperatives (Mayblin 2017; Sidnell, Meudec, and Lambek
2019, 3). Despite these critiques, an opposition between ethics (as the cultivation of various conceptions of the good) and instrumental power retains
a great deal of force with continuing implications for the representation of
religious practices.

Embodied practices of ethics, morality, or the good (regardless of the
various ways to distinguish these three terms) obviously involve questions of
power. This empirical reality begs the question of why instrumental power
should be opposed to ethical life in so many representations. An obvious
answer is that the separation of power from ethics resonates with the foun-

dational purifications of Western modernity between public and private, market and sentiment, reason and emotion, secular power and religion, or instrumentality and love. Talal Asad (1993), of course, opens his foundational essay on the construction of religion as an anthropological category by showing how the separation of religion from power was a founding act in Western modernity and liberal secularism. Subsequent scholarship, however, has most often cited Asad's essay as a critique of a "Protestant bias" toward immaterial belief that explicitly or implicitly discriminates against the material rituals of Islam, Judaism, Catholicism, and/or charismatic Protestantism (which might be different from the ideal-type Protestantism this bias has in mind) (e.g., Hirschkind 2011; Houtman and Meyer 2012; Seligman et al. 2008). These critiques have often centered on discrimination against forms of the recognized "world religions," but the exclusion of obeah (or other terms for native and African religions) from the category of religion altogether raises some different questions. I suggest that the problem is not simply a crypto-Protestant bias toward belief but farther-reaching ethical distinctions between religion and instrumental power.

To counteract this bias, scholars have drawn on Asad's (1986) suggestion to treat religious practices as traditions that train the pious in ethical modes of life, focusing on the embodiment of virtues rather than an internal disposition of belief (e.g., Hirschkind 2006; Jouili 2015; Mahmood 2005). Drawing heavily on classical virtue ethics, particularly MacIntyre's (1981) revival of Aristotle's writings, these approaches insist that ethical traditions are disciplines that achieve their realization through their very practice, transcending an economy of means and ends. Wearing a headscarf or holding a door open for someone do not simply reflect the obligations of a code of duty or the means to attain social distinction; they are themselves the embodied realization of ethical ends. Lambek (2010, 3), drawing on both Aristotle and Arendt ([1958] 1998), thus defines a programmatic emphasis on "ordinary ethics" as activity that lies outside of instrumental considerations of means and ends, as lived moments when action and values of the good merge (cf. Sidnell, Meudec, and Lambek 2019). Saba Mahmood (2012) similarly insists that her interlocutors in Egypt conceive of embodied practices of piety as ends in themselves, eschewing the idea that these practices are instrumental activities meant to garner status or other external goals. This perspective presents the pious embodiment of normative values as an alternative to the liberal individualism of Western feminist thought and its emphasis on resistance to norms.[10] Within these revivals of Aristotelian ethics, instrumental activity would thus seem to bear an ambivalent relationship to virtue, even as power forms a part of the training necessary to internalize ethical habits.

What is less often realized is that these conceptions of ethics can echo the very foundations of the modern category of religion in its constitutive separation from the instrumentality both of magic and of modern politics. To take but one influential example of the former purification, Malinowski, drawing on the earlier definitions of Frazer, Tylor, and Marrett, defines magic as "a practical art consisting of acts which are only means to a definite end." Religion, on the other hand, is a "body of self-contained acts being themselves the fulfillment of their purpose" (Malinowski 1925, qtd. in Otto and Stausberg 2014, 156). Writing in 1964, in *A Dictionary of the Social Sciences*, Edmund Leach asserts that "the core of magic" is essentially an instrumental "effort at control" that separates it from the devotional orientation of religion (qtd. in Otto and Stausberg 2014, 187). These distinctions echo the Durkheimian ethical separation of individualistic magic from communal religion. For Durkheim ([1912] 1964), there can be no "church of magic" because it is an individualized practice. Religion, in contrast, is the very basis of moral community and social solidarity. In surprisingly familiar language, key figures in anthropology separated instrumental magic from communal piety while making the former characteristic of "primitive" attempts at science rather than religion proper.

More recent defenders of the validity of the magic category have similarly defined magic's fundamental difference from religion in terms of its instrumentality or individualism (see, e.g., Chireau 2006; Sørensen 2014). In her work on African American "black magic," Yvonne Chireau (2006, 3) sums up these Western distinctions between magic and religion: "In contrast with religion, [magic] is efficacious. . . . Magic is used for specific, personal ends. It operates mechanically—as opposed to prayer, which is communal, devotional, and noncoercive." This entrenched opposition between religion as devotional and magic as instrumental or coercive has provided the ethical substance for religious and racial hierarchies in the modern world, even as "magic" might be replaced with other words such as "superstition," "voodoo," "terrorism," or "fanaticism," which conjure the specter of nonsecular violence and coercion. Many defenses of the continuing use of the term "magic" in religious studies, therefore, still invoke the idea that religion is devotional while magic is instrumental and concerned with power. Ironically, this discursive separation of religion from power, which forms the foundation for post-Reformation secular ideals, was arguably the main target of Asad's (1993) original critique. The correctives of virtue ethics that emerged from Asad's critique have reproduced this separation in some ways, precisely because they are focused on the secular-religious dialectic (or distinctions between recognized religions) rather than on the separation of religious piety from instrumental magic.

More than being a scholarly question, such ideal-type categories of religion and magic have legitimated the criminalization and popular moral stigmatization of African-identified spiritual workers like Bishop Dawes or Baba Khan. In contrast to either the Aristotelian virtue ethics or Kantian duty ethics that have defined recent scholarly debates, Bishop Dawes was not simply trying to embody the norms of a tradition, obey social taboos, or approximate an exemplary ethical order through his mortuary rites.[11] Instead, he was trying to produce an unexpected future through counternormative practices of facedown burial (see chapter 2). These practices were "good" not by virtue of embodying ethical practices or avoiding taboos, but by virtue of contravening ethical practice through enacting taboos. Dawes's justice-seeking work, as he himself knew, would have been regarded as grotesque, debasing, or simply evil by many of those gathered at Arlena's funeral. Rather than embody norms, he intentionally inverted and violated the normative orientations and ordering of a good burial for someone he loved.

When Bishop Dawes embraced potentially reprehensible means that were quite emphatically different from his ends, it would seem that his practices would not be admissible to the opposing sides of scholarly debates over the constitution of religious traditions, whether defined in terms of duty ethics or embodied virtue. Yet this exclusion of Dawes's rites from ethical practice makes sense only if one considers spiritual workers' ends of achieving justice to be a virtue like other virtues. If justice can involve breaking the law and violating accepted norms, even to the point of harming others, then justice is a virtue that is not necessarily virtuous (at least in many understandings of virtue, even utilitarian or consequentialist ones). Dawes wanted to achieve justice for Arlena by afflicting the police and violating the norms of a good burial, utilizing means that many regarded as morally ambivalent—means that also produced allegedly dangerous or harmful ends. Rather than the formulation of virtue as means that are the practice of a tradition's ethical norms, justice can be conceived of as an end that does not necessarily involve the practice of a legal or religious tradition's conceptions of the good, and that could involve the "pure means" of divine violence (Benjamin 1986; Khatib 2011).

Whether people in Rio Moro thought that Arlena's death was the product of divine justice or an instance of extrajudicial violence that occasioned justice-making (and harming) spiritual work, they saw justice not as an exemplar of virtuous action but as an intervention that suspended the law. The real question was where the exceptional power to suspend ethical and state laws resided—in the police, in God(s), or in obeah. The ethical value of religious practice—and the value of justice-making obeah—was determined by the disputed location of this power. In the end, religion was not what its well-worn opposition to magic presupposed at my field site. Rather than a sphere that either eschewed power and violence or was focused on the embodiment of ethical norms, religion represented contested claims about the locus of the power to break the law and suspend norms, enacting violence in the name of justice. The locus of this power in the aftermath of the deaths of Arlena and her friends hinged on whether it was their time to die.

PLAYING DEAD TO CATCH CORBEAUX

We were sitting in the shade of Maureen's front porch at the peak of the afternoon's heat during 2012's dry season. She slumped in her chair. She wanted to take a nap, but her grandchildren were coming home from school soon, and she had to mind them. In the coconut palm above us some *corbeaux* (vultures) were gathering. They flapped their wings as they landed in the branches, and their feathers sounded as dry as the dry season's afternoon heat.

Maureen was telling me that God worked in mysterious ways. Her twenty-nine-year-old brother Otis was one of Arlena's friends whom police shot and killed at Number Twenty-One Junction. "We might cry for them that dead, but it was their time to dead," she said. Maybe if the officers had not shot her brother, she told me, those same police would still be out there doing wickedness. Other families would be shedding tears. In the months since her brother died at the hands of the seven police, there had been only one police shooting in south Trinidad: a crime of passion in which a policeman shot his lover's husband. Since the arrest of the officers involved at Number Twenty-One Junction, the wicked police in south had stopped killing people for hire. The death of Maureen's brother, then, was a sacrifice for others. "God works in mysterious ways," Maureen said. "We does cyah [can't] question."

She told me that her brother and Arlena were still alive after the police opened fire on their car and it spun around in the middle of Number

Twenty-One Junction. Her brother jumped out of the car with his hands up and Arlena fell out of the passenger-side door, as she had been hit with a stray bullet in her leg and couldn't stand up. The female police officer who would later be a state witness helped Arlena to stand and begged her commanding officer to call an ambulance. Instead, they handcuffed Maureen's brother and threw him and Arlena in the back of a police van. The woman driving the borrowed car was slumped in the driver's seat, and they put her dead body in the same police vehicle next to her friends. It was getting dark, and they drove between the abandoned cane fields and through the junctions, named after the number of cane scales that had marked the former sugar company's weighing stations. That was where the bull carts had brought the cane and the company had paid the farmers. There were still access roads that burrowed through the crooked and uncultivated stalks that lined either side of the road. The police van turned down one of those roads and drove into the cane. With only the stalks as witness they shot Arlena and Maureen's brother point-blank. The female police officer testified that she was pleading with her colleagues, saying that they had already killed one innocent person. The officer said that Maureen's brother was pleading for his life on his knees in that cane field.

As Maureen told me this, in the near distance her grandson made his way down the path that led to the gallery. His backpack was far too large for his six-year-old body. Both of his hands were on its straps, and he was walking distractedly. His head was turned upward and his eyes transfixed by the *corbeaux* gathering on the palm branches. Maureen and I both watched him watch the birds.

"You could say what," Maureen told me breaking the silence, "it still have police execution in Trinidad." While the south had gotten quiet, northern Trinidad still saw semiregular police shootings and community protests. After the female police officer had delivered her incriminating confession, Maureen told me, somebody disabled the brakes on her car. She went into witness protection afterward.

Maureen's grandson had stopped in the middle of the track, looking up at the *corbeaux*. Behind the palm tree where the birds perched was a wire fence, and behind the fence a patch of abandoned cane grew like oversized grass. I was thinking about what it must be like to plead for your life, like Arlena or Maureen's brother did, in the face of imminent death—in the middle of cane fields no less. Did God work in mysterious ways? Could we accept Maureen's brother's death as a sacrifice and make him a Christ in the cane field? Should we leave justice in the hands of the Lord and the law?

"Come now, boy!" Maureen shouted at her grandson. He began to walk distractedly again but did not turn his head from the vultures. "You study *corbeaux* like that," she warned him, "they going to come for *you*."

"Playing dead to catch *corbeaux*" is a saying in Trinidad. One pretends to die so that the vultures will descend. Metaphorically, it references a situation in which someone plays stupid, seeming to become an enemy's prey to ultimately trap the predator once they get close enough. It is a particular kind of tactic—one in which feigned quiescence and deceptive appearances lead to capture. Maureen's brother did more than play dead; for Maureen, he was sacrificed by God so that predatory police could be caught in a trap. But was this really an instance of strange justice? Was it his divinely ordained time to die at the age of only twenty-nine?

TIME TO DEAD?

When Bishop Dawes told me that he worried about people calling the ethics of his justice-seeking work "evil," he was not simply concerned about the opinion of the anonymous public. Among Arlena's own family and neighbors there was no agreement about whether the spiritual work of Dawes and others was justified and ethical. The value of this spiritual work hinged on whether it was time for Arlena and other victims of police and interpersonal violence to die—whether this was evidence of human wickedness that demanded intervention or simply strange divine justice.

This question was debated on one of the last nights of Arlena's wake. I showed up to the gathering with Mother Jackie Cooper, an experienced Spiritual Baptist who lived the next trace over from Arlena's family. Mother Jackie had mourned extensively, traveling not only to the usual destinations of India, Africa, China, and the Depths, but also to Germany, the North Pole, and the bottom of the sea. She had descended to the furthest level of the Depths, where she stole a key from Satan that she brought back to the carnal earth. She was an "all nations woman" and a well-known Spiritual Baptist, but when I asked her if she engaged in spiritual work, she told me that she tried not to "indulge" in the practice. Nevertheless, in the debate that ensued at the wake, she would be the one advocating for spiritual work to avenge Arlena's death.

We walked up to a relatively small gathering of older women seated in plastic chairs against the shoulder-high wall surrounding the family's

Orisha *palais*, where they usually held a large yearly feast. Everyone looked tired. While most wakes are lively affairs characterized by drumming, drinking, and card playing—a fact that consistently offended European observers' sensibilities about the proper affect toward death in Trinidad— Arlena's wake that night was a somber, palpably subdued affair. There was no music, alcohol, or card playing, but simply a row of older women seated in plastic chairs outside of the walls of the *palais*. They had been keeping the all-night vigils for almost two weeks while Arlena's body was unburied, kept in cold storage, as they pooled funds and waited for an independent autopsy to be performed on Arlena's corpse, as most assumed that the state autopsy would be biased toward the police. Even for people accustomed to all-night wakes and nocturnal feasts, it was a long stretch to be up all night. Arlena's grandmother looked exhausted and distraught as she motioned for a granddaughter to bring some more plastic chairs from inside the house for Jackie and I to sit.

While we were waiting for the chairs, I made out Arlena's aunt, Mother Lisette, among the older women. Lisette was the head of an Orisha shrine atop a hill about a mile away from Arlena's home. The last time I had seen her, we were sitting on the benches that surrounded the open dirt floor of her Orisha *palais* while she fiddled with her cell phone, looking for the contact of an Orisha *mongba* (ritual leader) she wanted to give me. Arlena's name was still the first to show up in her contacts list, she told me, as she looked down on the small screen of her Nokia device. Even though her niece was dead, she did not have the heart to erase her.

"It was her time to dead," Lisette was telling the women in the plastic chairs. "Everyone have a time on this earth, and none of we can know the hour or the reason."

"You think she was supposed to dead at twenty-one?" Mother Jackie countered. We were still standing up waiting for the chairs. She told Lisette that while it was true that we all have a divinely allotted time on earth, there were "unnatural deaths," cases in which "human wickedness" cut a life short.

Lisette disagreed. Two weeks prior to Arlena's death, the Orisha Ogun had manifested through a woman at her shrine's feast. Holding his cutlass aloft in one arm, Ogun had come up to Arlena in the middle of the *palais* and prophesied her own death, warning her not to leave her home and lime (hang out) if she wanted to avoid imminent trouble. Maybe her death was a kind of punishment for disobeying the Orisha's orders, Mother Lisette speculated. Instead of going into the bush to work obeah on the police, Lisette said, the family should "turn the other cheek. Trust in God and let the

FIGURE 3.3. Young Blood DVD Club. Photograph by Gigi Gatewood, 2011.

law handle it." Lisette's comments were directed to Arlena's grandmother, who had gone into the bush earlier that day to do some justice-seeking spiritual work.

Lisette and Jackie continued to argue for a while, but the conversation eventually turned into an awkward silence. After half an hour or so, Mother

Jackie told me she had to get back to her house, so we bid the women good-bye. As we walked through the yard in front of the house, we passed the small plywood stand that Arlena had built to sell copied DVDs. The name of her business, Young Blood DVD, was spray-painted across the plywood. The name, as I later learned, was meant to signify the "young blood" that Arlena had injected into the town and the business community by being such a remarkably young and ambitious business owner. It was the first time I had noticed the name, and it took on for me a chilling, ominous, and disturbingly prophetic meaning. As we left Young Blood DVD behind us, Mother Jackie told me that Lisette did not know what she was talking about. Like Bishop Dawes, she thought that Arlena had been senselessly murdered in cold blood, a symptom of a racist and corrupt policing system, and that those who God had given the science to do so needed to return the lash rather than turn the other cheek.

WHAT BAD IS GOOD FOR

Disagreements about the ethics of spiritual work, as Mother Lisette, Jackie Cooper, and Maureen all suggested, were disagreements about the correct location of the sovereign power to legitimately use force in the name of justice. Who could rightfully wield the sword of justice—God(s), the police, or spiritual workers? Were the ethical injunctions of religious traditions—such as Jesus's commandment to turn the other cheek no matter the context of the blow—universal laws or simply guidelines with pragmatic limits in situations of power? The deaths of Arlena and her two friends were not the only events that highlighted these fraught questions for spiritual workers in Trinidad. By virtue of the same racialized distinctions that had made obeah illicit and instrumental (not-)religion, African-identified spiritual workers dealt with clients' most pressing and intransigent conflicts. Spiritual workers were often a last resort when doctors and lawyers had failed clients, or when they could no longer afford the aforementioned professionals. Their labor thus involved them in an inherently agonistic field of power, and for the spiritual workers I knew, intervening in the criminal justice system was their most common work. Such interventions often involved spiritual workers in a racialized division of labor, in which persons turned to stigmatized forms of religious practice when societal and religious norms, which upheld the rule of law or the sovereignty of God, were unable to provide answers.

In this respect, a spiritual worker named Mother Siddiq was no different. She had lived much of her life in "the Trainline"—a neighborhood in the southern Trinidadian city of Marabella—but had come back to live in her family's home in Rio Moro to get away from what she called the "crime situation" (the Trainline was notorious for violence in the national imagination). Alongside labor that would be more easily construed as the healing of psychosomatic ailments, she had also performed numerous interventions in the criminal justice system, performing spiritual work out of her home. She had worked for those who had been "set up" by the police (including police officers who felt their superiors had set them up), as well as those who were wrongly accused of a crime, wanted to get family members out of jail, wanted to win a dispute in court, or wanted justice for loved ones killed by the police. Unlike many of my other interlocutors, she had lived a *physically* transnational existence (all of the spiritual workers I knew lived *spiritually* transnational existences by virtue of mourning). She had migrated to the northeastern United States in her early twenties. Like so many other Trinidadians, she did not encounter the financial success that she sought in the United States. She became profoundly ill during her first winter and was unable to work. While laid up in bed, she kept hearing what she called "African drums." She could not get the drums out of her head, and she took it as a sign to return to Trinidad to mourn.

She mourned in a church in the Trainline, right next to the old tracks of the now-defunct San Fernando–Port of Spain railroad that gave the neighborhood its name. As with other mourners, she first had to go down into the Depths, dying a spiritual death. In her church, the pointers were female, and women could also baptize, breaking a gender taboo held in many Spiritual Baptist churches. After her pointing mother laid her down on the "mourning ground" in the church's secluded chamber, Siddiq left her body where it lay and opened her "spirit eyes." Mother Siddiq found herself beside a river in the twilight of the Depths, shielding herself from blows. Her mother was beating her. Her mother used to give "a real good cut-ass, used to cut my tail bad," she told me. Even in Rio Moro, where corporal punishment of children was generally acceptable, Mother Siddiq's childhood friends remembered her mother's beatings as excessive. So Siddiq asked out loud, "What? Even here you fucking beating me?" And she turned around and jumped on top of her mother, bringing her to the ground, but when she looked at her mother beneath her, she saw it was not her mother's face. Instead, it was a face of bone, without skin. Later, her pointer told her that she had met Ezekiel—the Old Testament prophet that God had sent down into the valley to make dry bones live. With Ezekiel's visitation, Siddiq became a woman of Ezekiel's realm in the Depths, which Spiritual Baptists call the Valley of Dry Bones.

When Siddiq first recounted this experience to me, she caught power where she was standing in her newly tiled kitchen in Rio Moro. She entered what Spiritual Baptists call a "'doption" (from "adoption" by the Spirit). The 'doptions involve repetitive bodily movements, mouth drumming, and breathing techniques, and they comprise vehicles of travel. They have numbers that also link them to the order of sounds in the alphabet; the mouth drumming of the Number-One 'Doption, for example, involves repetitive "a" sounds sung in time while bending at the waist. This mouth drumming is performed with heavy exhaling and inhaling, such that scholars have called 'doption a form of mind-altering hyperventilation (Glazier 1983; Simpson 1966; Winer 2009, 5). Closer to what Siddiq and other practitioners said, however, the heavy breathing of 'doption was important because one had to "pull 'doption" as if one were drawing power up from the earth. The 'doptions take persons to different places; when someone is in a 'doption in the "carnal world," his or her spirit is at a certain location in the "Spiritual Lands." Number-One 'Doption can take Spiritual Baptists to different locations, serving divergent purposes for practitioners on the islands of Trinidad as well as St. Vincent (see Zane 1999, 101). For Siddiq, this 'doption took her down into the Depths, as she kept bending rhythmically at the waist and pumping her arms midair in her kitchen after recounting how Ezekiel came to her. She then stood upright and began to speak in tongues, saying, "Tayo, tayo," while swaying from side to side. She had gone back to that place where Ezekiel was from, the Valley of Dry Bones, and she moved in place on the newly tiled floor with her eyes closed. Eventually, she stilled herself and reached a trembling hand toward the counter to feel for a cup. With her eyes still closed, she filled the cup from the tap and poured three evenly spaced drops onto the tiles. Then she took a drink of water for herself and asked her boyfriend to bring her a cigarette.

Like Bishop Dawes, Mother Siddiq had extensive experience in the Depths—or "the cracks and crevices of the earth," as she also called it. Like Dawes, she was also involved in the study and practice of the Trinidadian Kabbalah and Yoruba-inspired Orisha practices, which she had come to through her Spiritual Baptist mourning travel in Africa and the Depths. In her travels to Africa, she learned that Ezekiel's form on the Orisha side was Shakpana (an Orisha probably deriving from a West African smallpox deity) and that his female counterpart was the ancient Egyptian goddess Isis, who had put the bones of her dismembered brother back together to make him live again. In the Depths, Mother Siddiq had also learned that the skeleton Ezekiel had brought back to life in the valley represented the Kabbalistic entities of Mr. Skull and Cross (the head of the skeleton) and Mr. Emmanuel Bones (the skeleton's body).[12] The different "sides" of the figure Ezekiel, as well as mourning travel between Depths and Nations, thus knit together the three paths of African religion in Trinidad. She called Ezekiel her "husband," and while he was a biblical figure, he was a multisided persona that held her Spiritual Baptist, Kabbalistic, and Orisha affiliations in a partially connected assemblage.[13]

The Depths illustrates the complexity of ethical distinctions and the relationship between bad and good for many African Trinidadian religious practitioners. The Depths, in some ways, is similar to Christian conceptions of hell, evil, and bad; the Depths are populated by demons, skeletons, those who died "bad" deaths, and—at the deepest level, according to Mother Siddiq and Mother Jackie—Lucifer himself. Yet in esoteric Spiritual Baptist and Kabbalistic understandings, the Depths occupies a position very different from hell. While the vertical relationship of heaven and hell models the hierarchical moral universe of good and bad, the Depths confuses such a relationship of moral antinomy. One of the most common Spiritual Baptist maxims is "Deeper depths for higher heights," and these words dictate that one can ascend into the spiritual heavens only to the distance one has gone down in the Depths. That is part of the reason why mourners, on their initial journey to the Spiritual Lands, have to go down into the Depths first (another reason is that the mourner must die a spiritual death and be resurrected). Both the Heights and the Depths are arranged in hierarchical "levels" (usually said to be seven each), but they do not form a vertical moral hierarchy as heaven and hell do (see also Lum 2000, 245). Rather, they are like inverted images of each other. In short, these seemingly opposed realms were inseparable, which is why it seemed so natural for Arlena to pick up both good and bad in her mourning journey rather than choosing one basket, thus showing her "African" spiritual self.

Like Bishop Dawes, Siddiq also used the powers of the unjustly dead and the Depths to work on behalf of families whose members had suffered death, injury, or extortion at the hands of the police. In these cases and other difficult court matters, she used a Kabbalistic entity known as Frank Mahan, who was said to have murdered his entire family before ending up on the hangman's gallows.[14] Her clients were often Christians who were not Spiritual Baptists, and she frequently told me how such people navigated the ambivalent feelings that the figure of Mahan tended to provoke in them. As we were sitting on her porch one afternoon in 2012, I began to talk about the spiritual work surrounding Arlena and her friends' deaths. Drawing on her own experience in similar cases, she summed up the situation in this way:

> [The relatives of the slain persons] said, "Let we take care of we problem." You understand? Because they fighting against the police, they don't see themself getting any recourse, any kind of justice. So you fight them with spirit. Attack the police. Attack they family. When people angry, they not going to follow the tenets of the Bible. If you oppressed, you turn your cheek away and bam! [clapping her hands together to simulate the blow.] You know, [you] follow that ideal that they follow. Otherwise they call you evil. God say that he will take vengeance, but when you feeling pain, that kind of pain, you don't care about redemption or salvation. When you have problem out here, you don't want to wait 'til you dead. You in the fast-food business. You want it done right now. Even if you shame to say the word "obeah" in your church, you will go looking for obeah. [We laugh.] You going to go by the obeah man saying, "That is where I will get my justice!" You see, black people don't have the courts. Black people don't have the court system. . . . So that is what we have — obeah — that is our . . . our justice system.

As on other occasions, Siddiq drew on the ideal type of noninstrumental, nonviolent Christian ethics (i.e., turning the other cheek to receive another blow) as a contrast to her own ethics of justice and spiritual work. This distinction echoed in a host of other ethical and temporal oppositions that she often evoked: fast food versus home cooking, male versus female, black versus white, Kabbalah versus Orisha, Depths versus Heights, pain versus salvation, retributive justice versus forbearance. In the process, she seemed to reproduce a set of familiar distinctions between good and bad, slow and fast, or instrumental expedience and nonutilitarian Christian values. These were the very distinctions that those who objected to Dawes's and Siddiq's justice-seeking interventions mobilized to cast their spiritual work as improperly instrumental and morally dangerous affronts to the sovereignty of both God and state law.

It would be easy enough to understand these contrasting terms as a choice between mutually exclusive, opposed "baskets" of good and bad, with ethical action as the choice between them. Yet echoing Arlena's obviation of this choice by picking up both baskets, Mother Siddiq saw these contrasting terms as she saw the Heights and the Depths themselves—as complementary and inextricable forms of power. When inserted into the framework of the Heights and the Depths, good ethical value and bad instrumentality took on different shades of meaning. Still, I wondered how she could invoke strict ethical standards in her own work, refusing to take on cases that involved harming others for reasons she deemed unjust or unwarranted, while using the spirit of someone who had been executed for killing his own family to achieve her ends of justice. She responded to me by drawing on Marlon Brando's character in the movie *The Godfather*: "They [the spirits of murderers or those who died violent deaths] are still good . . . still good for certain things. Remember the Godfather. The Godfather is a bad man. You know what I'm talking about? He was a bad man. But when a man daughter raped and she father wanted justice, it was him he went to. He said, 'Godfather, we want justice. My daughter raped. Take care of this problem for me. We don't want to know how it done.'" While the Kabbalistic entity Frank Mahan or Mario Puzo's Godfather were murderers, Siddiq insisted that such a capacity for violence and vengeance, if properly directed, could be particularly useful in contexts of injustice. Making a rhetorical move that I have heard in both Trinidad and Haiti, Siddiq asserted that forces that have been represented as evil or morally ambivalent, both in popular and in anthropological representations of certain African religious practices, are good for the redress of injustice or the protection from harm.

Siddiq's contrast between the ethic of turning the other cheek and the "fast food" ethics of an appeal to the Godfather does not represent an opposition between virtue and evil. These divergent ethics are good for different situations. Spiritual workers even insisted that following some of Jesus's injunctions from the Sermon on the Mount might be bad in many contexts. In this sermon, Jesus commanded his disciples to "resist not evil" and to respond to various kinds of abuse with love, no matter the context. Jesus is quite clear that whoever does not follow his injunctions "shall be called the least in the kingdom of heaven" and "shall be in danger of hell fire" (Matthew 5:19, 22). For many of my interlocutors who identified as Christians, it was no small action to insist that Jesus's commandments could be bad for certain things.

Yet how could it be bad to meet violence with love? Spiritual workers' insistence on the limits of an ethics of turning the other cheek brought an unlikely interlocutor to mind, one buried in the dim memory of my undergraduate years. Writing on the eve of the founding of national socialism in

Germany, Max Weber ([1919] 2009, 119–20) produced a resonant critique of Jesus's injunctions in his "Politics as a Vocation":

> By the Sermon on the Mount, we mean the absolute ethic of the gos-
> pel, which is a more serious matter than those who are fond of quoting
> these commandments today believe . . . take the example, "turn the other
> cheek": This command is unconditional and does not question the source
> of the other's authority to strike. Except for a saint it is an ethic of indig-
> nity. This is it: one must be saintly in everything; at least in intention,
> one must live like Jesus, the apostles, St. Francis, and their like. Then this
> ethic makes sense and expresses a kind of dignity; otherwise it does not.
> For if it is said, in line with the acosmic ethic of love, "Resist not him that
> is evil with force," for the politician the reverse proposition holds, "thou
> shalt resist evil by force," or else you are responsible for the evil winning
> out. He who wishes to follow the ethic of the gospel should abstain from
> strikes, for strikes mean compulsion; he may join the company unions.
> Above all things, he should not talk of "revolution."

Regardless of how one feels about Weber's obviously hostile interpretation of the Sermon on the Mount, his critique recalls some common themes that Siddiq, Dawes, and Baba Khan all raised. The unconditional commandment to "resist not evil" had to be limited by contexts of power and justice. For Weber, however, this context for an ethics of not turning the other cheek is "politics"—a realm that for him is incommensurable with the ideals of religion (or at least Christianity) as a sphere of values and virtues rather than power. Although Weber's conception of value is a bit more complex than subsequent interpreters have made it seem (see Starr 1999), this con-trast between Jesus's injunctions and the pragmatic realities of politics could easily recapitulate the secular division of ethical religion from instrumental action, or Weber's own distinction between value rationality and instru-mental rationality. This, of course, is the same division that has so often made African spiritual workers, concerned with the uses of power and the making of justice, not religious.

But is it really possible for any kind of lived religion to exist in a world of universal ethical commandments that transcend particular situations of power? Is the idea that this is possible actually dangerous, morally authoriz-ing acts of reform that are profoundly violent or turning a blind eye from the ethical complexities of the world and toward the comforts of transcendent ideals? These were open questions that my interlocutors debated within lived contexts of power that often contradicted what Weber would call "value ratio-nal" norms. One response to such a situation was to create a world of even more purified ethical oppositions—a spiritual and physical war between absolute good and absolute evil, which chapter 6 explores by examining neo-Pentecostal Christian "spiritual warfare" against obeah in Rio Moro. There was, however, a different ethical response that spiritual workers intimated.

When spiritual workers affirmed contrasting spheres of ethical value appropriate for different contexts, or when Arlena picked up both baskets rather than choosing one, their aim was not purification but appropriate balance. Scholarly and popular misreadings of this balance of ethical con-trasts as an amoral stance toward good and evil, however, have led to the profound distortion of many African-identified religions. Instead of an em-brace of evil, spiritual workers' ability to balance contrasting ethical realms reveals what Weber ([1919] 2009, 127) probably would have considered a more "mature" ethical stance, one he called an ethic of "responsibility" rather than "absolute ends." This ethics means, as Starr (1999, 419) notes in his exegesis of Weber, that persons "must rightly balance" the demands of contrasting ethical frameworks, after realizing that "no ethics in the world can dodge the fact that in numerous instances the attainment of 'good' ends is bound to the fact that one must be willing to pay the price of using morally dubious means or at least dangerous ones" (Weber [1919] 2009, 121). This alternate ethics of balance, as Fassin (2014) notes, diverges from the con-trast between virtue and duty ethics that has dominated recent scholarly approaches (see also Mittermaier 2010, 140–41). Such an ethics of difficult balance also helps redescribe long-standing moral distinctions not simply between African (not-)religion and religion proper but also between con-trasting forms of African-identified practice.

AFRICAN TRADITION AND
BLACK MAGIC

The racialized division between instrumental magic and sincere religion continues to affect the rights and protections of African-identified spiri-tual workers. As the debates on the ethics of spiritual work at my field site showed, such distinctions were not simply imposed by outsiders. Members of Arlena's own family alleged that the spiritual work used to seek justice for her death was dangerous or unethical, as Mother Lisette's comments at the wake or the hauntings that later afflicted Arlena's family showed (see interlude 6). In much of the rest of the African diaspora, similar ethical divides between instrumentality and proper religion are no less common. Indeed, studies of African religion in the Americas have often reproduced resonant distinctions between the devotional orientation of morally upright African traditions and other powers that are depicted as morally suspect, less authentically African, and/or instrumental. There is a long list of such distinctions, but a partial inventory of the best-known cases would include the distinction between Yoruba-inspired Candomblé and Quimbanda, Macumba, or Umbanda in Brazil (e.g., Engler 2012; Hayes 2011), the Rada-Petwo opposition in Haiti (see Apter 2017; Mintz and Trouillot 1995), and the allegedly antagonistic relation between Myal and Obeah in Jamaica (see Brodber [1988] 2014; cf. Stewart 2005). Perhaps, however, the best-known of such distinctions is that between Yoruba-inspired Santería (also known as Regla de Ocha or simply Ocha) and Kongo-inspired Palo in Cuba.

Numerous scholars have elaborated on this alleged distinction between the filial devotion of Ocha and the mercenary instrumentality of Palo, but one of the most iconic accounts is that of Stephan Palmié. Palmié (2002) enumerates the well-worn oppositions between Ocha devotion and Palo instrumentality but rejects the scholarly conclusion that such a contrast is the result of the difference between Yoruba and Kongo origins of the two practices (a perspective he calls the ethnic "theme park" approach to African religion). Rather, the moral opposition between Ocha and Palo seems to stem from the historical conditions of slavery, which bifurcated worlds between heavily alienated, instrumentalized regimes of labor and the humanized realms of affective relations and religious morality. Palo, Palmié argues, models both the objectification of slave labor and slaves' martial resistance, as humans assume a commanding, aggressive, and instrumental relationship to the Palo realm of spirit power—the dead. Unlike the dead, the spirit powers of Ocha—the Orichas—stand in a relationship of parental sovereignty to humans, who can only supplicate the Oricha deities.

In a critique of Palmié's description, Todd Ramón Ochoa (2010a, 396) argues that a fairly clear division between Palo as sorcery or magic and Ocha as proper religion emerges in this account:

> Palmié transposes these judgments to suit Palo, which he places within a similarly Protestant moral framework wherein: Palo is at times described as "reversed and perverted," "ghastly," and "grisly." Having accomplished

the conceptual and moral negation of Palo, Palmié then extends these judgments to his analysis of Cuban religion in general, depicting the relationship between Yoruba-inspired Santo/Ocha (Santería) and Kongo-inspired Palo as a moral opposition between good and bad. . . . This opposition is then resolved into a coherent "system" by sublimating Palo as a minor power destined to operate in the shadows of Santo/Ocha's "spiritually" ascendant light. In fact, these philosophical and moral positions in Palmié reveal not so much a Santo/Ocha-centric point of view (which characterizes his work), so much as they reveal that the intellectual resources he brings to bear on Palo are inevitably Hegelian.

Although Ochoa characterizes this moral opposition between Palo and Ocha as reflecting a Protestant bias or a Hegelian framework, this opposition, as I have shown, extends beyond the confessional boundaries of Protestantism or the limits of Hegelian thought. The principal ethical opposition of the religion-magic divide remains: should humans yield to the rightful sovereignty of God(s) (or the law), or are humans (in concert with other powers) themselves responsible for making justice in an inherently conflictual and unjust world? Echoing the terms of scholarly distinctions between magic and religion, Palmié asserts that, within an Afro-Cuban "indigenous sociology" of religious formations, Santería is supposed to represent expressive or devotional forms, whereas Palo works through expedient relations of contract labor in which the human can command and control supernatural power primarily through relations with the dead.

While Ochoa takes Palmié to task for recapitulating this magic-religion divide, Palmié himself takes an ironic or critical distance from these moral oppositions. For this reason, Palmié's summary of the distinctions between Palo and Ocha made by many contemporary practitioners of Santería is tempered by his Cuban interlocutors' constant recognition of how these moral dichotomies break down in practice. Palmié's interlocutors thus echo one of the points that Mother Siddiq made—that morally contrasting forms of religious practice are not necessarily good or bad, but they may be good for different things. Palmié (2002, 165) thus writes that "to a large extent, such conceptions [of a moral opposition between Palo and Ocha] do not derive from ascriptions of an inherently amoral or evil nature to the spirits of the dead [*muertos*]. . . . Different problems, people say, require different solutions."

Palmié ends his discussion of this opposition by hinting at a different reason for the moral contrasts between Palo and Ocha. These distinctions solidified only in the early 1900s, displacing the relative integration of Ocha and Palo in the nineteenth century. The prerevolutionary twentieth century, of course, marked the height of violent policing of African religions and the lynching of black *brujos* (witches) in Cuba. Yoruba-Cuban religious specialists of Ocha and Ifá, Palmié tentatively suggests, could have displaced negative images of instrumental witchcraft onto Kongo-identified Palo in their struggles for legitimacy, authority, and respectability that David Brown (2003) details so well.

In this way, it was not substantive moral distinctions between Kongo-inspired "sorcery" and Yoruba-inspired "religion" that drove the Ocha-Kongo divide but rather the process of religion-making in contexts of power. As I have argued throughout this work, this process of making religion depended on the making of religion's others. This process of religion's making and unmaking happened not simply between racial or religious groupings but also within them. Yet, as Palmié speculates, this process also increasingly divorced idealized images of religion from everyday problems, weakening the immediate efficacy of Ocha as it became proper "religion" in public representations. The result was an idealized moral dichotomy between magic and religion that was empirically untenable but productive of different forms of power. If Ocha and Ifá ritual modalities could capitalize on Santería's positioning as authentic African religion, then the methods of Palo could claim to be the ones that solved people's immediate problems in a more expedient manner.

By the end of his chapter, Palmié admits that the "indigenous sociology of religious forms" that he has elaborated is "bad sociology" (I take "bad" here to mean reductive). It is not simply "indigenous" practitioners but countless works of "nonindigenous" sociologists and anthropologists that, as Palmié notes, have propagated this somewhat-reductive picture of magic versus religion. While Palmié focuses on elaborating this "bad sociology," he does not focus as much on alternative ways of viewing reductive moral dichotomies between magic and religion. My project in this chapter has been to assert that such alternatives already exist amongst practitioners of African-inspired religions. My interlocutors could have different ways of doing an "indigenous sociology of religious forms," which produced divergent ontological and ethical worlds. The differences between these worlds did not necessarily map onto recognized borders between discrete ethnicities or religions (i.e., what Palmié calls the ethnic-theme-park approach). Rather, to draw on Marisol de la Cadena's (2015) "indigenous cosmopolitics," multiple worlds—that is, points of disagreement and/or incommensurability—

exist within what would be called "a religion," "an ethnicity," "an island," or "a culture." In other words, practitioners of African religion might disagree on the sociology of religion that is valid (as scholars also disagree on such things). While the bifurcation of Ocha and Palo along the lines of idealized images of filial devotion versus instrumentality continues to exert moral force, it continually breaks down in practice. In lived contexts of power, practitioners of African religions have ethical frameworks that construe the value of contrasting forms of practice differently.

OBEAH, KABBALAH, AND THE
MORAL ECONOMY OF THE DEPTHS

Like Palo, obeah has embodied a trope of instrumental magic intimately bound to accusations about intercourse with the dead as opposed to the filial devotion to God(s) that true religion supposedly embodies. Across the anglophone Caribbean, however, those accused of obeah tried to show that they were involved in legitimate "religion," defending their practices as forms of devotional prayer that left power in the hands of God rather than with humans or the human dead. Charged with practicing obeah in Trinidad in 1929, Victoria Doyle, for example, told the arresting officer that "she didn't work obeah but only makes prayers," having told her client (who turned out to be an undercover police officer), "I do things to make a [court] case drop but I don't work obeah" (qtd. in Paton 2015, 191). Defendants claimed to be engaging in prayer rather than obeah, with the line between these forms of action determined by the same distinction between supplication of God(s) and the instrumental "assumption of supernatural power" that seems to arbitrate moral distinctions in Afro-Cuban religion or Western dichotomies between religion and magic. Yet the line between prayer to God(s) and the instrumental assumption of "supernatural power," as Diana Paton (2015) notes, was never clear, and cases seemed to draw this line in contradictory or arbitrary ways. What *was* clear was that the burden of proof for drawing the line between magic and religion rested on the shoulders of the subaltern accused, who were found guilty roughly 80 percent of the time in such trials (Paton 2015).

Judging from the archival records of obeah trials and the distinctions between Afro-Cuban religious forms, it is tempting to argue that Caribbean peoples had to digest and internalize the European moral distinction between devotional religion and instrumental magic, creating purified ideal types that would correspond to this division, thus allowing them to refute charges that African traditions were prone to the latter. It is important to note, however, the complex play of race in these distinctions, and that "black magic" and Africanness are not necessarily equivalent. In the African diaspora and the transnational sphere of African traditional religion, Yoruba-identified practices of Orisha devotion have become the representative of African religious tradition par excellence over the course of the twentieth century (see Brown 2003; Clarke 2004; Matory 2005). The Yoruba-inspired African tradition of Ocha, as Palmié's ideal-type depiction suggests, is more like religion proper than sorcery in many scholarly representations, even as other forms of African practice assume the racialized denigration of (not-) religion. Similarly, in Trinidad it is not simply Euro-American Christianity that stands for religion proper, but (at least for Afrocentric cultural reformers) the most "African" practice of the threefold path—the Yoruba-inspired Orisha faith. Ironically, the most ostensibly white or European-influenced practice of the threefold path—the Trinidadian Kabbalah—is the tradition that typically plays the morally denigrated foil for the Orisha faith in this Yoruba-centric Trinidadian sociology of religious forms.

This manifestation of the distinction between instrumental, morally dubious magic and noninstrumental religious devotion was readily apparent in the ways that some Orisha devotees condemned Bishop Dawes's and Siddiq's justice-seeking work for the dead. Mother Mariella, for example, herself no stranger to Kabbalah banquets, claimed that Bishop Dawes's work with the dead was a "dark" and "dangerous" Kabbalistic practice that ultimately stood in a relationship of inferiority to the supplication of the Orishas. According to Mariella, two days before the arrest of the police officers was the date Arlena had set for a thanksgiving ritual to offer gratitude to the Orishas for the success of her recently opened Young Blood DVD Club. Now that the police had cut her life short, friends and relatives had decided to mark the date with memorial prayers. However, instead of holding this meeting at the family's Orisha shrine, as would have been the usual custom, people marched together into the forest where, Mariella said, the power of the Orishas was more immediate.

Mother Mariella believed it was their petitions to the Orishas that had brought the police to justice, but she made a sharp distinction between the power of the Orishas and the conjuring of dead spirits that had also been contracted to bring the officers to trial. When I described to her the repeated stories I had heard of coffin preparations to attain justice, she told

me that I had crossed out of the Orisha faith and entered a little understood, "deeper" and "darker" practice that dealt in "trapping" and "oblig-
ing" spirits of the dead to do work. For Mariella, that practice was the Kabbalah, which dealt with the fallen angels (demons) of the Christian tradition
and the unrestful dead. As Mariella's analysis showed, Kabbalah often operated as the unethical, coercive other for both European Christianity and
Yoruba-inspired religion, which both allegedly operated through supplication of God(s) rather than instrumental command of power. While there
is no elaborated discourse on a Kongo tradition in contemporary Trinidad,
some of the same oppositions between Yoruba-inspired African traditional
religion and Kongo-inspired Palo in Cuba still obtained. Orisha was devotional, whereas the Kabbalah was manipulative. The Orishas were forgiving
and benevolent, whereas Kabbalistic entities were dangerous and volatile.
Humans could only supplicate the sovereign Orishas, whereas Kabbalistic
practitioners could manipulate or be manipulated by the objects of their
devotion. Finally, the Kabbalah, like Palo or obeah, was associated with the
dead, whereas the Yoruba-inspired Orishas seemed to model something
closer to European conceptions of angels or gods. This was not because of
geographical proximity or immigration between Trinidad and Cuba, but because the magic-religion dichotomy is a "North Atlantic universal" (Trouillot 2003) integral to the making of religion as a key category through which
rights and respectability are conferred.

Mariella's circumspection about justice-seeking spiritual work using
the dead seemed to echo in some community members' appeals to leave justice "in the hands of God," replacing instrumental human action with the
supplication of sovereign powers. Yet most spiritual workers, like Mother
Siddiq herself, insisted that it would actually be unethical to not take matters into their own hands and use their divinely gifted knowledge. Referencing biblical accounts of Jesus's or Solomon's command over spirits, Bishop
Dawes told me that the Bible made clear that God had given humans the
power to control spirits. "I don't think God would give you such knowledge
for you not to use it," he said, defending his justice-seeking spiritual work.
Another spiritual worker named Philip Lemoine echoed Dawes's sentiments about biblical affirmations of the power to use spirits, but he com-
plained that present-day humans "run from the power." In cases of extreme
injustice, to run from this power and seek refuge in transcendent notions
of moral value implied responsibility for, in Weber's ([1919] 2009, 119–20)
words, "evil winning out." In fact, Mother Mariella herself also thought
it was necessary for humans to intervene in cases of injustice; she simply

thought that the Orishas were more effective, and less dangerous to use, than the powers of the dead.

In other words, there was no consensus on the limits of ethical action among my interlocutors. While Palmié's (2002) "indigenous sociology of religious forms" seems to recapitulate a long-standing magic-religion distinction in terms of instrumentality and devotion, the situation for practitioners of Afro-Cuban religion, as Palmié himself notes, remains more complex. As Julie Skurski (2007) briefly argued in a critical review of Palmié's (2002) work, his hard-and-fast opposition between Palo and Ocha ethics does not reflect the everyday experiences of practitioners of Afro-Cuban religion, who are very often initiated into both Ocha and Palo (while also practicing some forms of Espiritismo). As Skurski also notes—and as Palmié (2002, 194) admits—the Orichas are not necessarily the model of benevolence and parental care that Palo-Ocha distinctions often depict. The experiences of my interlocutors in Trinidad also showed that the Orishas were capable of harming, paralyzing, or relentlessly afflicting humans either to get their attention or to express their dissatisfaction with the way humans were treating them. As Ochoa (2010a) also asserts, reducing Palo to a recapitulation of slavery and objectified labor misunderstands the ways that Palo practitioners experience their devotion and work (see also Crosson 2017a, 2017b).

It is not simply Hegel, Protestantism, or popular notions of Afro-Cuban religion that have primed scholars to often misrepresent ethical distinctions in the African diaspora as moral divisions between magic and religion; it is also an enduring conflation of religion with what Weber might call an ethics of "absolute ends." In this view, religion proper models moral maxims that transcend worldly contexts, with ethical action defined by the realization or embodiment of a noninstrumental good. Yet it is difficult to show how any religion models such ideals consistently, and that is why the endless purification of (not-)religion is necessary. As Palmié (2002) notes, it was probably this dynamic of purification among Cuban practitioners of heavily stigmatized African traditions in the late nineteenth and early twentieth centuries that incited the Yoruba-Kongo, Ocha-Palo moral economy.

In sum, the long line of scholars who depict these distinctions between ethically contrasting practices of African religion as a division between mutually exclusive religious forms misses the experiences of my interlocutors. Even Mariella or Lisette, who both ethically opposed justice-seeking work with the dead and represented the Kabbalah as an inferior or suspect practice, had extensive experiences in attending Kabbalah banquets and interacting with Kabbalistic entities. Mariella had been the right-hand woman of the former head of the national Orisha organization, who was known to be a "grand master" in the Trinidadian Kabbalah. For those who advocated for justice-seeking work with the dead, the situation was no different. Like many practitioners of African religions, Bishop Dawes's first and most prominent affiliation was with the Spiritual Baptist faith, and he had come to his Orisha, Hindu, and Kabbalah devotions through the spiritual travel of mourning. Mother Siddiq had also begun as a Spiritual Baptist before shifting toward Orisha and Kabbalah practices. Certainly, there are practitioners of each of these paths who draw hard-and-fast borders between religious formations that should not be crossed. Indeed, in terms of collective rituals there was sometimes controversy over whether a manifestation in an Orisha feast was really a Kabbalistic interloper. The point is not that there were no distinctions, but that they were not the same as ideal-type distinctions between religions as mutually exclusive confessional communities or between black magic and religion as mor(t)ally opposed entities. Rather, the ability of practitioners to inhabit multiple practices that displayed contrasting ethical frameworks reflected what Weber ([1919] 2009), following his critique of the Sermon on the Mount, argued: we do not live in one value-rational world of good and bad but in multiple worlds with conflicting modes of ethical action that are appropriate for different contexts (see also Starr 1999). Even if one thinks the Kabbalah or obeah is bad, as Mother Siddiq argued, bad can still be good for certain things.

Most importantly for my argument here, apparent distinctions between good and bad can be understood through ethical frameworks that differ from those that have epitomized a Western conception of religion (or many scholarly critiques leveled against that category of religion). It would be easy enough to render the differences between the Heights and the Depths, Kabbalah and Orisha, or Palo and Ocha as reproductions of well-worn moral hierarchies between religion and magic, good and evil, the dead and God(s), or the underworld and the heavens. Most of my interlocutors did not see it this way. Even as the moral distinction between the assumption of supernatural power and noninstrumental religion became an integral component of how spiritual workers justified their own practices (and criticized the practices of other spiritual workers), such distinctions take on radically different meanings within the framework of the Heights and the Depths. In this world, what is so often represented as "bad" — whether the dead, demons, or other morally ambivalent entities — is not a moral antinomy to be shunned but a fearsome depth to be plumbed for one to enact a more-than-shallow ethical sensibility in lived contexts of power.

In contrast to Christian imperatives to turn the other cheek, my interlocutors elaborated an ethics that they identified as peculiarly African. The Africa that this framework proposes is not simply a continental landmass but also an ethic of difficult balance between contrasting forces (see also Chernoff 1979; Eglash 1999; Guerts 2002; Karp and Bird 1987; Stewart 2005). Importantly, this ethos of balance does not imply universal moral injunctions or a fixed concept of tradition. As one initiated priest in the Lucumí (i.e., Cuban-Yoruba) tradition writes,

> The Lucumí worldview is tremendously complex, embracing paradoxes and opposites as part of a complex and constantly changing balance rather than the rigid and . . . dualistic view of the world found in most Western European thought. . . . We see the universe as well as ourselves as being in a constant struggle to achieve, maintain, or restore balance. This is because we are surrounded by a multitude of forces perpetually confronting and interacting with one another each with their own trajectories and aims. . . . Balance is a precarious thing, or as martial artist Bruce Lee once put it, "Balance is running like hell to keep it." (Eyiogbe 2015, 151–52, 154)

In other words, rather than recapitulating Western notions of an equilibrist tradition that precedes the linear development of modernity, an ethics of balance is incredibly dynamic.

While inextricably bound to colonial and postcolonial experiences of governance, obeah signals something else in addition to a colonial legal category or an internalized legacy of the post-Enlightenment opposition between devotional religion and instrumental magic. Obeah, I suggest, expresses a generative ambivalence of power—an ethics of cultivated balance between opposing forces—noted as a pervasive theme in West and West Central African–inspired religions (Karp and Bird 1987, xv; Mintz and Trouillot 1995; Stewart 2005, 177–84). The anti-African denigration of (not-) religion can be read as a willful mistranslation of this aesthetic of balanced forces into a Western ethical framework of good and evil. This mistranslation made possible modern ideas not simply of race as a moral-chromatic hierarchy between white and black but also of narratives of redemption that structure contemporary projects of reform in postcolonial worlds. Invectives against African religion as dark or evil recapitulate the moral-chromatic antinomy that, as Frantz Fanon ([1952] 1986, 146) notes, under-girds much racial thinking: "In Europe, whether concretely or symbolically, the black man stands for the bad side of the character. As long as one cannot understand this fact, one is doomed to talk in circles about the 'black prob-lem.' Blackness, darkness, shadow, shades, night, the labyrinths of the earth, abysmal depths, blacken someone's reputation." Although Fanon paints a rather dismal picture, inserting blackness into the cosmology of the Heights and the Depths transforms the pressing moral-racial problem he highlights. Blackness and "abysmal depths" are not evil in this reckoning. Rather, they are deep—and the Depths are not simply abysmal. Both dark and light have their place in the situated ethics of spiritual workers, as Baba Khan insisted with his metaphor of the car battery. The contrasting polarities of spirit are not inherently good or bad; they are good for different situations, and their contrast generates power. Like Arlena, spiritual workers often asserted that one had to pick up both good and bad to walk with power and balance.

CONCLUSION

Oppositions between instrumental magic and religious devotion have con-tinued to undergird scholarly and popular conceptions of religion and ethics, as well as the racialized exclusions enacted in their names. While the evolutionary hierarchy that accompanied this magic-religion dichotomy in Frazer (1922) or Tylor (1871), as well as the hierarchy of complexity that accompanied Malinowski's ([1925] 1954) resonant distinction, are probably offensive to contemporary anthropologists, some recent conceptions of ethics or piety have unwittingly taken on this rather Western distinction in their attempts to critique Western categories of religion and morality.

The alternative to this alternative is not an unethical, amoral universe where it is all right to commit murder if it leads to desired ends. Rather, the alternative proposed here is a virtue of justice as the difficult balance be-tween opposed or antagonistic forces. Unlike most representations of pious ethics in recent scholarship, this virtue is not necessarily the enactment of (what one's religious tradition defines as) the good. Because power must have oppositional polarities to flow, spiritual workers engaged with con-trasting ethical values to make justice through experiments with power.

Life involves complex and contradictory ethical situations. One way to deal with this is to create an idealized and purified value-rational sphere of religion or ethical tradition, which allegedly presents moral guidance in the face of modernity's ethical incoherence (e.g., MacIntyre 1981). Perhaps, however, such a noninstrumental notion of ethics and the purifications of religion and magic (or religion and power) enacted in its name present potentially dangerous ideals incapable of navigating complex situations of power (Weber [1919] 2009). Certainly such distinctions between religious conscience and power were fundamental to both the denigration of obeah and the practice of violent injustice under the banner of enlightened ideals during the civilizing mission of British colonialism in the Caribbean.

For some people who have stronger beliefs in the authority of law or have seldom been on the wrong side of the police state, the justice-seeking ethics of some of my interlocutors might seem patently devoid of ethical standards. Spiritual workers, however, quite clearly believed that there were ethical limits and guidelines in their works, although they did not all agree on what these might be or think that they were necessarily independent of the particulars of ethically complex situations. For the spiritual workers I knew, the problems that surrounded them in their communities, as well as their popular association with "black magic," meant that these ethically vexing situations darkened their doors on a not unusual basis. It took them away from the value-rational world of ideal-type religion and toward the world of knowledge and action they called science, obeah, experiments with power, or work.

Do any religions really model such ideals of noninstrumental ethical traditions and value-rational worlds on a consistent basis? Catholic priests regularly performed exorcisms at my field site, and many of my interlocutors asserted that they were some of the best "obeah men." Pentecostal-charismatic spiritual warriors battled the demons of obeah and commanded spirits in the name of God. Certainly the litany continues of "sorcerous" behavior within recognized non-Christian "world religions." In Trinidad, Muslim imams gave people healing and protecting oils or manufactured what Hindus and Muslims in Trinidad call *tabej* (an Arabic-derived South Asian word for "talisman"). Hindu pundits, particularly in Kali *puja* temples, made their living performing protective rituals on people's cars, healing the sick, fabricating *tabej*, giving bush baths, and doing money magic for clients. Nevertheless, African-identified healers in Trinidad have borne the disproportionate brunt of obeah accusations (Paton 2015), and obeah itself continues to be popularly conceived as non-Christian, African atavism. While some scholars continue to insist on a substantive distinction between religion and magic, these distinctions are highly flexible and polemical, inflected by racial and religious biases for people who actually have to navigate such categorical distinctions.

Despite their often counterempirical nature, distinctions between instrumental practices and religion proper continue to undergird moral invectives in contemporary worlds, and this is patently evident in the continuing intolerance exhibited toward obeah and African spiritual work in the Caribbean. The next chapter highlights one of the key ways in which these counterempirical distinctions are naturalized, through what my interlocutors call "blood." At my field site, "blood" refers not simply to race and consanguinity but also to the practice of "blood sacrifice." The chapter follows the "blood lines" that separate proper religion from animal sacrifice, Christianity from Africanness, religion from obeah, and respectable Hinduism from South Asian superstition in Rio Moro. "Blood" shows how the limits of religion are inextricable from racial polemics, but rather than a figure of shared lineage and origin, "blood" articulates the disavowal of ritualized violence that has formed the basis for civilized religion in colonial and postcolonial settings. This ostensible supersession of violence, as the previous chapters have shown, actually becomes the justification for violence toward religious and racial minorities in modern nation-states. Just as an ideal of noninstrumental piety can exist only through the foil of black magic, proper religion can only hope to disentangle itself from violence through the disavowal of blood.

2
THE NATIONS

Where the Ganges Meets the Nile, I

Arlena heard the turbulence before she could see the rapids, a roar, she tells me, something like the sound of the waves when the sea got "brave" (rough) in Rio Moro. But this roar was not coming from Rio Moro's ocean, for she was far from the southern shores of Trinidad. After descending into the Depths, her spirit had traveled to the Nations, where she found herself walking on a tongue of land between two iconic rivers. She had been enjoying her view from this strip of ground between the Ganges and the Nile, admiring the Spiritual Nations of Africa on one side and India on the other, but she came to the point where the two rivers met and there was no way forward except to cross over to one of the Nations. "That place, where the Ganges meets the Nile, is trouble," she tells me, "because it have what we does call a 'crossover spirit,'" a set of racially ambiguous forces that could interfere with a mourner's ability to choose between Spiritual Nations.

When Arlena found herself at the tumultuous conjunction of rivers, her progress on her mourning journey was premised on choosing to cross over to one of the Spiritual Nations that also signified the homelands of Trinidad's two most populous ethno-racial groups, Indo-Trinidadians and Afro-Trinidadians. While mourners have told me of their journeys to the North Pole, under the sea, or to the land of the Apache, Africa and India were the Spiritual Nations that most often helped to define a mourner's "true identity"—a spiritual identification that might have no direct connection to a mourner's everyday notions of ethnic heritage.

Arlena thus faced a consequential choice at the confluence of the Ganges and the Nile, one that presented her with some difficult options. Eventually, Arlena would cross over into Africa and meet the market vendor who would make her a "calabash woman" (interlude 3). But standing on the tip of land between Nations, Arlena pondered the changes that each Spiritual Nation might demand of her in her daily "carnal" life. She remembered the Afro-Trinidadian man who crossed over to India and had received instructions from the spirits there to wear a dhoti (South Asian cloth wrap for men) to church. People laughed at him on the public minibus he had to ride to services until he bought a long robe that covered what his detractors referred to as his skirt.

For Arlena, a more salient hurdle in choosing either Africa or India was not a change in clothing but an alteration in her relationship with animal blood. One of the most difficult things about crossing over into Africa was the potential that she would be called into the Yoruba-inspired practice of Orisha, whose collective feasts usually involved animal sacrifices, or "blood," as the offerings were often known in Rio Moro. In contrast, one of the hardest things about crossing over into India was that Arlena might find a Hindu spiritual identity and be asked to become vegetarian and give up eating meat. Over the course of the twentieth century, vegetarianism and the abandonment of popular Hindu practices of animal sacrifice had profoundly shaped ideals of respectable Hinduism in Trinidad. Giving up meat and offering animals were both sacrifices for Arlena, who, like most contemporary Trinidadians regardless of race or religion, consumed meat but had never killed an animal. As Arlena stood before Africa and India, the difference between these Nations was drawn by both streams of tradition—the Ganges and the Nile—and by lines of animal blood.

BLOOD LINES

Race, Sacrifice, and the Making of Religion

"BLOOD"

In Trinidad, the word "blood" carries charged meanings. "Blood," of course, could signify the concerns with violence that saturated public discourse. As I write these words, news media has proclaimed January 2018 to be the "bloodiest month ever" in Trinidad and Tobago's history, due to an unprecedented murder rate (Seelal 2018a; "January 2018 Is Bloodiest Month" 2018; "T&T Police Appeal" 2018). Meanwhile, the blood of lower-class black people killed by the police is often celebrated as expiatory by middle-class Trinidadians, communicating the heavy racial and class distinctions that accompany questions of violence in Trinidad (see Ramsaran 2013; Welcome 2018). "Blood" has long carried these racial overtones, with the sordid history of race in the Americas arguably beginning with the "blood cleaning" (*limpieza de sangre*) of the Spanish Inquisition (Martínez 2008) and the pro-toracial idea of Christian blood (Anidjar 2011). The contemporary meanings of "blood" in Trinidad (and the Americas) show how issues of race, class, and violence continued to be entangled. Arlena's death at the hands of the police was just one pointed manifestation of this entanglement.

In Rio Moro, however, the word "blood" also conjured associations that were less familiar to me. "Blood" referred to practices of animal sacrifice, and one could be "in blood" (practicing animal offerings) or "out of blood" (having forsworn such obligations). While initially unfamiliar to

FIGURE 4.1. "Young Blood" T-shirt. For Arlena's burial her friends made T-shirts embla-zoned with her nickname, "Young Blood," which had expressed her youthful vitality. The word "blood," however, also conjured the violence of a life cut short, with the phrase above her photo stating, "Gone Too Soon." Photograph by the author, 2011.

me, these associations with animal sacrifice still conjured the issues of race, religion, and alleged violence that have permeated blood's genealogy in the West. In Arlena's vision of the Ganges and the Nile that precedes this chapter, she drew Trinidad's predominant ethno-racial border between Africa and India not with human bloodlines but with lines of animal blood. On the one hand, a sacrificial Africa reflected the centrality of animal offerings for devotees of Trinidad's iconic African religion, Orisha. The rejection of animal sacrifice, on the other hand, defined respectable ideals of India and Hinduism for Arlena. To make matters more complicated, for many Afro-Trinidadian Christians a quasi-human sacrifice (i.e., the blood of Jesus) rendered practices of animal sacrifice sinful acts or harmful obeah. Yet rather than a shared substance, "blood" (as a popular term for animal sacrifice) was often an object of disavowal. These disavowals arbitrated the limits of respectable religion for many Hindus and Christians in Trinidad, with the rejection of "blood" often signifying one's distance from the alleged harm of obeah.

As many of my Hindu and Afro-Christian interlocutors disavowed "blood," however, they were less concerned with the divide between Africa and India than with their own links to the sacrificial practices of their forebears. African-identified Spiritual Baptists, Pentecostal Christian spiritual warriors, or Hindu pundits could all "dismiss blood," healing people of obeah by nullifying the relationships of animal sacrifice that their progenitors from India or Africa had allegedly established with spiritual powers. Other Spiritual Baptists and Hindus, however, defended animal sacrifice as a practice of care and commensality, denying these accusations of harmful obeah and the denigrations of aspects of Indian or African traditions that they communicated.

The questions of harm, religion, race, and sacrifice that congealed in the word "blood" are no trivial matter. The moral condemnation of animal sacrifice continues to be a cornerstone of religious intolerance across the globe, alleging that others' practices are unimaginably cruel (an accusation that, ironically, motivates acts of symbolic and physical violence against religious minorities). As I was writing this chapter, a reporter from Texas requested an interview from me after eleven practitioners of Afro-Cuban religion in San Antonio were arrested on charges of "animal cruelty." To make this coincidence more jarring, I had just been teaching about the resolution in Hialeah, Florida, that had sought to outlaw Afro-Cuban religion on the grounds that animal sacrifices violated public morals (e.g., Palmié 2013). These projections of cruelty onto minority religions were not limited to the

United States or the Caribbean. In India, charges of animal cruelty against cows have been a key justification for growing violence by Hindu nationalists against Muslims and Dalits, and in Sri Lanka the Buddhist-majority government has condemned Hindu practices of animal sacrifice as illegal savagery (e.g., Boaz 2019; Ghassem-Fachandi 2012). In Brazil, African religious practices have also been targeted for criminalization as allegedly being cruel to animals (Boaz 2019). Why, when most Trinidadians, Brazilians, and Americans consume meat, have they been so concerned about a relatively small number of animals killed under ritualized conditions of purity that sought to both consecrate the animal and minimize its suffering at death?

My answer in this chapter is that attitudes toward animal sacrifice are more concerned with the moral and racial limits of religion than with animal welfare. These attitudes foreground how religion is a race-making project in Western modernity, which has taken shape through the projection of violence onto sacrificial not-religion. As I have argued in previous chapters, the making of good religion in the story of liberal secularism presents itself as the separation of moral religion from instrumental force, whether in idealized separations of religion and magic or of church and state. Yet the deritualization of killing that supposedly separates tolerable religion from sacrificial not-religion has authorized violent forms of intolerance, especially toward African religions in contemporary worlds. Meanwhile, other forms of violence are celebrated or tolerated. In Trinidad, the daily violence of the security state even occasions moral praise. On my most recent stay in Trinidad, in 2018–2019, the police commissioner's shoot-to-kill policy was celebrated in much popular and political discourse (see, e.g., Hassanali 2019). In a reversal of the logic of sacrificial substitution, the cruelty toward (certain) humans was less problematic for many than was the sacrifice of animals. In Texas, even as those responsible for placing human asylum seekers into cages at the US-Mexico border faced no legal punishment, Texans who sacrificed domestic farm animals in religious rituals were placed in jail. It is not the scale of violence or the species killed that determines which acts are legitimate and which provoke legal sanction. Instead, it is the intertwined distinctions of religion, class, and race that separate acceptable from unacceptable harm.

This chapter begins by paying closer attention to the dismissals of animal sacrifice that Hindus and Spiritual Baptists in Trinidad used to heal afflicted clients and to distinguish their own practices from obeah. The chapter then examines the historical and contemporary links between disavowals of "blood sacrifice" and attempts at morally cleansing religions and nations of violence, focusing on discourses of race and sacrifice in the Caribbean. Next, I show how many Africans and Indians in Rio Moro were sometimes less concerned with forging lines of ethno-racial difference than with disavowing connections to their own progenitors and coreligionists who practiced animal sacrifice. Finally, I look at the actual practices involved in animal sacrifice for a Spiritual Baptist threefold practitioner who holds an Orisha feast. A focus on "cruelty" and the act of killing in representations of animal sacrifice, I argue, erases the long-term practices of animal care that are central to Orisha devotion. As practitioners devote significant amounts of their daily time (and money) to minding animals, they show how devotion to the Orishas is inseparable from devotion to the gods' animals. I then close by reiterating that the incredibly persistent racial invectives against animal sacrifice have more to do with the colonial making of (not-)religion and the projection of anxieties around violence onto obeah. As both Indians and Africans faced accusations of obeah in Trinidad, the disavowal of "blood" reflected not so much contrasting racial essences but a moral and racial discourse of religion that has defined subaltern respectability in colonial and postcolonial settings. By disavowing obeah and blood, Hindus and Christians distanced themselves from the popular practices of their own ancestors and attempted to disentangle themselves from past and present violence.

DISMISSING BLOOD

"The price of wealth is blood," Mary told me, after settling herself into a chair on her second-story balcony. Mary was an Afro-Trinidadian Spiritual Baptist (whose "true identity" was Apache), and she made her living by performing spiritual work for a range of clients across Trinidad.[1] By "blood," Mary meant animal sacrifice, and her work the previous day had been to "dismiss blood," nullifying an intergenerational obligation of animal offerings that she had diagnosed as the cause of her clients' afflictions.

Across the road from Mary's balcony, a child waded through the tall grass of the overgrown football pitch to retrieve a tethered goat before the sun set. Mary rubbed her eyes. She had just woken from one of the day-long naps that she took after performing some particularly taxing spiritual work. Her clients generally lived in other regions of Trinidad, and she had to travel extensively on public transportation to reach them. The family she had worked for the previous day were, like many of her clients, Indo-Trinidadian Hindus. "Indian people does obeah for richness and land," Mary told me, and she had been hired to counteract the "obeah" that her clients' previous generation had performed through animal sacrifice to lay claim to the property on which they still squatted.

Mary attributed potentially harming acts of obeah and blood sacrifice to her well-worn racial stereotype of Indian greed for land and wealth, even though obeah is popularly understood as an African practice in the anglophone Caribbean. As Mary suggested, however, animal blood and instrumental motives could turn Indian practices into denigrated obeah (just as her own disavowal of blood made Mary an Afro-Trinidadian Christian that had rejected her mother's animal sacrifices for the Orishas). While Mary diagnosed Indian clients as enmeshed in obeah because of their own greed, these same clients worried that the presence of Mary, as a black practitioner of a formerly criminalized African-inspired religion, would incite neighborhood accusations of obeah against them. The family lived in a predominantly Hindu neighborhood, and the matriarch requested that Mary not ring her handbell when she performed her spiritual work. In most rituals of purification, as well as in their church services, the clang of handbells is a distinctive marker of the African-inspired Spiritual Baptist faith, and the colonial law that prohibited the Spiritual Baptist religion in Trinidad from 1917 to 1951 had also outlawed bell ringing. "How I'm supposed to work without bell ringing?" Mary asked me rhetorically. She agreed to the family's request, however, as she had agreed to refrain from bell ringing for Hindus, Muslims, and mainstream Christians who did not want the neighbors to know they were dabbling in an African practice that made them liable to accusations of obeah. Through the shared discourse of obeah's disavowal, competing racial stereotypes of Indian greed and African atavism could both be expressed in a common linguistic marker of racialized superstition.

Like many working-class Trinidadians, Mary's clients were squatting on the land they occupied, possessing no formal title to the property on which they built their house. Such situations lend themselves to land disputes regardless of the race of those involved, and in this case, another branch of the family was claiming rights to the property. So that no one would move them from the land, Mary told me, her clients' forebears had performed blood sacrifices to the (typically) dark-skinned Hindu goddess Kali at the base of a pomerac tree in their backyard. Kali has "both a good side and a bad side," Mary says. On the bad side, "you offer blood to her to get money and land, to work obeah. On the good side you pray to her for help without

FIGURE 4.2. Spiritual Baptist handbell with spiritual oils, flowers, and Bible, Trinidad. Photograph by Olivia Fern, 2011.

offering blood." Now the family cannot rest, she says, because a deity, once offered animals, will grow angry if it does not receive more blood. Mary told them they had to cut down the pomerac tree and perform a blood sacrifice of the same type of animal, in this case a goat. This time, however, they would douse the goat's carcass in puncheon (160-proof rum) and burn it.

She would write her "key," a special biblical phrase given to her during Spiritual Baptist initiation ceremonies of blindfolded spirit travel (i.e., "mourning"), on a piece of parchment and bury it at the base of the tree. In the hole she would pour some "dismissal oil," a fragrant oil available in spiritual stores and some pharmacies. This is the way to "dismiss blood," Mary tells me, and stop a cycle of unpropitiated intergenerational obligation.

As the shape-shifting racial polemics in Mary's narrative suggest, disavowals of obeah and blood sacrifice are about more than the well-being of animals. These disavowals enact the race-making project of separating moral religion from harmful not-religion, and this project cut across the racial divide of African- and Indian-identified religion in Trinidad. In distinguishing between "good" religious devotion and harmful obeah, Mary employed the well-worn divide between moral religion and instrumental magic. While the former was characterized by prayerful devotion, the latter was preoccupied with wealth, land, power, and harm. While Mary turned this invective on Hindus (and on blood devotion to Kali, in particular), the attribution of instrumental harm to African-identified religions has also hinged on their alleged relationship to sacrifice.

RACE AND SACRIFICE

Sensationalized representations of animal sacrifice have formed one of the most potent—if not the most potent—supports for the denigration of African-inspired religious practices within and beyond the Caribbean basin. In the landmark 1993 US Supreme Court case *Church of the Lukumi Babalu Aye v. City of Hialeah*, it was the sacrifice of animals, more than any of the other stigmatized aspects of West African diasporic religious practice, that instantiated questions about the limits of "religious freedom." The racist vitriol of Hialeah residents toward the Regla de Ocha (Santería) congregation was popularly articulated through sensationalized representations of animal suffering. Local newspapers featured such hyperbolic headlines as "Ritual Sacrifices Turn Miami River Red," and the invocation of "animals shrieking" remained a focus of those Cuban Americans in Hialeah who were working to ban the practices of this Afro-Cuban religion for violating "public morals" (Palmié 2013, 150).[2] A nearby meatpacking factory, engaged in mass killings of animals who spent their lives confined in cages or hung upside down, was entirely unproblematic, but the periodic offering of animals within the confines of a legally recognized church raised accusations of unimaginable cruelty.

Similarly, in the arrests in March 2018 in San Antonio, Texas, the principal legal and moral charge brought against the eleven Santería practitioners was "cruelty." In response, the head of the domestic shrine where the eleven were arrested went on the local ABC television affiliate to deny these charges. The news interview was entitled "We Are Not Cruel People." Asserting that only "vegans" had the right to call them cruel—since all others consumed killed animals—the head of the shrine explained that the animals were not abused in any way. Indeed, ritual norms in Orisha devotion sought to minimize animal suffering at death. Nevertheless, the alleged "cruelty" of what happened in the suburban San Antonio garage shocked the moral conscience of neighbors and police.

In the Caribbean, the racist representation of animal sacrifice as unimaginably cruel has often depended on the imagined threat of another kind of sacrifice: the sacrifice of human life, and most particularly white humans. The child murder cases of the early 1900s, in which black spiritual workers were accused of murdering white children for their blood and were then lynched in Cuba and other parts of the Caribbean (Palmié 2002; Putnam 2012), or the sensationalized accounts of human sacrifice in Haitian Vodou that helped justify the US Marine occupation of Haiti (1915–1934) and fueled the American "voodoo craze" (see Hurbon 1995) are just some examples of how animal sacrifice has conjured racial fears of another form of violence. Indeed, back in the United States, accusations of cannibalism and child sacrifice formed a part of residents' vitriol in the Hialeah city council meeting that led to the prohibition of animal sacrifice and in the moral panic surrounding Afro-Cuban religion in Texas (Palmié 2013).[3] It is telling that these stories of alleged Afro-Caribbean human sacrifice so closely echo anti-Semitic "blood libel" in Europe—a widespread accusation that Jews used the blood of sacrificed Christian children in their rituals (see McAlister 2004; Putnam 2012). The specter of human sacrifice and the ritual usurpation of Christian blood, then, have been key accusations against African religious practitioners in the Caribbean and United States and against Jews in Europe.

In the parts of colonial India from which many of Trinidad's indentured laborers hailed, this sensationalistic conflation of animal and human sacrifice centered on the dark-skinned Sanskritic goddess Kali. In the British colonial imagination, a group known as the *thuggees* supposedly honored Kali with human blood (the English word "thug" derives from this group).

While the extent to which a fraternal group of highwaymen known as *thug-gees* was a product of colonial anxiety is debatable (see van Woerkens 2002), the transformation of *thuggees* into a religious cult devoted to sacrificing humans is undoubtedly the product of racist colonial representations of aspects of Hinduism—particularly those that involved animal sacrifice—as malevolent savagery. These colonial anxieties over *thuggees* were not limited to the Indian subcontinent; they also traveled across the British colonial world. In the 1890s, a Trinidadian newspaper speculated with alarm about the presence of murderous *thuggees* on the island.[4] These salacious representations have also entered popular culture, with a scene of *thuggees* worshipping Kali with human sacrifice featured in *Indiana Jones and the Temple of Doom* (1984).

In the anglophone colonial Caribbean, moral panics surrounding religious violence were inevitably bound to accusations of obeah.[5] And, like accusations of obeah, invectives against sacrifice were ultimately tied to colonial ideas of unredeemed blackness. They could also, however, be mobilized against other subaltern groups. In colonial and postcolonial Trinidad, heated debates regarding the sacrifice of animals have centered on two religious practices: the Kali (or Shakti) *puja* and the West African–inspired Orisha faith. Polemics against these practices have often hinged on the question of the value of animal sacrifice, pejoratively referred to simply as "blood" in these debates. These "blood lines," at different moments, divided Trinidad's mainstream Sanatanist Hindus from Hindus who worshipped at Kali temples, drove a wedge between "vegetarian" and "nonvegetarian" Kali worship, or drew the tenuous line between Orisha devotees and (some) African-inspired Spiritual Baptists.

Echoing colonial denigrations of sacrifice in Africa, India, or the Caribbean, contemporary polemics against animal killing sometimes bled into concerns about the violent consumption of humans. When I told middle-class Trinidadians that I was attending the rituals of the Kali *puja* and the Orisha faith, they sometimes warned me about secret practices of human sacrifice. Despite my protestations, one woman from the island's capital insisted that Trinidad's reputation for human trafficking from South America (usually attributed to local and transnational prostitution rings) was in fact used to deliver sacrificial victims to Orisha congregations. The violence of human trafficking in Trinidad, which consumed and enslaved Spanish-speaking women from South America, was thus projected onto African-identified rites. Echoing justifications for transatlantic slavery or the US occupation of Haiti, characterizations of African-identified religions as cruelly sacrificial masked and misplaced the locus of the violent consumption of life for profit. Taking a contrasting line of critique that attacked the island's bourgeoisie, working class residents in Rio Moro sometimes attributed Trinidad's possession of one of the highest per capita murder rates in the world to the human sacrifices that the powerful who profited off of narcotics, arms, and human trafficking allegedly made to accrue wealth (often to feed their moneymaking spirit-dwarfs, or "bucks"). Rising murder rates thus reflected the consumption of human life that profitable networks of narcotics and human trafficking necessitated.

For my subaltern interlocutors in Trinidad, however, the supposed instrumentality and harm that obeah and animal sacrifice often represented did not simply emanate from racial and religious others. As groups of bound labor who had been subjected to the colonial making of respectable religion (albeit in different ways), Indians and Africans in Trinidad often stood in an ambivalent relationship to the practices of their own forebears who had sacrificed animals. These intimate relations of consanguinity could form the basis for affliction, occasioning the "dismissal of blood" by spiritual workers. While invectives against animal sacrifice have sought to other religious minorities around the world, the disavowal of both "blood sacrifice" and obeah in Trinidad's majority-minority society reflected the potentially intimate nature of spiritual harm. Instead of white children, however, these invectives were concerned with the violence that afflicted the descendants of enslaved and indentured laborers in the Caribbean.

"EVEN HINDUS USED TO DO THIS THING"

"Even Hindus used to do this thing," Mitra told me as we sat in his living room in upper Rio Moro. "Even they used to take parts of animals—like a black cock—to do bad and work obeah." Like most Trinidadians, Mitra regarded obeah as a quintessentially African tradition, yet he continually used the category to refer to certain Hindu practices that he associated with the sacrifice of animals. The most salient of these were the Di *puja*, Kali *puja*, and hog *puja*, and Mitra regarded these practices as deriving from a past that bore an awkward relation to another past—the diasporic horizon of India.

While Mitra remembers his Indian neighbors performing *pujas* in which animals were offered and then consumed, his Hindu parents, he claims, never allowed him to attend such functions. "It was always forbidden by my family to go to those things," Mitra explains. "It was seen by my family as being an evil thing. Coming from a Hindu background, we don't eat meat. . . . So sacrifice by blood, or offerings by blood, wasn't accepted." I asked Mitra if he and his Hindu family ate meat growing up. After a long pause, Mitra emitted a drawn-out, hesitant yes. "But we did not eat . . . the only thing we ate as a child was chicken, you know, and that came about, in my view, when we came to the Western world. It's like I could ask you today, 'Do Muslims eat pig in Trinidad?' And the answer is yes. So it's that kind of shift that took place. We came from an Eastern background, from India, into the Western world and we started to pick up the traditions of the West, like killing and eating animals."

Like many Hindus in Trinidad, Mitra drew a line between two different pasts using the blood of animals. As with most middle-aged Hindus in Rio Moro, Mitra remembered Hindu rituals that involved the killing and consumption of animals as a familiar occurrence in his youth. These memories, however, were bound to a past of indenture and dislocation, when Indo-Trinidadians struggled to conserve their culture under conditions of dire hardship and struggle. The result, in popular wisdom, was that these ancestors had produced a "mix-up" (untutored, confused) form of religious practice that had to be brought in line with another version of the past: the diasporic horizon of Indian culture and tradition. Muslims eating pork and Hindus offering animal sacrifices were some of the most salient markers of this "mix-up" indentured past, and vegetarian offerings and diets had become integral to Hindu claims of allegiance to proper homeland practices in the present.

Aisha Khan (2004a, 41) has pointed toward the paired duality of these two pasts for Indo-diasporic Trinidadians. On the one hand, "when Indians' context and point of reference is India, they are not 'white,' but they are 'Aryan,' they are 'Caucasian.'" On the other hand, when the point of reference is indentured labor and immigration to the Caribbean, they become "'coolies,' increasingly 'black,' both because of and irrespective of their claims to Hinduism." This colonial narrative was based on two opposed pasts, one of whitened homeland tradition (associated with colonial racial theories of "Aryans" as light-skinned peoples who had mixed with the darker "Dravidian" or "Madrassi" natives of South Asia) and another of menial and coerced labor. These two pasts reflected the paired dualities of British colonial representations of South Asian culture between elite and peasant, Aryan and Dravidian, North Indian and "Madrassi," or civilized and superstitious practices. Blood sacrifice was one of the most salient arbiters of the

lines between the terms of these dualities, joining practices of spirit manifestation or ritual uses of alcohol as markers of colonially denigrated Hindu
practice in the Caribbean.

While a separation of carnivorous and noncarnivorous deities and vegetarian and nonvegetarian social classes has been identified in studies of
South Asian society as a principal arbiter of social status (Srinivas 1965),
this division was often one of complementarity rather than disavowal (e.g.,
Dumont 1957). Carnivorous deities—those that accepted animal sacrifice—
were often inseparable from vegetarian gods and goddesses, functioning as
their protectors and mediating between human and divine concerns (see
Fuller 1988). Nevertheless, elite South Asian reform movements that arose
during the nineteenth and early twentieth centuries were preoccupied with
the abolition of animal sacrifice in Hindu practice. In Trinidad, influential Arya Samaji and Sanatanist missionaries from India, who advocated
for very different kinds of Hindu standardization in their campaigns, were
particularly concerned with expunging this practice. Over the course of the
twentieth century, repudiating animal sacrifice was a cornerstone of these
efforts to make popular South Asian practices into a respectable world religion known as Hinduism, which was clearly separable from other recognized religions (see Rocklin 2019). As this chapter shows, the concern in
contemporary Trinidad is not usually with the complementarity of "blood"
and "vegetarian" deities and offerings. Reflecting the colonial logic of the
magic-religion duality, the concern is with the purification and separation
of these two kinds of worship and the different forms of value they yield.
These two pasts form two different diasporic horizons: one of homeland tradition or proper religion and one of indentured laborers' untutored, violent,
or overly instrumental (not-)religious practices.[6]

Against the diasporic horizon of India, Mitra believed that Trinidadian
Hindus had often performed illegitimate and malevolent practices. Yet *pujas*
involving animal sacrifice were arguably more characteristic of popular religious practice in the areas of North and South India from which indentured
laborers hailed than was the respectable Hinduism that was often supposed
to epitomize an authentic homeland past in the present. Arguments about
past origins, however, elide the relations of power that have been so important in shaping what counts as religion. For both Mitra and Mary, connections to a fraught past could be severed through the annulment or denial of
blood sacrifices. Against more legible discourses on African or Indian tradition in Trinidad, the kind of genealogy of religious formations that this
chapter offers does not indicate a line of descent traced continuously from

a shared past, as many dictionary definitions of "genealogy" assert. Rather, this genealogy signals forms of disavowal and erasure that are central, yet often unacknowledged processes in the making of consanguinity and tradition. Afro- and Indo-diasporic practices of animal sacrifice are some of the most salient arbiters of these disavowals.

DISMISSING BLOOD:
KALI PUJA AND SANATANIST HINDUISM

When Mitra asserted that "longtime" Hindus used to perform animal sacrifices and do works of obeah, he mentioned the head of the local Shakti or Kali Temple, Baba Narayan, as someone who still practiced such "obeah." As Mitra conflated the Kali *puja*, animal sacrifice, and obeah, he articulated a popular, if inaccurate, equation. While the Kali *puja* was a Hindu practice, Mitra insisted that Hindu tradition prohibited animal sacrifice and that the practice of killing animals resulted from the influence of "the West." Despite this popular understanding, by most mid-twentieth-century accounts, animal sacrifice formed an important and widespread part of popular Hinduism in Trinidad (see Klass [1961] 1988, 176–78; McNeal 2011, 164–65; Niehoff and Niehoff 1960). Throughout the twentieth century, animal sacrifice and practices of spirit manifestation that formed integral parts of popular Hindu practices in both South Asia and Trinidad were gradually expelled from a Brahmanical, Sanatanist Hindu orthodoxy that exerted hegemony in the domains of both Indo-Trinidadian politics and religion (see Van der Veer and Vertovec 1991). McNeal (2011, 171) asserts that, while still forming some part of domestic Hindu rituals, collective practices involving animal sacrifice had become moribund in Trinidad by the 1960s.

By the late 1970s, however, as part of a wider postcolonial reevaluation of colonially stigmatized religious practices among both African and Indian Trinidadians, the first Kali or Shakti temples in Trinidad (with help from Guyanese devotees) reintroduced collective practices of animal sacrifice and ecstatic mediumship in weekly *pujas*. Hindu practices of animal sacrifice thus became identified with this temple-based neo-Hindu movement that, reproducing colonial racial logic, identified its stigmatized practices as peculiarly "Madrassi" (a colonial racial category signaling dark-skinned, Dravidian, and/or South Indian persons and practices). In the early to mid-1980s, however, Krishna Angad's *mandir* (temple) became the first Kali *mandir* in

Trinidad to reject the practice of animal sacrifice, aligning itself with the disavowal of animal offerings in both Brahmanical Hinduism and the popular
Sathya Sai Baba movement on the island (Guinee 1992, 177; McNeal 2011,
175). Today, most Kali temples in Trinidad staunchly oppose the practice of
animal sacrifice, adopting a "vegetarian" or *sada* practice of offering deities
only fruits and flowers. Like obeah, the practice of animal sacrifice has become an accusation and a moral stain for Kali *pujaris*, one that was endlessly
deferred and disavowed in most contexts during my fieldwork.[7]

As if Baba Narayan had heard Mitra's accusations of blood sacrifice and
obeah at his Kali temple, his *satsang* (religious gathering) address that week
focused on these popular stigmas associated with Shakti/Kali devotion.
After a coterie of heterodox and orthodox Hindu deities had manifested in
the bodies of devotees who placed flaming camphor cubes in their mouths
to prove the authenticity of their manifestations, Baba Narayan picked up
the temple's microphone. "You always hear Christians talking about how
they going to church, like they proud," Narayan began, "but Hindus afraid of
what people will say if they talk about doing *puja* or praying to the sun. And
when someone go to a Shakti temple, the fear is worse still. They say we sacrificing fowl and drinking their blood. But we shouldn't be ashame to come
here. Because if we come here hush-hush, people going to think we coming
here for obeah." For that reason, Baba Narayan was organizing a procession
down the main road of upper Rio Moro the next week. A pickup truck with
large speakers would play *bhajans* (devotional Hindu music), and another
truck would carry the new *murti* (statue or icon) that they were installing in
the temple. A line of *pujaris* ecstatically manifesting various deities would
follow the vehicles while a pickup carrying *tappu* drummers would com-
plete the motorcade: "This a part of [us] worshipping freely, like everyone
else in the country," Baba Narayan said, "showing people how we worship
so they don't talk about [us] working obeah."

The next person to pick up the microphone was the *pujari* David. He
began by denouncing the "backbiting" among Hindus and the allegations
of obeah that had been leveled against him for attending a Kali temple. "But
we can't be backbiting and condemning others for dealing in blood," he
said, referring to the strong moral stigmas reserved for the minority of Kali
temples that still performed animal sacrifice in Trinidad. "We must help to
bring people out of blood and into *sada* [vegetarian practice]. If we turn
devotees away because they dealing in blood, then we not practicing what
we preach." Indeed, in much of his spiritual work, Baba Narayan aimed to
shanti (pacify) or "dismiss" obligations of blood that he diagnosed as the

FIGURE 4.3. Tappu drum played at a Kali Temple in Rio Moro. Tappu drums are open-frame goatskin drums specific to Kali Puja worship in Trinidad and Guyana. Photograph by Gigi Gatewood, 2011.

cause of his clients' afflictions. These afflictions most often stemmed from
the actions of a blood relation who had performed the sacrifice of an animal to a deity that now remained unpropitiated. Narayan's work was to dismiss this intergenerational obligation by propitiating the deity or "power"
through *sada* offerings of fruit and flowers. *Pujari* David thus continued his
address by claiming that he personally knew families who did not properly
shanti their obligations of blood sacrifice, and within a month one member
was dead. He pointed to Baba Narayan and proclaimed that Narayan had
brought nearly a hundred people over to the *sada* side, "*shanti*-ing" their
potentially harmful sacrificial obligations.

As persons came to Baba Narayan, Mary, and other spiritual workers
on both the African and the Indian sides for healing from affliction, these
spiritual workers often performed the dismissal of blood offerings that dis-
solved ties with the stigmatized practices of these clients' blood relations,
neighbors, or religious forebears. Even in the Kali temples that still practiced blood sacrifice, a moral line was often drawn between offering goat or
chicken and swine, with devotees' afflictions often diagnosed as a result of
their ancestors who performed the "hog *puja*" (the same hog *puja* for the
Hindu goddess Parmeshwarie that Mitra condemned). In his study of Kali
temples that performed animal sacrifice, Guinee (1992, 9) asserts that the
attribution of affliction to the hog *puja* "negotiates the most uncomfortable
aspects" of his interlocutors' relations to their own traditions.

Various forms of blood sacrifice thus instantiate shifting and contingent boundaries between beneficial and malicious Hindu offerings in Trinidad. For mainstream Sanatanist Hindus, the entire Kali *puja* often evokes
a realm of morally questionable sacrificial praxis, whereas for the majority
of *sada* practitioners of the Kali *puja*, nonvegetarian Kali temples represent this moral limit. For practitioners of the nonvegetarian Kali *puja*, the
offering of hogs rather than goats or fowl represents the boundary between
healing and potentially afflictive offerings. These moral boundaries are often
uncomfortably close to many contemporary Hindus, whose own family and
neighbors may have performed these practices in the not-so-distant past
(or do so in the present). These afflicted persons are then called back into a
relation with these disavowed carnivorous spirits, but it is a relation forged
through the experience of affliction and the act of dismissal. These ritual
disavowals of blood, however, are not peculiar to Hinduism in Trinidad.
As I show in the next section, both practitioners of Afro-diasporic religions
and Pentecostal Christians are heavily invested in lines of blood as arbiters
of relation to the alternate pasts of homeland tradition and objectified labor.

DISMISSING BLOOD:
SPIRITUAL BAPTISTS AND THE ORISHAS

In the anecdote that opens this chapter, Mary, an Afro-Trinidadian Spiritual Baptist, claims that Kali has two sides, a "bad" one involving blood sacrifice for instrumental gain ("money and land") and a "good" one involving vegetarian offerings where the object is devotion. While Mary has never set foot inside of a Kali temple, these divisions of blood would be familiar to her precisely because they are the same lines that she evoked to distinguish herself from the majority of Orisha practitioners in Trinidad. Like many Spiritual Baptists, Mary maintained ritual relations with the West African–inspired Orishas, manifesting them in collective rituals, and even organizing her own "Orisha thanksgivings." Yet she drew the line at blood sacrifice, thus dissociating herself from most Orisha feasts that offered animals to deities.

This tenuous blood line between Orisha devotees and Spiritual Baptists was usually articulated with reference to the sacrifice of God's son (Jesus) and the consequent revisioning of Mosaic law. One Spiritual Baptist leader expressed these sentiments during a thanksgiving performed at the house of a Rio Moro congregant:

> God don't want no death sacrifice. God say, "I am a God of life" not "I a God of death." We are no longer under the ceremonial laws. No more sacrifice of bull or goat or turtle dove. And anyone who is still doing such things is committing an abomination unto God.
>
> You are the sacrifice. Your flesh and blood—that you live a life that is pleasing to God. Your life is the sacrifice. Jesus came and shed his blood to end the ceremonial laws—the laws of sacrifice—and gave us the gift of grace. Grace allows us to come to God when we have sinned and ask forgiveness. We no longer must offer sacrifice to atone for our sins.

This Spiritual Baptist leader delivered his thanksgiving address with full knowledge that some in his congregation attended Orisha feasts where animals were offered. After the thanksgiving, I talked to one such congregant, Derron, a man who had held his own Orisha feasts in which he offered the prescribed animal sacrifices. While attaining some notoriety for his work with the Orishas, he had recently attained the rank of bishop within one of the Spiritual Baptist organizations. He had stopped holding his Orisha feasts, he told me, because the Orishas themselves told him not to offer animal sacrifices to them. He turned to keeping what he called an "African thanksgiving table" for the Orishas every year, where he offers fruits, cooked foods, and oils to the "African powers." He still keeps stools and altars to the Orishas at his home, but he offers prayers and candles rather than animals there. His newfound position of authority in the Spiritual Baptist organization thus coincided with a change in his devotion to the Orishas and the removal of animal sacrifice from his ritual repertoire.

Certainly, Spiritual Baptists are far from the only Christians who invoked Jesus's crucifixion to disparage practices of animal sacrifice. The sacrifice of Christ, as the Pentecostal leaders I knew in Rio Moro avowed, had superseded the need to make animal sacrifices. While in the early Christian church, the rejection of animal sacrifice was a basis for Christian supersession of ancient Mediterranean practices, in Trinidad, Christianity superseded Indian and African rather than Jewish and Pagan traditions. Through a sacrifice that early Christians first compared to regnant practices of animal sacrifice (i.e., Jesus as the sacrificial lamb of God) and then, by the fourth century was said to supersede animal offerings, Christian elites were able to position themselves as a people distinct from and morally superior to their Jewish and Pagan neighbors by virtue of Christ's blood (Ullucci 2011). The plot of Christian supersessionism through the rejection of animal sacrifice thus continued to inform Christian polemics and the making of palatable diasporic horizons in Trinidad. These condemnations of animal sacrifice, however, exceeded the bounds of Christianity. Hindu claims to orthodoxy also assumed these blood lines, ostensibly separating Brahmanical homeland tradition from the degraded practices of indentured laborers.

As Kali devotees attended Sanatanist temples and honored mainstream Hindu deities, and as Spiritual Baptists attended Orisha feasts and maintained devotional relations with the Orishas, the shifting line of blood often determined who and what could attain moral value for practitioners of both Indo- and Afro-diasporic religions. Certainly these disavowals of blood sacrifice elucidate how streams of ethno-religious tradition have been defined and separated in Trinidad. Like modern ideals of mutually exclusive nations, religious orthodoxies were supposed to have clearly defined borders, further strengthened by the disavowal of instrumental not-religion. Yet many spiritual Baptists devoted to the Orishas took part in feasts where animals were offered, emphasizing to me the centrality of animal care in these practices.

The considerable time and labor that went into raising consecrated animals was a significant sacrifice in and of itself—one that highlighted a different view on the meaning of animal sacrifice.

MINDING BLOOD:
SPIRITUAL BAPTISTS AND THE ORISHAS

Mother Evelyn was a Spiritual Baptist who came to the Orisha work through her mourning journeys to Africa. While growing up in Rio Moro, she had relocated to one of the densely populated working-class neighborhoods just east of Trinidad's capital city, from which her husband hailed. She lived amid a hilly network of narrow roads and tightly packed houses, but behind the gates of her compound, it seemed like the countryside again. Animals took up most of her small parcel of land. Ducks, goats, chickens, sheep, and turtles roamed freely on a relatively large piece of earth beneath her open-air Spiritual Baptist praise room and adjoining enclosed mourning room. The two rooms also served as her Orisha *palais* and *chapelle*, and I arrived at her home as she was making preparations for her annual Orisha feast. A Spiritual Baptist leader, who also worked on the Kabbalah and Orisha sides, would preside over her feast that year, serving as *mongba*.

Unlike other Spiritual Baptists who drew the line of their Orisha devotions at blood offerings, Evelyn told me that she was proud to offer the animals she had raised with her own hands at her yearly feast. The labor for her feast did not simply occupy the week of its celebration but was also reflected in the year-round activity of caring for all the animals that would become the sanctified food for the Orishas and their devotees. The odor of animal manure was faint, but not overpowering, as Evelyn and her shrine members bustled about the tight spaces of her compound in preparation for the feast's first night. The braying of goats, the complaints of ducks, and the crowing of a cock punctuated the din of human voices and laughter. I had never seen so many different kinds of animals coexist, and I was surprised to see how geese and goats drank from the same water trough in relative harmony.

"Minding these animals," Evelyn told me, "is about keeping the Orishas and God in mind." For Evelyn, the animals' care was the most time-consuming part of preparations for the feast. Such care involved intimate contact with animal bodily fluids, sicknesses, and smells. This care, she told me, was essential to her devotion to the Orishas. Rather than through words

FIGURE 4.4. Mother Evelyn's yard. Photograph by the author, 2011.

alone, Orishas communicated with humans through the medium of food. Orishas were hungry for the care and sustenance of humans, and hunger was a key modality through which devotion was expressed in the various lineages of Orisha devotion in the United States, Cuba, Nigeria, and Trinidad (see Pérez 2016).

Instead of an act motivated by instrumental cruelty, scholars have interpreted animal sacrifice as a kind of commensalism (i.e., eating together) that sustains relations between humans and gods. "The gods' hunger is no more a metaphor than their reality," Elizabeth Pérez (2016) writes in her exquisite examination of cooking and eating in an Afro-Cuban lineage of Orisha devotion in the United States. Pérez breaks new ground in studies of religion by focusing on the cooking and killing of animals rather than simply the human words and prescribed gestures that have typically been the focus of ritual studies.

Yet cooking and killing was only a fraction of the story at Evelyn's shrine. For my interlocutors, the care of living animals is a more time-consuming and mundane activity than their slaughter, cooking, and consumption.[8] Like Pérez's focus on cooking, this attention to care opens a new window onto what the practice of religious devotion can mean. It also powerfully refutes the notion that animal sacrifice is simply about cruelty or killing.

Affirming the care that animals are given in Orisha devotion is particularly important to counteract the accusations of "animal cruelty" that have led to the arrest of practitioners in the United States, their demonization across the Americas, or calls for their extermination by certain animal rights groups. Nevertheless, conflating care with the ideal of romantic love that structures normative human-nonhuman relationships in some parts of the world would be equally misleading. Such a characterization would turn sacrificial animals into pets. While this would probably be the ultimate moral redemption from "animal cruelty" in the eyes of many of their accusers, relationships between human devotees and sacrificial animals are not devoid of coercion, constraint, and (ultimately) killing. Yet in the United States relationships with pets, who are regularly caged, kept in small apartments, used for therapy, or "put to sleep," are not devoid of such less-than-romantic dimensions.

Rather than romantic ideals, practices of animal care in Orisha shrines highlight that the word "care" itself also implies worries, concerns, and burdens. Sometimes the Orishas' desires for nonhuman animals inspired devotees' resentment over the considerable financial obligation that these animals represented in a petrostate where goats and sheep were extremely expensive commodities. It also involved a concern over the spiritual retribution that might occur if one were financially unable to meet this obligation. Would the Orishas, denied the bond of animal blood that tied them to humans, react with anger? Dismissal, therefore, was not simply the concern of those who morally abjured animal offerings. It was extremely important for those who needed to discontinue the bond of blood, either because they did not have the money to realize such offerings or because a shrine head died without an heir that would maintain the shrine. Just like the sometimes-overwhelming demands that blood kin implies, bonds of animal blood between humans and Orishas could signify obligations that were overbearing.

While this chapter has focused on the polemics against sacrifice and obeah that set the bounds of proper religion for many in Trinidad, it is important to remember that animal sacrifice involves mundane and time-consuming practices of minding animals that are inseparable from the care

FIGURE 4.5. Ogun's stool. Goat horns, cutlasses (machetes), and rebar are planted in the earth of an Orisha shrine in Claxton Bay, Trinidad, forming the assemblage of Ogun's stool. Ogun is offered male goats and is the Orisha of iron, metal working, and technology. Each Orisha's stool is composed of the particular animals and material implements that define their tastes, capabilities, and domains of power. Photograph by Gigi Gatewood, 2011.

for the gods. The sickness of a sheep or goat put the possibility of feeding an Orisha (and the success of an entire feast) in danger, and these animals were much more than scapegoats. Rather than discarded repositories of sin, consecrated animals in Orisha devotion were extensions of the gods that were consumed by humans and Orishas. The horns or feathers of consecrated animals became important parts of the material assemblages (or "stools") where the Orishas literally sat in the domestic shrine. Both gods and animals were a part of Evelyn's household, becoming the subjects of domestic care that "blood" has typically implied in Western genealogies of family. Rather than reflecting the actual practices of devotees, representations of animal sacrifice as unimaginably violent have more to do with policing the moral and racial boundaries of religion, boundaries that have authorized symbolic and physical violence against subaltern religious practitioners across the Americas and South Asia.

CONCLUSION

In this chapter "blood" has signified not so much the difference between Indians and Africans as groups that possess contrasting racial essences but rather the common logic of nonsacrificial religion that British colonial authorities (and Protestant or Hindu reformers) used to define moral subjectivity and the exit from heathenism. It is extremely important to note, however, that in colonial racial theories, Africans and Indians could make the claim to nonsacrificial religion in different ways (see Munasinghe 1997, 2001; Segal 1993). According to these colonial theories, New World Africans possessed no religion or civilization, making (the right kind of) Christianity the only way to attain moral subjectivity in colonial reckonings. Indians, in contrast, had religion and civilization, but only to the extent that they could demonstrate their religion as "Aryan." Nineteenth- and early twentieth-century European racial theories asserted that the "Vedic peoples" (the so-called Aryans) had entered the Indian subcontinent from elsewhere, racially and religiously mixing with the darker-skinned natives (see Khan 2004a). The indentured laborers who came to the Caribbean from North and South India between 1845 and 1917 were not cultural elites, and they were particularly vulnerable to British allegations of negligible Aryanness. To have a respectable religion, South Asian religious elites would represent their religions as "scientific," "Vedic," "Aryan," or "Protestant" (see Lopez 2008;

McMahan 2004; Prakash 1997). For both colonial officials and the Hindu religious reformers of the Arya Samaj who came to Trinidad in the early twentieth century, indentured laborers could have a proper religion only if they refrained from their popular practices that involved embodied pain—most especially, animal sacrifice, cults of affliction, and fire walking. Colonial officials and reformers often reinscribed these practices as the property of darker-skinned "Madrassi" or "Dravidian" South Indians, thus purging Aryan Hinduism of such practices (see Khan 2004a; McNeal 2011). Racial distinction for both Indians and Africans in British colonial regimes in Trinidad was thus based on ideas of proper religion that demanded the excision of the animal sacrifices essential to popular practices in West Africa and South Asia. As such, blood sacrifice arbitrated the lines between past superstition and present reform, instrumental magic and moral religion, whiteness and blackness, colonial degradation and venerable tradition.

What my interlocutors' talk of blood made me realize is that the race-making properties of religion are not only about the assertion of shared essences. Rather than "bloodlines" that signaled consanguinity, my African and Indian interlocutors often asserted blood lines that were markers of division. Instead of lines of descent, the dividing lines between those who were in and out of blood expressed a remarkably resonant language of religious distinction that seemed to cut across the dominant lines of race in Trinidad. Perhaps, alongside the idea of blood as a shared racial substance, the foundation for notions of race in the Americas has also been an idea of moral religion based in the supersession of blood sacrifice and violence. For the growing number of African American and Latino persons in the United States who practice Yoruba-inspired religions such as Santería, animal sacrifice is a key site at which racism and exclusions from moral citizenship continue to be enacted in overtly religious terms. In Trinidad, European norms of religion, informed by the Christian rejection of Semitic, Pagan, or "heathen" practices of animal sacrifice, played a central role in colonial race-making and religion-making. Certainly, debates surrounding the value of animal sacrifice did not begin with Christianity or European colonialism.[9] Yet in the areas of Africa and South Asia from which most Trinidadians arrived, animal offerings were integral parts of popular religious practices in the eighteenth and nineteenth centuries. Contestations over these practices were intimately bound up with colonial projects of religion and race that Africans and South Asians faced on the island.

More than an act of Christian supersession buried in ancient history, the rejection of animal sacrifice continues to articulate a wide variety of distinctions between and within religious categories. In contemporary India, polemics about sacrificial offerings and animal cruelty motivate Hindu nationalist attacks on Dalits and Muslims (e.g., Ghassem-Fachandi 2012). Turning the tables on Hinduism, the Buddhist-majority government of Sri Lanka has mobilized moral invectives against the supposedly "primitive" or dangerously violent nature of animal sacrifice to ban such practices in Hindu temples (Boaz 2019). In contemporary West Africa, the Caribbean, and Brazil, the demonization of blood sacrifice and the attribution of cruelty to "African traditional religions" have underwritten arrests, stigmas, and legal regulations.[10] Perhaps the nexus of race and religion in modern worlds derives not simply from ideas about shared biological essences but also from polemics about sacrifice and religious violence. The rejection of animal sacrifice has been a (if not the) key arbiter of these racialized invectives, and the contemporary confluence of racial and religious intolerance has much to do with this moral separation of good and bad forms of killing. Somehow, the sacrifice of a few animals is more morally offensive to many contemporary Americans or Indian Hindu nationalists than are killings of Muslim civilians enacted under the banner of these countries' religious nationalisms. Race and religion are both ways of separating legitimate from illegitimate violence, and we need more accounts that trace the religious genealogies of the redemptive violence of the modern state (see Asad 2007; Fessenden 2012). These entanglements are not limited to or definitive of any particular form of Christianity, but they might be essential to the concept of religion that arbitrates the making of race and moral citizenship in contemporary worlds.

As Arlena told me what it was like to stand on the strip of land between the Ganges and the Nile in the realm of the Spiritual Nations, it was not simply her own relation to "blood" that made her pause there. As she faced the turbulent confluence of the two rivers ahead of her and looked at the Nations of India and Africa to either side, she told me that she remembered her own experience of standing in between the lines of race and religion that often divided her everyday life in Trinidad. In particular, she remembered her best friend from childhood. As a young woman growing up in a part of Rio Moro that was home to roughly even numbers of African and South Asian–descended inhabitants, she spent much of her childhood around her Indo-Trinidadian friend's house. Arlena remembers being fascinated with her friend's straight hair, which (as a child) she regarded favorably in comparison with her own. Their differences, however, were otherwise unremarkable until her friend married a man from a more monoracial sugarcane growing area that abuts Rio Moro. He did not like Africans, and he made no attempt to hide his distaste when Arlena visited his wife. This hurt her. "Down here that kind of thing does not fly, because here it's fifty-fifty, Indian and African, and we have to live together."

Eventually the two friends stopped visiting each other, but shortly before Arlena's ritual travel in the Spiritual Nations she recognized the husband's truck coming down her trace. It was dark by the time she again heard the telltale sound of worn-out wheel bearings signaling his exit from her neighborhood, but as the truck passed her porch, the engine sputtered out. It pulled over to the side of the junction and Arlena walked down the steps of her porch to stand under the stilts of her board house. "I stay in the shadows," Arlena told me, "and call out to him, bawling 'I could make you stay here all night for what you did to me.'"

"'Come out the shadows now,' he says to me. 'Let me see your face.'"

"'No,'" Arlena recalled, "'but I'll make sure your car gets fixed.'" Arlena called out to one of her neighbors who was a mechanic. "'Fix this man's car—and make *sure* he pays you.'"

After his truck was fixed, she came out from the shadows beneath the eaves of her house and walked up to him. "I'm the 'n—— woman' you hate so much, your wife's friend, and if it wasn't for me you'd be spending the night here."

Arlena recounted these experiences as she described what it was like to stand in the place where the Ganges meets the Nile. Her best friend's husband had taught her which side of Trinidad's ethno-racial divide she occupied, narrowing a spit of land between Trinidad's two predominant cultural streams. Once again, at the confluence of the Ganges and the Nile on her journey in the Spiritual Nations, Arlena was forced to choose one side of this divide between Africa and India or to forge headlong into the tumultuous mixture of these two streams. Yet just as she would eventually refuse the choice between good and bad upon entering into Africa, she decided to refuse this decision. Instead of going forward with her journey, Arlena closed her eyes, said her secret password, and turned around.

When she came back to herself on the earthen floor of the "mourning room" in her Spiritual Baptist church, Bishop Dawes seemed to know where she had been, chastising her for not setting her foot down on either the African or the Indian side. Until she chose a Nation, she would be in a transient place of what he called "crossover spirits." These spirits that inhabited the spit of land between Spiritual Nations confused inexperienced spiritual travelers and possessed no fixed nationality. In short, Arlena stood in a dangerous place of powers that represented neither a single ethno-religious stream nor the confluence of recognizable traditions. While she could name the Spiritual Nations and rivers that lay to either side of her, she had no name for the ground on which she stood—the narrowing strip of land she refused to leave—or for the crossover spirits that inhabited that ground between traditions.

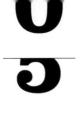

A TONGUE BETWEEN NATIONS

Spiritual Work, Secularism, and the Art of Crossover

BETWEEN THE GANGES AND THE NILE

As one of the most ethnically and religiously diverse places on the planet, Trinidad provides a unique lens for questions of racial and religious difference. In the preceding interlude, Arlena's vision of the Spiritual Nations at the meeting of the Ganges and the Nile reflected this diversity on an island whose two largest ethnic groups self-identify as either "African" or "Indian" (each group comprising around 35 percent to 40 percent of the island's population, according to census data). At this confluence of rivers, Arlena refused to make a choice between two seemingly exclusive alternatives—the Spiritual Nations of India and Africa that lay to either side of the Ganges and the Nile. Eventually, on a subsequent mourning journey, Arlena decided to cross over into Africa, where she again refused a different kind of binary choice to become a member of that Spiritual Nation (see interlude 3). This chapter pauses, as Arlena did, on the unnamed spit of land between the Ganges and the Nile, which Bishop Dawes characterized as a dangerous place of crossover spirits.

Strips of land between rivers are often called "tongues."[1] In the previous chapter, I showed how the making of religion has been forged not simply through shared identities but also through a common tongue of denial. The disavowal of practices categorized as not-religion defined streams of respectable tradition across colonial and postcolonial settings. In the anglo-

FIGURE 5.1. Originally from Rio Moro, Mr. Alvarez stands next to his family's stool for Osain, the West African Orisha that ruled his head. For grassroots practitioners Osain was often known as "the Indian man," and Mr. Alvarez first met Osain when he traveled to the Spiritual Nation of India during Spiritual Baptist mourning. Afterward, he began to have visions of the South Asian saint Sathya Sai Baba, who he also incorporated into his Orisha devotion and spiritual work. Photograph by Gigi Gatewood, 2011.

phone Caribbean, obeah remains a potent boundary category, in some ways analogous to the dangerous "crossover" tongue in Arlena's vision, defining streams of respectable Hinduism or Christianity by being excluded from their flow. Yet these negative denials of obeah, which often defined the banks of streams of religion, tell only half the story. After all, Arlena stood on a tongue of land that she did not want to leave, and this intervening space suggests a productive ground for rethinking what constitutes religion. This chapter argues that obeah's exile from the category of religion forms the basis for a tongue of crossover between traditions.

At the meeting of the Ganges and the Nile, Arlena faced both essential difference (the two separate rivers that defined Nations) and what Homi Bhabha (e.g. 1994) called the "third space" of hybridity (the mixture and meeting of the streams). While Arlena's vision could be placed within this common dialectic of mixture and hybridity—a dialectic that has structured projects of nation making and racial categorization across the Americas— the tongue of crossover represented a "fourth space" that existed outside the flow of the two separable streams and the rapids that represented the "third space" of their mixture. Taking its inspiration from Arlena's vision, this chapter theorizes spiritual work as a tongue of crossover that navigates ethno-religious difference without producing mixed or syncretic amalgams. As such, (what gets called) obeah presents an alternative to both racial essentialism and hybridity as ways of thinking about ethno-religious difference. North Atlantic ideals of secularism (and, as the next chapter discusses, science) have been defined through the transcendence of difference—a transcendence that subaltern peoples have often been excluded from in colonial representations of the tribal, ethnic, racial, and religious differences that supposedly overdetermined nonwhite people. This chapter, however, looks at spiritual work as a crossover art that incorporates difference without transcending the ethno-religious divisions that help compose spiritual powers. Spiritual workers experimented with difference rather than purporting to transcend, mix, hybridize, or segregate streams of tradition.

MIXTURE, DIFFERENCE, AND CROSSOVER

And of all these rivers that shaped this land
Two mighty ones move like a sculptor's hand.
—David Rudder, "The Ganges and the Nile" (1999)

Across the Americas, national narratives have claimed to realize the secular dream of transcending difference through ethnic mixture. Arlena's vision of the meeting of two racially marked rivers reflected the power of this dream in Trinidad. As Arlena herself told me, this confluence referenced a popular calypso, "The Ganges and the Nile," by the renowned calypsonian David Rudder. This song—which provided the soundtrack for a beach video promoting Trinidad's Miss Universe swimsuit competition in 1999—proclaims Trinidad as the place where the Ganges (as a metonym for Indo-Trinidadians) has met the Nile (as a metonym for Afro-Trinidadians).

The lyrics depict the process of diaspora as the journey of these rivers from their homeland sources to a confluence that makes a new, mixed river (i.e., Trinidad). Like so many celebratory nationalist visions of racial, cultural, and sexual mixture in Latin America and the Caribbean, Rudder's calypso lauds this mixture as a way of erasing the divisive ethno-racial differences that are said to structure postcolonial racial or political conflict. By avoiding "politricky situations," Rudder proclaims, Trinidad can be "one lovely nation, under a groove," where "the Ganges has met the Nile."

In contrast with Rudder's celebratory tones, Arlena's vision cast this process of mixture in more ambivalent terms, as she faced the turbulent confluence of rivers and recounted the racial tensions between Africans and Indians that had interrupted a childhood friendship. Like countless academic critiques of national narratives of creolization or *mestizaje* in the Americas, her dilemma at the tip of this tongue of land highlighted the friction between racial categories that occasioned tropes of mixture in the first place (e.g., Gould 1998; Khan 2004a; Munasinghe 2001; Téllez 1999). As these critical accounts have asserted, nationalist visions of mixture in the Americas, while articulated as inclusive, have also reinforced racial, religious, and sexual exclusions. The melting pot of the United States can accommodate only ethnic whiteness, for example, and the idea of Brazil as a "racial democracy" of hypermixture masks extremely high levels of everyday state violence against black and brown populations (see Smith 2016). As I detail below, the popular narrative of Trinidad as a harmonious ethnic "callaloo" (i.e., puree) was limited by a patriarchal Christian axis of creolization, which presumed a hierarchical binary of whiteness and blackness as the basis for ideas of mixture.[2] A middle-class, Christian, and Afro-creole vision of the postcolonial nation as callaloo mixture excluded African religions, Indian culture, and non-heteronormative sexuality in divergent ways (e.g., Alexander 1994; Hintzen 2000; Kamugisha 2007). Ostensibly uniting the nation through (an exclusionary process of) mixture, this "creole nationalism" dominated political projects in the anglophone Caribbean following independence from Britain in the mid-twentieth century.

Nationalist visions of mixture, however, also presumed the other conventional model of difference that Arlena encountered—the mutually exclusive ethno-religious "Nations" on either side of the Ganges and the Nile. While seemingly opposed, these models of mixture and difference were an intertwined dialectic, with processes of creolization or *mestizaje* presuming a racial grid of unmixed identities that would form the ingredients of national melting pots. Like visions of national mixture, assertions of mutually exclusive ethno-racial identities can yield liberatory or oppressive overtones. Certainly, the notion of separate races and religions has fostered conflict, segregation, and inequality in modern nation-states. However, the multicultural paradigm that arose in Trinidad in the 1990s to counter the creole nationalist exclusion of certain forms of identity also asserted the "right to difference" (most especially religious difference from Christian normativity) as its clarion call (see also Brereton 2010; Castor 2017; Fernando 2014; Ryan 1999). Echoing widespread efforts to recognize groups excluded from national identities across the world, these multicultural efforts have also been critiqued for reifying and domesticating difference, substituting the recognition of difference for the redistribution of substantive rights (e.g., Fernando 2014; Kelley 1999; Prashad 2001).

Caught between separate ethno-racial streams and their confluence, Arlena's predicament not only mirrored a dialectic of cultural mixture and ethno-racial division that characterizes nation-making projects in the Americas; it also seemed to echo the dialectic of syncretism and orthodoxy that shapes popular ideas about religion. As Shaw and Stewart (1994) note, the envisioning of religions as rivers—what they call the "streams of tradition" trope—has long structured ideas about what happens when religions meet. In a popular theorization of religion, Thomas Tweed (2006) takes up this trope, arguing that religions are "aquatic flows." That is, religions flow as separate streams (forming orthodoxies) and mix together to form new streams. Tweed conceives of this process of syncretism as the "crossing" of traditions, implicitly suggesting the heteronormative trope of crossbreeding that has consistently dogged European theories of race, evolution, and speciation (as well as eroticized visions of national mixture in Latin America and the Caribbean) (see Darwin [1859] 2004; Fraunhar 2002; Hartigan 2017; Pravaz 2012; Young 1995).

Yet what struck me most about Arlena's vision was not this familiar racial dialectic of crossing and purity, but the tongue of land in between this dialectic—the unfamiliar territory of crossover between the Ganges and the Nile that Arlena did not want to leave. As Bishop Dawes's admonitions about crossover spirits suggested, the word "crossover" can carry ambivalent meanings. "Crossover music," for example, can make hits on multiple charts, but it can also imply racial appropriation or inauthenticity.[3] Even as crossover artists move between styles of performance, questions of power attached to musical, racial, or gender categories persist (and this is precisely why crossover affords something that metaphors of mixture or purity do not). Like the tongue of crossover spirits on which Arlena stood, crossover music reflects neither a geography of mutually exclusive genres nor a fluid mixture of the boundaries between genres. Certainly, the ability to perform crossover and not be accused of opportunistic fakery has been easier for some subjects than others. Crossing over racial and religious lines has been significantly harder to navigate for nonwhite people, and subaltern spiritual workers who performed a variety of religious traditions were often inconceivable anomalies or frauds within colonial classifications. The colonial trope of the obeah practitioner as charlatan depended on such accusations of racial inauthenticity. African-descended persons arrested for obeah who claimed to be practicing science, spiritualism, or Hinduism were construed as racial impostors bent on profiting off their clients (see Rocklin 2016).

One striking example of such an arrest involved the prosecution of a black man "of the bold negro type" listed in court records as Baboo Khandas, arrested for obeah in 1919 in Trinidad (see "Alleged Assumption" 1919; Paton 2015; Rocklin 2016). He described himself as "a sadhu" (a Hindu term for a wandering holy man or ascetic) who had been born in Africa. He spoke "Hindustani" through an Indian court interpreter who translated his words into English for the judge. A month earlier, however, Baboo Khandas admitted to having given his name to police as "James Williams" and identifying as an Anglican Christian. He was arrested through the usual tactics of undercover police entrapment for spiritual work and was found in possession of the English-language European *grimoires* (spell books) that were evidence for obeah across the Caribbean (see Paton 2015; Rocklin 2016). His case combined elements of what might be called Hinduism, Islam, African traditional religions, European forms of Christianity, and/or "Western" esotericism. Khandas's lawyer drew analogies between Roman Catholic practices and Khandas's spiritual work, but the judge found that Khandas did not practice any one kind of appropriate religion and ruled him guilty of obeah ("Alleged Assumption" 1919; Paton 2015; Rocklin 2016). While Khandas's eclectic self-presentation could be read as an attempt to circumvent the stigmas associated with blackness and Africanness, he did not adopt a Hindu identity to displace his Africanness. He identified as both African and Hindu, presenting a multiple identity that made little sense within a colonial framework of mutually exclusive racial and religious categories.

Spiritual workers who experimented with a variety of traditions and techniques were usually unable to prove that they were the proper subjects of one tolerable, state-recognized religion—the claim necessary to avoid guilt in the eyes of the law. Obeah-practicing men and women who experimented with multiple traditions, therefore, were often "crossover artists," with all the negative connotations that phrase can carry. Beyond questions of racial and religious authenticity, however, "crossover" points to an alternate way of understanding both ethno-religious difference and spiritual work. Rather than racially pure or mixed subjects, "crossover" suggests a multiplication of the self through performance (see Szwed 2006). Instead of judging my interlocutors' crossover performances as inauthentic, profit-driven, and fraudulent (thus reproducing the trope of obeah as fraud), this chapter dwells on this multiplication of the self as a subaltern practice of spiritual mobility that exists outside the urbane nodes of cosmopolitanism.

Rather than resulting in a unitary mixture, performances of difference can make one multiple through the very lines that are supposed to divide identities. Spirit possession, carnival masquerade, comedy, and theater all epitomize this multiplication of the self to cross between identities. This tongue of crossover, however, is not inherently liberatory. These performances often rely on crudely stereotyped forms of difference that echo racial and religious hierarchies. Spiritual Baptists who travel to the Spiritual Nation of China, for example, often come back having learned kung fu and speaking a form of "spiritual Chinese" that can sound like the stereotypical "ping-pong" mockery of Chinese in Trinidadian comedy and song.[4] Along with this potential reliance on racial stereotypes, "crossover" also disrupts fixed identities. In contrast to a census chart of ethno-religious data, which often assigns a single person to a single identity, this modality implies an ability to cross over to identities, and to cross back. Because this process is reversible and multidirectional, it is not one of conversion. Rather than a unidirectional change from one fixed identity into another, crossover implies a capacity for temporary and repeated transformation. These transformative encounters with difference are not always willed or wanted; spiritual workers often experienced the manifestations, afflictions, visions, and dreams of spiritual powers as draining, annoying, or vexingly foreign (Crosson 2017a).

While neither inherently liberating or oppressive, this tongue of crossover provides an undertheorized way of approaching dynamics of religious and racial difference. In contrast to commonsense notions of community in Western social theory, which see groups as amalgams of persons who share an identity, a tongue of crossover sees persons as multiplicities composed of the divisions that organize society.[5] In this way, crossover focuses less on identity-related questions of authenticity and more on performative powers. How can a subject, already heavily circumscribed by racial, gender, and class markers, mobilize the powers of being otherwise in particular ways? This power, of course, was heavily limited in colonial regimes of governance for nonwhite persons, who were assumed to be provincialized by their racial origins. Yet as Robin D. G. Kelley (1999) has suggested, there has always been an alternate way of conceiving of nonwhite heterogeneity, which he calls "polycultural." Rather than answering the persistent question "What are you?"—thus fixing himself within a multicultural grid of mutually exclusive identities—Kelley calls for the recognition of "the people in me" that compose him as a heterogeneous black being.

Although Kelley does not talk of spirit manifestation or spirit travel, these practices obviously foreground a multiple or "polycultural" notion of personhood, with my interlocutors manifesting West African deities or Indian and Chinese "spiritual" selves that diverged from their "carnal" identities. This is the modality of crossover that I want to explore as a means for understanding the practices of spiritual workers that get called obeah or science. More than the racial inauthenticity that allegations of crossover raise, this multiplication of the self gave my interlocutors spiritual and physical mobility through the very ethno-religious lines that have often divided rural subaltern people in Trinidad.

OF OBEAH AND ALTERITY

My argument—that spiritual work, popularly glossed as obeah, models alternate ways to conceive of religious heterogeneity and relations through ethno-racial difference—might seem counterintuitive to anyone familiar with the popular imagination of the obeah man or woman in the Caribbean. The ideal-type obeah practitioner is often thought to hail from the rural margins of the island or nation, where it is presumed that African tradition has survived in a more isolated and racially homogeneous setting. This premise underlies not only popular representations of obeah as the rural, folkloric past, encountered in Trinidad's Best Village competitions or Tobago's Heritage Festival, but also some of the foundational anthropological studies of the region. When Melville and Frances Herskovits came to Trinidad in search of African survivals, they bypassed the urban environs of the capital, where the practice of Rada- and Yoruba-inspired religion more closely modeled the kind of "Africanisms" they sought, in search of the rural, isolated village. They thus assumed that rurality and isolation equated to Africanisms, reproducing a troubling opposition between modernity and African-inspired cultural practice. They found the Africanisms they were searching for only in the "Shango cult" as they passed back through the capi-tal on their way out of Trinidad. Their study, *Trinidad Village* (1947), focused not on these urban locales of African religious practice, but on the rural vil-lage, which they represented as freer of European or South Asian cultural influence (see Paton and Forde 2012, 18; Rocklin 2012).

This equation of the rural village with ethno-racial homogeneity, iso-lation, underdevelopment, and tradition was not limited to Trinidad or the Caribbean. Instantiations of "community" have functioned as rural pasto-rals of homogeneity and consensus, or, alternatively, as oppressive, nondi-verse, and backward dystopias, since the romance of community's loss in early industrial Europe. The nostalgia for rural community and cohesion did not simply characterize modernization in England, as Raymond Wil-liams (1973; 1983, 75–76) shows, but remains a pervasive sentiment, whether idealized in new urban and New Age discourse or in romantic visions of the modern nation as an "imagined community" (see Creed 2006). The nostal-gia for community that accompanied industrialization, proletarianization, and enclosure in Britain, furthermore, was preceded by and premised on another radical disruption of locality: the transatlantic slave trade. Despite the unprecedented, nonlocal dislocations of the slave trade and indentured labor schemes, the Caribbean never garnered the cosmopolitan status that European metropoles were able to evidence as a result of the disruption of emplaced communities.

Thus, while obeah is a peculiarly modern formation, forged out of the colonial regulation of religion, coerced or forced dislocation, and the mass labor-based migration of nineteenth- and twentieth-century Caribbean peoples, it is popularly figured as a phenomenon whose incidence increases with rural isolation. It is no coincidence that the site of my field research, Rio Moro, simultaneously figured as one of the most backward, isolated, and underdeveloped regions of the island and as the nation's cradle of obe-ah. Other studies have attempted to counter these pernicious stereotypes by stressing the urbanity of many of those arrested for obeah in the Carib-bean (Paton and Forde 2012) or by emphasizing the role of intra- and extra-Caribbean labor migration in the circulation of obeah discourses (Putnam 2012, 2013). By emphasizing urbanity or nodes of labor migration, though, these studies still leave unexamined the possibility that marginalized rural regions might offer alternative histories of cosmopolitanism. This alterna-tive cosmopolitanism might be based not only on migration as it is usually conceived but also on the more-than-physical mobilities of spiritual travel, spirit manifestation, and spiritual work.

As scholars have noted, the isolated and homogeneous rural village or pacific island served as the foundational sites for Western ethnographies of non-Western peoples (Kuklick 1996). While the diasporic diversity of Caribbean islands misaligned with this ethnographic fiction of the homogeneous community, ethnographies of Trinidad have often kept this fiction alive by treating subaltern ethno-racial groups as self-contained islands. A fairly persistent organizing frame for these ethnographies, therefore, has been ethnically identifiable, ostensibly bounded religious communities, defined as either Afro- or Indo-diasporic. In the ethnographies of the Herskovitses (1947) and Klass ([1961] 1988), there was a concerted attempt to elide evidence of subaltern mobility, rural cosmopolitanism, and interracial traffic that did not fit into anthropologists' ideas of what Indian or African tradition in village settings should look like (see Rocklin 2012).

Thus, the use of Hindu ritual paraphernalia by rural Afro-Trinidadian Spiritual Baptists, while noted in the Herskovitses field notes, never makes it to their published work (and the prevalent use of allegedly European esoteric texts by African spiritual workers is de-emphasized) (Rocklin 2012, 68–69, 73). In *Trinidad Village*, the Herskovitses note that Afro-Trinidadians were not influenced by East Indians, citing a police officer who asserted that the influence traveled only in the opposite direction (Herskovits and Herskovits 1947, 20; Rocklin 2012, 73). These assertions go against the ways that Spiritual Baptists were self-consciously appropriating Hindu ritual paraphernalia. The subaltern cosmopolitanism of the Spiritual Baptists was rendered as inauthentic invention, an affectation to impress the anthropologists and garner interview payments, in the Herskovitses' field notes (Rocklin 2012).

Subaltern religious practices often failed to align with anthropologists' visions of the traditional village or ethnic group, and a principal area of misalignment was undoubtedly obeah, spiritual work, and conceptions of the powers of the dead (see Khan 2003, 2004a). Most often defined as "African," practices considered obeah bore the recognizable influence of some Hindu-identified religious practices, and Indo-Trinidadians were arrested, albeit less frequently, under anti-obeah laws (Khan 2003, 770; Forde 2011; Paton 2015; Rocklin 2013b). In addressing spiritual work and the powers of the dead, a foundational ethnography of Indian culture in Trinidad (Klass [1961] 1988) makes a sharp distinction between Indo- and Afro-Trinidadian religious communities, despite evidence to the contrary. Overlap between Indian and African conceptions of spiritual power surfaces in Klass's ethnography as his semirural Indian interlocutors use an African name for spirits of the dead: "jumbie." While "jumbie," a still-popular noun and verb

in the Trinidad English/Creole, probably derives from central African linguistic roots (the same roots from which "zonbi" and "zombie" derive),
Klass found that his Indo-Trinidadian interlocutors made extensive use of
the term.[6] "East Indians, like [Afro-]Creoles, may be troubled by 'jumbies,'" Klass ([1961] 1988, 33) writes, noting that "the East Indian definition
of 'jumby' is not unlike at least one definition given to the Herskovitses [by
their Afro-Trinidadian informants]." Nevertheless, Klass insists that "the
Trinidad Negro's jumby—as an agent of an Obeah Man, as an 'emanation
from Satan,' etc.—is on the whole a substantially different phenomenon."
For Klass the ethnic identification of the spirits of the dead rests upon a
sharp distinction between "satanic" African traditions (obeah) and the East
Indian spiritual work that his interlocutors call *ojha*. While the work of *ojha*
is strictly healing and protection, Klass insists that the obeah practitioner
can harm through the use of the dead, although he provides no specific evidence to underwrite this racial distinction. As I have argued in different
ways, this projection of spiritual violence onto African-identified customs
(despite empirical evidence to the contrary) also forms the basis for moral
economies of obeah, race, and criminality in contemporary Trinidad.

Certainly, Klass's distinction between obeah and *ojha*, which maps onto
the Western divide between instrumental magic and ethical religion, may
have some ethnographic basis (though not the objective basis he purports
to offer). As I detailed in the previous chapter, obeah remains a denigrated
category for Hindus in contemporary Trinidad, and Hindu disavowals of
obeah (like many Afro-Trinidadian disavowals) can have the effect of projecting religious violence onto atavistic Africanisms. This racial distinction
between healing work and the potentially harmful manipulation of the spirit
world also appears in other midcentury ethnographies of Indo-Trinidadian
communities. Clarke (1986, 109) asserts that "exorcism of spirits . . . was the
task of the *ojha* man, but manipulation of the spirit world, in malevolent
as well as protective ways, was thought to be more within the competence
of *obeah* men—usually Creole blacks, engaged by both East Indians and
lower class Creoles."[7] For this very reason, there were numerous cases of
Indo-Trinidadians contracting Afro-Trinidadian obeah men and women
for the work of protection. That Indo-Trinidadians formed a significant per-
centage of Afro-Trinidadian spiritual workers' clientele was the rule rather
than the exception in my field research, and this often had to do with the
moral-racial economy of the types of spiritual work to which Clarke refers.
In my own fieldwork, African spiritual workers sometimes marveled at the
"wicked" things that some Indian clients wanted them to perform (com-

mentary that in turn recapitulated racist images of Indians as ruthlessly greedy and money grubbing). A racist image of African obeah as amoral and the making of twentieth-century century Hinduism into a respectable religion were the intertwined phenomena that helped to drive this inter-racial dynamic of spiritual work. Klass's or Clarke's moral distinctions be-tween obeah and Hindu practices may have been extremely reductive and (in practice) inaccurate, but these distinctions certainly exerted power and influence in the racial imaginary.

Despite Klass's and Clarke's insistence that obeah is an Afro-Creole phenomenon, the principal interlocutor in one of the few ethnographic studies of obeah in Trinidad was an Indo-Trinidadian, referred to as "Boy-sie" (Borofsky 1968). Throughout this study, which includes extensive tran-scripts of patient consultations, it remains impossible to assign a single reli-gious affiliation to either the "obeah man" or his clients. While the patients in fifteen of the twenty-two consultations Borofsky observed self-identified as Indo-Trinidadian, Boysie's principal healing methods could not be bound to Hindu, Muslim, or Christian traditions. Rather, he drew most frequently on esoteric books distributed through mail order by the Chicago-based De Laurence publishing house, especially two texts purporting to reveal Kab-balistic spells and ancient Egyptian magic. Like the other African-identified spiritual workers interviewed in Borofsky's thesis, Boysie was hired to rec-tify domestic problems, heal psychophysical ailments, and/or transform socioeconomic fates. The clients' self-diagnoses and Boysie's own readings assigned these forms of social suffering to unnamed spirits, which envious social familiars had contracted to "pull down" the patients. As did Klass, Borofsky found that both Indo- and Afro-Trinidadians were troubled by jumbies, which signified both the spirits of the dead and a more general category of "ethereal agents" that could afflict, possess, and empower the living (Khan 2004a, 113; Khan 2007, 660–61; see also Vertovec 1998, 251).

Like Borofsky, I found that spiritual work evidenced a subaltern reli-gious cosmopolitanism rooted in the practicalities of treating a diverse cli-entele. This cosmopolitanism was not simply inspired by the mail-order publications of De Laurence but also by the cosmopolitanism of grassroots African religion, particularly the spiritual travel of mourning. Like Arlena, mourners traveled to a variety of "Spiritual Nations," learning African, Indian, or Chinese linguistic and religious practices even as their physical bodies stayed in Trinidad. Contrary to popular representations of calcified African tradition, grassroots African religion thus offered a dynamic religious cosmopolitanism that spiritual workers could draw on in their work with diverse clients.

To take one example, Bishop Dawes identified as "Indian in the spirit" after having traveled to the Spiritual Nation of India as a mourner, with his primary power being the elephant-headed Hindu god Ganesh. In front of his family's Spiritual Baptist church, they hired Hindu pundits to perform *pujas* (religious ceremonies) and plant *jhandis*, or flags, for various Hindu deities. Eventually, by watching the pundits, Dawes and his family felt confident performing the *pujas* themselves, buying do-it-yourself *puja* kits from the island's Hindu spiritual stores. When Bishop Dawes had to treat a Hindu client, this spiritual cosmopolitanism provided him with a common language of deities and ritual actions. This did not mean that Bishop Dawes had "converted" to Hinduism or ceased identifying as a practitioner of African religion. Rather, the Hindu "side" to his devotions complemented the Orisha, Kabbalistic, and Spiritual Baptist "sides" of his avowedly African practices.

To take one more example of cross-racial dynamics in African-identified spiritual work, a practitioner known as Mother Lennie grew up in an Orisha shrine and maintained a leadership position in a Spiritual Baptist church, but she also regularly had visions of Hindu deities and had traveled to the Spiritual Nation of India during mourning (although she identified as African in the spirit). One example of these visions occurred when an Indo-Trinidadian brother and sister arrived at her house while I was interviewing her in 2011. A hired car had brought them from a more monoracially Indian area, formerly devoted to sugar cultivation, about forty-five minutes away. The man could hardly walk, and the driver of the car helped him limp into Lennie's yard. When Mother Lennie saw clients with serious health problems, she usually asked if they had been to see a medical doctor at a health center before performing any treatments. The man's sister said that no doctor had been able to explain the cause of the man's ailments, and he had been getting progressively weaker since his wife had left him. Mother Lennie's chin dropped to her chest and she bent at the waist, her fists rolling over each other in front of her chest in rapid circular motions. She began to speak in tongues, repeatedly shouting "Jai Sita Ram!" Later she told me that she had a vision in which an "Indian spirit" with a monkey's head had come to her playing an instrument (most likely the monkey god Hanuman, the protector of Sita and Ram). She could not remember the name of the musical device, she told me, but she made the motion of someone pumping a billows with her hand. "A harmonium?" I suggested, to which she concurred (harmoniums are a common accompaniment for Hindu devotional singing in Trinidad and beyond).

The spirit spoke to her in "Indian language" but also whispered the English translation of its message in her ear. The man had to offer "a prayers" (i.e., *puja*) to "the monkey god," which the couple readily understood as the Hindu deity Hanuman, or else he would die. She told him that he was to abstain from alcohol until the prayers were completed. Five weeks later, Lennie told me that the couple returned and the man was still more gaunt. His body and breath exuded the odor of rum. No prayers for Hanuman had been kept, and Lennie told me that she again caught power in her yard. After she came back to herself, she told the couple that she had suddenly seen a lilac-colored coffin in front of her. As she backed away from the box sitting in her yard, she saw two women in white saris standing to either side of the open casket. She saw her client lying inside of it.

When the woman heard this she vowed to offer a prayers for Hanuman immediately and invited Lennie to come to the Hindu temple where it would be held. But at the prayers, Mother Lennie told the pundit in charge of the *puja* that she had seen the Hindu goddess Saraswati crying in a white sari inside the temple. At one point during the *puja*, she watched the sick man sitting in the temple stand up and walk outside into the bush surrounding the temple. After he disappeared into the bush, however, she realized that he was still sitting in the same spot in the temple. She told the pundit that the man's body was just a shell at the point, and his spirit had already left.

Mother Lennie told me that the man died the next day. It was only the sister who wanted to keep the prayers; the man himself couldn't be bothered. "When you promise God something," Lennie said to me, "you must deliver. God ain't no fool." She then paused and added, "Indians need to give up the Hindu thing and stick to worshipping God."[8] While Mother Lennie had visions of Hindu powers and treated Hindu clients, she sometimes employed this long-standing Christian or colonial critique of alleged "Hindu idol worship" to condemn her Indian clients' practices as not properly monotheistic. Rather than converting to Hinduism or mixing it with her own African-inspired Christianity, Lennie traversed the differences that constituted spiritual power through visions, spirit manifestation, and spiritual travel. As a crossover artist she sought to perform difference, but only to the extent necessary to make her own practices legible to a racially and religiously diverse audience (who were also consuming the power of her racial difference as an African obeah woman).

Bishop Dawes, Mother Lennie, and other African-identified spiritual workers in Rio Moro treated a religiously and ethnically diverse clientele, often embodying Hindu deities and prescribing Hindu rituals. Certainly, these workers treated clients who identified as practitioners of African religions. Their work, however, often demanded the ability to move between an African-identified lexicon of other-than-human power and those of their Hindu, Muslim, or mainstream Christian clients. The ability to make analogies across traditions was characteristic of grassroots African religion in Trinidad. As scholars have shown, West African Orishas often have sides that are Hindu deities or Christian saints in grassroots shrines (Mahabir and Maharaj 1989; McNeal 2011). While it is impossible to say definitively how this happened, the pragmatic experiments with difference that spiritual workers performed knit together diverse persons and practices to solve problems, creating a language of "crossover" between traditions.

Unlike a model of discrete and self-contained ethno-religious traditions, what got called obeah involved extensive religious border crossings. This little-recognized insight into the practice of subaltern spiritual work questions the stigmas of atavism and rural isolation that attach themselves to both obeah and my field site. Emphasizing the cosmopolitanism of obeah and Rio Moro contests the equation of African tradition with the insular and ethno-racially homogeneous village. Yet the border crossings of obeah do not necessarily yield the mixture of religious streams that Arlena encountered at the confluence of the Ganges and the Nile. Neither Bishop Dawes nor Mother Lennie understood themselves to be practicing a religion that was a syncretic mixture of Hinduism and other practices. They embodied Hindu deities or had visions of them without converting to Hinduism or claiming to make a single amalgam of Hinduism, Christianity, and African traditions. Indeed, Mother Lennie went so far as to criticize Hinduism, employing a well-worn colonial Christian invective against its alleged polytheism, even as she engaged extensively with its powers. In contrast, Bishop Dawes possessed a more extensive and respectful knowledge of Hindu material practices and considered himself "Indian in the spirit" by virtue of his mourning travels. Even for Dawes, though, the lines of separation between his various practices of devotion were what gave them their power. Hindu, Kabbalistic, or Orisha forces were good for different kinds of problems (see chapter 3), and metaphors of mixture served only to muddle or dilute the differences between traditions. Such narratives of mixture also missed the racial and religious tensions that might coexist with, or be the basis for, the subaltern cosmopolitanism of spiritual work.

Precisely because obeah was, in many ways, about the power that difference could produce, the aim of spiritual work was not the creole mixture and syncretic melding of the differences between traditions. Rather, obeah evinced a language of crossover that lay between the territories of pure traditions and the rapids of mixture that Arlena faced where the Ganges met the Nile. This tongue of crossover significantly revises common narratives of the national melting pot and the secular transcendence of difference. Before further delving into how (what gets called) obeah performs the work of crossover, it is worth detailing the ways that subaltern forms of cosmopolitanism in Rio Moro unsettle these narratives of nation and secularism in the Americas.

CREOLE NATIONALISM VERSUS MULTICULTURALISM

When Arlena stood on the tongue of crossover between the Ganges and the Nile, she recounted her powerful memories of both friendship across racial lines and racial tensions between Indians and Africans. Accounting for both of these seemingly contradictory experiences means elaborating a model of race relations that diverges from ideas of harmonious mixture, on the one hand, or rigidly opposed ethno-religious groupings, on the other. When Arlena recounted stories marked by both interracial tensions and cross-racial affinities, she was not alone among my interlocutors in Rio Moro. While Arlena's story focused on the antiblack racism of Indo-Trinidadians as an impediment to these affinities, my friend Tony remembered how the anti-Indian racism of his grandmother, Tantie Dunn, intervened in his boyhood friendships with Indians. An Afro-Trinidadian Rasta in his late thirties, Tony grew up in a predominantly Indo-Trinidadian section of my rural cosmopolitan field site in southern Trinidad. When the surrounding neighbors held "Hindu prayers," the devoutly Catholic Tantie Dunn forbade them to leave the house, scorning their religious rituals as "idol worship" (surely an ironic distinction, considering Reformation discourses on Catholicism). Tony and his brothers, however, cried and carried on until she reluctantly let them go. Tony begged to go not only because he preferred the Indian cuisine offered at the "Hindu prayers" to his own grandmother's cooking but also because his closest friends were Indo-Trinidadians. At every "prayers," the hosts asked after Tantie Dunn and sent the boys home with a plate of food

for her, but Tantie refused to eat what she derisively called "coolie food" —
"coolie" being a derogatory term for South Asians used commonly in British
colonial and postcolonial settings.[9] When Tony began working in the out-
door produce market in town as a teenager, she again used this racial epi-
thet for Indian laborers, telling him "that [is] coolie work" (agricultural
labor often being associated with Indians in Trinidadian racial imaginaries). "Tantie Dunn," Tony stated bluntly, "hate Indians."

These experiences of interethnic rivalry and racism are clearly legible in
analyses of southern Caribbean society. In Trinidad, as V. S. Naipaul (1962)
acerbically remarked on the eve of independence from Britain, the primary
rivalry was not between a white or whiteish minority and the nonwhite
laboring classes they exploited, but between Afro- and Indo-Trinidadians.
Since independence, political competition has been popularly expressed not
through reference to ideological differences but through this racial polarity of African and Indian. Thus, the People's National Movement, which
has ruled Trinidad for nearly four out of its five decades of independence,
is commonly understood as the "African party," while the hegemon of two
recent national governments, the United National Congress, is understood
to be the "Indian party."[10]

Ideas about religious difference have been absolutely central to these
narratives of ethno-political antagonism. Categories of religion and race
were not clearly separable under British colonialism, with the word "Hindu"
often functioning as a marker of all persons from South Asia and "Christian"
marking the way African-descended peoples could attain moral citizenship
(to a degree heavily dependent on class and color hierarchies).[11] An ethno-
political divide between African and Indian in Trinidad thus often morphs
into a confrontation between Christians and Hindus (Ryan 1999), despite
interreligious alliances or sizeable populations of Indian Christians (who
might still also be Hindus).[12] Indeed, African-identified religious groups
have formed coalitions with the Indian rather than the African party, precisely because of a shared opposition to the hegemony of Euro-Christian
norms in determining the limits of "spiritual citizenship" in the nation (see
Castor 2017). These interreligious solidarities between the Indian party and
Spiritual Baptist or Orisha organizations point toward the concerns of this
chapter. Despite such solidarities between Hinduism and African religions
in contemporary Trinidad, the popular narrative of ethno-political rivalry
remains that of Afro-Creole Christians versus Indo-Trinidadian Hindus
(see Ryan 1999).

As David Scott (1999, 56) has shown, Western notions of religion in

FIGURE 5.2. Former prime minister Kamala Persad-Bissessar at Spiritual Baptist Liberation Day Celebrations, 2011. Bissessar wore a pink head wrap to African religious celebrations, leading to speculation that she was a devotee of the Orisha Oshun (whose color was pink). Bissessar also identified as Hindu, Indian, and Baptist. Photograph by the author.

many ways obliged colonized peoples to define themselves as "one exclusive . . . community *against* others" to articulate claims for power and recognition within colonial and postcolonial civil society. An important critique of the effects of colonialism in Trinidad, therefore, has emphasized the ways that colonial power was exercised through concepts of antagonistic, separable ethno-religious groups. This critique asserts that the colonial and postcolonial state positioned the African and the Indian in separate niches of the economy, resulting in interracial labor competition or geographic segregation (see, e.g., Munasinghe 2001, 77; Prashad 2001, 85; Puri 1997, 120). Like the mechanisms of colonial governance they aim to critique, these accounts posit bounded and oppositional ethno-religious solidarities as the baseline subaltern condition, rendering illegible other forms of association. Central to this historical narrative is the assumption of urban-rural, oil-sugar, Christian-Hindu, or north-south divides, in which Indo-Trinidadians filled the barracks of sugar estates south of the Caroni River, after ex-slaves and indentured Africans had vacated the barracks in favor of urban, northern locales or more skilled occupations. "In popular wisdom," as Aisha Khan (2004a, 68) notes, the result remains "a mutually exclusive geography where an Afro-Trinidadian, urban 'north' is elevated in contrast to an Indo-Trinidadian, rural 'south.'" While there is ample evidence that Indo- and Afro-Trinidadians would have interacted even on the sugar estates (e.g., Abraham 2007), one authoritative history asserts that "Indians interacted with members of other races as little as possible" and supposedly saw blacks as polluted untouchables within South Asian caste hierarchies (Brereton 1979, 188–89). In short, relations between Indians and Africans, according to this standard history, were characterized by "mutual contempt" (Brereton 1979, 189).

Elsewhere, I have offered a more extensive critique of this narrative, drawing on oral histories from Rio Moro to show how the rural regions of preindependence southern Trinidad evidenced "rural cosmopolitanism" and "altered solidarities" across and through ethno-religious lines (Crosson 2014). In brief, the common story of Indian laborers "saving" the sugar plantation economy after emancipated Africans abandoned agricultural labor and fled to the cities might be a foundation for present-day racial stereotypes, but it is largely inaccurate. Rather, in the nineteenth and early twentieth centuries, both African-descended people (including the large numbers migrating from Venezuela and a host of other Caribbean islands) and Indians sought a qualified autonomy from the plantations by gravitating toward Trinidad's relatively large reserves of undeveloped land (cf. Munasinghe 2001, 77). Laborers from India, Venezuela, and Africa, and emancipated slaves from surrounding islands or the United States, all converged in Rio Moro, developing linguistic and religious lingua francas. Such rural cosmopolitanism, however, was not simply the cause for harmonious relations; subaltern Trinidadians leveraged the racial and religious categories of colonial Trinidad both to launch disparaging attacks and to make connections across racial, linguistic, and religious differences. Rather than simply "mixing" their cultures, these people were (and are) engaged in acts of both ethno-religious distancing and crossover.

Despite such rural cosmopolitan counterhistories, the narrative of the colonial segregation of Indians and Africans still forms the basis for popular ideas about the colonial past. Two alternate narratives, however, allegedly overcome this past of subaltern racial and religious tensions, and these were the commonplace models of mutually exclusive traditions and their mixture that Arlena encountered at the confluence of the Ganges and the Nile. This latter model of mixture asserts that Trinidad is a land of racial and cultural blending, with hopes for national unity and the overcoming of interethnic antagonisms pegged on the recognition, affirmation, and further practice of these forms of mixture.[13] Complementing these sanguine (yet fraught) discourses of mixture is the former model of mutually exclusive ethno-religious groups. While popular discourse asserts that Trinidad is a "callaloo nation" of mixture, an equally popular saying, drawn from the national anthem, asserts that Trinidad is a place "where every creed and race [can] find an equal place." This is not a paradigm of mixture but one of separate yet equal differences. As the national anthem implies, "creed" is most often conflated with "race" in this multicultural model, for it is through ethno-religious traditions that the compartmentalized units of difference can be identified, recognized, and cataloged by the state. Within a Trinidadian discourse of proper religiosity, it is clearly not appropriate to assert that Hindus, Muslims, Christians, and Orisha devotees will so thoroughly mix their practices as to erase their differences, creating a callaloo religion.[14] Thus, the affirmation of recognizable difference, if embodied in authorized ethno-religious practices, is appropriate in this idea of pluralist harmony.

This pluralist framework of separate ethno-religious traditions seemed, in some ways, comparable to Arlena's Spiritual Baptist cosmology of "Nations," where each ethno-religious formation is clearly demarcated by a flag, color, certain type of dress, and various religious or folkloric practices. Wearing a dhoti and becoming vegetarian marked one of her fellow Afro-Trinidadian Baptists as spiritually Indian, just as a brass "om" symbol or a yellow flag (yellow is India's color in the threefold path) were markers of the Nation of India in Spiritual Baptist churches. Yet the tongue of land between the Ganges and the Nile did not seem to fit this spiritual cosmology that (at least on the surface) mirrored the geopolitical idea of modern nation-states. "That place between the Ganges and the Nile," Arlena told me, "is not a Nation like Africa and India with language and flag." While adherents of the Nations of Africa and India could speak in the spiritual tongues of those lands and often wore the colors of those Nations' flags as their church uniforms (red for Africa, yellow for India), the land between the Ganges and the Nile did not have its own language, banner, or religion. While it was a common experience for mourners I interviewed to stand on this nameless tongue of land, it was not a place that conferred a recognizable position in church organizations or the religious geography of the Nations. It was a place, as her pointer Bishop Dawes noted, of "crossover spirits."

While this place of crossover did not fit into a geography of multicultural nationalism, neither did it yield the alternate image of harmonious puree or fluid mixture. As Arlena's vision haunted me, I began to wonder whether this tongue was something like what liberal political theory has called the secular—a neutral space that ideally stands apart from the divisiveness of particular identities. As Talal Asad (2003, 5) has suggested, the secular is, in many ways, the purported transcendence of these differences through the modality of citizenship in the modern nation-state (see also Seales 2013). Yet as Asad also argued, this transcendence is premised on the abstract equality of citizens—an equality that ignores the particular exclusions and differences that have made nationalism possible. In the United States, for example, the idea of a multicultural or melting-pot nation masks the white nationalism and "Judeo-Christian civilization" that continue to define the formal and informal rights of citizenship (see Berry 2017; Silk 1984). In Trinidad or Brazil, as in much of Latin America and the Caribbean, the fantasy—both sexual and political—of national racial mixture occludes (and reveals) continuing forms of exclusion and racism (e.g., Fraunhar 2002; Mohammed 2009; Puri 2004; Tanikella 2003).

Yet the tongue of land where Arlena paused lay apart from these problematic rapids of mixture and the attendant geography of mutually exclusive ethno-religious essences. Instead of a place that transcended divisive differences through mixture, enacting the fiction of the secular state and the melting-pot nation, I began to wonder whether this tongue of crossover was composed of those differences. Rather than crossing as an act of mixture, crossover signaled an act of relation that did not lead to a mixed identity. Within the field of ethno-religious identifications in Trinidad, obeah represented this space that was neither a recognized tradition nor a creole mixture of such traditions (cf. Khan 2013). As the previous chapter showed, obeah has often been the disavowed ground that defined the banks and boundaries of religion for many Afro- and Indo-Trinidadians. Rather than an empty strip of land that simply served to define streams of tradition, though, obeah has often represented a tongue of relation through difference. It is a language of occluded relationships and powers that reveals the underrecognized dynamics of subaltern cosmopolitanism. As the following anecdote illustrates, these relationships of spiritual work provided an alternative to secular transcendence, creole mixture, or state multiculturalism as a means for grappling with the politics of difference.

"MUSLIMS DOES GO INTO THE SCIENCE TOO"

Preacher was late for "school." As we zigzagged through a network of back-street shortcuts off the main road, he kept telling me that his work was about "timing." He was never late for his appointments at the cemetery, which he referred to as his "science school," but his clients had not been waiting for him at the side of the highway as instructed. Even though it was nearing midnight, he decided to double back to see if her driver's black Lancer was there. We finally found them, waiting on the wrong side of the road.

"What the ass is this?" Preacher asked the young dreadlocked driver when we pulled up next to them. Mala and Mother Vera, the two clients whom Preacher was going to treat, were sitting in the back seat of the car. "You real lucky, boy," Preacher told the driver. "School in session and you sticking so?"[15] Preacher sucked his teeth, making an audible sign of disapproval. "Well, let we go now."

Mala and Mother Vera had both come to Preacher during the preceding week for help with pressing problems. The police had been harassing Mother Vera, an elderly woman who was the head of a Spiritual Baptist church. Officers had searched her house multiple times, finally claiming that they had found marijuana there. Vera insisted that the police had planted the marijuana (though Preacher told me privately that he thought the marijuana might belong to her son). Because she was the owner of the house, Vera had been facing a protracted criminal trial for drug-trafficking charges. In addition, Vera had a mysterious swelling in her foot. When she showed up to her initial consultation with Preacher, I had to help her up the stairs, and her foot was wrapped in thick bandages. Foot injuries were commonly attributed to obeah, the product of stepping on a spot of ground where a harming spiritual work had been buried. Vera felt that her neighbor, also a Spiritual Baptist, was working obeah against her to usurp her authority in the church. Preacher had told her to meet him at the end of the week so that he could take her to his "operating table," a grave mound in an Indian-dominated part of central Trinidad about an hour's drive from Rio Moro.

The cemetery was in the broad expanse of flat land that had been the island's sugarcane belt before the definitive closure of the industry in 2007. Preacher had chosen this cemetery as his science school for at least two reasons. First, there was a hotel frequented by the nearby town's prostitutes in front of the graveyard's gates, and late-night traffic thus aroused no suspicion from the neighbors. Second, the cemetery was what he called a Hindu graveyard,[16] and Preacher was an Afro-Trinidadian threefold practitioner who often worked on the Indian side. Preacher called the dead man he worked with "Sahib," and told me that Sahib had been a Hindu sadhu in life.[17] Tonight he would beat the packed earth of Sahib's grave with the palm of his hand and ask him to help Mala and Mother Vera with their problems.

As we pulled up to the gates of the cemetery, Preacher was still complaining about the driver of the other car making us late. School started at midnight, and being late for school was an offense to the spiritual keepers of the graveyard. The dreadlocked driver of the first car jumped out to open the metal gates of the cemetery, which were emblazoned with "om" symbols, wrought in the South Asian Devanagari script. We all reached our arms out of the windows of our cars as we passed underneath the cemetery's arch, dropping our "shillings" (twenty-five-cent pieces) at the gate to pay the two keepers of the cemetery—the Kabbalistic entity Mr. Bones (associated with Ezekiel on the Spiritual Baptist side) and Oya (the Orisha of cemeteries whom Preacher also associated with the Hindu goddess Kali). Preacher hailed a homeless Indian man with matted locks who lived in the cemetery and was familiar with his works there. "Eh, Ras," he said as we drove past.

When we stopped, I took Mother Vera's arm to help her out of the first car, as she hobbled on her one bandaged and swollen foot. She leaned into me as we walked in the dark over grass swollen with the mounds of graves, making the ground uneven and hard to navigate. Preacher led us to the last row of graves, to an earthen mound, about the length of a human, with a small tree planted where the corpse's head would be. This was the grave of Sahib. Beyond his grave, the cane fields began, and their flat dark expanse stretched all the way to the glittering lights of urban North Trinidad, with the dark bulk of the Northern Range behind them.

Preacher began to draw a circle on the grave mound with handfuls of sweet-smelling corn flour. He divided the circle into fourths with two lines of flour and placed a dot inside of each quadrant, after which he added other esoteric designs. Finally, he tossed handfuls of grains in the four directions. Preacher then took a half bottle of puncheon (160-proof rum) and poured a liberal amount into the circle as he started to beat the grave mound vigorously with his bare palm. "A pleasant good morning to you," he said, awakening the spirit of Sahib with a greeting that inverted human senses of time.

Preacher beckoned to Mala and had her sit down inside the white circle drawn on top of his "operating table." Mala had come to Preacher earlier in the week complaining of abdominal pains and acute domestic strife. Mala was a Hindu, but her husband was a devout Muslim, a not unusual occurrence in Trinidad. Mala, however, began to visit Preacher, an African-identified spiritual worker, after her husband began violently quarreling with her. Preacher told me that her husband's genitalia had been infected with a spiritually harmful substance he acquired through intercourse with an "outside woman." He then infected Mala's womb, which began to "rotten."

On a previous visit, Preacher had advised her to set an egg in their bedroom, standing it on its end in an open location for twenty-one days, as eggs are spirit magnets that absorb any harmful influences lurking around their bed. The egg was then to be smashed on a tombstone after the allotted period of time, thus returning the harmful powers to their sender. Mala, however, said her husband would never allow such a thing. It would be a sign of the "simi-dimi," "obeah," or "superstition" that he found inimical to his Muslim faith.[18] He had already harangued her for visiting an "obeah man," saying she was mocking his religious devotion. "I don't pray five times a day for nothing," he told her. According to the husband, then, prayer and religious devotion were the proper paths to achieving desired effects in life, and obeah was not. Mala continued to consult Preacher, but she consciously concealed the signs of "obeah" from her husband. She bathed to wash off the smell of the red lavender Preacher used to give her "bush baths" and hid the spiritual oils that Preacher told her to rub on her body to bring domestic harmony.

Yet on a different occasion, after another quarrel, Mala's husband told her, "You know, it have Muslim oils we could use." He was suggesting that in place of the spiritual oils Preacher prescribed to bring domestic tranquility, they might try the oils his imam purveyed. Despite his disavowal of obeah and its patently material means of accessing supernatural force, it was not simply the physical discipline of prayer that held power for her husband.

FIGURE 5.3. Spiritual oils. A conventional pharmacy in urban Trinidad stocks spiritual oils next to smelling salts. Photograph by Olivia Fern, 2012.

"Muslims does go into the science too," Preacher had remarked to me with a half grin on his face, upon recounting this story.

As Mala and Mother Vera underwent healing in Preacher's science school, a number of religious traditions evidenced his "science"—material practices that solved problems with spiritual powers. Like many spiritual workers, Preacher called his own work science, drawing on a long-standing lexical equivalence of "obeah" and "science" in the anglophone Caribbean. The next chapter details the impact of this equivalence on understandings of science itself. For the purposes of the present argument, however, it is worth pausing to consider the impact of Preacher's cemetery science on understandings of religion, racial difference, and secularism.

In the above anecdote, Preacher's subaltern cosmopolitanism allowed him to tack between Muslim, Hindu, Yoruba, Kabbalistic, and Christian traditions for his multiracial clientele. As with North Atlantic cosmopolitanism, this ability to move across difference was epitomized for Preacher by the word "science." "Science," in modern discourses, has been widely celebrated (and critiqued) for its alleged ability to transcend cultural difference through repeatable experiments that demonstrate "facts" about a universal nature. Like the secular, science is supposed to provide a value-neutral realm that can offer this cosmopolitan transcendence. Yet as numerous scholars have noted, this notion of science is a fiction that has abetted the gendered and racialized hierarchies of the West (e.g., Haraway 1991; Harding 2008, 2015; see also chapter 6). Numerous critiques have thus sought to provincialize "modern science" as a product of the West, subject to political, social, and cultural contexts of power.

The science of Preacher and other spiritual workers yielded a different kind of cosmopolitanism. Rather than transcending difference, Preacher performed his spiritual work with the powers that religious difference could yield. He firmly identified himself as a practitioner of African religions, with a strong background in Kabbalistic, Spiritual Baptist, and Orisha practices. This was how the clients that I knew saw him: as a black practitioner of African-identified obeah. Yet Preacher's "real partner" in his spiritual work was a Hindu holy man (Sahib), and his clients had a variety of different religious backgrounds. The place where he performed most of his spiritual work with these clients, his cemetery science school, was a meeting ground for powers that had Hindu, Orisha, Kabbalistic, and Spiritual Baptist sides. For Preacher, "science" was not isomorphic with one of the mutually exclusive traditions of the paradigm of world religions, and he avowed that there could be "Muslim science," "Hindu science," and "Yoruba science." Science allowed him to cross over between traditions without converting or mixing. Preacher did not claim to be a Hindu because he worked with Sahib and treated many Hindu clients, sometimes drawing on the ritual repertoires of Trinidadian Hinduism to solve their problems (he had performed hog *pujas* for the Hindu deity Parmeshwarie as part of his spiritual work, for example).

Rather than provincializing science as a product of the West, Preacher talked about science in a way that provincialized a Western framework of religion, which had insisted that religious traditions (with the frequent exception of Euro-American Christianities) were culturally circumscribed and mutually exclusive systems. To practice more than one of these systems at a time, in this framework, was evidence of a syncretic or mixed religion. Afro-Caribbean religions have most often been understood as "syncretic" or "creole" religions because they seem to combine multiple traditions. Yet all recognized world religions are syncretic in the terms of this definition. Various forms of Christianity, for example, today bear the indelible imprints of Judaism or European Paganism. Euro-American Christianity, however, is not often called syncretic, precisely because such a label would make it into a mixture of various religions rather than the representative of a world religion in its own right. Attributions of syncretism involve questions of power, and it is no coincidence that African-identified religions bear the disproportionate burden of the label "syncretic." Yet inverting this framework, it perhaps makes more sense to think about Christianity as a syncretic religion—it combines various traditions but represents itself as a singular whole—and grassroots African practices in Trinidad as world religion, because they open to the heterogeneity of the world without reducing its complexity to a single tradition.

Preacher's science or obeah, however, offers another alternative besides syncretism or world religion for thinking about what happens when religious traditions meet. Instead of irrevocably crossing religious traditions together to produce a hybrid religion, Preacher was a kind of crossover artist who experimented with difference to solve specific problems. This subaltern cosmopolitanism was not simply based on commonalities between traditions—like the fact that spiritual workers and imams might use the same oils. Because obeah intimated harm as well as protection, subaltern fluency in multiple religious idioms was as much about deciphering commonalities as sources of spiritual attack. Because religious and racial difference were sources of spiritual power, they had the potential to both heal and harm, to connect and repel, yielding neither harmonious mixture nor mutually exclusive differences.

SPIRITUAL WORK, INTIMATE HARM,
AND SUBALTERN MOBILITY

As this ethnographic slice of Preacher's work shows, spiritual workers often treated people who did not share their own everyday or "carnal" ethno-religious identifications. Initially this puzzled me and provoked certain theoretical questions, but I was not the only one who wanted to theorize about this phenomenon. Philip, an Afro-Trinidadian labor union organizer from Rio Moro, had been conducting his own observations and drawing some conclusions. "From my observation, when I look around to see the experience of my neighbor there," Philip stated, pointing toward the house of a spiritual worker I also knew, "90 percent of the people you see [going by her] is Indian people. When I check the experience of Treadwell in Moreau or Mother Clara in Petit Riviere," Philip said, invoking the names of other well-known Afro-Trinidadian "Baptist" spiritual workers in his area, "it is the same thing. You know [Hindu] pundits is very good in this thing. Pundits are very good spiritual workers too. But you find that East Indians comes to Africans because they don't want to expose their business to their own kind. They prefer to expose it to the African." From these observations, Philip concluded that this was "a cultural thing" that "we don't ever look at . . . when we talk race in this country."

Certainly, Philip's assertion that 90 percent of the clients of African-identified spiritual workers were Hindus might be overstating the case to prove a point. In my experience, however, Philip's words expressed an important and unexpected dimension of spiritual work. The Trinbagonian anthropologist J. D. Elder is one of the few scholars to remark on this tendency.[19] In an unpublished 1970 lecture, he noted, "Persons needing supernatural assistance travel out of their own locality, village, or island to engage the services of look-men [spiritual workers]. . . . The Tobago seeker travels down to Moruga Road [in southern Trinidad], while the Trinidadian goes over to Les Coteaux [in Tobago] or even to the Warau [i.e., Warao indigenous nation] or the Bucks [Amerindians] of Guyana." While Obeah, in popular representations, has typically connoted rural isolation—a more accurate history of the spiritual work of healing and justice-making reveals constant, semiclandestine movements. Scholars have largely focused on longer-distance mobilities, particularly intra-Caribbean and circum-Atlantic labor migrations of Caribbean peoples (e.g., Matory 2005; Putnam

2013). But smaller-scale mobilities have been understudied, especially those that did not necessarily lead to lasting residency and were conducted with some degree of secrecy. Owing both to obeah's illegality and its association with acute interpersonal conflicts, clients often traveled outside their own communities to keep their spiritual work and their problems a secret from their social familiars.

The potential of obeah to represent both healing and forms of intimate harm helped to explain why spiritual workers and clients so often hailed from different ethnic groups or geographical regions. While clients' afflictions could often be attributed to problems with institutional powers— particularly the justice system, the police, and workplace supervisors— spiritual workers also diagnosed cases of social suffering as the result of the envy or ill intentions stemming from those closest to the client. Thus, during my fieldwork, spiritual workers often located the source of a client's affliction in the envy, or "bad mind," of neighbors, family members, or lovers. This envy occasioned both semiconscious forms of harm (*maljo*, or "evil eye") and intentional acts of injury (a neighbor's alleged contracting of a spiritual worker to perform obeah against the client). These were the intimate forms of harm that often, but not always, motivated clients to travel outside of their mundane social circles for spiritual assistance. Because the problems of Mala and Mother Vera emanated from their own neighbors, coreligionists, or domestic partners, it made sense for them to look for help outside their immediate social circles.

Because these relations of spiritual work were based on shame surrounding personal problems, suspicion regarding the motives of those close to oneself, or the social stigmas attached to seeking out "obeah," they did not always reflect the kinds of intimacy and trust that have formed the basis of models of relationality in social science (see also Geschiere 2013). Obeah, therefore, not only provides a different way of thinking through law and justice in the Caribbean but also presents a counternarrative of race relations between the groups of enslaved and indentured laborers who came to the region from West and Central Africa and from South Asia. These relations of crossover neither negated the Africanness of (those who were called) obeah men and women nor necessarily led to a "creole" mixture of religions. Practicing Hindus who were healed on the Spiritual Baptist or Orisha sides would most often (though not always) continue to identify primarily as Hindus.[20] To assert a process of syncretic or creole mixture would imply the muting of the very differences that help to make relations of confidentiality possible between many healers and clients. Difference was also a key

FIGURE 5.4. "Envy/Welcome." Tobago. Photograph by the author, 2011.

way of generating and intensifying spiritual power. Obeah thus suggests a generative space between the models of mixture and mutually exclusive tradition that have tacitly determined the authorizing limits of religion in the Caribbean.

Rather than fit the confessional mold of mutually exclusive religious communities, the relations of power that comprise imputed acts of obeah challenge the limits of this mold. In colonial situations North Atlantic secularism implied two contradictory imperatives: the transcendence of difference and the parsing of populations into opposed ethno-religious constituencies. While the former transcendence was implicitly reserved for white men, the latter imperative marked subaltern peoples as overdetermined by difference. To overcome the alleged problem of conflictual difference, postcolonial nation-making projects in the Americas have posited national melting pots that produce one people out of many (although more recent multicultural projects have critiqued the limits of this unifying mixture) (Brereton 2010). The dynamics of spiritual work, however, ask us to think beyond the dialectic of mixture and purity that this contradiction of liberal secularism has provoked in postcolonial settings, offering a nontranscendent framework for the negotiation of difference.

CONCLUSION

Although the persistent association of obeah with potential harm has proved a stumbling block in scholarly approaches and attempts to achieve legal recognition for obeah (as discussed in chapter 1), obeah's apparent lack of an identifiable constituency has been an equally powerful impediment. Even though other formerly prohibited and stigmatized African diasporic religious practices in Trinidad, such as the Orisha and Spiritual Baptist faiths, now have a national holiday, state-funded schools, or grants of government land for their religious associations, obeah has received no equivalent state recognition. In part, this is because there seems to be no identifiable organization to recognize and no apparent community of avowed believers who politicians can woo and mobilize as a potential constituency. There are also no identifiable churches or temples of obeah in Trinidad and no religious organizations that identify themselves with the term. Even the few people who publicly identify as obeah practitioners have used terms other than religion (e.g., "art," "science," "work," "way of being," "philosophy") to describe it (Best 2019; Clarke 2001; Sankeralli 2010).

As Paton (2009) has argued, the difficulty of writing obeah into the category of religion, and thus writing it into legality and state recognition, has much to do with the creation of obeah as a category of criminality that isolated certain aspects of Caribbean religious practices that did not fit into a

Western model of religion. A central tenet of this model was the assumption that religions were mutually exclusive confessional communities of identifiable believers who congregated in public places of worship and collectively assented to certain propositions of belief. In contrast, magic was an individualistic pursuit opposed to the collective morality of religion. Following in the tradition of Durkheim ([1912] 1964), religion has often epitomized the solidarity that shared bonds occasion, forming the basis for models of social life. This bias in the constitution of religion was also a means by which religions could be regulated and governed through state recognition under modern secular regimes. If state power could not isolate a community and locate its institutional manifestations, then the legal rights and state recognition that the category of religion conferred did not apply. In this way, the Western dichotomy of magic and religion, in which, as various anthropologists and scholars of religion affirmed, magic is an individual pursuit and religion a group one, formed the basis for the stigmatization and prohibition of practices that did not align with this model of religious community.[21]

Rather than simply reflect these colonial stigmas, obeah's lack of a confessional community points toward an alternate logic of personhood, relationality, religious practice, and difference. Precisely because the practice of (what gets called) obeah does not conform to a model of mutually exclusive groups, it affords a different kind of negotiation of difference than secularism. While liberal secularism aims for the transcendence of religious difference, what gets called obeah often forms relations of crossover through these very differences. The art of crossover does not negate my interlocutors' "authenticity" as competent practitioners of African-identified religious practices. A crossover artist is defined by the ability to be rooted in a particular genre of performance while also bringing this competency to bear on other genres in a convincing way.

Far from dismissing questions of racial or religious authenticity for subaltern persons, grassroots spiritual work continues to provoke accusations of charlatanry and fraud. That obeah remains illegal in much of the anglophone Caribbean testifies to the real effects that colonial categories continue to exert in authorizing practices that look like Western ideas of religion and delegitimizing those that are characterized as magic. This opposition depends on modern dichotomies between community and individual and between devotion and instrumentality, but it ultimately depends on asymmetries of power in defining what counts as religion and state-recognized cultural tradition. While we must pay attention to the effects of these colonial purifications of religion and magic, it would be an oversimplification to read subaltern subjects as simply determined by these discourses. Rather than being passive victims of colonial prohibition and the demonization of Afro-diasporic religious practices, subaltern peoples in Trinidad have worked the hegemonic polarities of these stigmas to produce counterdiscourses on power, mobility, justice, and relationality.

As we saw in chapter 2, one of the words that instantiates this subaltern creativity is "science." A long-standing synonym for obeah in the anglophone Caribbean, "science" (rather than the confessional community of religion) represents the language of "crossover" and experimentation that practices called obeah involve. In Western modernity, science has often been assumed to be a bridge over difference, but this notion has often depended on the transcendent universalism of science—a universalism linked to Western secularism's assumed transcendence of race, gender, sexuality, and religion. Yet just as obeah questions the indifference of the secular, spiritual workers' theories of experimentation question these transcendent ideals of science. As the next chapter shows, science in Rio Moro is about the ambivalence of power rather than the transcendent neutrality that scientific practice commonly epitomizes.

3

THE HEIGHTS

FIGURE 6.1. Spiritual work with Arlena's casket in the crossroads. Photograph by Olivia Fern, 2011.

INTERLUDE 6
Arlena's Haunting

Arlena's half-sister Aiesha pointed beyond her porch into the darkness that had descended around us, indicating a square of light that glossed the cellophane packages of snacks hung behind a shop's black chicken-wire grid. It had been almost a month since Arlena and her friends were murdered by police officers at Number Twenty-One Junction, but Aiesha's daughter Maria kept dreaming that her deceased aunt was standing in front of that shop, smoking a cigarette. In her dreams, Arlena's backlit silhouette beckoned to Maria, saying, "Come now." Her aunt's words were not an innocuous invitation; Arlena wanted Maria to join her in the world of the spirit, but that meant that Maria would have to die.

Shortly thereafter, a turn of events would threaten Maria's life right in front of the shop, and Aiesha herself would be the unwitting instrument of that harm. "[Maria] keep on dreaming her," Aiesha told me as she pointed toward the shop, "dreaming her by the parlor [store] right there. And Arlena telling her, 'Come now,' but [Maria] say, 'No, leave me alone.' In that very said spot I reverse my father's car and bounce [hit] my daughter—pinning her there on the wall." Her daughter was pregnant at the time, and Aiesha rushed her to the nearest hospital, one hour away by car. Maria spent four days there until her damaged ligaments had healed enough for her to walk again. Aiesha worried about the child in Maria's belly and felt that Arlena's spirit had willed the collision. The accident, she reminded me, had happened in the same spot where her half-sister stood smoking in the dreams. Aiesha went to see Mother Yanique, a spiritual worker, to find out what their beloved and dead relative wanted from her daughter.

Mother Yanique assured Aiesha that the spirit of Arlena was "looking for a next soul to help fight stronger now, to help find [the killers] now," and that she would not rest until her murderers were brought to justice. Her appearance in Maria's dreams was not simply a troublesome haunting; it called on those who were close to her to refuse to bury the memory of her violent and unjust death. But Arlena's spirit was also calling Maria over to the other side of life, to join her as a spirit fighting for justice.

The haunting of spirits that died unjust deaths was a double-edged sword in Rio Moro, the result of what many residents called the "science" or "obeah" performed by spiritual workers with the dead. Just as surely as the vengeance of those killed was a justice-making force for the families of the slain, the continued presence of these spirits was potentially dangerous to those whom they loved. After Maria was afflicted by the spirit of her aunt, Aiesha felt intensely ambivalent about the "science" that Bishop Dawes and others had performed to incite the spirit of her half-sister to search for justice. "I say whatever they did in the cemetery, [Arlena] not resting so please undo it," Aiesha told me. "It affecting my family. And let the law handle it now."

While residents of Rio Moro often appealed to the sovereign power of God or the law as alternatives to the "science" of spiritual workers, these powers were no less fraught than "obeah" (as the first three chapters of this book argue in a variety of ways). The enforcers of state law, after all, had just killed Aiesha's sister and her friends without any provocation, and she remained doubtful as to whether the "law" would provide justice. "Nothing wasn't happening until we decided to protest," she told me. "We needed to talk to somebody—*somebody*—because nobody wasn't coming. So the oniliest way we would get that to happen was by protesting, blocking the roads where everybody's going to feel it and something, hopefully, will come out of it now." Over a month after her sister was gunned down, in the midst of the state of emergency, she still did "not know what would come out of it" (and eight years later the jury trial against the officers has yet to begin). While she had chanted about the power of obeah to bring justice during the protests, she wondered whether the justice-seeking violence of obeah would harm her own daughter. Yet the faith in the law that she proposed as an alternative remained just as tenuous and conflicted as her own attitudes toward spiritual work with the unjustly dead.

In the end, the shortcomings of the law would play a tragic role in Aiesha's own life. As we talked on the porch that night about Arlena's haunting, I could not have known that Aiesha herself would soon cross over into the spirit. Shortly after our meeting, Aiesha would move away from Rio Moro. When I called her a few months later, she told me she had left Rio Moro to get away from an abusive relationship. Aiesha would die an incredibly tragic death two years later, as the jealous boyfriend from Rio Moro literally hacked her into pieces with a cutlass (machete). In the end, despite repeated trips to the police, the law that Aiesha had appealed to as a justice-making force in Arlena's death would not protect her from the domestic violence that would end her life. As the murderer remained at large and the memory of Aiesha's untimely death haunted her friends, some loved ones again called for a "science" of spiritual work that could handle what the law failed to address.

Hauntings, science, and domestic abuse would again converge in Rio Moro during my field research, in a series of spiritual afflictions dubbed "mass hysteria," which closed down the local secondary school on a number of occasions. Just as Arlena's haunting had been both a justice-making and a harming force, so too the hauntings at Rio Moro's secondary school intimated a reckoning with past crimes that caused afflictions in the present. For many, it was science that could dispel these school hauntings, ushering in a rational modernity freed of the spiritual afflictions of the past. For others, however, science was the cause of these possessions, and this science echoed the concerns with justice that Aiesha's and Arlena's deaths left in their wake. Did obeah represent the violence of the past that science could rationalize and overcome, or was "science" a synonym for obeah's reckoning with the opaque and intransigent powers of the present?

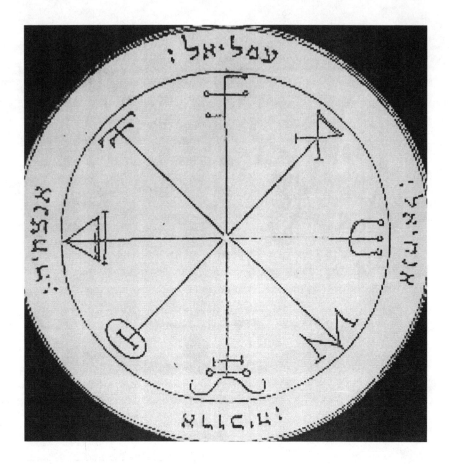

FIGURE 6.2. A printout of a "seal" from the Renaissance grimoire (spell book) *Clavicula Salomonis* (republished by L. W. de Laurence in 1914 as *The Greater Key of Solomon*). The book describes the necessary drawings to perform what the text describes as "experiments." A spiritual worker downloaded this experimental design, known as the Third Pentacle of Saturn, from the website CarolinaConjure.com at an internet café in the closest city to Rio Moro. Photograph by the author, 2012.

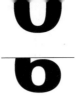

HIGH SCIENCE

THE AFFLICTIONS OF SCIENCE

Before I had the 1980 Ford Cortina, traveling from Trinidad's sprawling urban north, which contained the island's sole commercial airport, to Papoy and Vita's house in Rio Moro was a four-hour journey that involved five different "route taxis." These taxis are the major form of public transportation in Trinidad; they are private cars that follow more or less fixed (yet often-unmarked) routes, packing five to six people inside of a sedan. When I returned in 2010 for long-term field research, I was wedged into the middle of the back seat of the fourth taxi—the one that would take me into Rio Moro proper—when the national call-in show on the driver's radio turned its attention to this region in southern Trinidad and the forces that had gripped its secondary school. Starting in 2010 and continuing for two consecutive years in the weeks preceding All Souls' Day, Rio Moro Secondary had to be closed down due to disturbances enacted by between ten and thirty female pupils. These students yelled obscenities, spoke in men's voices, broke the straps of ambulance stretchers, and resisted police officers with a force that seemed to exceed their thirteen- and fourteen-year-old frames. Similar disturbances had, in fact, happened at other schools in the nation, but the secondary school's location in Rio Moro, a rural area popularly marked as the national epicenter of obeah, ensured that the incidents became a media spectacle, pitting discourses of both scientific rationality and born-again Christianity against the spectral forces that supposedly existed at the limits of the island's petroleum-fueled modernity. Several full-page articles had appeared in the various national newspapers detailing the episodes of "demonic possession" at the school and linking them to Rio Moro's reputation as Trinidad's capital of "obeah," a word that the articles equated to "witchcraft."

As we drove down the tenuous asphalt of Rio Moro's main road, slowing intermittently for deep potholes and unrepaired landslides cordoned off by bamboo poles, the radio debate centered on the question of whether obeah signaled the backwardness of Rio Moro, a sign of the area's failure to join in a forward-looking narrative of national development, or whether obeah was actually a sign of the moral predicaments of the present. Many callers espoused the former opinion, and Rio Moro's alleged obeah provoked a kind of postcolonial shame at the apparent inability of the island to be properly modern (see also chapter 1). One caller, for example, expressed outrage that such "unscientific belief in spirits still exist in the twenty-first century." As an emblem of both relative underdevelopment and African obeah in the national imagination, these callers associated Rio Moro with a lack of scientific aptitude and rationality, leading one exasperated caller to ask, "Why these sort of things don't happen in developed countries?" While episodes dubbed "mass hysteria" or "demonic possession" have been integral features of twenty-first-century school disturbances and neo-Pentecostal movements in the "developed" United States (McCloud 2015), the respondents assumed that such "beliefs" were products of Rio Moro's African-associated atavism, backwardness, or "underdevelopment."

The comments seemed to perform a familiar conflation of science and modernization, as projects of increasing transparency, development, and rationality. This notion of modernity has its foundations in the project of the Enlightenment, which self-consciously defined itself as a beam of reason that illuminated and dispelled the occult forces of superstition.[1] However, other callers invoked a very different vision of modernity—one that was equally palpable in Rio Moro, the Caribbean, and much of the contemporary world. As we made our way down the main road in the route taxi, callers insisted on the existence of negative spiritual forces, resenting the unscientific backwardness that this belief apparently implied. According to one caller, those who sought to discredit the reports of spirit possession had been "seduced into believing that we must abandon spiritual beliefs to aspire to first world status." "Demons are real!" another caller exclaimed, asserting that the island's dramatic increase in murders and violent crimes over the past decade was evidence of a contemporary "demon infestation"—a peculiarly twenty-first-century malaise in which Trinidad was "not nice again" because of citizen insecurity.[2]

In the following week, similar debates broke out in the responses to the national newspapers' coverage of the school's events. On one side was a teleology of progress—a materialist, rational, and scientific modernity, whose advance was hampered by backward beliefs in spirits. For these readers, science was a modern antidote to the superstitious credulity of Rio Moro's obeah. On the other side, however, were those who identified modernity not with the triumph of scientific explanation or development but with increasingly threatening and occult forces. For these born-again Christians, modernity represented an arc of decline, with the current moment defined as an end-time battle with demons and crime (see McAlister 2014; O'Neill 2015). The demons were the cause of contemporary Trinidad's rising murder rates, and they were ultimately driven by allegedly demonic practices like obeah. Against the story of these twenty-first-century ills (a narrative of increasing violence and spiritual warfare that characterized not simply Trinidad but also much of Latin American and the Caribbean), the born-again proponents of religious reforms targeted the same problem that advocates of science decried: obeah. While seemingly opposed in popular discourse, Christian religion and modern science in these responses were actually both antisuperstition machines, united by the obeah they fought. In practice, the project of modernity was defined by neither science nor progress but by the third term of African-identified "black magic" that both science and religion sought to reform at Rio Moro's secondary school.

While Rio Moro's demons provoked a familiar opposition between "black magic" and science or religion, residents of Rio Moro often had a different story to tell about the events at the school. On the one hand, my interlocutors were painfully aware of the stigmas of superstition that they bore in this debate about the limits of rationality and moral community in Trinidad, stigmas that had justified Rio Moro's exclusion from national programs of development and narratives of economic progress. On the other hand, they often had a story to tell that did not sit easily on the side of either African superstition or modern rationality and Christian moral reform. It was a story encapsulated by the word "science."

"Science," according to the *Dictionary of the English/Creole of Trinidad and Tobago*, is the appeal to occult forces to achieve effects, ranging from attempts to influence the ambivalent forces of the criminal justice system to efforts at resolving an intransigent affliction that biomedical doctors are unable to cure (Winer 2009). "Obeah" bears almost the same definition in the dictionary, and "science" and "obeah," as previous chapters have explored, are long-standing synonyms across the anglophone Caribbean. Thus, when I asked Ashok, the father of one of the afflicted pupils at Rio Moro Secondary, what had caused the disturbances at the school, he told me matter-of-factly, "Science." My own image of science was far removed from spiritual harm, and I asked him how science could possibly cause the afflictions at

Rio Moro Secondary. Surely, at this early point in my fieldwork, I thought modern science would be the least likely motive behind the very forces that so many had tasked scientific reason with dispelling. "It have both good and bad science," he said by way of explanation. Science could perform beneficial works and harm, Ashok avowed, and science was not simply a triumphant force of explanation and rationality but also a source of esoteric and potentially dangerous knowledge. Instead of dispelling the occult forces of superstition, science actually represented the ambivalence of these occult powers.

Like the spiritual workers I knew in Rio Moro, Ashok asserted that science could index morally ambivalent, opaque, and potentially dangerous powers—a characterization that unsettled my own preconceptions of a science constituted by the divide between matter and spirit, nature and supernature, facts and fetishes, or the benign pursuit of knowledge and malevolent intentions. As I talked about science with my interlocutors over the course of the next five years, my "epistemic disconcertment" (Verran 2001) at the equation of obeah and science led me to ask what the events at Rio Moro Secondary could say about the omnipresent adversaries of secular modernity—science and religion—that structured projects of reform at the school. My contention is that this story of secular modernity is missing a third term—variously described as "black magic," "voodoo," "obeah," "superstition," or "witchcraft." While opposed in the popular reactions to the events at the secondary school (and in countless contemporary discourses), science and religion attained coherence only by uniting against a common enemy of racialized and gendered false belief. At Rio Moro Secondary that enemy was obeah, as well as a host of others—"voodoo," "wizardry," and "witchcraft"—that religious and scientific reformers could indiscriminately equate with Rio Moro's African-identified atavism.

As such, science and religion were eminently modern projects, reflecting a continuous antisuperstition current that has run through the history of Western modernity, from the Reformation and the Enlightenment to twenty-first-century Pentecostal-charismatic spiritual warfare or new atheist defenses of science (see, e.g., Gross and Levitt 1994; Kaden and Schmidt-Lux 2016; McCloud 2015). These definitive antisuperstition currents show how modernity, as Nils Bubandt (2014, 14–15) has argued, is a "heuristic cover term" for visions of a definitive break from the past that promises to render occult forces transparent to the gaze of reform. Whether such a break is to happen through the facts of science, the rule of law, or the spiritual warfare of Pentecostal and charismatic Christianity, these projects promise to dispel different kinds of hidden powers—superstition, corruption, drug trafficking, or demons. As Bubandt shows, this promise of the modern, which should have already been fulfilled, is constantly being foiled by opaque and ambivalent powers. In Bubandt's study, such forces come under the heading of a term he translates as "witchcraft." His account replays a common story of modernization, in which witchcraft represents the persistence of occult forces that science, religion, and development come to (hopefully) dispel.

My interlocutors, however, asserted that science itself pointed toward the occult and hidden nature of power in the world rather than the transparent elucidation of facts. Many studies have questioned the biases of Western modernity by revaluing non-Western "magic" as rationality (Evans-Pritchard 1937), technology (Malinowski [1925] 1954), or natural science (Harding 2015; Wiredu 1979). These liberal projects of inclusion have bestowed the labels "rational" and "scientific" onto the activities of "non-Western traditions," provided that the activities involved "objective investigation" of "what the West would refer to as the natural world" (Wiredu 1979, 137; Harding 2015, 90). These liberal projects of inclusion have attempted to recognize certain aspects of non-Western practices as "science," but none of them has fully questioned the very notion of scientific rationality (and "nature") on which these projects ultimately rest. Was science really about natural facts and rational explanations that dispelled occult forces, or did science signal a practice of experimenting with occult powers? By making a "recursive" movement (Holbraad 2012) from science to obeah and back again in this chapter, my interlocutors' conceptions of science transform what this term (and modernity itself) can mean. Such a transformation fundamentally alters the terms by which "indigenous" or "traditional" knowledge has been included in or excluded from the categories of science and religion.

Before elaborating a notion of science as a practice of experimenting with what the architects of (what is now known as) the Scientific Revolution called "occult qualities"—immanent forces that are hidden or hard to perceive—I give a brief genealogy of magic and science in the modern era and describe the projects of religious or scientific reform at Rio Moro Secondary.[3] These projects attempted to dispel what spiritual workers saw as the inescapably opaque and ambivalent nature of power. While working to project the ambivalence of power onto an atavistic African past, these projects of reform at Rio Moro Secondary were caught up in peculiarly contemporary forces of gender violence, the internet, and transnational trafficking. Was the inability of the present to fulfill the promises of modernity an

occasion for redoubled efforts at reform, or did the deferral of such promises necessitate a science of working with occult power? The answer to this
question hinged on the contested relationship between science and obeah.

A BRIEF GENEALOGY OF SCIENCE
AND/AS MAGIC

The story that this chapter tells—of science and modernity as occult,
experimental projects—is contradicted by a pervasive and powerful story
about modernity and tradition. In this story, modernity breaks with and
dispels the superstitious belief in occult forces that non-Western traditions allegedly embrace. Within modern racial frameworks, it was African-
identified traditions that bore the heaviest burden in this reformatory narrative. In nineteenth-century evolutionary hierarchies, scholars would place
African "fetishism" at the very bottom of developmental frameworks, with
another newly coined term, "scientist," superseding Christian monotheism
as the pinnacle of modern reason (Hegel [1837] 1956; Comte 1853; Frazer
1922; Tylor 1871).[4] Science was thus pitted (and defined) against black magic,
charged with a project of reform in nineteenth-century evolutionary discourses. As one widely republished 1892 newspaper editorial titled "How
to Kill Obeah" asserted, "The rise of natural science in Europe and the fall
of [African] fetishism are only two ways of looking at the same thing."[5]
The best medicines against the Caribbean fetishism of obeah, the author
asserted, were the plain and simple "natural facts" of science. In this view,
science was a truth-making discourse, demonstrating facts and discarding
superstitions.

As a triumphal program of progress and reform that reveals "facts," the
word "science" has long exerted the force of what Michel-Rolph Trouillot
(2002) called a "North Atlantic universal." It is necessary, however, to make
a tentative distinction between such popular, triumphal discourses and the
actual practice of a heterogeneous array of sciences, which can use very different methods that are not necessarily concerned with visible "facts." During my period of long-term field research, for example, Papoy and many of
his neighbors were employed as manual labor on a seismic petroleum survey that quite clearly involved a less-than-transparent practice of "science."
The contours of subsoil formations under Papoy's feet were visible to no
one, including the geologists and geophysicists who sat in offices in the capi-

tal or in an air-conditioned, heavily guarded computer trailer at my field site. These scientists remained as invisible to Papoy and other manual laborers as the geological formations that the survey was trying to "see." While these scientists were literally hidden from view, their actual practices of mapping subsoil formations were no less straightforward. In new onshore petroleum fields, the predictions of geologists are wrong 75 percent to 80 percent of the time (or 85 percent to 90 percent of the time for new deepwater surveys), resulting in the drilling of dry holes (see Weszkalnys 2015). Relying on the reflected shock waves produced by buried dynamite or underwater air cannons, these scientists performed the highly mediated task of transducing sound waves into visual images. Depending on different months-long ordeals of computer processing or the interpretations of different geologists, the surveys could produce divergent representations of what lay beneath the ground from the same seismic data. But the representations were all dependent on the negotiated expertise and cooperation of local labor. It was local laborers' knowledge of terrain that allowed them to successfully lay the seismic cables through dense forests, circumnavigating marijuana fields that were often protected by potentially deadly trap guns attached to trip wires. Offshore surveys depended on tense company negotiations with the fishermen unions whose boats would provide transport and local knowledge of maritime navigation for the surveys.

As was quite clear to the residents of Rio Moro who worked on these seismic surveys, science was a less-than-transparent pursuit that depended on transnational relations of capital, the highly mediated sensing of invisible phenomena, local knowledge of terrain, and negotiations with labor. While so often invoked in the singular, "science" denoted a heterogeneous range of methods and epistemologies in Rio Moro, referring to the divergent practices of school psychologists, petroleum geologists, geophysicists, and spiritual workers. Yet none of these sciences was simply about the demonstration of readily perceptible "natural facts." Broadly speaking, there were thus two ways of talking about science that exerted power in Rio Moro. The first discourse, saw science as a transparent practice that dispelled occult superstitions like obeah. The second discourse insisted that science was a heterogeneous and occult practice, which included (what got called) obeah.

Philosophers of science have made a roughly analogous distinction between two ways of talking about science. On the one hand, sciences are heterogeneous practices of experimentation that seek to produce novel conditions in which generally invisible or hard-to-perceive forces (e.g., subsoil fluids, electrons) could take shape as things that seemed to speak and act for themselves (even as specialists spoke for or manipulated them in highly mediated ways). The philosopher of science Isabelle Stengers (2012) calls this experimental encounter with the unknown the "adventure of sciences," contrasting this adventure with the great narrative of Science (with a capital "S") disenchanting non-Western or premodern worlds. The almost-deified Science is closely related to what other scholars have called scientism—a popular ideology of science as a reformatory organ of truth. This scientistic discourse, as Peter Gottschalk (2012) notes, was particularly forceful in colonial settings. During the secondary school possessions, this notion of science thus joined a host of other purported North Atlantic universals—such as Christian religion, national sovereignty, or development—as categories through which the (in)adequacy of Rio Moro and its students was articulated.

What often goes unnoticed in this scientistic narrative, however, is the way that science has often been the double of magic, rather than its other, in modern Western representations. Ostensibly, this doubling has revolved around attempts to denigrate and/or legitimize practices typically considered "magic" in Western genealogies of religion. Indeed, a key trope in Western anthropologists' representations of non-Western cultures has been that their "magic" is like "Western science," making it rational or materialistic (but ultimately inferior to modern science). Non-Western or premodern magic was, in Frazer's (1922) famous turns of phrase, "false" or "bastard" science—a kind of primitive precursor to the modern European scientific endeavor (see also Tylor 1871).

These foundational notions in anthropology sparked the protracted "rationality debate," which I also delve into at the end of this chapter. Considering anthropology's entanglement with Western racial theory, it seems no coincidence that this debate centered on Western anthropologists' representations of African "magic" or "witchcraft." These practices were "rational" or "scientific" to the extent that they sought to uncover the hidden forces responsible for empirical social phenomena. However, they failed to engage in the open-ended, empirical experimentation that was the hallmark of Western science, instead relying on the rote explanations of African tradition (e.g., Evans-Pritchard 1937; Horton 1967b; cf. Hogg 1961). "African magic" was also unlike "Western science" in that science could predict phenomena using the mechanistic laws of an impersonal nature, whereas magic could seek only to influence empirical reality in line with personal ends (e.g., Beattie 1966, 65). Ultimately failing to attain the transcendence of Western science, African magic was also unlike religion by virtue of these attempts at manipulating the world in many accounts. The hidden forces of religion proper (i.e., "gods") were ultimately devoted to the elaboration of a "moral order," whereas African magic tried to instrumentally influence the order of the world (Mair 1974, 215). Not moral enough to be religion and too interested or subjective to be science, racial tropes of African magic were the constitutive others of these "universal" Western domains.

Throughout this work I have questioned the conflation of religion with "moral order" that a wide variety of people have selectively employed to elaborate racist ideas of "black magic." In this chapter, however, I want to critique the notion of science that also made "African magic" not-religion (and a "bastard" double of scientific practice). More recent accounts of experimentation stemming from advances in quantum physics have suggested that scientists cannot stand apart from a law-governed nature, simply predicting outcomes without influencing the world around them. Experimentation with subatomic phenomena (according to one widespread interpretation in quantum physics) has shown that every measurement necessarily involves a transfer of energy that is transformative (Barad 2007). Scientists, in other words, "interfere" in the world, rather than simply "peering" at phenomena from an objective distance (Hacking 1983). Experimentation is thus an ethically fraught act, even if one experiments only with seemingly innocuous nonhuman particles (the atomic bomb being the ultimate realization of this fraughtness) (Barad 2017). Feminist science studies scholars have also roundly critiqued the idea of the objective scientist, divorced from the interests of power or interference in the world, as a masculinist colonial fantasy (e.g., Haraway 1991; Harding 2008). In short, Western anthropologists have relied on scientistic tropes of objectivity or rationality to make African "magic" into a negative double of science. The doubling of science and obeah, however, suggests something quite different.

In contrast with the evolutionary condescension of these accounts of non-Western practices, movements that scholars have (mis)placed under the heading of "Western esotericism" have equated science and magic to argue that spirit channeling or ceremonial magic are progressive, rational, and empirical practices. Nineteenth-century spiritualists claimed to provide a scientific basis for the afterlife, and Theosophists enamored of the mysteries of the East claimed to have uncovered a universal "spiritual science," intellectually superior to most forms of "organized religion" (McMahan 2004; Noakes 2019; Stolow 2008, 2013). The best-known ceremonial magician of the twentieth century (Aleister Crowley) claimed to be elaborating a purely scientific form of magic, scoffing at the intellectually inferior and superstitious approaches of magicians that preceded him (Asprem 2008).

These legitimizing invocations of "occult" or "spiritual" science were not limited to what has been narrowly conceived of as the West. In Brazil or Cuba, a spiritist language of science has helped to establish class boundaries, racial hierarchies, and claims to authoritative rationality (Bastide 1967, 5; Espírito Santo 2015, 97–154; Hess 1991). In Iran, movements of spiritual seeking and occultism have embraced science to define their projects as attempts at "cleansing metaphysical knowledge of superstition" or "rationaliz[ing] the unseen" (Doostdar 2018, 4–5). The first known text written by an avowed obeah practitioner (who, as Alexander Rocklin has recently discovered, turns out to have been a Scottish Theosophist who owned a plantation in Tobago) speaks about obeah as a science. Echoing Theosophical reformatory discourses of occult scientism, this author (known only by the pseudonym Myal Djumboh Cassecanarie in the text) claims to purify "true" obeah of superstition, material fetishes, and charlatanry.[6] It would seem only logical, then, that Caribbean spiritual workers would follow this post-eighteenth-century global trend in defining their practices as rational, advanced, and nonsuperstitious by calling them science.

All of these uses of science, however, are intensely scientistic, adopting "science" to help denote universalism, class superiority, rationalization, evolutionary advancement, and/or the eradication of superstition. This is precisely why the idea that Caribbean spiritual workers' talk of science reflects a mimicry of North Atlantic occult scientism, whether culled from spiritualism, Theosophy, or esoteric texts republished in the nineteenth and twentieth centuries, is insufficient. Apart from denying spiritual workers their own agency, creativity, and intellectual capacities, scientistic discourses of "spiritual science" misrepresent what science meant for my subaltern interlocutors. Science did not signal moral superiority or rational advancement, and it was not simply a legitimizing discourse. It was an ethically fraught process of accessing hard-to-perceive powers that was both potent and dangerous. This was why science, rather than an antisuperstition project, could be the cause of the afflictions at the secondary school for my interlocutors in Rio Moro.

WE UNITE TO FIGHT: OCCULT SCIENCES AND MODERN TRADITIONS

The two-story concrete-block buildings of Rio Moro Secondary sit at the top of a small hill off Rio Moro's main road, a few miles before it dead ends at the sea. The school was built on the land of Mr. Pierre, known by those that remembered him as a man knowledgeable in "science," who had owned a library of mail-order ritual implements and what Hogg (1961) calls "science books" (also popularly known as "bad books" at my field site). When Mr. Pierre's sister was raped by the neighbor's son, so the story goes, he used his knowledge of science to destroy the neighbor's family. The son went to jail for two years, and the rest of the family went mad. The incarcerated man's brothers began taking boards off the house they grew up in, slowly dismantling it to make cooking fires. After the son got out of jail, he vowed never to go back to Rio Moro. Still, he knew his brothers had gone mad and lived in poverty, so he drove one day to deliver groceries to them. Once he set foot in the yard where he had grown up next to Mr. Pierre's property, my friends tell me that whatever Pierre had set there was waiting for him. When he left to drive back to the city at nightfall, the lights of his Ford Cortina went out and he drove into a tree, sustaining injuries that ended his life before he reached the hospital.

My friend had told me that the son of Mr. Pierre still lived in a house by the secondary school and that many residents were attributing the possessions at the school to the continued presence of the "science" Mr. Pierre had unleashed around his property to avenge his sister's rape. The son had sold ten acres of his father's land to the government for the construction of the school in the 1980s and lived in the remaining property of his father. So, around two months after the initial disturbances, I turned my own Ford Cortina off the main road—coincidentally I had just bought the same rare model of car that Mr. Pierre's science had destroyed—and I drove up the hill to look for the son, passing the razor-wire fence that marked the school's property. I noticed that the gates of the school were open and the guard booth unmanned, an unusual state of affairs on a Saturday. From the open windows of my car, I heard the high-pitched tremolo of a double-tenor steel drum and the mixed voices of a crowd coming from up the hill.

The last time I had passed by the school on a Saturday, almost three months earlier, I had heard the distinctive glossolalia of a Pentecostal congregation permitted by school officials to exorcise (or in their terms, "deliver") the grounds after the school was first shut down by the spate of possessions. I turned up the school's drive, and when I crested the hill, the music grew louder. Through the open doors of the auditorium I could see a crowd of shifting bodies, and I noticed the family whose daughter was the first student possessed at the school standing by the doors. They told me that the man speaking on the microphone in a gray dashiki was Kenneth Rush, the

Afro-Trinidadian pastor of a Pentecostal Open Bible church in the main city of central Trinidad, a two-hour drive from this part of Rio Moro.[7] The most popular gospel radio station in Trinidad, 98.1 FM, had sponsored this "crusade" at Rio Moro Secondary. Rush paced the stage, shouting "Fight!" Behind him, a banner spelled the word "hope" in large, pastel capital letters. He continued:

> We declare that Rio Moro shall not be known any longer, it shall not be in the memory of the people of this nation, as a place of obeah. We declare by the bounty of the strength of the living God.
>
> We release this community. We release the future generations. We release the future generations. We decree and declare it's a new season. A community of holiness. A community of righteousness. A community of unity. We drive out from the eastern coast. We drive out from the western coast. We drive out from the northern coast. We drive out from the southern boundary by which Rio Moro keep watch over the law of Trinidad and Tobago. We drive out everything of the evil of generations of the past. We declare new life through Jesus Christ. We declare new vision through Jesus Christ. We declare that there shall be no continuance of obeah [cheers]! There shall be no continuance of voodoo [cheers]! There shall be no continuance of any form of ignorance. In the kingdom of God, there will be no forms of witchcraft, no forms of wizardry. We unite to fight against the spirits of the past. We leave behind all ways of sacrifice, except the one true and living sacrifice. It's a new day. A place of life! A place of life! A place of life! A place of life! A place of unity!

As he spoke, the pulse of the bass guitar and the high-pitched tremolo of steel-drum notes rose and fell, punctuating the pastor's words. He began to command the ocean that formed the southern channel separating Rio Moro from South America: "We command the ocean to give up every vessel of human trafficking, every vessel of drug trafficking. We command the ocean to swallow them up. In the name of Jesus Christ. We release the holy spirit to fill every law enforcement agency." The pastor then commanded the Colombians, who he said were making cocaine, to repent to the Lord. The energy of the auditorium was palpable as shouts of affirmation greeted the pastor's proclamations.

Instead of continuing on my way to investigate the science of Rio Moro, I had been drawn into a Pentecostal and charismatic "crusade" against Rio Moro's obeah. Pastor Rush seemed to make some firm and characteristic distinctions between Rio Moro's past of obeah and a liberated future. Stranded somewhere in between was a present full of illicit and less-than-transparent powers: the infiltration of the island by drug cartels, cocaine, and human trafficking and prostitution networks (with the culpability for these occult networks, according to the xenophobic logic of Trinidad's anti-crime fervor, projected onto Colombia or Venezuela).[8] Rio Moro and the "rebellious" bodies of the students who inhabited its school were a national threshold for these forces, existing at the literal and figurative borders of both the nation's modernity and the narrow channel of water that separated Rio Moro and the anglophone Caribbean from the Spanish-speaking mainland of South America (Venezuela being visible on a clear day from Rio Moro's fishing port). Rio Moro was both the African past and the modern national threshold of a demon-infested twenty-first century.

Straddling this geo-temporal threshold at Rio Moro Secondary, Kenneth Rush's crusade exorcised possessed bodies on a variety of different temporal and spatial scales. The bodies of the students, of the community, and of the nation were all subject to external forces that threatened to overwhelm their capacities for moral action. These forces supposedly emanated at once from a past of "African witchcraft" (epitomized by "obeah" or "voodoo") and from the present vicissitudes of supply-chain capitalism and transnational flows of guns, humans, media, and cocaine. For Pentecostal and charismatic Christians in Trinidad, the forces at the school were demonic, and the antidote was the "infilling" of bodies, whether of the nation, of the students, or of law enforcement agencies, with the Holy Spirit. This "infilling" effectively sealed the borders of these bodies off from the demonic forces that roamed the earth, fallen and rebellious angels or spirits of native religions that caused social problems such as alcoholism and violent crime (see McCloud 2015).

Across the world, "third wave" Pentecostal and charismatic Christians engage in what they call "spiritual warfare" against demonic forces that they often allege are worshipped in Muslim, indigenous, African, or pagan traditions (see Macedo 1990; McAlister 2014; McCloud 2015; McGovern 2012; Meyer 1999; Roeder 2019; Shaw 2007). The "true nature" of humans for the Pentecostal leaders I knew in Trinidad was inherently good, but without the infilling of the holy spirit, humans were spiritual vacuums, permeable to native or demonic forces that were extraneous to their "true personalities." Besides a vacuum, the Pentecostal pastors I knew persistently likened a person's spirit that had not been infilled to an empty house whose doors and windows had been left open—a sure magnet for criminal or demonic trespass. These pastors told me that they were able to distinguish between the Holy Spirit and a host of intrusive spirits that inhabited the earth precisely because the former worked within the bounds of one's "personality," while the latter exerted power over one's true self to realize their illicit desires. Drug addiction, mental illness, and the "rebellious behavior" of females were all explicable as the result of demons or the ancestral spirits of native religions that had taken possession of those individual humans not filled by the Holy Spirit.

National media responses to the events at Rio Moro Secondary often pitted the reform efforts of these born-again Christians against an allegedly rival explanatory theory — "science" (represented primarily by psychology). An editorial in a national newspaper following the possessions summed up the ostensible conflict in its title: "Bring Psychologists Not Exorcists." Another editorial, "Education not Exorcisms Will Help Rio Moro 'Possessions,'" claimed that these irrational and charismatic pastors encouraged the already obeah-laden "stench of superstition and irrational beliefs" in Rio Moro. The psychological diagnosis of "mass hysteria," this northern Trinidadian claimed, provided an "objective" explanation that made the events at the school analogous to overzealous girls "fainting at a Michael Jackson concert." By equating the behavior of the pastors to the irrationality of those in Rio Moro, this editorial leveled the same charge of superstition that drove the Christian exorcisms at the school in the first place. Christian exorcisms were as embarrassing as the obeah of Rio Moro in this scientific antisuperstition discourse, and "science" represented the antidote of education, development, and progress.

Ostensibly, in the context of this media battle between "exorcists" and "science," the Pentecostal ontology of demons was a far cry from the approach of authoritative psychologists, who held high-ranking positions in both the national mental hospital and the University of Trinidad and Tobago. These mental health experts identified the cause of the school's disturbances not in the external force of ethereal agents but in the "weakness" of the female students' personality structures. The leading university and government psychologist who diagnosed the disturbances with the misogynist and somewhat anachronistic term "mass hysteria," for example, told me that the "weak ego structures" of the female students rendered them susceptible to "excitement." The result was "copycat behavior," he said. "One girl starts to beat up and the rest of them follow suit." The weakness of their ego structures, he emphasized, was a product of "poor education" in Rio Moro and "a belief in obeah"—the power of supernatural forces—rather than what he called the "power of the ego to discern between fantasy and reality."

In this diagnosis of weak ego structures and hysterical females, some school officials found a rational explanation for the unusual behavior of the students. "There is a scientific explanation for this," the Afro-Trinidadian Muslim school principal told me, "and the descriptions I read of mass hysteria online are exactly what we had here. . . . If you want to hear about obeah," she continued, "go down the road to the village." Like many of the callers to the national radio show, the principal thought that "scientific explanation" could dispel the force of false beliefs in Rio Moro. This project of "science" was enacted through and against gendered notions of irrationality (mass hysteria) and racialized concepts of atavism (village obeah).

While newspapers touted a supposed battle between science and religion, the neo-Pentecostal and charismatic pastors and the champions of a "scientific explanation" associated the problematic porosity of female students or national borders with the obeah that Rio Moro conjured in the national imaginary ("obeah" that my interlocutors in Rio Moro often resignified as "science"). For the pastors, the "infilling" of the bodies of the female students or the body of the nation with the Holy Spirit fortified the boundaries of these bodies against the atavistic forces of obeah (and the menace of the Latin American trafficker). In a different yet resonant way, the university psychologist believed that fortifying the ego structures of the female students could render them immune to the influence of atavistic superstitions. Whether the strengthening of the boundaries of the ego, of the nation, or of an individual's spirit, these projects of purification shared a similar ethos that depended on an opposition to "African traditions" (popularly epitomized by obeah or Rio Moro) and the related problem of nonsovereign porosity and possession. In this way both religious and scientific interventions enacted projects of modernity, which sought to drive a wedge between a traditional past and a liberated present, premised on a purification of the human subject of false agencies. This familiar battle recapitulated the idea that modernity enacts what Charles Taylor (2007) called the break between "porous" selves open to a world of spirits and the "buffered" self that has sealed itself off from such external agencies. This combat was not simply a battle of religion against science, as these conventional narratives of secular modernity and the national reactions to the events at the school would often have it. While recent anthropological critiques of secularism have not often mentioned the word, "superstition" was the third term that religion and science both opposed, and this enemy was the failed sovereignty instantiated by racialized pasts of obeah and porous female bodies.[9]

This promised liberation from past superstition at the school, however, was also a liberation from a present of networked powers that put the sovereignty of the human subject and the boundaries of Trinidad and Tobago in question. The powers that threatened the bodies of the students and the nation were simultaneously the past of obeah and the very contemporary forces of transnational networks, "science," and the internet. Alongside obeah or "African witchcraft," the most common explanation for the students' possessions at my field site was their access to science on the internet at the school. Community members avowed that the internet had allowed students access to the same "science books" that Mr. Pierre had acquired by mail order from Chicago and used to avenge his sister's rape. Inspired by the internet's digitized copies of these out-of-copyright books, the female students were awakening some of these same forces without being skilled "scientists" who could control such powers.

This was the kind of science that Ashok and other interlocutors in Rio Moro referenced when they attributed the events at the school to scientific forces. What my interlocutors called "science books" or "bad books" were texts that had circulated widely throughout the anglophone black Atlantic via mail-order catalogs since the late nineteenth century, purporting to reveal Hebrew, Hindu, Hermetic, Kabbalistic, and Egyptian occult sciences. In another twist on presumptions about the relationship between obeah and modernity, the disturbances at the secondary school in this reckoning were caused not by atavistic African practices but by access to the internet.[10] All of the most popular occult scientific texts that had originally circulated via mail-order catalog, and had been somewhat difficult to acquire, since they were illegal for being the chief "implements of obeah," were now readily available free-of-charge on the web.[11]

Just as publishers have freely pirated and reproduced these texts, spiritual workers in Rio Moro acquired photocopied versions of these books or formed reading groups to share a single copy. The internet, however, took such duplication and access to a different level, as numerous websites featured free downloads of these books (fig. 6.2). As the secondary school was the only place where most people had access to the internet at that time in Rio Moro, it would make sense that students would be able to read the books only on computers at the school. Obeah was alive and well at Rio Moro Secondary, but this obeah was not simply a representative of an atavistic

African past, as Pastor Rush and other reformers alleged. Obeah reflected long-standing Atlantic networks of esoteric texts—transnational occult networks that the new technology of the internet seemed to intensify. The connection between "modern science" and these texts was far from idiosyncratic. These Renaissance and Enlightenment esoteric compilations were, according to various historians, inspirations for the movement known as the Scientific Revolution of Europe, with an interest in occultism continuing to form a part of the story of "Western science" over the course of the past century (e.g., Asprem 2018; Henry 1986; Yates 1964, [1972] 2013). Far from simply European books, separable from obeah or Africanness, these books were often attributed northeastern African origins.[12] After all, the principal figures said to inspire these texts—Solomon, Moses, and Hermes Trismegistus—were all associated with Egypt or Ethiopia.[13] Both European devotees of "Western esotericism" and Trinidadian students of the Kabbalah have taken these figures as key sources of inspiration, and these esoteric influences, in turn, are an important part of the story of "modern science."

The reactions to the events at Rio Moro Secondary showed that it was not so easy to relegate obeah to an atavistic past, separable from both science and concerns of the present. While projects of scientific and religious reform asserted as much, allegations of obeah were entangled with some of the most salient forces of the twenty-first century: drug trafficking, border security, the internet, neo-Pentecostal Christianity, and science. The narrative of modernity, whether enacted in the name of born-again Christianity or science, promised to render occult forces transparent to the gaze of reform, but Trinidad's modernity represented a proliferation of such forces. Rather than an archaic notion of occult science, which Western science had allegedly left behind as it modernized (e.g., Lakatos 1978), my interlocutors' articulations of science better reflected the experience of transnational networks (whether of drug trafficking or the Internet) that characterized late modernity. These seemingly invisible networks showed that the borders of modern body politics were porous rather than buffered, and this was just as true of the individual female bodies that bore the weight of the occult powers at Rio Moro Secondary. Did science emanate from these occult powers of obeah and the internet, or was it a force for dispelling the occult and making the students into rational and buffered subjects? Other less-than-transparent forces, however, haunted the female students at Rio Moro secondary—forces that echoed the violence that had led to Mr. Pierre's original acts of science on the school grounds.

TO MAKE A BREAK WITH THE PAST?

As Kenneth Rush ended his purification of the school and the nation, I turned to leave, bidding goodbye to the first of the demon-afflicted students and her parents. Her mother, Parvati, had told me the previous week while we were sitting on the front porch of their home, off a dirt track bordering an abandoned cane field, that spirits of the past were to blame for the events at the secondary school and the affliction of her daughter. The twisted stalks of cane that sometimes rustled in a breeze beside us were reminders of the iconic past that had brought Parvati's own great-grandparents to the Caribbean to work as indentured labor on sugar plantations. Parvati's daughter had begun to have episodes in which she would act out at school, cussing at teachers and taking off articles of clothing. The pastor at the Pentecostal church that she attended diagnosed these episodes as the product of an "ancestral spirit," specifically the Hindu goddess Kali to whom her Hindu ancestors had performed animal sacrifices prior to her own generation's conversion to Christianity.

Forgoing the material rituals of exchange that Hindus or African Spiritual Baptists used to dismiss troublesome ancestral obligations of "blood" (see chapter 4), Pentecostal-charismatic attempts to make a break with the past focused on severing relations with demons and non-Christian spirits through the moral behavior of the individual. Through born-again faith and lack of sin, Parvati's daughter could make herself immune to the past forces that haunted her. Echoing a discourse I heard from the families of other students, Parvati said her daughter would have to become "white as snow" to evade the forces of science unleashed at the school. Her mother kept repeating that phrase — "white as snow" — when I would see her around Rio Moro, for her daughter was engaged in a daily discipline of purification, which included counseling with multiple Pentecostal pastors and faith-healing sessions, to avoid the bouts of possession that afflicted her. The mother told me that this process of purification concerned not simply sinful acts but even sexual thoughts or fantasies. The student, whose mother was always present during our conversations, agreed that she would have to learn how to control such fantasies to master her bouts of demonic possession.

Parvati told me that her brother, a Pentecostal pastor at a different church from the one they attended, could give a better explanation of her daughter's afflictions. When I reached her brother's house, he brought out a book called *The Shepherd's Staff* and began to read passages on demonic spiritual warfare, explaining that his niece's afflictions were caused by the "demons" that Africans and South Asians had formerly worshipped. The book, I later learned, was distributed by the US Christian organization called World Map, which claims to have distributed more than a million copies of *The Shepherd's Staff* to church leaders in "developing nations." The organization's own literature often condemns African-identified religions, with one of their newsletters promising that *The Shepherd's Staff* would dismantle the "cradle of lies" that African "voodoo" represented (Balser 2013).

Other community members and school officials told a different story about the source of these disturbances. Rather than demonic spirits or the sinful thoughts of the students, the principal and the teachers at the school themselves admitted to me in private conversations that some of the afflicted students were known to have suffered forms of sexual abuse. Two of the students (in the presence of their mothers) told me that their episodes began after seeing a man with horns in a stall of the secondary school's girls' bathroom who tried to assault them. It would be impossible for me to equate these visions of spiritual attack with sexual assault; nor is it possible to make generalizations about the causes of all the students' afflictions. For some time, I hesitated to even write about this dimension of the school disturbances, but the underrecognized prevalence of domestic sexual abuse in Trinidad (and beyond) led me to feel that this social problem deserved further attention (see Barclay 2009). Certainly, scholars have shown how episodes of spirit possession across the world represent alternate ways for women to articulate forms of violence that men enact against them (e.g., Boddy 1989; Ong 2010), and it would be inaccurate to deny that talk of such gender violence played a significant role in the events at Rio Moro Secondary.

Even the Pentecostal pastors' discourses of demonic possession were haunted by the language of sexual assault. Echoing an explanation I heard from other residents, one pastor in Rio Moro attributed the disturbances at the school to an "incubus," a male spirit that forcibly has sex with women, also known in French patois as "gumbo glissay" in Rio Moro. "This is not very uncommon," he told a newspaper reporter who came to cover the school disturbances. "I believe it is caused by a demon, incubus, who preys on young girls. We need to do special prayers." "So Incubus is the name of the demon who preys on young girls?" a reader identified as "Daisy" wrote in the comments that appended the online version of the article in which the pastor's explanation appeared. "They have about 500,000 incubus [*sic*]

in TT [Trinidad and Tobago]," she concluded, wryly linking sexual and domestic abuse in the nation (whose total population was roughly 1.3 million)
with the gendered dynamics of demonic possession at the school.

Sexual assault was certainly part of the history of another afflicted student I knew well, who had twice made rape allegations against her mother's
boyfriend, only to rescind them after being paid off by the man. Indeed,
his intermittent payments significantly ameliorated a financial situation in
which the mother's weekly income of approximately US$80 from the un-
employment relief crew was the family's only income in a petrostate whose
consumer prices equaled or exceeded the cost of goods in the United States.
Yet despite such a history, following the teachings of a Pentecostal pastor,
she told me that she attributed her afflictions at school to her own sinful
thoughts and fantasies, which invited demons to enter her.

Modernity is a project with two linked imperatives: to break with the
past and to undergo continual processes of reform and purification (Seligman et al. 2008; Latour 1993). By promising a break from the past through
the reform of their thoughts and feelings, born-again Christianity fore-
grounded this project of modernity. In a different way, "science" at Rio Moro
Secondary also promised a break from a past of superstition and the reform of individuals (through psychological diagnosis or education rather
than spiritual interventions). Among these explanatory frames for what
happened at the school, it was only the alternate story of science (as told
by my interlocutors in Rio Moro) that explicitly focused on justice-making
and crimes of sexual violence. The science at Rio Moro secondary had been
unleashed in response to the crime of rape, but the punitive force of this science was inherently ambivalent in the present, threatening to afflict those
who had suffered the same injustice as Mr. Pierre's sister. Science, at least for
the spiritual workers I knew in Rio Moro, represented something besides a
project of purification or a break from a troublesome past. This science was
about the potential ambivalence of more-than-human powers to redress
past injustices that would not go away. Rather than a purification of humans
from nonhuman agencies or a definitive burial of the past, science addressed
the skillful practice of making justice with and against forces that had lives
of their own. Becoming "white as snow" was not the object, or even a fea-
sible option. Instead of individual moral reform, the emphasis fell on the
complexities of interpersonal justice and injustice.

The popular notion that science is simply the rational observation of
facts assumes that science is a morally neutral enterprise. Science, however,
was not neutral and thus removed from contexts of power for my inter-

locutors but inescapably immersed in these contexts and thus profoundly ambivalent—always potentially capable of protection and harm. The majority of cases among the spiritual workers I knew centered on forms of injustice that one could not reasonably expect state law to address in Trinidad. When one came up against the powers of trafficking organizations or the monetary dependence on one's abusive stepfather, the law-and-order world purified of harm and occult powers that Pastor Rush and others offered might seem particularly dubious. Rather than the observation of facts, science in Rio Moro is about intervention in this world of networked, opaque forces. Like more recent conceptions in the philosophy of science and feminist science studies, scientific experimentation was not about "peering" at a world of transparent forces but about "interfering" in this world to produce an altered state of affairs (Barad 2007; Hacking 1983).[14] Rather than a fact-based march into a liberated future, scientific experimentation bore the weight of ethical complexity and justice-making for past violence. These were the associations that my interlocutors in Rio Moro spoke of when they attributed the events at the school to science.

"WE ARE ALL SCIENTISTS"

I was first drawn to Dark Man's yard by the dry thunder-and-lightning sound of a metal roof shaking in a gust of wind. I had pulled into the shadows of the high wall that surrounded Dark Man's yard so that Giselle, the daughter of the family I lived with in Rio Moro, could deliver her homemade mango preserves to the neighboring shop. The heat of the thirty-year-old Ford Cortina's engine had been pouring over our legs, making a dry-season day even hotter, and I took advantage of Giselle's sale to escape the heat inside the car, catching a breeze in the shadows of Dark Man's freshly painted concrete wall. It was then I heard what seemed like thunder—a welcome, if unlikely, sound on an oppressively clear dry-season day. When I looked up, I found the source of the noise in a steeply pointed cone composed entirely of bent sheets of corrugated metal roofing that towered above the rim of the wall. A gust of wind had rattled the rust-edged galvanized metal, patched together like strips of papier mâché to form what looked like an inverted cyclone.

I was paying so much attention to the peculiar roof that I did not notice the man standing in the green wall's half-opened gate. Noticing my fascination, he told me that the metal cone was the minaret of his mosque, where he taught Bible lessons on Sunday and performed works of healing the rest of the week. He introduced himself to me as Philip Antoine, but everyone in this area of Rio Moro, as I would later learn, knew him as Dark Man, a name that referred both to his complexion and his popular association with obeah. Although his neighbors called his practice of healing and protecting spiritual work "obeah," thus identifying him with both African origins and a colonial category of superstition that had made obeah illegal, he referred to his chosen profession as science and worked with a range of Hindu, Muslim, and Kabbalistic powers. He did not leave his house much because his spirit familiars—Mr. Mohammed Khan, Emmanuel Bones, and the Hindu deity Shiva—could manifest on him at unexpected, inopportune times, render- ing him volatile or unconscious of his actions. His clients, therefore, came to him in his home, and he gave them spiritual baths or protective "seals" on pieces of parchment paper, designs that he derived from his study of the aforementioned "science books," which were full of such invocatory draw- ings.

On that first meeting, he told me to come back the next afternoon, as he was tending to a client who appeared to be an Indo-Trinidadian man in his thirties. I returned the next day but found Dark Man transformed. The exuberant person who had greeted me the day before sat slumped and despondent on his porch. He was indulging in a kind of 160-proof rum called puncheon, the drink of choice in Rio Moro. A young man from the neighborhood had come to him the previous night asking for his help in locating an important possession, as the finding of stolen or lost objects has been an important task of spiritual workers in the area for as long as people could remember. Invariably, the powers of the famed scientists of the past included the ability to locate or induce the return of stolen goods. In this instance, however, the stolen object in question was a brick of cocaine. After the US-supported campaigns against the dominance of Colombian cartels and the subsequent decentralization of cocaine trafficking over the past two decades, the narrow strip of water separating Trinidad from Venezu- ela had become an important crossing point for cocaine bound for Europe, the United States, and domestic Trinidadian markets (Figueira 1997, 2004). Like neoliberal supply-chain capitalism, this decentralized drug trafficking operated through the hierarchical subcontracting of risk, whereby persons occupying structurally subordinate positions assumed the financial and cor- poreal dangers of doing business in a deregulated market. In Trinidad, this meant that bricks of cocaine had proliferated as a currency that minted violently enforced relations of debt in a material substance worth far more than its weight in gold (Figueira and Labrousse 2008). If the young man did not find the brick, he was liable to be killed by the man who supplied it to him, as it would be impossible for him to come up with the cash value of the cocaine he was to have sold. Even as most murders resulted in no conviction or publicly substantiated motive in a nation that had recently experienced an upsurge in violent crime, my interlocutors recognized many killings as ways of fighting over or disciplining the illicit supply chains of transnational trafficking. So Dark Man decided to help his client out of a difficult, life-threatening situation by naming the location of the brick in question.

He began to perform what he called an "experiment," instructing his client to hold a key that hung at the end of a thread. Dark Man then opened the Bible to Psalms and closed it on the key, pressing the Bible between his palms and saying "what he had to say." He released the key from the pages and asked his client to begin calling the names of those he suspected of stealing the brick. The key hung motionless in front of his client's face, but eventually he called the name of one of his neighbors and the key began to spin on the end of the string. Dark Man told him that he would find his brick at the house of that individual.[15]

The next morning, Dark Man found out that the person whose name he called as the thief had been shot dead in the middle of the night. He had known the murder victim well. He felt the weight of the dead man on his chest and began to drink puncheon to dilute the feeling. Whether we like it or not, he told me, "every single thing we does is science . . . and all of we [are] scientists." Science was not an innocent or transparent pursuit, as the weight of the dead man reminded him. It was about living and working with powers that inhabited and exceeded human frames of corporeality and understanding in often uncomfortable or painful ways.

Dark Man had to live with powers he could not totally master or control. On the one hand, he lived amid the relations of local violence that held together an extended and transnational supply chain of guns and cocaine. For my interlocutors, these partially occult and illicit networks led to the upper echelons of domestic society or the metropolitan centers of northern nations. Although Dark Man, Kenneth Rush, and others perceived these powers to emanate from afar, these networked forces also produced intimate forms of violence and legal problems for some of the clients of spiritual workers. Apart from these forces of illicit supply chain capitalism, Dark Man also lived with unpredictable powers that confined him to his own home, because, as he told me, the powers could come upon him unannounced like a gust of wind. Sometimes he cursed them, but he could not get away from them. He had already tried to resist them when he first began to experience spirit manifestations as a teenager, begging the spirits not to come on him. Like many other spiritual workers I knew he had initially undergone exorcism and deliverance in a variety of Christian churches before coming to accept the forces as empowering, if demanding "coexistences." Although his own experience of living with the exogenous powers that he (like Mother Mariella) called "coexistences" was particularly potent, Dark Man claimed that we are all scientists—that we all have to live skillfully with powers that both exceed and inhabit our frames. A liberatory exorcism was not an option, and power could never be purified into a transparent, rather than partially occult, force.

With this understanding of the relationship between persons and powers, Dark Man viewed the actions of reform at Rio Moro Secondary as profoundly misguided. Violent exorcisms would only provoke the ire of science; one had to enter into a relationship with the forces that afflicted the girls to find out what they wanted. "Them people does try to run [get rid of] spirit," he told me, "but I does try [question] the spirit." I began to realize that the perception of the students' possessions as an affliction was only one interpretation, one that made perfect sense within a modern project of reform that sought to separate persons from false agencies. Yet maybe Mr. Pierre's science was not as ambivalent as it might have seemed to me, especially in the face of the sexual abuse that teachers, students, and other community members attributed to many of the "rebellious" students' domestic situations. Perhaps these possessions at Rio Moro Secondary were vengeance for the continuing crime of rape, a vengeance that could reach fruition if one "tried" the spirits—that is, questioned the forces that inhabited the students to find out what they wanted—rather than exorcising them.

Science was a process of questioning ritually prepared objects (e.g., a key suspended from a string), afflicted persons, or powers bound to certain natural forces, landscapes, and histories. Dark Man worked with powers that dwelt in what he called "the cracks and crevices of the earth," and the fissures in the earth's crust were what he called his "school." Down the road, the spiritual worker I knew best, Mother Mariella, also performed what she called her "experiments" by questioning charged objects and powers. She lived with these powers, who dwelled in the "stools" she would constantly "feed" with "lights" (candles) and their favored libations. She did not work "by guess," she avowed, but questioned the powers to find out how she should proceed with afflicted clients on a case-by-case basis. Sometimes she

cussed the powers when they demanded difficult things or refused to intervene in certain situations. It was not simply a harmonious relationship, and
the process of housing these powers in her body was sometimes a taxing and
physically painful experience for Mariella.

Originally, I had wanted to counteract the social stigmas against Mariella's experiments by arguing that they belonged within the legitimating cor-
pus of "Western science," to claim along with Palmié (2002, 207) that what
obeah and science share is "a fundamental rationality that is hard to deny."
As on other occasions, Mariella did not agree with my intent; there was a difference between her science and what she called "laboratory science." This
difference hinged precisely on the notion of rationality that Palmié (2002)
used to place obeah and science in a relation of equivalence. In this reckoning, rationality implies the human control of objectified and predictable
forces to maximize their productive capacities. This was the modern economic rationality that bound slavery, science, and obeah together as techniques of controlling both humans and nonhumans for certain ends. Yet
Mariella did not presume to control the powers that she lived with and that
made her spiritual work possible. The work of these powers was premised
on tenuous relations of exchange—the offerings of animals, oils, alcohols,
and candles that kept lines of imperfect communication open with powers
that often exceeded human frames of understanding. For Mariella, this was
the difference between the science that came to dispel inchoate forces at Rio
Moro Secondary and her own experiments with power.

The last time I saw her, Mariella reminded me of this difference from
the top of her stairs as she looked down at the altar to her principal Orisha, known as Mama Lata, tucked away behind the brightly colored leaves
of some coleus bushes in the corner of her yard.[16] Embodied sensations
were the evidence of Mama Lata's power, but these tremors, dreams, and
changes of body temperature represented the presence of an other-than-
human force that was not totally comprehensible to Mariella or identical to
her human body. Her relationship with Mama Lata was a very intimate alterity, in which other-than-human powers inhabited and exceeded human cor-
poreal, ontological, and epistemic frames. This ontological limit to knowing
for Mariella separated her science from what she called "laboratory science."
She told me that when she was younger, she had wanted to understand how
the power worked, to come up with some kinds of regular laws that governed the power's actions. Yet as Mariella told me from the top of the stairs,
she had "give[n] up on proof." She could not know exactly how the power
worked (although she knew that it worked effectively). She could, however,

question, experiment, and listen to nonhuman powers that exerted unpredictable forces and sometimes offered difficult answers.

SCIENCES OF THE OCCULT

By giving up on proof and transparency, had Mariella effectively given up on science, as it is understood in the modern West? The idea that science is inherently "occult" and morally opaque does not jibe with the progress narrative of modernity, which is a story of increasing transparency and understanding. Just as the ideal of unmediated witnessing and visual observation structured the methods of experimental philosophy, so too the gaze of the consumer, facilitated by new technologies of steel and glass construction, became the model for consumer capitalism (Benjamin 2002). In one pithy turn of phrase, as Dutton, Seth, and Gandhi (2002, 137) write, "Science turned on observation, and modernity, it seems, both in the scientist's laboratory and down at the local shopping mall, was all about the gaze."

Yet as is transparent enough for scholars of the experimental sciences, few experiments happen simply through the unmediated observation of the human gaze. Against a popular notion that science is about the ready observation of visible matters of fact, Bruno Latour (2010) asserts that laboratory science is about the highly mediated accessing of hard-to-perceive forces, which are too small, too far away, or too slow to be directly perceived by humans. Much of science, in other words, addresses "occult" forces that are perceptible to scientists through complex and delicate material apparatuses in experiments that are replicable only through a tenuous assemblage of humans, instruments, computer processing, and nonhuman forces that usually yields the visual representations that the public views. To "see" an electron, a galaxy, or subterranean geomorphology requires the use of sonic shock waves, charge differentials between subatomic particles, or radio frequencies that scientists (and the powerful computers they use) transduce into visual representations that might differ from other scientists' representations of the same material evidence (see Lerche 1997; Weszkalnys 2015). In other words, much of what we call science is not really about gazing or passively observing but rather involves the active movement between very different media and scales of existence. This does not mean that the diverse techniques of sciences are not accurate or that they do not engage with a material reality that actually exists. What it means is that the actual practices of sciences are different from the modernist telos of visibility, which renders occult realities transparent to the gaze of the rational observer, thus objectifying formerly inchoate forces.

In fact, what is now called the Scientific Revolution was revolutionary because it was a turn away from medieval Aristotelian methods of deductive proof, which confined natural philosophy to mechanical causation, and toward experimentation with "occult" and invisible phenomena like vacuums, gravity, or even witchcraft (Lakatos 1978; Hutchison 1982; Shapin and Schaffer 1985). Rather than deductive proof, the main figures of the Scientific Revolution asserted that these experiments could only produce probabilistic knowledge about invisible forces (e.g., Feyerabend 1975; Lakatos 1970; Shapin and Schaffer 1985). In many ways, therefore, Mariella's giving up on proof and my interlocutors' insistence on a science of occult forces remained closer to the ethos of the so-called Scientific Revolution than modernist notions of science as the unmediated observation of facts and known truths.

Nevertheless, this modernist telos of science was incredibly important to the antioccult force of "scientific explanation" at Rio Moro Secondary. The school principal and others who insisted on such explanation said that science could dispel obeah by clearly identifying the cause of the disturbances in chemical imbalances or psychological diagnoses. In contrast, my interlocutors in Rio Moro who talked instead about science as the cause of the disturbances insisted that science was a potentially dangerous process of accessing occult forces. The promise of modernity's exemplar was not a break between the occult and the new life of proper understanding that advocates of both scientific explanation and Pentecostal-charismatic spiritual warfare promised. Science represented a morally ambivalent process of harnessing occult forces, whether spirits or subatomic particles, in the interests of power (see also Barad 2017).

In more general terms, for both my interlocutors and the reformers at Rio Moro Secondary, the modernity they inhabited was marked by a profusion of occult powers that could not be observed directly, from transnational trafficking networks and high-level corruption to the long shadows of domestic sexual abuse that the principal and teachers alleged had marked the possessed students. While there were laws against all of these occluded phenomena, exceptional economic and gendered powers often trumped these laws. This was not exactly a situation of intractable unknowing or total occlusion, for everyone simultaneously knew that such occult abuses of power existed, although relatively few had actually observed them directly. To take an example from the natural sciences, just as few people have "seen" electrons, many people know that they exist. Residents knew that large quantities of cocaine and arms passed through Rio Moro and other coastal areas of Trinidad, and information circulated about who was profiting, how the police and coast guard were involved, or how the largest businessmen in Trinidad controlled the trade. Yet the conversion of such information into actionable evidence was a different story, for there was no place in which evidence could be separated from relations of power.

Science, for my interlocutors in Rio Moro, was not about the distanced observation of facts; it was not "all about the gaze" of modernity and its telos of transparency. Scientific and religious reformers at Rio Moro Secondary, in contrast, held onto the horizon of modernity's promise—a definitive break with a past of superstitious forces and a present of illicit networks that would signal a liberated future. Two different kinds of ethical frameworks thus presented themselves around the events at the school. One framework was premised on the constant work of reform that defines the tradition of North Atlantic modernity (Seligman et al. 2008), promising a continually deferred horizon of transparent truth, human equality, an end to violence, and/or the shared prosperity of national economic development. None of these promises seemed to be materializing for my interlocutors; in some cases, particularly in terms of violence, prosperity, and equality, the recent march of modernity had been a story of regress rather than progress. In the twenty-first century, Trinidad's rising gross domestic product, fueled by a natural gas "boom," had been accompanied by drastically increased murder rates and social inequality. This did not stop the thrust of reform. Rather, such apparently daunting conditions signaled the need for redoubled efforts at religious or scientific reform to dispel the occult forces of past superstition or contemporary criminality.

In contrast, those African spiritual workers likely to be accused of obeah presented a different ethical framework. There was no imminent horizon of transparency and equality that would liberate humans from the ambivalent workings of power. Rather, there was a continual process of work within a field of more-than-human forces and imperfect human intentions (see also Brown 2001). Spiritual workers did not see their work as moving toward an imminent endpoint of redemption. "We [African spiritual workers] are not waiting for the trumpets of glory to sound," as Mother Mariella often said, sarcastically differentiating herself from Euro-American Christian eschatology. Arguably, neither were the Pentecostal-charismatic spiritual warriors simply waiting, as their born-again ritual warfare was supposed to hasten the global victory of Christianity and these trumpets of glory. Neverthe-less, there was a fundamental difference between these cosmologies. In the Heights and the Depths, good and bad, darkness and light were entangled and inextricable qualities, which could be good for different situations. In the framework of heaven and hell, however, these forces were mortal ene-mies engaged in a battle that would produce an end to death and suffering (at least for born-again Christians). In a resonant way, modernity, as Bruno Latour (1993, 10) observes, "designates a combat in which there are victors and vanquished," with the sides of this battle often represented as science versus superstition or religion versus magic (Styers 2004; Seng-Guan 2016). Instead of African spiritual workers' practice of balancing and experiment-ing with the inherently ambivalent polarities of power, the Christian proj-ects of reform at Rio Moro Secondary were quite literally conceived of as a war (see chapter 3).

As Nils Bubandt (2014) has argued, modernity, in the guises of national development, Christianity, or science, has promised to dispel "aporia" — a condition of intractable contradiction and incomplete knowledge that Bubandt aligns with (what he translates as) "witchcraft." For reformers at Rio Moro Secondary, "African witchcraft" did indeed seem to oppose modernity's liberatory promises, echoing Bubandt's observations. My inter-locutors' conceptions of the science at Rio Moro Secondary, however, told a different story. This science did not represent an antisuperstition project but was the very source of the occult forces at the school. Was this notion of sci-ence simply a local (mis)understanding, or did it have something profound to say about the stories of modernity, religion, and Western rationality that continue to permeate projects of reform around the world? In an unex-pected detour through what has come to be known as the Scientific Revo-lution in Europe, one practitioner of African religions in Trinidad asserted the latter in the wake of the events at Rio Moro Secondary.

IMPLEMENTING OBEAH

As Rio Moro Secondary reopened its doors and students began attending classes again after the first spate of disturbances in 2010, the questions sur-rounding the place of obeah in the national imaginary continued to cir-culate. Particularly for those who practiced African-identified religions, the media representations of obeah connected with the school's closure dramatically illustrated just how strong the stigmas against African religion continued to be, despite the recent government recognition of Orisha and Spiritual Baptist groups (see Castor 2017) and the repeal of anti-obeah laws in 2000 (see Paton 2015). Even for some of those who did not practice African-identified religions, the salacious national images of demonic obeah provoked a reconsideration of Trinidad's much touted ethnic and religious tolerance.

It was in this atmosphere of debate that organizers of an arts and cultural center in the Barataria neighborhood of the densely populated working-class suburbs just east of Trinidad's capital, announced an evening of discussion on obeah. While the event was in honor of the birthday of LeRoy Clarke, a controversial patriarch of the visual arts in Trinidad, the timing of the forum on the heels of the media spectacle of Rio Moro's malevolent obeah was not coincidental. Clarke had openly professed to being an obeah man, also avowing that his art was a form of obeah (see Clarke 2001), and the theme of the event was intended to celebrate him by celebrating obeah. Yet the event also reflected an urgent call by the organizers to combat the negative representations of obeah that had been recently circulating in the popular media after the national coverage of the events at Rio Moro Secondary. The founders and contemporary organizers of the cultural center (Studio 66) had been participants in Trinidad's Black Power movement of the late 1960s and 1970s. After the Black Power Revolution of 1970 nearly led to the overthrow of Prime Minister Eric Williams's regime in Trinidad, the government violently suppressed the remaining armed elements of the movement (see Meeks 1999). Instead of armed resistance, however, a large number of Black Power participants, in the words of one of the movement's key leaders, "came to the traditional African religion as an act of political and ideological self expression" (Springer, qtd. in Henry 2003, 95). Black Power arguably shifted its emphasis in the 1970s from the seizure of national political power to the cultivation of Afrocentric religious and cultural sovereignty, contributing significantly to what has been called the "Orisha resurgence" in Trinidad (see Castor 2017; Henry 2003; McNeal 2011). Due to the strong Afrocentric and Black Power orientations of the organizers, Studio 66 was one of the few spaces in Trinidad where an event honoring both obeah and a self-proclaimed obeah man made perfect sense.

The final speaker, who preceded the address of LeRoy Clarke himself, was Burton Sankeralli, an Orisha devotee, self-published philosopher, educator, and *parang* singer. The title of his speech, "Implementing Obeah," was meant to parody a whole genre of documents, familiar to many in Trinidad, about "implementing" various neoliberal ideals (good governance, rule of law, austerity, transparency). Sankeralli's message for Trinidad and Tobago was that the country must work to implement obeah, and the tone of the talk in some ways echoed the Calypsonian Mighty Chalkdust's counsel that Trinbagonians, instead of implementing the neoliberal structural adjustment policies offered by "Washington" in the wake of falling oil prices in the 1980s, should "try obeah" as a political and cultural solution to the nation's socioeconomic ills (see Bilby 2012, 64–65). Similarly, Sankeralli held out hope of obeah as an effective response to these problems, one that was at once religious, economic, political, and philosophical.

Yet what exactly did "obeah" mean for those gathered at Studio 66 to celebrate the term? Most participants in the night's events offered Yoruba etymologies derived from the "obi seed" used as a tool of divination in Orisha, bringing obeah under the umbrella of the Yoruba-centric religion to which so many Black Power participants had turned. One other participant contested this definition by offering Igbo etymologies that traced obeah to a root meaning "doctor" or knowledgeable "scientist" — an etymology convincingly supported by scholarly revisions to the less-than-complimentary Ashante roots that British colonial observers had used to translate obeah as "witchcraft" (see Handler and Bilby 2001). Taking a different approach, Sankeralli answered the question of obeah's slippery contours by opening with a quote that he said provided what "appears to be a good definition of Obeah":

> For they have made me see that it is possible to arrive at knowledge which is most useful in life, and that, instead of the speculative philosophy taught in the Schools, a practical philosophy can be found by which, knowing the power and the effects of fire, water, air, the stars, the heavens and all the other bodies which surround us, as distinctively as we know the various trades of our craftsmen, we might put them in the same way to all the uses for which they are appropriate, and thereby make ourselves, as it were, masters and possessors of nature.

The author of this definition of obeah, Sankeralli revealed after reading the quote, was a person whom he referred to as the "first modern philosopher and one of the pivotal architects of modern science" — René Descartes. A few members of the audience of about one hundred people erupted into laughter. The year of the quote, Sankeralli revealed when the audience had quieted down, was 1637. Western Europe then was on the cusp of what in hindsight is called the Scientific Revolution (see Shapin 1996). Sankeralli told the audience that Europe was also on the threshold of a split between two kinds of philosophy, which he called "speculative" and "experimental" (see also Antsey 2005). For Sankeralli, Descartes's definition accurately showed how both obeah and Western science did not embody an alleged modern embrace of rationality—as Palmié (2002) argues—but a rejection of what he called "Aristotelian rationality and the Western philosophical tradition" in favor of "the occult tradition." The architects of the Scientific Revolution, in other words, embraced experimental practices with what Isaac Newton and other early modern natural philosophers would shortly thereafter call the "occult qualities of nature" (Hutchison 1982). As Sankeralli asserted, and as a number of historians have argued, the "new experimental philosophy" of early modern Europe was intimately bound up with what (to contemporary eyes) would be patently "occult" pursuits, such as Hermetic Neoplatonism, Rosicrucianism, verification of witchcraft, and alchemy (e.g., Darr 2014; Yates [1972] 2013). Modern science, in this occluded genealogy, represented not an embrace of rationality but an occult tradition that emerged, in part, from the Renaissance explosion of interest in the occult sciences and the subsequent compilation and mass printing of occult texts during and after the Enlightenment (Davies 2010; Yates 1964), a process that yielded many of the books that the students at Rio Moro Secondary were allegedly accessing via the internet. Such a rejection of speculative philosophy, based on the deduction from first principles or mechanical causation, and an embrace of an experimental natural philosophy that dealt with "occult qualities," Sankeralli asserted, was "obeah indeed."

In Sankeralli's occult genealogy, "science" seemed to be something almost entirely opposite to what many anthropologists and scholars of religion have thought it was. These scholars used a popular, scientistic notion of science as the demonstration of truth to either denigrate or redeem non-Western "magic." In the infamous and protracted "rationality debate" in anthropology—a debate that to some extent is still unfolding—scholars rejected Evans-Pritchard's (1937) assertion that "African witchcraft" was subjectively true and rational but (in contrast to Western science) objectively false.[17] Drawing on Austin's (1962) distinction between performative and constative utterances, Tambiah (1990) and Winch (1964) argued that such a characterization of magic was ethnocentric. Instead of being false, magic simply operated under radically different conditions of felicity than modern science. While modern science was about true-false statements and transparent matters of fact, magic was a performative and persuasive endeavor. To judge "non-Western magic" on the criteria of true-false distinctions, Tambiah argued, was to commit an act of ethnocentrism designed ultimately to shore up the authority of Western science. A long line of anthropologists had committed this error, according to Tambiah, leading to the notion that magic was like science while still ultimately remaining "bastard science."

What Sankeralli's occult genealogy of science showed, however, was that these anthropologists' notion of science as an arena of transparent facts might itself be subjectively true but objectively false. Certainly this simplified notion of science as the fetishization of facts would have been appealing to the early modern philosopher whom Sankeralli used to define obeah. As a mechanical philosopher, Descartes would have been no friend to the occult dimensions of nature (sometimes including witchcraft) that many architects of the Scientific Revolution wanted to investigate (see J. Henry 1986; B. Henry 2018; Lakatos 1978). Indeed, across the English Channel, Descartes's contemporary mechanical philosopher—Thomas Hobbes— opposed the new experimental philosophy of the Scientific Revolution precisely because he detested occult properties and wanted to limit natural philosophy to plainly observable forces and deduction from first principles (see Shapin and Schaffer 1985). Since the nineteenth century, popular ideas of science—as a realm of mechanical causation, absolute truth, and visible facts—have ironically sided with these antioccult enemies of the Scientific Revolution. This is the notion of science that anthropologists and scholars of religion have so often mobilized in making non-Western "magic" either pseudoscience or a performative speech act. In the former case, magic is pseudoscience because it is concerned with practical results but fails to produce facts; in the latter instance, magic is unlike science because it is not concerned with true-false statements. What goes unnoticed is that these opposing sides of the "rationality debate" both rely on a straw-man version of science that is patently antioccult. One might reasonably ask whether the practice of experimental sciences is simply about the demonstration of truths and the embrace of "modern rationality," or whether the comparison with obeah actually reveals some less commonsense relations of similarity and difference, pointing toward more nuanced accounts of the history of science and the practice of experimentation that Sankeralli or science studies scholars have offered.

Yet Sankeralli's choice of Descartes to describe obeah in some ways undermined his own argument. The idea that science/obeah was, in Descartes's words, a process of making humans "masters and possessors of nature" was actually reflective of an antioccult project, and it did not jibe with the views on science that spiritual workers expressed to me. Nor did it nec-

essarily describe the Scientific Revolution and the preoccupation with the
occult that Sankeralli referenced in Europe. The quote does, however, presage
the ideology of scientism and the close connection between triumphal ideas
of science as mastery and European projects of colonialism. As Sankeralli
continued his address, he drew on Descartes's promise that humans would
be "masters and possessors of nature" to assert that this vision of the "obeah
of science" had been first implemented in the Caribbean—the initial scene
of Europe's colonial mastery and possession. In the Caribbean, of course,
a process of enslavement coincided with the so-called Scientific Revolution and Enlightenment of Western Europe, and some of the best-known
Enlightenment gentlemen were economically invested in the slave trade
(see Buck-Morss 2000). Sankeralli thus seemed to echo Palmié (2002, 207)
in asserting that obeah and Western science share "a fundamental rationality" that is ultimately "a vehicle of reification," ruthlessly commodifying
labor and nature (Tambiah 1990, 146, qtd. in Palmié 2002, 203). If science
reflects this "witchcraft" of modern rationality, as Palmié (2002, 201–10)
insists, then negative views of obeah in the Caribbean (as a kind of malevolent science) thus represent a critique of science's dehumanizing instrumentality, which reached its dystopic extreme in the Atlantic slave trade.
In quoting Descartes's dream of mastery, Sankeralli seemed to echo Palmié
in reproducing the negative trope of instrumental magic or witchcraft to
define both obeah and science. Yet in these descriptions of a science/obeah
of mastery and possession, spiritual workers did not describe their ends as
ones of domination, enslavement, or economic rationalization. Rather, they
spoke about experimentation with forces that could not be totally subjected
to human intentions or rational calculation.

If obeah simply reflected the vicissitudes of the project of modernity—
as scholars have argued about so many dimensions of Caribbean culture
(e.g., James [1938] 2001; Mintz 1966, 1985, [1974] 1989; Scott 2004; Williams
1944)—then the question of obeah's lexical equivalence with science might
end there. Yet Sankeralli ended his manifesto for implementing obeah
with a very different notion of science and experimentation. Drawing on
twentieth-century philosophy of science, Sankeralli noted the similarities
between obeah and another dimension of experimental practice: "Now
there is a viewpoint in the philosophy of science called 'operationalism.'
It asserts that science does not really provide us with a priori facts about
reality, rather it is the 'operation' of the scientific experiment that estab-
lishes the data. Hence the 'reality' of science is, in reality, generated by its

operations. . . . Our obeah also exists in its operations, in its process, in the 'wuk' [work]."

In using the Trinidad English/Creole word "wuk," Sankeralli was gesturing toward something different than the rationalized labor that the word "work" often signifies. Unlike a Cartesian vision of mastery—in which natural forces or other humans will perform labor for Man—"wuk" in Trinidad signifies an embodied process of transformation that suspends the subjugation of the laboring body. Rather than commodified wage labor, "hard work" is a particularly vigorous or liberating form of dance associated with carnival. In Trinidad's English/Creole, "work" is also what most academics would call "religion" (Winer 2009, 971–72). The Orisha "religion," therefore, was often referred to as "the African work" or "the Orisha work" by my interlocutors, just as Spiritual Baptist practices were also known as work (see also Simpson 1970, 69; Warner-Lewis 1996, 94). "Work," of course, also signified obeah/science—"spiritual work." In this sense, obeah or science was not about the instrumentalization of laboring bodies or the transparent observation of facts but about transformative and embodied interventions—the "wuk" or "work" of experimenting with more-than-human powers. In Sankeralli's estimation, this "wuk" signaled "our ownmost obeah" rather than the negative image of obeah (and work) as rational instrumentality and mastery of inert bodies—a negative stereotype also closely associated with popular fantasies about "voodoo" and "zombification" (see Hurbon 1995; Mintz and Trouillot 1995). This "ownmost obeah" was the "wuk" that Sankeralli wanted to implement, and it questioned the idea that science was simply about the project of making humans the "masters and possessors" of nonhuman forces.[18]

CONCLUSION

To grapple with the long-standing lexical equivalence between obeah and science that has puzzled scholars, we need not make obeah into an idealized (or dystopic) image of Western science. On the one hand, in the triumphal image, science indicates proof, transparent observation, and mastery, dispelling superstitious beliefs and inchoate forces. Yet as feminist science studies and the philosophy of science have repeatedly shown, such an image of science falters during experimental practice, which necessarily happens in social contexts of power and involves active interference or "intra-action" rather than distanced observation (e.g., Barad 2007; Hacking 1983; Haraway 1991; Shapin and Schaffer 1985).

On the other hand, the often-dystopic image of science employed in popular and scholarly critiques is not much different from the triumphal image. Science is still about mastery, but the moral valence of this mastery is reversed. Rather than providing the knowledge to control productive forces for human benefit and imputed progress, science recapitulates a Western project of domination, economic rationalization, and exploitation. With both images of science, obeah is scientific only to the extent that it involves the conversion of humans and more-than-human powers into objects that one can manipulate. The idea that African religions make humans into manipulable objects is perhaps best exemplified by the pop culture image of the "voodoo doll," but this idea permeates both alluring and repulsive popular fantasies about Afro-Caribbean religious practices more generally (see Hurbon 1995).

Rather than recapitulating these popular narratives of science (and African religion), obeah or science reconfigures the assumptions on which these narratives rest. Was science simply about rendering inchoate forces into transparent phenomena that could then be managed, controlled, and calculated? Was non-Western "magic" similar to science (and unlike religion) because it sought that control but ultimately failed to achieve it? Prompted by the theories of spiritual workers and the afflictions of students at Rio Moro Secondary, this chapter has been an exercise in obviating these questions.

As Ashok first suggested when I inquired into the causes of the "possessions" at Rio Moro Secondary, science is an ethically ambivalent project that deals with occult powers rather than a practice that passively observes visible facts. Arguably, modern science and technology have multiplied the invisible forces that many people assume that they live with, from radiation and X-rays to electrons and Wi-Fi signals (Stolow 2008, 2013; Noakes 2019). For my interlocutors, the same was true of a twenty-first-century modernity in which transnational trafficking networks, sexual violence, the internet, and the invisible hand of neoliberal economics represented forces that threatened the body of the nation and the bodies of students without being directly visible. Just because these forces are not immediately observable to many humans does not mean that they are not real. Rather than a theology of an invisible and otherworldly God that opposes a science of worldly matters of fact, science/obeah intimates pragmatic practices of living with immanent invisibilities that have bodily effects. Coming to terms with the resonance between "obeah" and "science" in the anglophone Caribbean, means that neither obeah nor science can be placed on one side of a racialized and gendered divide of modernity and tradition. What gets called obeah, as previous chapters showed, is often about past violence that refuses to rest in the present. Rather than a project of moral reform that would keep such violence in the past, science/obeah means a confrontation with the opaque powers that afflicted the students at Rio Moro Secondary.

EPILOGUE

The Ends of Tolerance

In 2011, almost a year to the date after the first spate of disturbances at Rio Moro Secondary, the school closed its doors again as female students began, in the words of one teacher, to become "extremely violent and speak in different languages." This time, the department of education brought in a private psychological firm to provide long-term counseling to the students. Rather than simply diagnose the students as hysterical and call their talk of spiritual afflictions superstitious (as government psychologists had done a year prior), these psychologists admitted that they did not know exactly what they were treating and did not rule out a "spiritual" cause. Instead of presuming knowledge, the psychologists began a long-term process of talk therapy with the students—an approach that has thus far effectively stemmed school closures. This psychological intervention was something closer to what spiritual workers had advocated a year earlier: an open-ended process of inquiry into the students' afflictions that remained closer to their own experimental ethos of "trying the spirit" rather than simply exorcising it.

These disturbances and the therapeutic response did not make the sensational headlines that they had a year earlier. By that time in 2011 the national news cycle was dominated by the state of emergency that had been declared in the name of fighting crime. Instead of the afflictions of Rio Moro's obeah, newspapers carried stories about the implementation of martial law and the designation of certain areas as "crime hot spots." Still, African-identified religious practices were implicated in this news on the state of emergency. The curfew that was imposed on Rio Moro and other areas designated as crime hot spots effectively meant that the collective rituals of Orisha and the Trinidadian Kabbalah could not take place. These ceremonies happened during the night, and asking the spirits to show up during noncurfew daylight hours was not within the realm of possibility for practitioners. As the oldest living Orisha shrine leader in Trinidad—Leader Arthur—prepared to hold his annual feast, the police denied him the curfew permit that would have been required for Orisha ceremonies. Since a daytime Orisha feast was unthinkable within his grassroots Trinidadian sensibilities, Leader Arthur was forced to replace the four nights of homage to the Orishas with an afternoon Spiritual Baptist thanksgiving, in which offerings of fruits, drinks, and sweets were arrayed on his shrine's giant, cross-shaped Kabbalah banquet table.

I sat next to Leader Arthur that afternoon as he watched members of his shrine distribute the contents of the thanksgiving table to local children. He was seated in a large velvet-backed chair that had the appearance of a throne. Each of his fingers bore gold rings emblazoned with esoteric seals associated with Spiritual Baptist and Kabbalistic mysteries. As a threefold practitioner, his life spanned the three interrelated traditions of African-inspired religious practices on the island: he was a respected Orisha elder, a noted Kabbalistic operator, and a Spiritual Baptist leader. He said he felt happy to see the children getting fed, but he was more than a little vexed about his inability to hold his annual feast. He repeatedly told me that he wanted to show me his copy of the Trinidad and Tobago constitution, specifically its article guaranteeing freedom of religion. Originally drafted upon the country's political independence from Britain in 1962, the very first chapter of its first section promised, in the rights-based Enlightenment language that characterizes the opening sections of most contemporary constitutions, to protect "the freedom of conscience and religious belief and observance." Leader Arthur was intent on pointing out the contradiction between the denial of his ability to hold an Orisha feast and his constitutional rights, hoping I would publicize the injustice taking place.

The constitution, however, was in the upper floor of his home. Leader Arthur was suffering from the complications of type 2 diabetes, and doctors had recently amputated his right leg after gangrene had set in. With only one leg, Leader Arthur could not easily ascend the stairs to look for the document. He promised me that he would ask someone to look for the constitution and would have it ready to show me the next time I arrived. If the curfew and state of emergency were lifted by February, he was planning to hold a banquet (as collective spirit manifestation practices of the Trinidadian Kabbalah are called), and I promised to return before the start of the banquet to review the constitution's guarantee of religious freedom with him.

Leader Arthur would die before he could show me his constitution or attempt to celebrate another Orisha feast. If I had ever been able to review the document with him, and we had read past the list of rights that headline the constitutions of virtually all liberal democratic nation-states, we might have run into a contradiction that also characterizes most liberal regimes of constitutional rights and the rule of law. In the rather extensive third part of the constitution, titled "Exceptions for Emergencies," the document specifically states that the rights previously enumerated might be violated, suspended, or abridged for a potentially interminable time if the government declares that a "public emergency"—an "imminent threat" to public order and safety—exists.

On August 21, 2011, the government declared that Leader Arthur's community and other crime hot spots presented just such an "imminent threat," asking the nation to "sacrifice" for its redemption from "marauding groups of thugs" (Ramsaran 2013, 133). In the imaginary of the middle and upper classes, these "thugs" were most often associated with the crime hot spots where the government imposed its curfew and carried out its mass detentions—largely lower-class black areas, like Leader Arthur's neighborhood, where the police and armed forces used the emergency powers to round up over seven thousand detainees during the 2011 state of emergency (see Achong 2018; Ramsaran 2013; Wilson 2018). Leader Arthur's illustrious career in the field of African religions would thus end in an unresolved conflict between his legal rights to religious observance and their suspension in the name of preserving the rule of law and security. As a wide range of scholars have argued, it is this contradiction that characterizes contemporary liberal governance, enacted not as a war against a particular state but as amorphous, seemingly interminable, officially undeclared, and moral wars against terror, crime, or drugs, enacted under exceptional emergency powers.[1] These powers nullify constitutional rights, especially for immigrants, noncitizens, and religious and racial minorities.

As a practitioner of African-identified religions, this state of exception from basic rights was less than exceptional for Leader Arthur. He was old enough to remember the police breaking up Spiritual Baptist ceremonies and arresting congregants during Trinidad's period of the "Shouter prohibition ordinance" (1917–1951), and for most of his life obeah was illegal. These chapters have dwelled on this seeming impasse between constitutional rights and the rites of African-identified religions, which Leader Arthur faced throughout his life. In the seven years between Leader Arthur's aborted feast and the completion of this book, this impasse has proved no less salient. Obeah continues to signal practices that fall outside the boundaries of legal rights, even if it is recognized as a religion. In recent episodes from Antigua and Barbuda to Canada, intolerance against obeah has converged with the anticrime and anti-immigrant campaigns of security states. These recent episodes have brought me back to the central contradiction that Leader Arthur wanted to show me at his aborted Orisha feast—a contradiction that suggests some fundamental limits to liberal ideals of religious tolerance.

In late 2015, I received an email from a national news network in the Caribbean nation of Antigua and Barbuda, asking me to take part in a radio discussion on the recent arrest and deportation of three South Asian "Hindu priests" accused of practicing obeah (Crosson 2018). Colonial anti-obeah laws still remained on the books in Antigua and Barbuda, and the radio host informed me that the discussion would turn from the deportation of the South Asian nationals to contemporary efforts to repeal anti-obeah laws in the name of "freedom of religion." Indeed, the moderator began the program by asserting that critics of the recent arrests "were quick to say the move went against the freedom of conscience provided for in the constitution." These critics, however, were met by popular support for the arrests, with a former police commissioner answering such charges by claiming that "freedom of conscience" was limited to those who abided by the founding of the nation under "the supremacy of God." Such questions about the limits of religion, conscience, and freedom had sparked what the moderator termed a "region-wide debate, with the sides fiercely divided."

I thus prepared myself for a rather heated exchange, but as it turned out, all the participants seemed to agree that obeah should be decriminalized. These discussants included a British historian—Dr. Diana Paton—who had written on the cultural politics of obeah. Joining us from neighboring Jamaica, where efforts to decriminalize obeah were also sparking intense debate and opposition, were the Protestant reverend and author Dr. Devon Dick and the attorney and member of Parliament Tom Tavares-Finson. While we all agreed that obeah should be decriminalized, what seemed less clear was how to justify this decriminalization in terms of liberal secular values of the freedom of religion. For Devon Dick and Tavares-Finson, obeah's freedom seemed bound to its status as an "ancestral" and fundamentally

African religion, as they used the words "ancestral practice," "African system of beliefs," or "African spirituality" to campaign for obeah's freedom. It was unclear, however, how this freedom would apply to three non-African Hindu priests who, like a significant portion of Antigua's labor force, were foreign nationals with tenuous immigration status in a predominantly Afro-Caribbean, Christian nation. The British historian, in contrast, said she preferred to talk about "freedom of conscience" rather than "freedom of religion." She explained that she was reluctant to use the term "religion" because of the colonial conditions of religion's making and unmaking in the Caribbean. Indeed, in her published work, Paton argued that British colonialism had separated out certain subaltern religious practices as not-religion based on Western ideas about superstition, magic, or witchcraft (Paton 2009).

These categories of not-religion were the very words that Antiguans who supported the deportation of the "Hindu priests" used to characterize the men's practices as illegal obeah. The self-proclaimed charismatic Christian "activist group," known as the Movement, which had staged a protest at the South Asian priests' place of business a day before the arrests, called the men's fairly standard Hindu practices "witchcraft" or "necromancy," warning that such practices would attract "unwanted evil to the country" (Gordon 2015). In making these accusations, the Movement drew on the same neo-Pentecostal spiritual warfare theology that had been on display at Rio Moro Secondary, asserting that Christian nations and persons were threatened by an array of non-Christian and demonic spiritual entities in the twenty-first century (McAlister 2012, 2014; McCloud 2015). After the subsequent police raid of the three men's place of business the following day, the attorney general of the nation echoed this language of spiritual warfare, stating, "We do not practice black magic in Antigua and we are going to stamp that out. We are a Christian society and I want to applaud the Christian community which got together and have moved forward to stop this practice" (Gordon 2015). Rather than religion, the attorney general asserted these "Hindu priests" allegedly performed "witchcraft" or "black magic," rendering such practices infectious crimes rather than religious acts protected under Antigua and Barbuda's constitutional guarantees of the freedom of religion and conscience.

This episode showed once again how European ideas of not-religion have framed the long-standing intolerance toward obeah. Just a few weeks before the radio show, a political advertisement that had aired during Trinidad's national election season had driven this point home. The ad accused the Afro-Trinidadian candidate for prime minister of practicing obeah by

FIGURE 7.1. Still from an anonymous paid political advertisement, Trinidad, 2015.

pairing a distorted audio track of his voice with images of early modern European witches Sabbaths, spiritual oils, and severed animal heads (presumably the product of African rituals of animal sacrifice) (see Alphonso 2015; "Emancipation Group Condemns" 2015). In the face of this conflation of African-identified practices with European images of not-religion, it would seem that an important way to counter such intolerance would be to insist that obeah is, in fact, a religion (or, as Paton suggested, an expression of one's conscience). In theory, obeah would thus be entitled to some of the fundamental rights that liberal constitutions promise. This was the tack that the Jamaican respondents or the British historian took when they insisted that obeah should be protected as a matter of either conscience or religion.

Yet even when obeah has been recognized as religion, what gets called obeah can still remain exiled from these protections — an exile that has to do with the assumed limits of ethical conscience and religion proper. To take one recent example, Canadian courts in 2006 and 2013 ruled in favor of a police tactic of impersonating obeah practitioners to obtain criminal confessions, despite siding with expert witnesses in declaring that obeah was a religion.[2] While all the trial and appeals judges recognized that the use of religious consultations as criminal evidence would be "shocking" if they involved confessions to a Catholic priest, they insisted that the obeah in question was not a matter of ethical conscience and thus not "sincere" enough to be protected as religion.

The police tactic of impersonating an "obeah man" was inspired by a Jamaican-Canadian spiritual worker who himself volunteered to record one of his clients. A Jamaican-Canadian man named Marlon Rowe had asked this spiritual worker, who performed rituals in the back room of his religious-supply store, for spiritual protection from the authorities during a robbery of a Canadian bank in which he was about to participate. The spiritual worker agreed but told his client that if anyone was harmed during the robbery he would turn in the man and his accomplices to the police. During the robbery his client accidentally shot a bank employee to death, and the spiritual worker went to the police offering his assistance. The police asked him for permission to wiretap his phone conversations and place hidden microphones in his consultation room. The spiritual worker called Rowe promising to protect Rowe and an accomplice from both law enforcement and the affliction of the person's spirit who had been shot and killed. When Rowe and his partner showed up at the spiritual store, the spiritual worker told Rowe that he could help him only if he recounted the exact details of what had transpired at the bank. This account was recorded and was presented as evidence against Rowe and his accomplices in the subsequent trial.

To admit this evidence, however, the prosecution had to argue that the "obeah" in question was different from other religious practices, whose spiritual consultations would not be admissible as evidence. As the supreme court decision on the Rowe trial noted, "Indeed, if the police were to impersonate a priest or a lawyer, their conduct could well shock the community" and would be a "dirty trick" inadmissible as evidence (*Rowe v. Her Majesty* 2006, 4). Yet because obeah allegedly served immoral rather than sincere purposes, the protections did not apply. Invoking the crime of fraud that had been the basis of obeah's criminalization in the post-emancipation Caribbean, the Supreme Court decision insisted that "the relationship between the applicant [Rowe] and [the spiritual worker] was not grounded in religious belief but, rather, corrupt business practices, a desire to facilitate criminal behaviour and an ambition to evade police detection" (*Rowe v. Her Majesty* 2006, 5). While the court admitted that the spiritual worker "did use superficial trappings of religious ritual," the motivations for such rituals were supposedly immoral and insincere, thereby excluding these practices from the protections granted to exercises of religious conscience.

A detective sergeant involved in the Rowe investigation was impressed by the efficacy of obeah in extracting a detailed confession. Apparently this detective looked up "obeah" in the Merriam-Webster dictionary and found out that obeah was not a religion but a form of "sorcery" (*Her Majesty v. Welsh* 2013, 14). Based on this information, he decided that it would not infringe on constitutional and common law guarantees of the freedom of religion and conscience if a police officer would impersonate an obeah practitioner to extract incriminating evidence from citizens. In testifying about his design of the obeah operation, the detective sergeant made clear that "he would not use a similar operation for an established religion." In their December 2006 approval of the legality of using Rowe's confession to an "obeah man," the Supreme Court of Canada had seemed to agree with the detective sergeant. Despite expert testimony asserting that obeah was a religion, the court ruled that the participants in obeah themselves arrived to their "'altar' with dirty hands" (*Rowe v. Her Majesty* 2006). This obeah was "dirty" not because killing someone was wrong (the spiritual worker obviously thought that was not ethical), but because the court insisted that the obeah rites involved instrumental ends, such as profit or protection from the police. Certainly, Christian churches have often functioned as places to protect persons from the police or to generate the profits that sustain religious specialists, but this did not alter the fundamental distinction between the obeah in question and properly religious motives.

With the ostensible approval of Merriam-Webster's dictionary and the Supreme Court, the Peel Regional Police Department asked an officer of British Caribbean descent to impersonate an obeah man named "Leon" to obtain confessions from persons of Caribbean descent in the area. Acquiring information that the Jamaican-Canadian mother of a murder suspect in the area, Ms. Robinson, was a "believer in Obeah," this undercover obeah man intentionally got into a traffic accident with the mother to ingratiate himself with her. After the accident, he told her that he would pay for the damages and that he felt "a vibe" upon talking to her. Leon offered to protect her and her family from a "duppy" [spirit of the dead], telling her that her family was being afflicted by a murder victim, a well-known Middle Eastern–Canadian drug dealer who had been killed shortly after he murdered one of her family's closest friends. Police had previously obtained information that Ms. Robinson, who had been like a mother to the drug dealer's murder victim, believed that the spirit of the victim was haunting her, demanding justice for his death. After the "obeah man" told her that the recently deceased drug dealer was also haunting her, the police staged several other incidents to convince her of the undercover obeah man's powers and the affliction of the dealer's spirit. Officers placed a dead crow on the Robinsons' doorstep after the obeah man told her son that he had a vision of him as a black crow surrounded by a flock of white crows, suggesting that he was a black man surrounded by the largely white police officers of the "Babylon system." The appearance of a dead crow and a variety of other staged acts were supposed to convince the woman that the obeah man was protecting her from the racist "John Crow system" of state policing and criminal justice (Humphreys 2008).

In response to these manipulations and the suggestion of the obeah man, the mother arranged a private meeting for her son and his friends with the police officer who was posing as the obeah man. The "obeah man" spoke to the youths about the immense powers of "science" and "obeah," impressing upon them the need to confess exactly what they had done so that he could free them from the affliction of the notorious drug dealer's "evil spirit." The young men seemed reticent, so the police arranged for the mother to be detained. In a subsequent meeting, the obeah man told the youths that the spirit of the dead drug dealer could manipulate the "John Crow system" and persecute the mother relentlessly until they told him exactly how this man had died. Only with that information could he successfully free the woman from police detention—a woman who was the biological mother or "like a mother" to all of the youths. Reluctantly, the mother's son said that he had been present at the shooting and had watched it occur. In the process, he told the obeah man that the gun used in the murder had belonged to his family—that he had once "touched" the gun and that his mother had once cleaned the gun.

Based on the confession that they had once touched and cleaned the gun, both mother and son were charged as accomplices to first-degree murder. As with the Rowe trial, however, defense lawyers argued that the police use of a confession to an obeah man was a violation of freedom of religion, akin to using confession to a priest as evidence. The defense called on four expert witnesses, including two cultural anthropologists (one of whom had testified in the Rowe trial on the basis of her field research in Trinidad), a Christian ethicist, and a professor of theology, all of whom asserted that obeah was indeed a religion. The testimony of the police sergeant who had invented the undercover obeah idea and scripted much of Leon's performance suggested that he had some inkling that he was treading on constitutionally dangerous ground, possibly violating religious freedom protections. To nullify such concerns, he relied not simply on Merriam-Webster's dictionary but also on the popular distinction between religion as an ethical tradition and black magic as an evil or instrumental practice that the dictionary definition of "obeah" recapitulated. The sergeant thus avowed that he made the undercover officer impersonating the obeah man named "Leon" "pure evil, in that nothing that [the obeah man] was going to do was going to be for the good of the system" (it was unclear if he was referring to the racist "John Crow system" or some other system) (Humphreys 2008). Such "pure evil," included the obeah man telling Ms. Robinson that he would protect her son from imminent danger, promising the young men that he could get their mother out of jail, and paying for the damages police themselves had inflicted on Ms. Robinson's car. To further reinforce all this "evil," the obeah man wore part of a Dracula costume that police had rented from a costume store for his role, replaying a long-standing entanglement between popular horror entertainments and representations of African Caribbean religion (see Hurbon 1995). The sergeant in charge also made sure to remove any "religious symbols" from the obeah consultations. His notion of religious symbols was constrained to the emblems of so-called world religions, belying a legalistic understanding of what counts as sincere religious expression that has also played a central role in other religious freedom cases in the United States (Sullivan 2005). "My belief was that if I could remove [religious symbols]," the sergeant stated, "it would take away any sort of challenge that defense [lawyers] could bring up saying that it was religious" (Humphreys 2008).

To a certain extent, the police sergeant turned out to be correct. Still, the presiding judges in the original case and in the 2013 appeal, followed unanimous expert testimony in declaring obeah was a religion. While accepting that obeah was a religion, because of what judges called the broad and "ill-defined" nature of the category (*Her Majesty v. Welsh*, 2007, 2013), the trial court and the court of appeal found that any police infringement on the defendants' religious rights was "trivial" or "insubstantial" (Humphreys 2008). In fact, by declaring obeah a religion, the courts could avow that they were not discriminating against obeah or compromising what the trial judge called Canada's "multicultural mosaic" (Humphreys 2008). Nor did police, according to the court decisions, compel the defendants' participation in religious rites thus violating a key component of religious freedom guarantees (apparently detaining someone's mother or damaging someone's car to involve them in religious rituals were not sufficiently compulsive actions). One of the most crucial reasons the obeah in question did not qualify is that it was not a reflection of a "sincere spiritual purpose" or "sincere participation in a religious rite" (*Her Majesty v. Welsh*, 2007). As in the Rowe case, a sincere purpose was equated to "penance" or "redemption." The courts implied that the existence of a kind of obeah that would be sincere and properly religious was possible, but such obeah would have to be about the unburdening of an individual's moral conscience rather than an instrumental goal of protection from malicious spiritual and security forces.

These decisions meant that obeah could be protected only to the extent that it did not pursue instrumental goals, which in these cases involved spiritual protection from a racist policing system. The fact that Christian churches have often functioned as places of refuge from state security forces did not seem to matter. The division between instrumental magic and non-instrumental religion was still very much at play, and such a division had the power to decide whether Canadians of Jamaican descent (including a mother and her son) would be spending the rest of their lives in prison. The fact that obeah was, at least abstractly, a religion under a liberal regime of tolerance and multiculturalism actually strengthened the state's position. The division between instrumental black magic and moral religion still fell along the same racialized lines that have run through the case studies of this book, making the liberal toleration and protection of obeah impossible in practice.

These court cases effectively show that making obeah a religion did not mean that it would garner the rights and recognitions that liberal constitutions often bestow on that category. *Experiments with Power* has focused on these limitations of religious recognition, drawing on the language of spiritual workers to suggest some alternatives to this project. Instead of legitimizing obeah by arguing that it is proper religion, this book has placed the burden of legitimacy back onto the category of religion itself. While the past decades have witnessed an eruption of critiques of the modern category of religion—showing how it privileges immaterial belief over practice—the pious alternatives that these critiques have offered implicitly recapitulate the moral and racial limits of this category (e.g., Asad 1986; Hirschkind 2011; Jouili 2015; Mahmood 2005). Spiritual workers' theories of experimentation, power, work, and science suggest some alternatives to pious ethics as the means to address the continuing problem of religious intolerance—a problem that ultimately rests on the assumed limits of ethical conscience.

This problem, of course, is not limited to obeah or Afro-Caribbean religions. Islam, in particular, has become an emblem of illiberal religion in contemporary worlds—an example of what happens when religious conscience is not separated from violence and politics. Making a link between Islamophobia and antiblack racism, Yassir Morsi (2017) has recently drawn on the work of the Caribbean postcolonial theorist Frantz Fanon to reflect on the limits of tolerance and the burden of conscience for contemporary Muslims. In *Radical Skin, Moderate Masks*, Morsi argues that the West enacts a "second-order colonialism" through liberal ideals of tolerance—ideals that mask economic and political imperialism as the spread of democratic values (see also Asad 2007). Obligated to shed their "radical skin" and prove that they are tolerant and nonviolent, Muslims can be recognized by the West only as model pious subjects or moderate liberals. This second-order colonialism happens on the plane of ethics, as moral subjectivity is defined by the nonviolent mask of Western liberalism—a mask that promises to make religion into a matter of conscience and politics into a matter of consent. Morsi argues that this is how beauty, reason, and ethical value often continue to be qualities that subjects marked by racial and religious difference must prove rather than possess.

These assumptions about the limits of religious conscience, which have shaped intolerance for both obeah and Islam, were driven home to me in the contemporary United States, at the Texas state capitol, just a few blocks from where I currently teach. In 2017, a group of "Texas Muslims" converged on the capitol hill in Austin to hold a press conference and rally. Like the Hindu priests who faced Antiguan protesters opposing their religious practices as fundamentally against the principles of the nation, these US Muslims faced demonstrators who saw Islam as inimical to the national polity. One protester, who continued screaming anti-Muslim sentiments throughout the press conference, demanded to know what right these people had to be there when the capitol was not "a Muslim capitol." "You don't own this property," he asserted. "This capitol is for Texans and you are blocking the sidewalk."

Despite having an official permit for the press conference and despite proudly proclaiming themselves as both Texans and US citizens, the protesters excluded those Muslims who gathered that day from the national body. While such sentiments might seem absurd to some, the recent "Muslim travel ban" and episodes of Islamophobia, including mosque burnings in Texas, show that they are not absurd to a large number of US Americans. As we formed a human chain to block the anti-Muslim protesters from entering the press conference, one of them attempted to break through the lines. "Allah is a demon," he shouted, echoing the discourse of the spiritual warfare theology that played such an important role at Rio Moro Secondary, "and you all are controlled by demons." One of the women in the human chain got a bloody nose in the altercation, and she stood afterward with her head tilted toward the sky in the shadow of a Confederate cavalry general's statue. Organizers had expected eighty people to show up to form this human chain in solidarity with their Muslim neighbors; instead, over a thousand people, from the community at large and a largely liberal Christian "interfaith" action network, gathered to secure a perimeter with lines that were four to five persons deep. The handful of anti-Muslim protesters, one of whom was armed with a large automatic weapon, had to stay outside this perimeter by force of sheer numbers.

Religious liberalism and secular tolerance seem to be hopeful alternatives to these increasingly illiberal currents in contemporary worlds. They certainly seem better than the kind of intolerance espoused by some charismatic Christian movements in the Caribbean or those anti-Muslim protesters who stood outside our circle at the Texas capitol. As I wrote this epilogue, however, I realized I had been far too focused on (and angered by) this kind of glaringly illiberal intolerance to have brought critical scrutiny to what was more important for this book's arguments: the burden of recognition that made a protective circle of amenable difference possible. The imam who opened the ceremonies at the Texas capitol, for example, read not from the Koran but from a Rumi poem about mystical love, even as his recital was peppered by accusations of protesters outside the circle that Islam was a violent religion, beheading Christians and mutilating female genitalia. Repeatedly, the speakers at the press conference avowed that Islam was a "religion of peace" and that those gathered within the circle had nothing to do with the violent intolerance of "extremist" or "fundamentalist" Islam. Certainly, this was a disavowal that the white liberal Christians who formed a good part of the protective circle would probably have shared with respect to the "fundamentalist" branches of their own avowed religion.

The master of ceremonies closed the press conference by proclaiming that the Texas Muslims were proud to live in the greatest state in the greatest country in the world. As they systematically disavowed the right of "true Islam" to enact any form of political violence (or, I would assume, resistance to the greatest country in the world's violent imperialism), the speakers at the press conference distanced what Saba Mahmood (2003b, 2006) has called "liberal Islam" from "radical" or "fundamentalist" Islam. As Mahmood (2003b, 2006) notes, in the era of the War on Terror, liberal Islam has become a focal point for efforts to reconcile Islam with liberal democratic values. Yet this process of reconciliation, she argues, travels in only one direction, with Islam expected to prove its compatibility with Western modernity and show that it is a tolerant, nonviolent religion. Western secular states and liberal regimes of tolerance, however, are far from nonviolent projects themselves, and Mahmood (2003b) asks what it might mean to bring the resources of Islamic theology and political history to bear on the ideals of Western liberalism. Bringing the theories of spiritual workers to bear on these ideals has been the work of *Experiments with Power*. Rather than providing an image of pious ethical practice to counter obeah's association with violence, I have questioned the very idea that religion (or science) can be innocent of violence in a world of injustice.

As these episodes of intolerance toward obeah and Islam suggest, the burden of proving that one is a citizen of good conscience falls on immigrants and religious minorities, rather than on intolerant Christian political movements in the Caribbean and the United States. Under this burden of proof, obeah is tolerable religion only to the extent that it is about making ethical subjects rather than intervening in the criminal justice system or protecting clients from the police. In a similar way, obeah becomes legible as "ethno-science" to the extent that its practices of healing and herbal medicine can be separated from the power of spiritual forces to make retributive justice. Driving a wedge between the legitimate use of force and religion has been the central act of liberal secularism since the Enlightenment and the aftermath of the Reformation's "Wars of Religion."[3] Unfortunately, it remains painfully obvious that activities recognized as religion in the United States and Europe are still entangled with violence. Rather than revealing contradictions within the project of Western liberalism, this apparent failure of liberal secularism to separate religion from violence can be projected onto the fanaticism and superstition of others.

The result of these limits of liberal secular tolerance is not simply invectives against the excesses of (not-)religion (i.e., fanaticism or superstition), but also a redemptive notion of what good religion really is. When scholars have defended religion against post-Reformation charges that it is a root cause of conflict, they have often dismissed the idea that religious formations might actually be inextricable from questions of violence as a myth (e.g., Armstrong 2015; Cavanaugh 2009; Phan and Irvin-Erickson 2016). Some scholars have sought to defend religion from these charges of violent extremism by offering a hopeful image of ecumenical tolerance, inspired by US religious liberalism and "the spiritual potentials of American democracy" (Kripal 2007, 10; Schmidt 2012). Whether implicitly or explicitly, these redemptive projects of religious liberalism seek to counter both a peculiarly American religious conservativism (see Hedstrom 2007; Schmidt 2012) and Anglo-American invectives against religion as a socially conservative force (e.g., Dawkins 2006; Hitchens 2007). These redemptions of liberal religion, however, implicitly reproduce the same limits of tolerance that condemnations of illiberal others explicitly display. The good kind of religion reflects liberal democratic values and promotes tolerance, redeeming religion from violence.[4] Rather than an assertion of power, religion, to quote one popular academic definition, is a special domain that "intensif[ies] joy and confront[s] suffering"—even as the example used to support this definition is, by the author's own description, the practice of Cuban American Catholic devotion as an antisocialist, procapitalist project that will help to oust the Cuban government (Tweed 2006, 167–68).

Taking a more critical approach, Winnifred Sullivan (2005) has suggested that liberal dreams of religious freedom are impossible, precisely because they require the separation of tolerable religion from intolerable notreligion (the same separation that undergirded obeah's criminalization). This, indeed, was the separation that made Diana Paton hesitant to use the phrase "freedom of religion" on the Antiguan radio show. Sullivan, however, continues to draw on the ideals of liberalism to propose her alternative to such impossibility, providing a rather libertarian solution. Instead of protecting religion, secular law should protect "the right of the individual, every individual, to life outside the state—the right to live as a self" (Sullivan 2005, 159). She suggests that this individual right (which sounds similar to the paradoxical idea that secular law must secure a place outside of state power for a privatized essence of religion) "may not best be realized through laws guaranteeing religious freedom but by laws guaranteeing equality." She thus upholds the central premise of liberal equality and universal human rights, of which the freedom of religious belief or "conscience" is but one example. From the US Declaration of Independence to the Universal Declaration of Human Rights, the premise of these proclamations is the sanctified freedom of a rights-bearing individual who is "born free and equal." In these reckonings, regimes of law are supposed to provide a place for the individual (and their conscience) outside of coercive power. Yet the reach of any regime of law is based on coercive power, making liberal dreams of systems of law (and religion) that transcend such power an impossibility.

Perhaps, in contrast to the fundamental premise of liberalism, human beings are not born free and equal; they are born profoundly unequal subjects with varying abilities to assert rights, and it is collective assertions of sovereignty—which must intimate the possibility of force, even if this show of force is avowedly "nonviolent"—through which rights are made. By replacing liberal values of freedom, natural rights, and equality with a focus on power, we can begin to see how ideals of "sincere" religion remain embedded in certain liberal values that continue the work of Reformation on different terms. To do the normative work of religious liberalism—to redeem Islam or obeah by separating "liberal Islam" from "political Islam" or obeah from harm—observers have made these forms of action into morally univalent practices of spiritual reverence divorced from coercive power. As I have argued throughout this book, such excisions perform a kind of redemptive work in which obeah can become (the right kind of) religion. Like any justice-making practice, however, the potential to enact some form of harm is a part of obeah's power.

For my interlocutors in Rio Moro, law, religion, and science were quite clearly about the ambivalent exercise of power. The police shootings at Number Twenty-One Junction and the state of emergency that followed shortly thereafter showed how state law exerted its power by nullifying the constitutional rights of certain individuals (chapters 1–3). The "demonic possessions" at Rio Moro Secondary showed how the science blamed for these events was about hard-to-perceive power rather than transparent facts (chapter 6). Religion itself, for spiritual workers, is devoted to "powers"— more-than-human forces, whether Orishas or the Holy Spirit, that manifest in human bodies. "Catching power" is thus a synonym in Trinidad for what scholars have called "spirit possession." For spiritual workers, power is not simply something held by authorities and resisted by people. Power also flows through persons, and more-than-human power has to be "manifested" or "caught" in embodied forms rather than solely existing in disembodied and transcendent heavenly beings. In this reckoning, "religion" is no different from other categories through which rights are claimed; it is made and unmade through performative acts of sovereign power. While Western political theology has tended to locate such power in transcendent entities (whether God, a head of state, or the law), African religions in Trinidad show how sovereign power is continually performed and worked in embodied experiments (see also Singh 2012).

The three "Hindu priests" in Antigua and the Texas Muslims faced performances of sovereignty in spiritual warfare that placed them outside the limits of nation, citizenship, and religion. These practices of Christian spiritual warfare in contemporary worlds dramatically illustrate how political and religious force converge in the embodied occupation of space. Employing a standard monotheistic distinction between religion (as piety that places sovereign power in the hands of God) and magic (as practices in which humans wrongfully assume such sovereign power), it would be easy enough to condemn charismatic spiritual warfare as the superstition it opposes. Such circular antisuperstition invectives remain wed to a mono-theistic political theology, which imagines sovereign power to reside in the Lord and the law alone (see Singh 2012). Certainly, some residents of Rio Moro asserted that only the state and the law could rightfully wield the sovereign power to make justice, and Pentecostal spiritual warriors in Rio Moro insisted that such power (at least in theory) could reside only with the Christian God (see chapters 3 and 6). While recognizing the power of God and state law, spiritual workers suggested that justice was made through em-bodied and agonistic experiments, presenting a different political theology of power. Yet it was not simply African-identified spiritual work that unset-tled the assumptions about sovereign power contained in much Western po-litical theory (and theology); the practice of any religion is involved in con-tests of power that take place through embodied performances. Substantive distinctions between good religion and bad (not-)religion miss the point, reproducing the moral and racial distinction that continues to undergird notions of proper piety and the exclusion of obeah from constitutional rights.

Alternatives to this language of exclusion, however, already exist. This book has focused on the theories of grassroots spiritual workers as a par-ticularly vital example of such an alternative. Spiritual workers described their practices using terms—like "power," "science," "work," and "obeah"—that have often been opposed to or excluded from a moral domain of reli-gion in Western modernity. At a different level of society, artistic repre-sentations of obeah in the Caribbean have also sought to find a language for religious practice that does not dispense with power. Directly refuting Tweed's (2006) definition of religion as that which "intensif[ies] joy," the avowed obeah man and Afro-Trinidadian visual artist LeRoy Clarke has bluntly stated that his work, and obeah itself, "is revolution; it's not about pretending at making you happy" (qtd. in Best 2019). Calypsonians and soca artists, most particularly Shadow and Bunji Garlin, have also worked to rep-resent obeah in a way that is neither derogatory nor dressed up as "good" religion.[5] As Clarke's comments suggest, obeah might be better understood as a "revolution" that inverts relations of power rather than a palliative prac-tice of healing or religious devotion that simply aims to make people happy.

As protesters occupied crossroads in Rio Moro after Arlena's death, chanting about and performing obeah, religious practice was quite obvi-ously about the assertion of some form of power that could invert an en-trenched state of affairs, punishing, protecting, and making justice. What remained subject to debate was whether this sovereign power was prop-erly located only in the hands of the Lord and the law or whether spiritual workers and the dead had a part to play. When a high-profile lawyer visited the protesters at Number Twenty-One Junction, urging them to stop blocking the roads, he assured them that a belief in "the rule of law" would lead to justice (see chapter 1). Other residents urged spiritual workers to leave justice in the hands of God and to desist from "obeah" (see chapter 3). In many cases, it remains useful to employ a conception of religion in which power is transcendent and law-giving. Yet such a focus on religion as a system of ethical injunctions and rules administered by a transcendent sovereign can never dispense with experimental situations of power in which norms are broken, overturned, and inverted. These were the situations that spiritual workers faced when a client sought justice for a loved one killed by police or when a police officer sought out protection from a vindictive superior.[6] Such situations called for the overturning of normal relations through experiments with power.

While the high-profile lawyer who visited Number Twenty-One Junction insisted that a belief in "the rule of law" would lead to justice, seven years after Arlena's death, as I write this epilogue, the jury trial against the police officers had yet to begin—the indictments for murder had not even been filed. When Bishop Dawes had justified his experiments with power to seek justice for Arlena's death at the hands of police, he kept reminding me how slow the justice system was in Trinidad. "It takes years," Bishop Dawes had told me, justifying his spiritual work in response to Arlena's death as an action that the unresponsiveness of the state justice system necessitated. The length of such trials in Trinidad, as Dawes had noted, meant that there was time for evidence to be lost and witnesses to get killed (the murder of witnesses has been a fairly well-established pattern over the last two decades in Trinidad). Indeed, one witness to the police ambush of Arlena and her two friends at Number Twenty-One Junction was shot and killed a few months before I started writing this, although police said the death was unrelated to the criminal trial. After alleged attempts on her life, the officer involved in the killings who turned state witness has had to live in a safe house for years waiting for the trial to start. My friends in Rio Moro say that the officer still goes mad periodically, haunted by the dead who she watched her colleagues kill point-blank.

In the meantime, the torpor of criminal justice has meant that legal efforts have turned toward civil suits. The high-profile lawyer who had urged protesters in Rio Moro to stop blocking the roads after the deaths of Arlena and her friends, promising to secure justice under "the rule of law," has filed a wrongful death suit on behalf of the families. Under the Compensation of Injuries Act, the attorney has asked for about US$700,000 in damages from the state (to be divided between the three families of the victims after legal costs). One of the accused police officers, represented by another high-profile lawyer, has brought his own civil suit against the state for the trial delay. As litigation turns from criminal to civil charges, the only certainty about the trial is that lawyers will be working on the case for some time.

Perhaps the families of the victims, the police, and the lawyers will all receive compensation for the shortcomings of the criminal justice system (and perhaps this is how that system is supposed to work). Yet as Papoy's daughter Giselle reminds me when we talk on the phone this week, monetary compensation cannot address what happened at Number Twenty-One Junction. "No amount of money can't bring back the dead," she tells me when I ask her about the civil suit, sucking her teeth with disdain.

While no compensation could bring a loved one back to life, the dead were still present for many people in Rio Moro. As Bishop Dawes and other spiritual workers experimented with power to keep the dead around, they intimated the justice-making force of what most people would call obeah. Even if state law would fail, family members asserted that this obeah would still take its course, enacting affliction in the name of justice.

From eighteenth-century slave rebellions to these contemporary responses to police brutality, obeah has been associated with the use of force to enact justice. This association has often been the basis for obeah's exile from the category of religion under regimes of religious tolerance and continues to justify the policing of obeah within and beyond the Caribbean basin. In response to similar invectives against Islam and forms of "extremist" religion in the twenty-first century, scholars have often defended (true) religion as a matter of piety and ethics, whose relationship to violence is incidental or reformatory (see chapters 1 and 3). Rather than defending obeah as a matter of piety or framing spiritual work as an ethical tradition, *Experiments with Power* has questioned the very idea of religion that tacitly underlies such a defense. In contemporary contexts of police brutality, spiritual warfare, martial law, and the security state, the theories and practices of Afro-Caribbean spiritual workers offer us alternative conceptions of religion and ethics. Describing their own justice-making practices as "work," "science," and "experiments with power," my interlocutors unsettled the moral and racial foundations of the category of religion, using words that have so often signified the opposite of religion in Western understandings. This reframing of religious practice as experimental provides a new basis for critiquing the limits of religion in liberal secular nation-states.

From Antigua and Trinidad to Canada and Texas, assumptions about these moral and racial limits of religion continue to have profound consequences for African-identified spiritual workers. The case studies of *Experiments with Power* have shown how these boundaries have undergirded the distinctions between religion proper and "black magic," structuring racial discourse and juridical rights from the Enlightenment to the present. Understanding religion as a race-making category means confronting these often-unspoken limits, and the theories of spiritual workers provide a means by which to experiment with other possibilities for conceiving of religious practice in contemporary worlds.

NOTES

INTRODUCTION

1. Throughout this work I use "Trinidad and Tobago" to refer only to the political and administrative formation of the twin-island nation-state. Because Trinidad and Tobago have different historical, religious, security, and racial contexts, I refer to "Trinidad" alone as my field site rather than conflating the two islands.

2. Motivations for the 2011 state of emergency remain contested. Labor leaders, among others, accused the government of imposing the state of emergency (which effectively outlawed public protests) to suppress a planned general strike by unions and growing unrest in the country (with the demonstrations in Rio Moro inaugurating a series of protests on various issues). Another popular theory noted that a relatively large quantity of cocaine had been seized by authorities at Trinidad's airport immediately preceding the state of emergency. In this story, the government called the state of emergency to preempt retaliation by those invested in this cocaine, which was often alleged to be an unnamed "Mexican cartel." Still others noted that the state of emergency was an ineffectual distraction intended to make the government appear to respond to Trinidadians' number-one issue of public concern—crime. If the government was really concerned about crime, these theorists insisted, they would pursue the "big fish" in charge of drug trafficking—in this case Trinidadian elites allied with the political class. These economic elites moved large quantities of cocaine in container ships. The logic of this explanation was expressed to me by using a popular metaphor about power that referenced pescatarian consumption—"small fish bone don't chook [stab, poke] hard." In other words, going after the "small fish"—lower-class black men with little economic or legal power—was a politically expedient way of appearing to address crime while leaving the "big fish" (whose bones did chook hard) uneaten. Certainly, the official rhetoric of the state of emergency as an exercise in fighting crime should be taken with a grain of salt. Political and economic motivations had some part to play, and the 2011 state of emergency was part of a much longer history of violent state interventions in lower class black communities in Trinidad.

3. On extrajudicial killings or levels of police impunity in Trinidad and Tobago, see Am-

nesty International (2012); Samad (2011); Scott (1986); Seaby (1993); and Welcome (2018).

4. For a detailed account of obeah's contested West African etymology, see Handler and Bilby (2001).

5. On the slippage between rights and rites in Trinidad, see Khan (2007).

6. Obeah has been decriminalized in Anguilla (1980), Barbados (1998), Trinidad and Tobago (2000), and St. Lucia (2004) but remains illegal in much of the region. Recent calls for the decriminalization of obeah in Jamaica as well as Antigua and Barbuda have met with considerable opposition, which argues that obeah is sinful, anti-Christian, and potentially damaging to national welfare (see Crosson 2018). In 2013, when Jamaica removed flogging as a punishment for obeah in order to sign the UN Convention against Torture, it left the criminal status of obeah untouched (Paton 2015). In Jamaica, however, there are ongoing efforts toward decriminalization, although they have achieved no lasting juridical success (see Crosson 2018).

7. All names of persons, excluding television personalities and national political figures, are pseudonyms throughout this book. This is in deference to the wishes of many of the spiritual workers I know, who do not want to be public figures (for an ethnography of more public forms of African religion in Trinidad, associated with post '70s Yoruba-centric reform movements, see Castor 2017). The names of places in Trinidad, apart from the capital city, are all pseudonyms. Identifying details in events of police brutality and spiritual work have been omitted or altered to respect the confidentiality of spiritual workers' clients and the legal integrity of ongoing court cases.

8. As in Afro-Cuban religion, networks of spiritual kinship often knit together grassroots practitioners in Trinidad in ways that exceeded Western conceptions of kin. A leader who initiated and mentored devotees thus became a spiritual "father" or "mother" to these devotees who became their spiritual children.

9. In Haitian Vodou, for example, Ogou represents a family of *lwa* whose characteristics resonate with Ogun in Trinidadian Orisha, Ogún in Cuban Santería, or Ogum in Brazilian Candomblé. There are, however, differences among the various manifestations of Ogun, Ogum, and Ogou. In Trinidad, the various types of Ogun are far less varied than in Haiti, with a principal Ogun (often associated with the Catholic St. Michael) and a lesser-known "Kongo Ogun" (often identified with St. George according to my interlocutors). For more on the proliferation of Ogun in the Americas and Africa, see Barnes (1997).

10. The majority of South Asian laborers hailed from Bhojpuri-speaking regions of north-central India, which were suffering from a famine induced by the British colonial disruption of irrigation networks in the nineteenth century. Indentured-labor schemes initially included large numbers of West and Central African, Chinese, and Portuguese Madeiran populations. Indentured-labor schemes in Trinidad lasted from 1834 to 1917.

11. Indo-Trinidadians identified as Hindus were arrested for obeah in Trinidad (although at a lower rate than those identified as African-descended persons) (Paton 2015). As I have discussed elsewhere (Crosson 2018), Hindu icons continue to occasion accusations of obeah in the present-day Caribbean. The historian Alexander Rocklin (personal communication, May 5, 2018) has also said that representations of the Virgin

Mary sometimes formed part of obeah accusations (although parallels with Catholicism were also a common part of defendants' attempts to legitimate their practices as "religion" rather than obeah).

12. For critiques of a "Protestant bias" toward belief and against materiality, see Hirschkind (2011); Houtman and Meyer (2012); Meyer (2015, 165–66); Morgan (2010); Ritchie (2002); Vásquez (2011, 214). For well-known works that have focused on piety, shared norms of tradition, and ethical subject making as an alternative to this bias, see Asad (1986); Hirschkind (2006); Jouili (2015); and Mahmood (2005). For more recent work that has critiqued this "pious turn" by emphasizing the importance of disagreements about ethical codes or the strategic circumvention of ethical norms in "everyday" practice, see Beekers and Kloos (2018); Laidlaw (2014); and Mayblin (2017).

13. It is important to note, however, that there are some cultural activists in Trinidad who publicly identify with the term "obeah," particularly within the Yoruba-centric circles of post-1970s Ifa lineages that Castor (2017) describes. The intellectuals and artists who have publicly championed obeah (namely LeRoy Clarke and Burton Sankeralli) have also used terms other than "religion." "Philosophy," "science," "work," and "art of the way to being" are some examples of the alternatives that these cultural activists have employed to describe obeah (see Best 2019; Clarke 2001; Sankeralli 2008, 2010). Certainly these urban Trinidadian reformers hailed from different class, educational, and geographical locations than did my grassroots interlocutors in southern Trinidad. Perhaps for this reason, they remained less reticent about identifying with a term that could tarnish one's respectability. They also had a tendency to conceive of obeah as a valuable cultural tradition rather than a problematics of power, leading to less ambivalent attitudes than those of my grassroots interlocutors. Nevertheless, the descriptions of obeah that these urban practitioners of African religions offered resonated (at least in some ways) with grassroots spiritual workers' theories of experimentation and science, calling attention to the limits of conventional notions of religion. For more on intellectuals' and artists' public avowals of obeah in the environs of Trinidad's capital city, see chapter 6 and the epilogue. It is important to remember that these cultural elites' attitudes did not necessarily reflect popular opinion in regard to obeah.

14. I draw the term "not-religion" from Rocklin (2015) and Sullivan (2005). I use the term to connect Rocklin's sense of the colonial making and unmaking of religion with Sullivan's sense of the separation of religion from not-religion under contemporary juridical regimes of "freedom of religion." Instead of "not-religion," I often use the term (not-)religion to indicate how polemics about witchcraft or superstition can often be applied to forms of bad religion or (in "new atheist" critiques) to all religion. The line between the category of religion and what it disavows is thus perspectival and shifting.

15. Obeah, according to British accounts, was allegedly used to seal rebel oaths and protect rebels in battle (see Lazarus-Black 1994a; and Handler and Bilby 2012).

16. This denial of moral citizenship to lower-class black Trinidadians could exceed the dominant lines of race (African versus Indian) and religion (Hindu versus Christian) in Trinidad. These invectives, as Forde (2018) or James ([1963] 2005) has posited, allowed nonwhite middle-class persons to distance themselves from negative colonial ideas of blackness. Middle-class persons identified as African or Indian, however, might enact

this distancing in different ways, reflecting the legacies of colonial racial ideas about different laboring populations and the degree to which they possessed religion, civilization, or amenability to Christian conversion (see Khan 2004a, 2004b; Munasinghe 1997, 2001; Rocklin 2019; Segal 1993). Since the 2011 state of emergency, these moral-racial discourses and support for the violent policing (or simple extermination) of lower-class black communities have continued to shape notions of who belongs to the nation and who is fully human. As Leniqueca Welcome (2018) has shown, when police shot an unarmed young man in the environs of the capital in 2018, many middle-class Afro-Trinidadians condemned community protests against the police shootings, inveighing against the protesters' alleged lack of moral discipline and productivity. During a recent research stay in Trinidad (in 2018–2019), the "African party" was in power, and national news headlines were dominated by the celebrated (and critiqued) shoot-to-kill policy of the government's recently appointed police chief (also a prominent member of the "African party") (see Hassanali 2019).

17. The most infamous example is a Ferguson police officer's description of Michael Brown as a demon (see Feldman 2018; Thomas 2014). On current violence against African religions in Brazil, see "Luto na Luta" (2017); and Roeder (2019). On the ways that ideas of "voodoo" as bloodthirsty and demonic have justified US military incursions in Haiti, see Hurbon (1995).

18. Originally attached to New Orleans and US black populations, representations of "voodoo" as threatening gained wide cultural salience in the United States during and after the US marines' occupation of Haiti (1915–1934). The leaders of a peasant resistance to the occupation and its regimes of forced labor were represented as "voodoo priests," prone to violence and cannibalism. In West Africa popular ideas of African traditional religion as malevolent play a central role in popular entertainment. Throughout this text I use the spelling "voodoo" to denote these popular fantasies while using "Vodou" to refer to the transnational Haitian tradition. For more on these issues, see Bilby (2012); Flesher (2006); Guerts (2002); Hurbon (1995); and Paton (2009, 2015).

19. In Trinidad, "manifestation" refers to what scholars have generally called "possession" or "trance." The word "possession" in Trinidad specifically refers to intrusive forms of spirit embodiment that call for exorcism, whereas "manifestation" refers to cultivated embodiments of spirit (see also McNeal 2011).

20. On the relationship between religious traditions and violence as baseless or incidental, see, e.g., Armstrong (2015); Crockett (2006); and Phan and Irvin-Erickson (2016). For work that focuses on "the pious Muslim," representing Islam as a matter of ethical subject making, see Asad (1986); Hirschkind (2011); Jouili (2015); and Mahmood (2005).

21. McNeal (2011, 253–58) provides a very different account of the place of liberalism in the Caribbean, arguing that the capitalist and individualist tenets of liberalism have seeped into the central principles of African-inspired religions in Trinidad. Building on Burton (1997), he argues that spirit mediumship in Afro-Caribbean religions recapitulates an orientation to the self as property and an experience of hierarchical political power. Elsewhere, I critique this use of possessive individualism as the frame for understanding the experience of spirit manifestation in the African diaspora (Crosson 2017a, 2017b). Although it is not a useful emic category for understanding manifesta-

tion in Trinidad, possessive individualism is useful for understanding scholarly notions of spirit possession (as the abject other of possessive individualism in Western thought) (see also Johnson 2011, 2014b).

22. Castor (2015) argues that the Hindu government recognized African religions, in part, to open a space for non-Christian religious forms on the national political stage, thus weakening Afro-Creole Christian hegemony.

23. The 2001 report by the government of Trinidad and Tobago to the United Nations on human rights achievements thus reads, "The Government in addition to enacting Equal Opportunity legislation has passed a Miscellaneous Laws (Spiritual Reform) Act, 2000 in an effort to decriminalize existing provisions of Trinidad and Tobago's statute law, which have been identified as discriminatory, in that they hampered the freedom of the Shouter Baptist and Orisa Baptist [sic] religious groups in the practice of their religions. This legislation amends the Summary Courts Act to remove references to 'obeah' and the offence of the 'practice of obeah'" (United Nations 2001).

24. In my reckoning, one reason that the Trinidadian Kabbalah is also known as Circle Work is because of the circular "seals" that are so important to its practice and which are often inspired by diagrams from popular *grimoires* (spell books) (see, e.g., fig. 6.2). These seals, however, are also important in the practices of grassroots Orisha and Spiritual Baptist practices, serving as designs that prepare offering tables, invoke spiritual powers, or protect clients and spiritual workers (fig. 0.4).

25. Mansions are understood not as "rooms of a house," the single units that make up a collective, but as complex entities in their own right. In a similar way, the Rasta phrase "I and I" (as a substitute for "we" or for the human-divine assemblage of the individual) expresses a nonreductive, multiple collective. A group of divine I's cannot be reduced to a singular we, and the individual cannot be reduced to a singular I. I do not know if Deleuze and Guattari ([1972] 2000, [1980] 2007) had any interaction with African diasporic religious thought, but their use of the assemblage (*agencement*) expresses a somewhat resonant idea of a nonreductive collectivity (on this point see note 73).

26. Houk (1993, 46) speculates that this practice was brought to the Caribbean by European colonizers and/or Sephardic Jews who were Kabbalists. He supports this theory by asserting that the Kabbalah is known as "white man's magic" in Trinidad. Staying closer to what the masters in that tradition have told me, the Kabbalah derives, to a good extent, from the secrets of King Solomon. Solomon and the Queen of Sheba are the progenitors of the Ethiopian Orthodox Christian church. Solomon (importantly, also the central figure in Freemasonry) thus leads back to East Africa and ultimately (for practitioners in Trinidad) to ancient Egypt, with the Papyrus of Ani (i.e., *The Egyptian Book of the Dead*) being a central text in the Trinidad Kabbalah. The grimoires (spell books) that circulated widely in the Caribbean for at least the past century also purport to reveal Kabbalistic secrets (although I do not think many contemporary practitioners of the Jewish Kabbalah would recognize them as central parts of that tradition). The most popular of these books in Trinidad, *The Sixth and Seventh Books of Moses*, uses the word Kabbalah to describe the "Hebrew" magical arts of Moses that the text purports to reveal. Other popular grimoires in the Trinidadian Kabbalah tradition purport to reveal Solomon's magical arts (i.e., *The Greater and Lesser Keys of Solomon*). The origin of

the tradition in Trinidad is not with "white men" (although this might be a lay interpretation) but with ancient Egypt and the "Hebrew" magical arts that allegedly emerged from that African tradition (especially through the figures of Moses and Solomon). I have also heard Kabbalah used in Jamaica to refer to this esoteric tradition, albeit much less frequently than in Trinidad.

27. In the early 1960s, in one of the first sustained academic studies of Shango (as practices of Orisha devotion were then known in Trinidad), George Simpson notes the importance of "mourning" practices (see McNeal 2011, 225). In contemporary grassroots Orisha shrines, it was often the case that *chapelles* (the enclosed rooms that held the Orishas' implements) also served as "mourning rooms" (the chambers where blindfolded spirit travel and relative physical isolation took place). Practices of blindfolded spirit travel were also central to the Trinidadian Kabbalah or Circle Work in my experience.

28. The "Spiritual Lands" is an umbrella term that encompasses the tripartite cosmology of the Depths, the Nations, and the Heights (see Zane 1999).

29. To "put a light [candle] in she ass" or to "put a light [candle] on she," for example, were common euphemisms for working obeah on someone in Rio Moro.

30. A *cocoyea* broom is an implement made out of bundled internal shafts of palm leaves. It is a common house-cleaning implement in Trinidad, but it is also a ritual implement in Trinidad Orisha practice, associated with a few different powers (most notably Shakpana and Osain). Probably the most popular Calypso representation of obeah — Mighty Sparrow's "Obeah Wedding" (cowritten with Byron Lee in 1966) — revolves around the attempted use of obeah to "tie a man" (i.e., compel a man to stay in a relationship). The Mighty Shadow's "Whop Cocoyea" (2003) reflects a humorous (but serious) use of the *cocoyea* beatings to signify obeah in popular song. All the popular theatrical representations of obeah that I witnessed (in both Trinidad's Best Village competitions and the Tobago Heritage Festival) centered on women attempting to tie men — a point that deserves further analysis than I can offer here. Again, such characterizations of the type of work that obeah involved were overrepresented in popular entertainments and underrepresented in my own experience of spiritual work.

31. On scientific practice as "situated knowledge," see Haraway (1991). For a good elaboration of science as a practice of situated translation between various forms of difference, see Tsing (2015, 217–26). On partial connections, see Strathern (2004); and De la Cadena (2015).

32. Marked bills were an important piece of evidence in most post-Emancipation obeah trials. However, there are also records of persons convicted of obeah in the twentieth century without any evidence of monetary exchange (Alexander Rocklin, personal communication, August 17, 2018).

33. Both my fieldwork and the ethnographic literature has recorded these uses of "work" as a marker of what might, in North Atlantic terms, be called religion. Grassroots practitioners often called Orisha the "African work" or "Orisha work." The Trinidadian Kabbalah was also known as "Circle Work." The Spiritual Baptist faith was also known as the "Baptist work." For more on these terms, see chapter 6.

34. MacGaffey (2012) also suggests that "healing" might capture Africana religious practices in a more positive light than "witchcraft," "magic," or "sorcery" while also avoiding

some of the problematic resonances that he perceives in the term "African traditional religion." MacGaffey notes, however, that Africana practices referred to as "healing" might often be far removed from Western ideas of sickness and medicine, a point which I have chosen to emphasize in avoiding the use of "healing" as a synonym for obeah. Certainly, spiritual work involves practices that could be construed as "healing" in Western conceptions, but it is also much more than that.

35. Various forms of Christianity, Islam, Hinduism, and Buddhism have claimed to be scientific or to have anticipated science since the genesis of the science-religion divide in the late nineteenth century (Numbers 2010). Evangelical "creation science" has been linked with efforts to refute modern science, but other claims to scientific religion, particularly in South Asia, were closely linked with attempts to reconcile Asian religions with Western science, thus proving them to be superior to Christianity (which was coming to be understood as a dogma opposed to science). Efforts at making "scientific" or "protestant" Buddhism by Theosophists and Sri Lankan reformers also revolved around internal reform efforts that sought to separate spiritual science from alleged folk superstitions within Buddhist practice (see Lopez 2008; McMahan 2004).

36. In the early nineteenth century Rio Moro was peripheral to the slave plantation system because of lack of reliable road access to the region. The Merikins thus formed a free black contingent in Trinidad that was largely outside the island's system of slavery. One origin narrative of the Spiritual Baptists asserts that the religion emerged in Rio Moro out of the Baptist practices of the Merikins.

37. For a good examination of how West African religion arguably bucks Western notions of primordial tradition, see Ogunnaike (2013). In contrast to a Western notion of tradition, scholars have shown how West African practices are dynamic and multilayered combinations of foreign and local, exoteric and esoteric, or normative and counter-normative powers (e.g., Apter 1991; McNeal 2011; McAlister 2002). In some ways, these two different kinds of Africa also influenced contrasting attitudes toward obeah among Yoruba-centric reformers and lower-class grassroots practitioners, with the former usually defining obeah through its alleged roots in the Yoruba word for kola nut, or obi seed (*obi abata*). Yet until recently, the obi seed used in Trinidad (and much of the anglophone Caribbean) was a two-lobed variety (*C. nitida*) unsuitable for Yoruba divination systems (which typically use the four-lobed *obi abata*). This two-lobed variety was more popular in Mande- and Akan-speaking areas of West Africa outside of Yorubaland (Lovejoy 1980). The word "obeah" had entered general usage in the Caribbean before instability in the Oyo Empire brought the first large influx of Yoruba enslaved persons and indentured laborers to the region in the nineteenth century. This direct etymological linkage between the Yoruba word for kola nut (*obi*) and "obeah," scholars have thus concluded, is somewhat questionable. Scholars have generally asserted Akan or Igbo rather than Yoruba roots for "obeah" (see Handler and Bilby 2001). The Yoruba-centric (and Ifa-centric) etymology of the obi seed was forwarded by many of the attendees at an art gallery event celebrating obeah in urban northern Trinidad in 2010, which I describe in chapter 6. However, one audience member also dissented from this opinion, emphasizing an Igbo root word (*dibia or obia*) meaning "power," "doctor," or "knowledge" (see Umeh 1997), emphasizing that obeah was a "philosophy

of power" rather than a facet of the Yoruba-centric Ifa tradition that middle-class reformers often championed.

38. In the twentieth century, Rastafarians faced intensive police persecution in the Caribbean, including arrests, forced cutting of dreadlocks, police raids, and at least one "mas-
sacre" enacted by state security forces (see Chevannes 1994; and Thomas 2011).

CHAPTER ONE

1. In March 2015, after his acquittal for Trayvon Martin's death, Zimmerman conducted
an interview with his divorce lawyer in which he defended his actions and blamed
Barack Obama for inciting racial aggression against him. When asked if he had regrets
about the killing, he responded, "As a Christian I believe that God does everything for
a purpose, and he had his plans, and for me to second-guess them would be hypocriti-
cal and almost blasphemous." See Schuppe (2015) and Golding (2015).

2. In this chapter, I use "violence," "harm," and "harming power" more or less inter-
changeably. I construe these terms along the lines of the World Health Organization's
definition of "violence" as "the intentional use of physical force or power, threatened or
actual," which intends to cause "injury, death, psychological harm, maldevelopment, or
deprivation." Violence, in this definition, can involve the use of power or physical force,
and harm can be actual or threatened, psychological or physical. The dictionary definitions of "harm" and "violence" are generally indistinguishable, with the caveat that
legal definitions of violence define it as harm that is against the law. Because I follow
scholars in seeing state law itself as violent (e.g., Benjamin 1986; Derrida 2002; Sarat
and Kearns 1993), I do not make such a distinction in this chapter. Nor do my interlocutors see the legitimacy of harming force as necessarily determined by the organs
of state law, as the police shootings and protests illustrated.

3. For more on contemporary efforts to decriminalize obeah in Jamaica, see Henry (2013).
For examples of Caribbean writers' and artists' efforts to vindicate obeah as valuable
cultural tradition, see Lovelace (2003); and Clarke (2001). For an example of scholarly
efforts to argue against the idea that obeah is not a religion, see Khan (2003).

4. As Paton (2015, 1) notes in a later work, "Efforts to rewrite obeah in more positive terms
have tended to come from the safe distance of the academy, of cultural nationalist politics, or of both." For good evidence of the pervasiveness of negative portrayals of obeah
(as well as some more complex attitudes), see Bilby (2012).

5. As Talal Asad (1993) has shown, medieval Euro-Christian conceptions saw the Church
as devoted to ethical training, but (in contrast with modern conceptions of conscience)
coercion, infliction of pain, and disciplinary power were essential to ethical formation
in this era. The post-Reformation attempt to separate religion from power thus laid
the basis for a qualitatively different conception of religion, conscience, or ethical subject making. The idea that humans (as inherently sinful beings) must be disciplined or
forced into being ethical persons does not seem amenable to liberal ideals of consen-
sual religion or governance, but (as scholars have noted) this notion of coercive moral

training (for certain populations) simultaneously became a foundation for state sovereignty, law, and disciplinary power in modern secular regimes (e.g., Sehat 2011).

6. As Cavanaugh (2009) has argued, the sectarian or religious motivations for the so-called Religious Wars were dubious. Nevertheless, the idea that religious divisions had helped create these conflicts was a widespread idea to which Enlightenment liberal thinkers and their heirs have continuously responded.

7. See Sulaiman (2019) for an overview of these anti-Orientalist approaches.

8. For representations of obeah as not-religion, see, e.g., Bell ([1889] 1893); Frye (1997); Olmos and Paravisini-Gebert (2000, 6; 2011, 155); and Williams (1933). For recent scholarly uses of "black magic" or "sorcery," see Chireau (2006); Parés and Sansi (2011); and West (2007).

9. Bilby and Handler (2004) do recognize that obeah has a diversity of values for Caribbean people, but they interpret such attitudes through a division between "positive" precolonial meanings of healing and the "negative" colonial meanings of harm, a colonial opposition which they assert that Caribbean people have so widely internalized.

10. This high-profile lawyer, however, stood to profit if any damages were awarded to the families of the victims in civil suits (see the epilogue).

11. In contrast with liberal ideals of secular law, Alexander Rocklin (2019) has shown how the prosecution of obeah involved the policing of religion in both public and private spaces. Most spiritual work happens in domestic settings, and undercover police officers entered these settings, posing as afflicted clients in order to entrap spiritual workers, in the nineteenth and twentieth centuries. In the 1860s, anti-obeah ordinances often split from antivagrancy ordinances and were increasingly framed legally as fraud and popularly as a threat to moral order and development (Paton 2015).

12. States of emergency—the conferral of executive powers that go beyond constitutional limits—are far from exceptional in modern states. Israel has been under a state of emergency since before its inception as a modern state, having perpetuated the Emergency Defense Act—originally promulgated by the British governance of Palestine—for more than six decades. The United States has been under a state of emergency authorizing exceptional policing, military, and intelligence measures since September 11, and the United States exercises emergency powers of economic intervention beyond its borders via the 1977 International Emergency Economic Powers Act. Since its independence in 1962, Trinidad and Tobago has been under states of emergency in 1970, 1990, 1995, and 2011. Recently, the opposition leader has called for another anticrime state of emergency in Trinidad (Ramdass 2018). Brazil is currently experiencing its own version of Trinidad's 2011 politically motivated "anticrime" state of emergency, with the 2018 declared emergency and martial law in Rio de Janeiro state. Mbembe's (2003) work suggests how colonialism itself was a vast state of exception to Euro-American liberal theories of the rule of law and constitutional proceduralism.

13. On obeah as lawmaking force, see Lazarus-Black (1994a, 1994b). On the inextricability of the force of state law and extralegal violence, see Benjamin (1986); and Derrida (2002).

14. Even Girard (1977), who posits an intimate relationship between violence and the

sacred, sees in religion an attempt to channel, limit, or mask violence. In Christianity, Girard (1987) sees the resources to supersede sacrificial violence altogether.

INTERLUDE TWO

1. "Spiritual eyes" or "spirit eyes" is a Spiritual Baptist concept. It refers to the idea that we can cultivate another pair of eyes that allows for visions (i.e., spiritual sight) rather than vision (i.e., carnal sight). As it was explained to me, that is why the physical eyes are blindfolded during mourning—to enhance the cultivation of spirit eyes by inhibiting the carnal eyes for an extended period of time. One should not run too far with ocular-centric conceptions of mourning travel. This travel is, in many ways, better conceived of through sound (see Zane 1999, 82).

CHAPTER TWO

1. To protect the anonymity of those involved in cases of police brutality—some of which are still open court cases—I have had to change some of the details, names, and dates of the events.
2. Shweder (2016, 478) defines justice as the imperative to "treat like cases alike and impartially apply rules of general applicability," as part of an argument for the fundamental importance of transcendent "moral absolutes" for human ethical life.
3. See David Brown (2003) for an excellent discussion of these debates. Brown himself emphasizes creole innovation and shows how the innovations of individuals in the late nineteenth and early twentieth centuries were struggles to redefine the authoritative norms of African traditions in Cuba, as well as to defend their legitimacy in an era of intense persecution. Spiritual workers' experiments, however, did not represent attempts to gain public legitimacy or install new norms in a tradition; they derived their force from being explicitly counternormative. This divergence between "experiments" and "innovations" reveals an important difference between theories of creolization and experimentation.
4. The idea that "premodern" or "non-Western" societies are "closed" echoes Lévi-Strauss's much-critiqued characterization of "cold" societies. Unlike the "hot" societies of moderns, cold societies are allegedly characterized by homeostasis and the idea of fixed natural and social orders (see also Latour 1993, 42).
5. See Feyerabend (1975) and Stengers (2000) for accounts that emphasize novel experimental achievements or "counterinductive" leaps in the making of scientific discoveries. While Kuhn ([1962] 1996) tells a progress narrative, in which long periods of norm-confirming science are punctuated by radical paradigm shifts, scholars have more recently noted how normal and counternormative approaches coexist in slower and more uneven processes of scientific change (see, e.g., Marx and Bornmann 2010).

6. Although Smith (1993) affirms the function of religious practice as ultimately over-coming "disjuncture" and reaffirming either a "locative" or "utopic" order, he does note a pervasive (yet less theorized) modality that does not seek to overcome dis-juncture. As an ordering phenomenon, ritual has often been interpreted as upholding what Smith (1993) called the "locative" function of religious practice—the tendency to reaffirm a centered social and sacred order. In contrast, Smith theorized a "utopian" tendency, which sought to flee worldly social (dis)order toward an ideal cosmos—a subjunctive world, opposed to the profane, that ritual could also be construed as con-structing (Seligman et al. 2008). Both of these dominant modes fail to describe the justice-seeking religious practices described in this chapter, which seek to neither up-hold a regnant social order nor enact a utopian, otherworldly vision. These counter-normative practices do, however, partially echo what Smith (1993, 300–302) theorized as a third modality of religious action, which he suggested was akin to a "practical joke." In contrast with the locative-utopia dichotomy, this modality lets disjunctures and oppositions stand, affirming that it is impossible to overcome them. Rather than overcoming oppositions, this modality plays between them to—in Smith's (1993, 309) estimation—"provide an occasion for thought." Clearly, the justice-seeking practices of my interlocutors were *not* practical jokes; nor were they simply intellectualist exercises in "modes of thought." They were deadly serious world-changing endeavors, exceeding the definitions and examples that Smith gives. Yet they shared what Smith (1993, 301) calls the use of radically counternormative practices to provoke a state in which "the normal expectation has been suspended and the unexpected intrudes relativizing . . . previous modes of thought." Although the idea that justice-seeking burials would be "practical jokes" or acts simply concerned with "modes of thought" is inconceivable, Smith points toward something important that this chapter explores—a third alter-native to his dichotomous (yet coeval) maps of religious practice as devoted to either normative tradition or otherworldly utopia.

7. It is important for practitioners to maintain certain distinctions between these paths and orders, even as they do *not* simply recapitulate the Western model of mutually ex-clusive confessional communities, with many practitioners following multiple paths simultaneously.

8. "Egungun" here refers to a Yoruba masquerade in which costumed dancers embody the spirits of ancestors.

9. Funerals in Trinidad are generally open-casket affairs that feature viewing and taking photographs of the corpse, so Dawes's sealing of the casket was highly unusual.

10. *The Dictionary of the English/Creole of Trinidad and Tobago* defines "lash" as both a physical blow and "an internal wound caused by obeah" (Winer 2009, 516).

CHAPTER THREE

1. Baba Khan is a pseudonym for the spiritual name of this spiritual worker. While an

Afro-Trinidadian Spiritual Baptist, he took an Islamic name to reflect his affinity with an Arab Kabbalistic entity known as Mr. Mohammed Khan.

2. One spiritual worker of the threefold path, again drawing on a knowledge of automotive electrical systems, extended this electrical metaphor further by distinguishing between two kinds of spiritual power: alternating current and direct current. Both forms of electricity involved an interplay between positive and negative polarities, albeit in different ways. In a car, alternating current is generated by the engine's rapid spinning of magnets inside the wire coils of the alternator, a rapid reversal of magnetic polarities that creates electricity (the same basic principle used by the dynamos of power plants). This alternating current is then converted to direct current to charge the car's battery, a direct current system in which a differential of charge between positive and negative poles causes electricity to flow through a circuit, powering headlights, windshield wipers, or audio systems. The spiritual worker likened alternating current to "divine energy." Alternating current, he reminded me, was also the kind of power that came through power lines to one's home (and had to be converted to charge cell phone batteries and other DC-powered devices). He then likened people to spiritual batteries, for whom this divine alternating current had to be converted in order to be stored in a material vessel with defined polarities. Through wisdom and knowledge, individuals could learn how to charge themselves and even to reverse these direct current polarities to simulate the oscillation of divine power. In other accounts of Spiritual Baptist practice, electricity and electrical grids of transmission have figured as central ways to express spiritual power (e.g., Keeney 2002). Electricity, of course, has also played a central role in new religious and energy-healing movements, such as mesmerism or spiritualism, since the eighteenth century (e.g., Stolow 2008, 2013). In 1799, for example, Moseley described how obeah "professors" treated their "patients" with a "rough magnetizing," recalling then-popular and controversial European healing practices of mesmerism, which used early battery technology to stimulate the "animal magnetism" of clients (qtd. in Murison 2015, 154).

3. The blame for this idea of religion is usually laid at Durkheim's ([1912] 1964) door, but this idea has a much older genealogy. The notion that true religion is about individual moral conscience was central to the Enlightenment (e.g., Kant [1793] 1960; Locke [1689] 1796), yet other scholars have posited an earlier point of origin for the conflation of religion and morality. Assmann (2009) dates the idea that morality is inherently religious (rather than something dictated by the political and legal power of sovereigns) to late antiquity and the rise of Christianity and Islam. Echoing this conclusion, the anthropologist of religion Webb Keane (2014a) has argued that "monotheistic" religions of the book (and ethnographies of these religions) tend toward idealized conceptions of piety that attempt to abstract ethical imperatives from specific contexts. Religion—as a realm of piety—thus comes to oppose the "profane" world of human contingency and ambivalent power, with its ethical injunctions aspiring to the universality that is a defining tendency of juridical ethics. As Keane (2014a) notes, recent critical approaches to religion have only underscored this ideal opposition by focusing on virtue, piety, and the embodiment of the shared norms of a tradition (see, e.g., Asad 1986; Hirschkind 2006; Jouili 2015; Mahmood 2003a, 2005; Robbins 2004).

4. Laidlaw (2014), in a critique of the ethical traditions approach inspired by Mahmood (2006) and MacIntyre (1981), thus focuses on moments of struggle and ambivalence in the everyday practice of ethics, when the norms of a tradition are not always virtuous within lived contexts. Extending and modifying the "ordinary ethics" approach promoted by Lambek (2010) and others, more recent work has recognized the problems with conflating ethics and the good (however that is defined) (see Sidnell, Meudec, and Lambek 2019).

5. The word "conduct" (*conduire*) was central to Foucault's own thoughts on ethics, though (at least to my knowledge) he did not expound in detail on the electrical charge that the word carries (i.e., to conduct is to become a circuit or channel with positive and negative poles). This electrical meaning shows how "to conduct" does not simply mean to guide, to drive, or to behave, but also means to become a channel for exogenous power (as in spirit manifestation—a key source of authority in African religions in Trinidad). Instead of these electrical resonances, Foucault focused on either the conduct of the self or the institutional conduct of self-conduct (e.g., Foucault 1982).

6. Relatively recent (2018–2019) popular representations of obeah and voodoo as morally suspect include the second season of Marvel's *Luke Cage* series and the second and third seasons of the Netflix series *Orange Is the New Black*. Popular representations of obeah and voodoo have most often been even less charitable than these recent examples (see Bilby 2012; Crosson 2017b; Hurbon 1995).

7. As Laidlaw (2014) has argued, the recent turn toward virtue ethics has often focused on shared ethical traditions (e.g., Asad 1986; MacIntyre 1981; Mahmood 2005), downplaying the conflicts, schisms, and fundamental disagreements that are a part of lived ethics (see also Keane 2014b). Naisargi Dave (2012) has suggested that these emphases on embodying the norms of a tradition belie a "juridical" emphasis in ethical theories from Aristotle and Kant to Durkheim and (anglophone appropriations of) Foucault.

8. For examples of contemporary intolerance toward obeah, enacted through deportations and denial of legal protections in the Caribbean and centers of Caribbean migration in North America, see Crosson (2015, 2017b, 2018); Khan (2013); and Paton (2015).

9. To take one recent example, the second season of the popular Marvel series *Luke Cage* revolves around a moral opposition between Afro-Caribbean and black American Christian forms of religiosity. The power-obsessed obeah of the Jamaican villain-antihero is continually contrasted to the black American Christian moral imperatives of the African American hero's father (who is the pastor of a church in Harlem). This opposition is not without its nuances. While obeah comes off as definitively dangerous, self-destructive, and malevolent, the African American hero struggles with the Christian moral imperatives (and his own relation to his father). For both the Jamaican villain and the protagonist, these moral struggles revolve around the use of violence to obtain what each defines as justice (and the fact that their notions of justice might be incommensurable).

10. Indeed, MacIntyre's own influential work on virtue ethics emerged in tandem with his conversion to Catholic Christianity, as answers to his profound dissatisfaction with the alleged instrumentality and individualism of Western modernity and its lack of guiding ethical traditions (see Fassin 2014). To some extent, this dissatisfaction is carried

over in the ethical turns within studies of religion, with secular Western modernity being the main target of this ethical traditions approach. In Saba Mahmood's (2005) *Politics of Piety*, for example, the emphasis on the pious conformity to the contested ethical norms of a tradition is the alternative to the liberal individualism of Western feminist thought and its emphasis on the resistance to norms. The polarities of individual and community, or freedom and tradition, continue to shape these approaches to ethics.

11. In many recent critiques, Aristotelian virtue ethics, based in an embodied habitus, have been the alternative to Kantian (or Durkheimian) duty ethics, based in individual reason (on this issue, see Mittermaier 2010, 140–41). Sometimes, this opposition has been represented using "ethics" to represent the Aristotelian position and "morality" to signal the Kantian perspective. This ethics-morality opposition, however, is far from consistent in the literature, with many scholars rejecting it altogether because of the vagaries of these terms' usages (e.g., Keane 2016). Following these scholars, I do not employ an ethics-morality opposition, not simply because it is widely inconsistent, but also because it reproduces certain fundamental assumptions.

12. The association between Mr. Emmanuel Bones and Ezekiel is quite strong, although its validity depends on the extent to which practitioners accept or condemn the Trinidadian Kabbalah as a legitimate path. Depending on the practitioner, Mr. Bones is either the entire skeleton that the biblical figure Ezekiel raised from the dead in the Valley of Dry Bones, this skeleton's body, or a side of Ezekiel himself.

13. I borrow the term "assemblage" from the translation of Deleuze and Guattari's ([1972] 2000, [1980] 2007) *agencement*. Assemblages are not organic wholes and thus provide an alternative to holistic conceptions of religions as mutually exclusive confessional communities.

14. There is no extended scholarly work on the Trinidadian Kabbalah and no convincing exegesis of the origin of many of its spiritual entities. My interlocutors sometimes mentioned the infamous US crime figure John Dillinger as a Kabbalistic entity, so, if I had to speculate, Frank Mahan might have been a similar outlaw figure from the early twentieth century (although I can find no records of this). Some (but by no means all) Kabbalistic entities are criminals, bearing a similarity to the spirits of the street (*povo da rua*) in Brazilian Umbanda or the *malandro* (bad ass, criminal) court in Maria Lionza devotion in Venezuela.

CHAPTER FOUR

1. Drawn from the Hollywood Westerns popular in the anglophone Caribbean, allusions to the Plains Indians of the Wild West formed an important inspiration for Carnival masquerades. In St. Vincent, these kinds of "Indians" were the more common inhabitants of the Spiritual Nation of India, probably reflecting the island's small number of South Asian people (see Zane 1999). In Trinidad, the Spiritual Nation of India more often reflected the Hindu and Muslim practices identified with South Asian indentured

laborers in Trinidad. "Apaches" or "wild Indians," however, were sometimes mentioned as an alternative kind of "Indian" who inhabited the Spiritual Lands.

2. The Hialeah City Council held an emergency public session on June 9, 1987. At the session, Councilman Silvio Cardoso stated that the religion is "in violation of everything this country stands for" and Councilman Julio Martinez noted (to audience applause) that in prerevolutionary Cuba "people were put in jail for practicing this religion" (qtd. in *Church of the Lukumi Babalu Aye v. Hialeah*, 508 U.S. 520 [1993]: 541). Hialeah's police chaplain testified that the church worshiped "demons," and the city attorney testified, "This community will not tolerate religious practices abhorrent to its citizens" (542). At the end of the session the city council passed a resolution announcing its commitment to prohibit "all religious groups which are inconsistent with public morals, peace or safety" (548). In September 1987, the city council unanimously passed three new ordinances that criminalized "sacrifices of animals for any type of ritual, regardless of whether or not the flesh or blood of the animal is to be consumed." The city council exempted Kosher slaughterhouses, regular slaughterhouses, hunting, fishing, pest extermination, euthanasia of stray animals, and feeding live rabbits to greyhounds.

3. In another Santería-related arrest in San Antonio, Texas, this year, a Santería practitioner known as "Cuban" was arrested as part of a sweeping police operation in the city's Eastside. While the man was technically arrested on outstanding charges of grave robbery, the rationale for his detention was framed in terms of long-standing popular connections between Santería and the specter of child sacrifice (Tepfer 2016). In Texas, these imaginaries recalled the ritual murder of a white University of Texas at Austin spring breaker on the Texas Gulf Coast in 1989. The murder made major national news and was connected to the practice of Mexico-US borderlands "Santería."

4. Evidence of late nineteenth-century moral panic about alleged *thuggees* in Trinidad was communicated to me by Alexander Rocklin (personal communication, April 29, 2019).

5. In Trinidad, the death of three-year-old Luther Barrow, for example, provoked fears of "Obeahism" as ritual murder in 1889 (Rocklin 2019, 253n19). In the early twentieth century in British Guiana, both Indian and African laborers were put on trial for the murder of a white child that was attributed to obeah (Alexander Rocklin, personal communication, April 14, 2019). Cases of murder and suicide among Indian indentured laborers on plantations were also said to be caused by obeah in newspaper accounts in Trinidad (Rocklin 2019, 113–15), echoing the use of obeah by British plantation owners to explain slave mortality as a consequence of obeah rather than deplorable working conditions (Paton 2015).

6. On the concept of diasporic horizons, see Johnson (2007).

7. A *pujari* is a devotee who manifests deities and assists with ritual offerings.

8. Most feast holders in Rio Moro raised their own animals. Even for those devotees in Trinidad who simply bought their animals, the acquisition of the sheep, goats, chickens, and land turtles that a full feast required was by far the most expensive and difficult material preparation, which often meant working overtime, taking out loans, or creatively piecing together thin financial resources to obtain these animals. In the postagricultural petrostate of Trinidad, animals (sheep and goats, in particular) were extremely expensive. Indeed, my interlocutors often cited the significant labor and

expense of animal offerings as a common reason why people left Orisha devotion for
other forms of religion (most particularly Protestant Christianities).

9. Scholars have noted how the rejection or limiting of animal sacrifice characterized a
wide variety of religious traditions, from Judaism to Buddhism, in late antiquity (e.g.,
Sanderson 2018; Stroumsa 2009). These accounts suggest that there was a profound
evolutionary shift in how religion was defined and that the waning of animal sacrifice
was an important part of this shift. However, the evolutionary thrust of these arguments about an "Axial Age" supersession of sacrifice inadvertently reinforces the race-
making idea that contemporary practices of animal sacrifice are atavistic survivals of
a previous stage of religion. Rather than focusing on evolutionary arguments about
religion, I have chosen to focus on the ways that the condemnation of animal sacrifice
continues to be instrumental to power relations, acts of distinction, and justifications
for the legal regulation of certain practices.

10. The attempts to legally prohibit African rites through the prosecution of animal sacrifice were not limited to Texas or Florida. In Brazil, for example, a white congresswoman
and animal rights activist was the author of a 2015 bill that prohibits animal sacrifice on
the grounds that it is unhygienic, cruel, and disturbing to the conscience of society. In
2018, Brazil's Supreme Federal Court was deliberating on the validity of the bill, with
a coalition of Afro-Brazilian religious groups mobilizing against the attack on their
"freedom of religion" (see Luto na Luta 2018). In Brazil, Pentecostal-affiliated spiritual
warriors have been linked to the destruction of Afro-Brazilian religious shrines and the
physical intimidation of practitioners of African-identified religions (see Boaz 2019;
"Luto na Luta" 2017; Roeder 2019).

CHAPTER FIVE

1. One definition of the noun "tongue" in the second edition of the *Oxford English Dictionary*, for example, defines it as a "narrow strip of land, running into the sea, or between two branches of a river, or two other lands; also a projecting horizontal point
or spit of ice in the sea, a narrow inlet of water running into the land, etc." "Tongue"
was an English-language synonym used by British authorities for the important North
Indian word *doab*, signifying the fertile land between confluent rivers, such as the *doab*
between the Ganges and the Yamuna (e.g., Thornton 1858, 791).

2. Trinidad-style callaloo is a puree of dasheen bush, okra, coconut milk, pumpkin, hot
pepper, and (sometimes) crab. This dish serves as a national emblem of Trinidad's
touted "hyperdiverse" cultural mixture (see Khan 2004a, 2004b).

3. "Crossover artists" can be performers who appropriate a racially circumscribed genre
of music, packaging it in a form that appeals to other racial demographics. Elvis, to take
one well-known example, whitened (and, according to many accounts, watered down)
the sensibilities of African American rhythm and blues to perform a crossover music
palatable to white US audiences in the 1950s.

4. One example of such mimicry or mockery is the 2005 hit song "Chinee Parang" by

Damien Joseph and Los Paramininos. The song's chorus features extensive use of phrases, such as "poong wang chong," which my interlocutors sometimes employed to perform a racially stereotyping and inaccurate imitation of "Chinee" (i.e., Chinese).

5. This notion of persons as "dividuals" composed of the divisions of society was developed by Marilyn Strathern (2004) and McKim Marriott ([1972] 1976) to describe a relational model of personhood that contrasted with Western individualism.

6. "Jumbie," according to Winer (2009, 474), derives from the Kikongo word *nzambi*, meaning "spirit of a dead person." The word for "jumbie" in Trinidadian French patois is "zonbi." Evidence of Indo-Trinidadians using the word "jumbie" occurs as early as the 1860s (Alexander Rocklin, personal communication, April 20, 2019).

7. "Creole" was a formerly popular racial term in Trinidad, analogous to "Afro-Trinidadian." This division between "Creole" obeah and Indian *ojha* is, of course, overly simplistic. There is abundant archival evidence of Indo-Trinidadians working with spirits in a variety of ways, with these practices sometimes called "obeah" by others.

8. Mainstream Hinduism in Trinidad also addresses this critique, constantly affirming that there is but one god, with the various *deotas* (Hindu deities) simply representing different facets of this singular entity.

9. Deriving from South Asian root words meaning "day laborer" or "slave," "coolie" reflected the stereotype of Indo-Trinidadians as non-Christian agricultural field labor in Trinidad. Indo-Trinidadians possessed the highest poverty and illiteracy rates of any ethno-racial group in Trinidad until the latter part of the twentieth century. While the idea that someone of African descent might claim structural superiority to a person of South Asian descent makes less sense in other racial matrices, this claim can be legible in Trinidad's matrix of race and religion (see Munasinghe 2001; Khan 2004a). Yet South Asians could also claim superiority over Africans by virtue of pervasive Western racial frameworks that denigrated blackness and/or Africanity.

10. Each party, however, contains a minority of members from the opposite racial group, and in Rio Moro political allegiances often cleaved to lines of patronage rather than race. For example, Afro-Trinidadian entrepreneurs who received unemployment relief contracts under the "Indian government" that took power during my fieldwork strongly supported the "Indian party" (while those who had their contracts taken away strongly resented both their own entrepreneurial neighbors and the Indian government). Nevertheless, popular understandings of an Indian and African party structure political controversies and rivalries up to the present.

11. In the nineteenth century, "Hindu" was often a racial term for British colonial authorities, with the word denoting persons from South Asia regardless of their religious leanings (what today would be Islam, Hinduism, Jainism, and so on). It was only in the early twentieth century that indentured laborers began to identify Hinduism as a religion with attendant rights. Nevertheless, Hindu remains conflated with race in Trinidad. As Aisha Khan (2004a) notes, when asked to put their race on a questionnaire, many Indo-Trinidadians of the late twentieth century wrote "Hindu." For more on this issue, see Rocklin (2016, 2019, forthcoming).

12. Until the legalization of non-Christian schools in the mid-twentieth century, Indo-Trinidadians had to attend Christian schools regardless of their religious identification.

Education and social advancement were heavily tied to an (at least nominal) Christianity, most especially Presbyterianism (with the Presbyterian Church sometimes known as "the Westernmost branch of Hinduism" due to Canadian Presbyterian missionaries targeting Indo-Trinidadian populations). However, the postcolonial reevaluation of Euro-Christian hegemony since the 1970s has led many Indo-Trinidadian Christians to reemphasize their Hinduness, often insisting that their Christianity was only a nominal addition to Hindu culture rather than an exclusive religious identity. To make matters more complicated, the inroads of Pentecostal-charismatic Christianity with Indo-Trinidadians has led to a new form of Christian conversion that tends to be less tolerant of simultaneous Hindu religiosity.

13. A more recent version of this redemptive story of mixture, particularly popular among some academics and cultural elites, is the equation of "douglarization," or Afro-Indo sexual mixture, with dreams of postcolonial racial democracy (see, e.g., Mehta 2004; Puri 2004; cf. Khan 2004b, 2007). These dreams of mixture, while promoting visions of harmonious equality, also imply contemporary problems and frictions. In the national narrative of creolization, ideas of social hybridity still exclude Indians (particularly Hindus) as supposedly resistant to mixing, and popular representations of douglarization in song typically exclude both Indian men and black women from this story of sexual and biological mixture.

14. Basdeo Panday, the first Indo-Trinidadian prime minister and the leader of the first government to officially recognize African religions in Trinidad and Tobago, summed up this common attitude toward religious syncretism during his address on the occasion of Orisha Family Day in 1999. While celebrating the "cultural syncretism in the creolisation of our [national] culture," he made sure to assert that "in no way am I suggesting religious syncretism" (qtd. in Castor 2013, 478). Separating religious from cultural mixture, Panday was thus able to celebrate a unifying national culture while affirming ethno-religious difference (and the right of both African and South Asian religions to find an equal place alongside Euro-American Christian denominations).

15. In the Trinidadian English/Creole, the verb "to stick" means "to tarry" or "to dawdle."

16. Cremation was prohibited (though not technically illegal) for most of Trinidad's colonial history and became a widespread Hindu practice there only in the 1980s (McNeal 2011). Prior to this, burial was the preferred mortuary practice of Indo-Trinidadian Hindus.

17. "Sahib" is an honorific title of Arabic origin. It is used in northern India as a term of address and can be translated as "proprietor," "master," "sir," or "mister."

18. In the Trinidadian English/Creole, "simi-dimi" means "superstition" and can be traced to Arabic root words.

19. I use the term "Trinbagonian" to refer to people that have long-standing ties to both Tobago and Trinidad or as a short-hand for appeals to the national citizenry that are meant to be inclusive of those on both islands. Since J. D. Elder grew up on Tobago and spent much of his professional life in Trinidad, I refer to him as Trinbagonian.

20. I did know a few practicing Hindus who became semiregular attendees of Orisha feasts after being healed by African spiritual workers, although this did not necessarily mean that they ceased to practice Hindu forms of worship. Again, Orisha- and

Hindu-identified practices were not necessarily mutually exclusive for many (but not all) African-identified devotees.

21. For examples of this seminal distinction between magic as individualistic and religion as communal, see Chireau (2006, 3); Durkheim (1912) 1964; Frazer (1922). In the Durkheimian valorization of social cohesion, this characterization of magic was negative, recapitulating the invectives of white Christian missionaries against African religion, as MacGaffey (1977, 18) has noted.

CHAPTER SIX

1. On the Enlightenment as an antisuperstition project, see, e.g., Hegel (1807) 1910; Locke (1689) 1796; Kant (1793) 1960; and Spinoza (1677) 2001. For a refutation of this narrative of disenchantment, see Josephson-Storm (2017).

2. In well-publicized and controversial remarks, the US televangelist Benny Hinn had made similar comments on his 2006 visit to Trinidad, on the invitation of then Prime Minister Patrick Manning (see Maharaj 2006; Castor 2017, 184n13).

3. On the central role of "occult qualities" in what has become known as the Scientific Revolution, see Hutchison (1982).

4. The neologism "scientist" was coined in 1833 by the British polymath William Whewell (see Numbers 2010). "Natural philosopher" was the common term to refer to the European men whom we now call scientists prior to the popularization of Whewell's neologism over the course of the nineteenth century.

5. This editorial, while reprinted in newspapers across the Caribbean, appears to have been originally published on 14 December 1891 in the *Jamaica Gleaner* by an anonymous author.

6. *Obeah Simplified, the True Wanga*, was published in 1895 by the offices of the *Mirror*, a relatively short-lived newspaper in Victorian Trinidad. Subtitled "A Scientific Treatise," the book promises in the opening pages to present "an introduction and aide-memoire to the science" of what the author calls "obeah-wanga." The author of the book is listed as Dr. Myal Djumboh Cassecanarie, a "Professor of Pneumatics in the Tchanga-Wanga University," consulting "quimboiseur" to the ex-president of Haiti, and "Member of the Principal West Indian and West African Scientific Societies." The author's name and credentials present an overtly transisland and transregional African identity. "Myal" is a term of Jamaican provenance for an African religious practice, *quimbois* is a rough French synonym for "obeah" still used in Martinique and Guadeloupe, and "Cassecanarie" is probably derived from the Haitian Vodou festival Casse Canarie. The author was active in transnational theosophical circles, for a version of *Obeah Simplified* appeared in serial form a few years earlier in 1891 in the journal of the International Theosophical Society (*Theosophist*), founded by Westerners but headquartered in South India, with the author listed as "Miad Hoyora Kora-Hon, F.T.S." (Fellow of the Theosophical Society). From 1884, Kora-Hon was listed as a regular contributor to the *Theosophist*, writing articles on the "mystic lore" of the "kolarian tribes" of eastern India and on alchemy

in Ireland. In this serial form, it becomes clear from the author's self-presentation that he is a foreigner in the West Indies who owned land and spent extended periods of time there. Stephan Palmié (2002) seems to assume that the author is of West Indian and African descent, presumably because he or she is an avowed obeah practitioner. Alexander Rocklin (forthcoming), however, has found that the author was a Scottish member of the recently founded Theosophical Society who owned a plantation in Tobago. For Cassecanarie (1895, 75), "true" obeah (which he also calls "wanga") is a "sound formula," and Cassecanarie proclaims that any obeah practitioner who uses material objects—"bottles, rags, or other rubbish"—as a necessary part of their practice is not a true obeah practitioner, but a "rascal" or "an impostor." In the final chapter, Cassecanarie provides anecdotes about "archaic" European witchcraft to show that these practices used objects—wax figurines or dolls—that rendered them more akin to "fetishism" than to the "science" of true obeah-wanga. Cassecanarie, closes his scientific treatise by stating that his purpose has been to educate readers about proper obeah—or what he calls the "true Wanga"—and if his work leads the public to discern between impostors who use objects and those true practitioners who rely primarily on spells, then he will consider that "the purpose of this pamphlet will have been accomplished." The science, then, is the "natural" power of "sound formula," and other material practices or objects are purely superfluous, making almost all Afro-Caribbean spiritual workers "rascals" or "fetishists." This notion of "true" obeah would prove central to the attempts of the best-known twentieth-century occultist—Aleister Crowley—to scientize magic (Asprem 2008; Josiffe 2013). Like most theosophical work, Cassecanarie's text is avowedly anti-Christian, offering allegedly non-Western practices as alternatives to dogmatic religion. Cassecanarie's distinction between true and false obeah, however, veers curiously close to post-Reformation distinctions between religion and superstition, with the former emphasizing words and the latter material practices (see Crosson, forthcoming).

7. Open Bible Churches form an association of Pentecostal congregations headquartered in Iowa, United States, affiliated with the major North American and global Pentecostal and charismatic organizations. The crusade at Rio Moro Secondary involved both local and national coalitions of Pentecostal churches. The charismatic movement refers more broadly to Christians, including Catholics or Episcopalians, who have taken up Pentecostal-like practices of glossolalia, faith healing, and/or spiritual warfare over the past decades.

8. The projection of culpability for Trinidad's "crime problem" onto Spanish-speaking Latin America has been a persistent feature of public discourse in Trinidad. One scholar who writes and teaches about the drug trade at the University of the West Indies, for example, once told me that Trinidad's "sin is geography," namely its geographical proximity to South America. In other words, Trinidad would be a nice place if it were not so close to Venezuela. In resonant forms of scapegoating, the state of emergency of 2011 was blamed on the alleged threat of an unnamed "Mexican cartel," with martial law the only measure that could forestall the unthinkable savagery this cartel supposedly wanted to unleash. Such racist explanations conveniently placed the blame on Latin America, rather than looking at police corruption or elite involvement in money laundering and transshipment that are present in Trinidad. Such scapegoat-

ing of Latin America can also de-emphasize the demand for cocaine in the United States or Europe as sources of culpability.

9. For recent accounts that have added "superstition" as an important third term to secular-religious binaries, see Josephson-Storm (2018) and Crosson (2018).

10. Disturbances at Caribbean schools inspired by the internet and attributed to obeah have gone beyond access to these grimoires. The "Charlie, Charlie" affair, which closed down schools across the region, was attributed to what was simultaneously characterized as an "African," "Mexican," and "satanic" rite that students had learned by watching a viral internet video (which turned out to be a trailer for a Hollywood horror movie) (Baverstock 2015; "Charlie Charlie Presents Challenges" 2015; Crosson 2017b). For more on the links between obeah accusations and the internet, see Crosson (2017b).

11. The most popular grimoires in Rio Moro were *The Sixth and Seventh Books of Moses*, *The Petit Albert* ("Titalbay"), *The Greater Key of Solomon*, and *The Lesser Key of Solomon* (although many others were also studied, including various South Asian–identified works referred to as *Indrajal*). Grimoires have long been associated with black Atlantic religion. *The Petit Albert*, for example, was recently republished as the supposed "Spell Book" of the "voodoo queen of New Orleans," Marie Laveau (Felix [1702] 2013). The book currently marketed as the "obeah Bible" is an 1898 volume written (or compiled) by the largest purveyor of grimoires in the Caribbean, the Ohio-born hypnotist William de Laurence, entitled *The Great Book of Magical Art, Hindu Magic and East Indian Occultism*. *The Sixth and Seventh Books of Moses*, a grimoire originally brought to the Americas by German immigrants (Davies 2010), was cited by Zora Neale Hurston ([1939] 2009, vii–viii) as one of the most important books for African American "hoodoo" practitioners.

12. In contrast, Littlewood (1993, 42) and Hogg (1961) differentiate between traditional obeah (as an African and rural practice) from "high science" (as a book-based, urban, and European practice). I found this distinction to be entirely untenable (and potentially racist); rural spiritual workers (like Western hermeticists) conceived of these texts as deriving from northeastern Africa, and they used them widely as another African source of inspiration.

13. This is not mere fancy but is a viewpoint entirely in line with the Hermetic and Solomonic traditions from which many of these "European" texts themselves emerged. The Hermetic tradition of Europe and Asia traces its knowledge back to the "thrice-great" Hermes Trismegistus of Egypt (see, e.g., Van Bladel 2009), and my interlocutors also studied *The Egyptian Book of the Dead* (or, as they called it, *Coming Forth by Day* or *The Papyrus of Ani*) as one of these "science books." Moreover, one of the greatest magicians of European grimoires is Solomon, who (along with the Queen of Sheba) was the founder of the Ethiopian royal lineage and is described as black or dark-skinned in the Bible. Solomon is a key figure in the Trinidadian Kabbalah. The other great magician of this grimoire tradition—Moses—has a long history in the Americas of being reinscribed as an African (slave) who learned his magic in Egypt (see Hurston [1939] 2009; Smith 1994, 33–45).

14. The philosopher of science Ian Hacking (1983) and the philosopher-physicist Karen Barad (2007) have insisted that scientific experimentation is about "interfering" in

material assemblages rather than simply "peering" at an a priori set of facts (see also Haraway 1991). For Barad, this view of science is confirmed experimentally by some of the most cutting-edge quantum physics experiments, which show how it is impossible for humans to measure something without seeming to "interfere" with the phenomena. Yet Barad goes further than Hacking by insisting that this is experimental evidence of what she calls an "intra-action" of human and matter, rather than simply human "interference" in the material world. This condition of nonpassive intra-action of human and nonhuman agencies is the basis for what Barad calls "agential realism."

15. Owen Davies (2010) has documented the use of Bible and key cleidomancy in Britain, and the use of this divination technique has also been documented in New England. A number of books that spiritual workers used also detailed the problem-solving uses of particular psalms, including the task of locating lost objects.

16. Mama Lata signifies "Mother Earth" in Trinidadian French patois, and she is an Orisha peculiar to the Trinidadian version of Yoruba-inspired religions in the Caribbean.

17. For more contemporary works engaged in this unfolding rationality debate, see, e.g., Bubandt (2014); Palmié (2002); Tambiah (1990); and Wiredu (1979).

18. With the word "ownmost," Sankeralli is referencing a key term in English translations of Heidegger as well as the way that the word "own" (rather than " 's") makes the possessive in the English/Creole of Trinidad and Tobago. In Heideggerian terms, "ownmost" signifies an ontological ground that is constitutive of one's being (rather than a self that one possesses). In his address, Sankeralli wanted to implement an "ownmost" obeah as an ontology that constitutes Caribbean ways of being and approaches to time, rather than as a set of practices or a creed. For more on Sankeralli's thoughts on obeah, see Sankeralli (2008).

EPILOGUE

1. Most "developed" nation-states have spent much of the twenty-first century under declared states of emergency, with the United States and Israel currently under official emergencies that have had particularly long durations. Beyond the official limits of the government or a codified emergency, a more generalized state of exception characterizes expanded powers of security—in "stand your ground" vigilance, militant xenophobia, extralegal surveillance, racialized police violence, and the booming business of private security in the Americas.

2. For a fuller analysis of this court case, to which my knowledge of these cases is indebted, see Khan (2013).

3. See Cavanaugh (1995, 2009) for a good history of how these wars shaped Enlightenment discourses of religious tolerance. Cavanaugh rightly doubts the extent to which the actual motivations for these wars were Christian sectarian difference. Nevertheless, the idea that these wars were the result of religious differences was an extremely powerful trope in Enlightenment thought, producing themes that echo in invectives against fanaticism and superstition today.

4. To a great extent, however, both "liberal" and "conservative" religious orientations in
    the United States remain closely wed to idealistic representations of "American democ-
    racy" (e.g., Kripal 2007; Schmidt 2012). In the scholarly domain, redemptions of liberal
    religion have often been yoked to the premature celebrations of globalization, multicul-
    turalism, transnational "flows," and the withering of nationalist divisions that peaked
    in most disciplines at the end of the twentieth century (with religious studies lagging
    a bit behind the curve) (see Appadurai 1996; Clifford 1988, 1992; Hannerz 1987, 1996;
    Tweed 2006; cf. Tsing 2004). Hopeful discourses of globalization have been a key fea-
    ture of what Povinelli (2006, 2016) calls "late Liberalism." As Povinelli (2016) suggests,
    militarized borders, increasing nationalism, a new cold war, and climate change indi-
    cate that late liberalism's time seems to have already passed.

5. To my mind, Bunji Garlin's 2011 song "Obeah" is the best example of a complex repre-
    sentation of obeah musically. In 2019, Trinidad's Lloyd Best Institute of the Caribbean
    presented Shadow's work alongside that of LeRoy Clarke's as an exhibition of "obeah
    as art" (see Best 2019).

6. Police officers could face dangerous situations of power with respect to superiors that
    led to them seeking out spiritual workers. In one case that I witnessed, a police officer
    came to a spiritual worker in Rio Moro after he was framed for stealing seized cash that
    had gone missing from the station's evidence room. The spiritual worker divined that
    his commanding officer had taken the money, and she performed certain inversions of
    the policeman's clothing and physical body to reverse his state of affairs. In Antigua, to
    take another example, a police officer who had brought complaints against a superior
    for sexual harassment was accused of practicing obeah in the police station to protect
    themselves and their job (see "Police Involved in Witchcraft" 2018).

REFERENCES

Abímbóá, Kólá. 2001. "Spirituality and Applied Ethics: An African Perspective." *West Africa Review* 3 (1): 1–29.

Abraham, Sara. 2007. *Labour and the Multiracial Project in the Caribbean: Its History and Its Promise*. Lanham, MD: Lexington Books.

Achong, Derek. 2018. "State Settles SoE Lawsuits." *Trinidad and Tobago Guardian*, March 1.

Agamben, Giorgio. 2005. *State of Exception*. Chicago: University of Chicago Press.

Alexander, M. Jacqui. 1994. "Not Just (Any) Body Can Be a Citizen: The Politics of Law, Sexuality and Postcoloniality in Trinidad and Tobago and the Bahamas." *Feminist Review* 48 (1): 5–23.

—––—. 2005. *Pedagogies of Crossing: Meditations on Feminism, Sexual Politics, Memory, and the Sacred*. Durham, NC: Duke University Press.

"Alleged Assumption of Supernatural Powers." 1919. *Port of Spain Gazette*, February 7.

Alonso, Ana M. 1990. "Men in 'Rags' and the Devil on the Throne: A Study of Protest and Inversion in the Carnival of Post-Emancipation Trinidad." *Plantation Society in the Americas* 3: 73–120.

Alphonso, Clyde. 2015. "Appalled, Disgusted by Dirty Obeah Ad." *Trinidad and Tobago Newsday*, September 5. https://archives.newsday.co.tt/2015/09/05/appalled-disgusted-by-dirty-obeah-ad/.

Amnesty International. 2012. "Annual Report: Trinidad and Tobago." http://www.amnesty.org/en/region/trinidad-amp-tobago/report-2012.

Anidjar, Gil. 2009. "The Idea of an Anthropology of Christianity." *International Journal of Postcolonial Studies* 11 (3): 367–93.

—––—. 2011. "Blood." *Political Concepts* 1. http://www.politicalconcepts.org/issue1/blood/.

Anjum, Ovamir. 2007. "Islam as a Discursive Tradition: Talal Asad and His Interlocutors." *Comparative Studies of South Asia, Africa and the Middle East* 27 (3): 656–72.

Ankeny, Rachel A., and Sabina Leonelli. 2016. "Repertoires: A Post-Kuhnian Perspective on Scientific Change and Collaborative Research." *Studies in History and Philosophy of Science Part A* 60: 18–28.

Antsey, Peter R. 2005. "Experimental versus Speculative Natural Philosophy." In *The Science of Nature in the Seventeenth Century: Patterns of Changes in Early Modern Natural Philosophy*, edited by Peter R. Anstey and John A. Schuster, 215–42. Dordrecht, Netherlands: Springer.

Anyangwe, Eliza. 2017. "Brand New Macron, Same Old Colonialism." *The Guardian*, July 17.

Appadurai, Arjun. 1996. *Modernity at Large*. Minneapolis: University of Minnesota Press.

Apter, Andrew. 1991. "The Embodiment of Paradox: Yoruba Kingship and Female Power." *Cultural Anthropology* 6 (2): 212–29.

———. 1992. *Black Critics and Kings: The Hermeneutics of Power in Yoruba Society*. Chicago: University of Chicago Press.

———. 2017. *Oduduwa's Chain: Locations of Culture in the Yoruba-Atlantic*. Chicago: University of Chicago Press.

Arcini, Caroline. 2009. "Buried Face Down." *Current Archaeology* (231): 30–35.

Arendt, Hannah. (1958) 1998. *The Human Condition*. 2nd ed. Chicago: University of Chicago Press.

Armstrong, Karen. 2015. *Fields of Blood: Religion and the History of Violence*. New York: Anchor Books.

Asad, Talal. 1986. *The Idea of an Anthropology of Islam*. Washington, DC: Center for Contemporary Arab Studies, Georgetown University.

———. 1993. *Genealogies of Religion: Discipline and Reasons of Power in Christianity and Islam*. Baltimore: Johns Hopkins University Press.

———. 2003. *Formations of the Secular: Christianity, Islam, Modernity*. Stanford, CA: Stanford University Press.

———. 2007. *On Suicide Bombing*. New York: Columbia University Press.

———. 2010. "Thinking about Terrorism and Just War." *Cambridge Review of International Affairs* 23 (1): 3–24.

Asprem, Egil. 2008. "Magic Naturalized? Negotiating Science and Occult Experience in Aleister Crowley's Scientific Illuminism." *Aries* 8 (2): 139–65.

———. 2018. *The Problem of Disenchantment: Scientific Naturalism and Esoteric Discourse, 1900–1939*. Albany: State University of New York Press.

Assmann, Jan. 2009. *The Price of Monotheism*. Translated by Robert Savage. Stanford, CA: Stanford University Press.

Atanasoski, Neda. 2013. *Humanitarian Violence: The US Deployment of Diversity*. Minneapolis: University of Minnesota Press.

Austin, J. L. 1962. *How to Do Things with Words: The William James Lectures Delivered at Harvard University in 1955*. Edited by J. O. Urmson and Marina Sbisà. Oxford, UK: Clarendon Press.

Ayala, Elaine. 2018. "S.A. Animal Sacrifice Was Santería Practice, But Was It Illegal?" *San Antonio Express-News*, March 23. https://www.mysanantonio.com/news/local/article/S-A-animal-sacrifice-was-Santer-a-practice-but-12773670.php.

Ba, Diadie. 2007. "Africans Still Seething over Sarkozy Speech." *Reuters World News*, September 5. https://uk.reuters.com/article/uk-africa-sarkozy/africans-still-seething-over-sarkozy-speech-idUKL0513034620070905.

Balser, Keith. 2013. "Dismantling a Cradle of Lies: *Shepherd's Staff* Needed to Oppose 'Voodoo.'" *World Map Digest* (Winter): 10–11.

Barad, Karen. 2007. *Meeting the Universe Halfway: Quantum Physics and the Entanglement of Matter and Meaning*. Durham, NC: Duke University Press.

———. 2017. "No Small Matter: Mushroom Clouds, Ecologies of Nothingness, and Strange

Topologies of Spacetimemattering." In *Arts of Living on a Damaged Planet: Ghosts of the Anthropocene*, edited by Anna Lowenhaupt Tsing, Heather Anne Swanson, Elaine Gan, and Nils Bubandt, 103–20. Minneapolis: University of Minnesota Press.

Barclay, Rosalie. 2009. *Literature Review: Child Sexual Abuse in Trinidad and Tobago and the Caribbean*. St. Augustine, Trinidad: Institute for Gender and Development Studies, University of the West Indies.

Barnes, Sandra T., ed. 1997. *Africa's Ogun: Old World and New*. Bloomington: Indiana University Press.

Bastide, Roger. 1967. "Le spiritisme au Brésil." *Archives de sociologie des religions* 24: 3–16.

Baverstock, Alisdair. 2015. "Children Hospitalised with Mass Hysteria, 'Mysterious Bruises' and a 'Mexican Demon': How a Video in the Dominican Republic Spawned the 'Satanic' Charlie Charlie Game Sending Teenagers into a Panic across the World." *Daily Mail*, June 9. http://www.dailymail.co.uk/news/article-3116725/Children-hospitalised-mass-hysteria-mysterious-bruises-Mexican-demon-video-Dominican-Republic-spawned-satanic-Charlie-Charlie-game-sending-teenagers-panic-world.html.

Beattie, John. 1966. "Ritual and Social Change." *Man* 1 (1): 60–74.

Beekers, Daan, and David Kloos, eds. 2018. *Straying from the Straight Path: How Senses of Failure Invigorate Lived Religion*. New York: Berghahn Books.

Beliso de Jesús, Aisha. 2015. *Electric Santería: Racial and Sexual Assemblages of Transnational Religion*. New York: Columbia University Press.

Bell, Catherine. (1992) 2009. *Ritual Theory, Ritual Practice*. Oxford: Oxford University Press.

Bell, Hesketh. (1889) 1893. *Obeah: Witchcraft in the West Indies*. London: S. Low, Marston & Co.

Benjamin, Walter. 1986. "Critique of Violence." In *Reflections: Essays, Aphorisms and Autobiographical Writing*, edited by Peter Demetz, 277–300. New York: Schocken Books.

———. 2002. *The Arcades Project*. Cambridge, MA: Harvard University Press.

Berry, Damon T. 2017. *Blood and Faith: Christianity in American White Nationalism*. Syracuse, NY: Syracuse University Press.

Best, Carmel. 2019. "Obeah Man, Answer the Question: A Tribute to Leroy Clarke and Shadow." *Trinidad and Tobago Express*, March 7. https://www.trinidadexpress.com/features/local/obeah-man-answer-the-question/article_23c0d7a0-4136-11e9-a899-4fa1817ea68d.html.

Bhabha, Homi. 1994. *The Location of Culture*. London: Routledge.

Bilby, Kenneth M. 2012. "An (Un)natural Mystic in the Air: Images of Obeah in Caribbean Song." In *Obeah and Other Powers: The Politics of Caribbean Religion and Healing*, edited by Diana Paton and Maarit Forde, 45–79. Durham, NC: Duke University Press.

Bilby, Kenneth M., and Jerome S. Handler. 2004. "Obeah: Healing and Protection in West Indian Slave Life." *Journal of Caribbean History* 38 (2): 153–83.

Boaz, Danielle. 2019. "The 'Abhorrent' Practice of Animal Sacrifice and Religious Discrimination in the Global South." *Religions* 10 (3). https://doi.org/10.3390/rel10030160.

Boddy, Janice. 1989. *Wombs and Alien Spirits: Women, Men, and the Zār Cult in Northern Sudan*. Madison: University of Wisconsin Press.

Bonilla, Yarimar. 2015. *Nonsovereign Futures: French Caribbean Politics in the Wake of Disenchantment*. Chicago: University of Chicago Press.

Borofsky, Robert. 1968. *Obeah: A Description of an Occult Medical System in Trinidad*. New York: Research Institute for the Study of Man.

Bouzar, Petra. 2012. "'She Is Always Present': Informal Authority in a Swiss Muslim Women's Association." In *Women, Leadership, and Mosques: Changes in Contemporary Islamic Authority*, edited by Masooda Bano and Hilary Kalmbach, 279–300. Leiden: Brill.

Boyarin, Jonathan. 2009. *The Unconverted Self: Jews, Indians, and the Identity of Christian Europe*. Chicago: University of Chicago Press.

Brathwaite, Edward Kamau. 1974. "The African Presence in Caribbean Literature." In *Slavery, Colonialism, and Racism*, edited by Sidney Mintz, 95–163. New York: W. W. Norton and Co.

Brereton, Bridget. 1979. *Race Relations in Colonial Trinidad, 1870–1900*. London: Cambridge University Press.

———. 1981. *A History of Modern Trinidad 1783–1962*. Kingston: Heinemann.

———. 2010. "'All Ah We Is Not One': Historical and Ethnic Narratives in Pluralist Trinidad." *Global South* 4 (2): 218–38.

Brodber, Erna. (1988) 2014. *Myal*. Long Grove, IL: Waveland Press.

Brooks, David. 2010. "The Underlying Tragedy." *New York Times*, January 15.

Brosses, Charles de. (1760) 1970. *Du culte des dieux fétiches, out Parallèle de l'ancienne religion de l'Egypte avec la religion actuelle de Nigritie*. London: Westmead, Farnborough, Hants.

Brown, David H. 2003. *Santería Enthroned: Art Ritual and Innovation in an Afro-Cuban Religion*. Chicago: University of Chicago Press.

Brown, Karen McCarthy. 2001. *Mama Lola: A Vodou Priestess in Brooklyn*. Berkeley: University of California Press.

Browne, Randy M. 2011. "The 'Bad Business' of Obeah: Power, Authority, and the Politics of Slave Culture in the British Caribbean." *William and Mary Quarterly* 68 (3): 451–80.

Bubandt, Nils. 2014. *The Empty Seashell: Witchcraft and Doubt on an Indonesian Island*. Ithaca, NY: Cornell University Press.

Buck-Morss, Susan. 2000. "Hegel and Haiti." *Critical Inquiry* 26 (4): 821–65.

Burton, Richard D. E. 1997. *Afro-Creole: Power, Opposition, and Play in the Caribbean*. Ithaca, NY: Cornell University Press.

Carter, J. Cameron. 2008. *Race: A Theological Account*. Oxford: Oxford University Press.

Casid, Jill H. 2002. "His Master's Obi: Machine Magic, Colonial Violence, and Transculturation." In *The Visual Culture Reader*, 2nd ed., edited by Nicholas Mirzoeff, 533–45. New York: Routledge.

Cassecanarie, Myal Djumboh. 1895. *Obeah Simplified: The True Wanga*. Port of Spain, Trinidad: "Mirror" Office.

Castor, N. Fadeke. 2013. "Shifting Multicultural Citizenship: Trinidad Orisha Opens the Road." *Cultural Anthropology* 28 (3): 475–89.

———. 2017. *Spiritual Citizenship: Transnational Pathways from Black Power to Ifá in Trinidad*. Durham, NC: Duke University Press.

Cavanaugh, William. 1995. "'A Fire Strong Enough to Consume the House': The Wars of Religion and the Rise of the State." *Modern Theology* 11 (4): 397–420.

————. 2009. *The Myth of Religious Violence*. New York: Oxford University Press.

"Charlie Charlie Presents Challenges for Caribbean Schools." 2015. *Antigua Observer*, May 29. http://antiguaobserver.com/charlie-charlie-presents-challenges-for-caribbean-schools/.

Chernoff, John. 1979. *African Rhythm and African Sensibility: Aesthetics and Social Action in African Musical Idioms*. Chicago: University of Chicago Press.

Chevannes, Barry. 1994. *Rastafari: Roots and Ideology*. Syracuse, NY: Syracuse University Press.

Chidester, David. 1996. *Savage Systems: Colonialism and Comparative Religion in Southern Africa*. Charlottesville, NC: University Press of Virginia.

Chireau, Yvonne. 2006. *Black Magic: Religion and the African American Conjuring Tradition*. Berkeley: University of California Press.

Clarke, Colin G. 1986. *East Indians in a West Indian Town: San Fernando, Trinidad, 1930–70*. London: Allen & Unwin.

Clarke, Kamari Maxine. 2004. *Mapping Yorùbá Networks: Power and Agency in the Making of Transnational Communities*. Durham, NC: Duke University Press.

————. 2013. "How Police Use Religion to Deceive Suspects." *Huffington Post*. http://www.kamariclarke.com/wp-content/uploads/2013/09/KC_Huff-Post.pdf.

Clarke, LeRoy. 2001. "My Work Is Obeah." In *Healing Cultures*, edited by Margarite Fernández Olmos and Lizabeth Paravisini-Gebert, 201–10. New York: Palgrave Macmillan.

Clifford, James. 1988. *The Predicament of Culture: Twentieth Century Ethnography, Literature, and Art*. Cambridge, MA: Harvard University Press.

————. 1992. "Travelling Cultures." In *Cultural Studies*, edited by L. Grossberg, C. Nelso, and P. Treichler, 96–116. New York: Routledge.

Coccari, Diane. 1989. "The Bir Babas of Banaras and the Deified Dead." In *Criminal Gods and Demon Devotees: Essays on the Guardians of Popular Hinduism*, edited by Alf Hiltebeitel, 251–70. Albany: State University of New York Press.

Comte, Auguste. 1853. *The Positive Philosophy of Auguste Comte*. Translated by Harriet Martineau. London: J. Chapman.

Covington-Ward, Yolanda. 2016. *Gesture and Power: Religion, Nationalism, and Everyday Performance in Congo*. Durham, NC: Duke University Press.

Creed, Gerald. 2006. "Community as Modern Pastoral." In *Seductions of Community*, edited by Gerald Creed, 23–48. Santa Fe, NM: SAR Press.

Crockett, Clayton. 2006. *Religion and Violence in a Secular World: Toward a New Political Theology*. Charlottesville: University of Virginia Press.

Crosson, J. Brent. 2013. "Invisibilities: Translation. Spirits of the Dead and the Politics of Invisibility." *Cultural Anthropology Field Notes*, June 20. https://culanth.org/fieldsights/invisibilities-translation.

————. 2014. "Own People: Race, Altered Solidarities, and the Limits of Culture in Trinidad." *Small Axe* 45: 18–34.

————. 2015. "What Obeah Does Do: Healing, Harming, and the Boundaries of Religion." *Journal of Africana Religions* 3 (2): 151–76.

————. 2016. "Cooking in Modernity's Crucible: Global Locals, Native Creoles, and the

Politics of Culinary Mixture." *Gastronomica: The Journal of Food and Culture* 26 (2): 94–96.

———. 2017a. "Catching Power: Problems with Possession, Sovereignty, and African Religions in Trinidad." In "What Possessed You? Spirits, Property, and Political Sovereignty at the Limits of "Possession," edited by J. Brent Crosson. Special issue, *Ethnos* 84 (4): 588–614.

———. 2017b. "What Possessed You? Spirits, Property, and Political Sovereignty at the Limits of 'Possession.'" Special issue, *Ethnos* 84 (4): 546–56.

———. 2018. "The Impossibility of Liberal Secularism: Political Violence, Spirituality, and Not-Religion." *Method & Theory in the Study of Religion* 30 (1): 35–55.

———. 2019. "Inventive Traditions: Authority and Power in African Diasporic Religions." *Religious Studies Review* 45 (4): 451–59.

———. 2020. "'Don't Study People': The Dangers of Studying Others in Trinidad and in Anthropology." *Anthropological Quarterly* 93 (1): 1093–1122.

———. Forthcoming. "Obeah Simplified? Scientism, Magic, and the Problem of Universals." In *Critical Approaches to Science and Religion*, edited by Terence Keel, Ahmed Ragab, and Myrna Perez Sheldon. Cambridge: Cambridge University Press.

Darr, Orna Alyagon. 2014. "Experiments in the Courtroom: Social Dynamics and Spectacles of Proof in Early Modern English Witch Trials." *Law and Social Inquiry* 39 (1): 152–75.

Darwin, Charles. (1859) 2004. *On the Origin of Species, by Means of Natural Selection of the Preservation of Favoured Races in the Struggle for Life*. New York: Routledge.

Dave, Naisargi N. 2012. *Queer Activism in India: A Story in the Anthropology of Ethics*. Durham, NC: Duke University Press.

Davies, Owen. 2010. *Grimoires: A History of Magic Books*. Oxford: Oxford University Press.

Dawkins, Richard. 2006. *The God Delusion*. New York: Houghton Mifflin Co.

De la Cadena, Marisol. 2015. *Earth Beings: Ecologies of Practice across Andean Worlds*. Durham, NC: Duke University Press.

Deleuze, Gilles, and Felix Guattari. (1972) 2000. *Anti-Oedipus: Capitalism and Schizophrenia*. Minneapolis: University of Minnesota Press.

———. (1980) 2007. *A Thousand Plateaus: Capitalism and Schizophrenia*. Minneapolis: University of Minnesota Press.

Derrida, Jacques. 2002. "Force of Law: The 'Mystical Foundation of Authority.'" In *Acts of Religion*, edited by Gil Anidjar, 228–98. New York: Routledge.

Dhalai, Richardson. 2011. "Jack: Demons among Us." *Trinidad and Tobago Newsday*, October 27.

Doostdar, Alireza. 2018. *The Iranian Metaphysicals: Explorations in Science, Islam, and the Uncanny*. Princeton, NJ: Princeton University Press.

DuBois, W. E. B. (1935) 2014. *Black Reconstruction in America: An Essay Toward a History of the Part Which Black Folk Played in the Attempt to Reconstruct Democracy in America, 1860–1880*. New York: Oxford University Press.

Dumont, Louis. 1957. *Une sous-caste de l'Inde du sud: Organisation sociale et religion des Pramalai Kallar*. Paris: Mouton.

Duncan, Carol B. 2008. *This Spot of Ground: Spiritual Baptists in Toronto*. Waterloo, ON: Wilfrid Laurier University Press.

Durkheim, Émile. (1912) 1964. *The Elementary Forms of Religious Life*. London: Allen and Unwin.

Dutton, Michael, Sanjay Seth, and Leela Gandhi. 2002. "Plumbing the Depths: Toilets, Transparency and Modernity." *Postcolonial Studies* 5 (2): 137–42.

Eagleton, Terry. 1981. *Walter Benjamin, or Towards a Revolutionary Criticism*. London: Verso.

Edwards, Brent Hayes. 2003. *The Practice of Diaspora: Literature, Translation, and the Rise of Black Internationalism*. Cambridge, MA: Harvard University Press.

Edwards, Bryan. (1793–1801) 1972. *The History, Civil and Commercial of the British Colonies of the West Indies*. Vol. 2. New York: Arno Press.

Eglash, Ron. 1999. *African Fractals: Modern Computing and Indigenous Design*. Rutgers, NJ: Rutgers University Press.

Elder, J. D. 1970. "Folk Beliefs, Superstitions and Ancestor Cult Activities in Relation to Mental Health Problems." Lecture given at the Nurses Training School, St. Ann's Mental Hospital, Trinidad, January 15.

"Emancipation Group Condemns Obeah in Political Advert." 2015. *Jamaica Observer*, September 4.

Engler, Steven. 2012. "Umbanda and Africa." *Nova Religio* 15 (4): 13–35.

Espírito Santo, Diana. 2015. *Developing the Dead: Mediumship and Selfhood in Cuban Espiritismo*. Gainesville: University Press of Florida.

Evans-Pritchard, E. E. 1937. *Witchcraft, Oracles and Magic Among the Azande*. Oxford: Oxford University Press.

Eyiogbe, Frank Baba. 2015. *Babalawo: Santería's High Priests*. Woodbury, MI: Llewellyn Publications.

Faavret-Saada, Jeanne. 1980. *Deadly Words: Witchcraft in the Bocage*. Cambridge: Cambridge University Press.

Fabian, Johannes. 1983. *Time and the Other: How Anthropology Makes Its Object*. New York: Columbia University Press.

Fanon, Frantz. (1952) 1986. *Black Skin, White Masks*. London: Pluto Press.

Fassin, Didier. 2014. "The Ethical Turn in Anthropology: Promises and Uncertainties." *HAU: Journal of Ethnographic Theory* 4 (1): 429–35.

Faubion, James D. 2003. "Religion, Violence, and the Vitalistic Economy." *Anthropological Quarterly* 76 (1): 71–85.

Feldman, Allen. 2018. "Histories of Violence: Living with Disappearance." *LA Review of Books*, February 26. https://lareviewofbooks.org/article/histories-of-violence-living-with-disappearance/#.

Felix, Talia, trans. (c. 1702) 2013. *The Spellbook of Marie Laveau: The Petit Albert*. Los Angeles: Papaveri Press.

Fernando, Mayanthi. 2014. *The Republic Unsettled: Muslim French and the Contradictions of Secularism*. Durham, NC: Duke University Press.

Fessenden, Tracy. 2012. "Religious Liberalism and the Liberal Geopolitics of Religion." In

American Religious Liberalism, edited by Eric Leigh Schmidt and Sally Promey, 359–73. Bloomington: Indiana University Press.

Feyerabend, Paul. 1975. *Against Method*. New York: New Left Books.

Figueira, Daurius. 1997. *Cocaine and the Economy of Crime in T & T*. Freeport, Trinidad and Tobago: H. E. M. Enterprises.

———. 2004. *Cocaine and Heroin Trafficking in the Caribbean: The Case of Trinidad and Tobago, Jamaica and Guyana*. Lincoln, NE: iUniverse.

Figueira, Daurius, and Alain Labrousse. 2008. "Évolutions récentes de la géopolitique de la cocaïne." *L'espace politique* (4). https://journals.openedition.org/espacepolitique/691.

Finley, Stephen, Margarita Guillory, and Hugh Page Jr., eds. 2014. *Esotericism in African American Religious Experience: "There Is a Mystery . . ."* Leiden: Brill.

Flesher, Paul V. M. 2006. "Film and the Christianization of Nigeria." *Religion Today*, October 22–28. http://www.uwyo.edu/relstds/_files/reli_today/2006/10-22-06.pdf.

Forde, Maarit. 2002. *Marching to Zion: Creolisation in Spiritual Baptist Rituals and Cosmology*. Helsinki: University of Helsinki Department of Anthropology.

———. 2011. "Obeah and the Production of Difference: Legacies of Colonial Government of Religion in the Caribbean." Paper presented at the annual meeting of the American Anthropological Association, Montreal, November 16–20.

———. 2012. "The Moral Economy of Spiritual Work: Money and Rituals in Trinidad and Tobago." In *Obeah and Other Powers: The Politics of Caribbean Religion and Healing*, edited by Diana Paton and Maarit Forde, 198–219. Durham, NC: Duke University Press.

———. 2018. "Fear, Segregation, and Civic Engagement in Urban Trinidad." *Journal of Latin American and Caribbean Anthropology* 23 (3): 437–56. https://doi.org/10.1111/jlca.12343.

Foucault, Michel. 1982. "The Subject and Power." *Critical Inquiry* 8 (4): 777–95.

———. 1988. *Technologies of the Self: A Seminar with Michel Foucault*. Amherst: University of Massachusetts Press.

———. 2003. *Society Must Be Defended: Lectures at the Collège de France, 1975–76*. New York: Picador.

Fraser, Tony. 2012. "Failure to Counter Crime: We to Blame." *Trinidad Express*, January 18.

Fraunhar, Alison. 2002. "Tropics of Desire: Envisioning the Mulata Cubana." *Emergences* 12 (2): 219–34.

Frazer, Sir James George. 1922. *The Golden Bough: A Study in Magic and Religion*. New York: Macmillan.

Frye, Karla Y. E. 1997. "'An Article of Faith': Obeah and Hybrid Identities in Elizabeth Nunez-Harrell's When Rocks Dance." In *Sacred Possessions: Vodou, Santeria, Obeah, and the Caribbean*, edited by Margarite Fernández Olmos and Lizabeth Paravisini-Gebert, 195–215. Rutgers, NJ: Rutgers University Press.

Fuller, C. J. 1988. "The Hindu Pantheon and the Legitimation of Hierarchy." *Man* 23 (1): 19–39.

Geertz, Armin, ed. 2013. *Origins of Religion, Cognition and Culture*. New York: Routledge.

Geschiere, Peter. 2013. *Witchcraft, Intimacy, and Trust: Africa in Comparison*. Chicago: University of Chicago Press.

Ghassem-Fachandi, Parvis. 2012. *Pogrom in Gujarat: Hindu Nationalism and Anti-Muslim Violence in India*. Princeton, NJ: Princeton University Press.

Girard, Renee. 1977. *Violence and the Sacred*. Translated by Patrick Gregory. Baltimore: Johns Hopkins University Press.

———. 1987. *Things Hidden since the Foundation of the World*. Translated by Stephen Bann and Michael Metteer. Stanford, CA: Stanford University Press.

Glazier, Stephen. 1983. *Marchin' the Pilgrims Home: Leadership and Decision-Making in an Afro-Caribbean Faith*. Westport, CT: Greenwood Press.

Gluckman, Max. 1953. *Rituals of Rebellion in Southeast Africa*. Manchester: Manchester University Press.

Golding, Shenequa. 2015. "George Zimmerman Calls Trayvon Martin Shooting Divine Order." *Vibe*, March 23. https://www.vibe.com/2015/03/george-zimmerman-blames-obama.

Gordon, Theresa. 2015. "Two Indian 'Obeah Men' Arrested." *Daily Observer*, November 11. https://antiguaobserver.com/two-indian-obeah-men-arrested/.

Gottschalk, Peter. 2003. "Dead Healers and Living Identities: Narratives of a Hindu Ghost and a Muslim Sufi in a Shared Village." In *The Living and the Dead: Social Dimensions of Death in South Asian Religions*, edited by Liz Wilson, 177–200. Albany: State University of New York Press.

———. 2012. *Religion, Science, and Empire: Classifying Hinduism and Islam in British India*. New York: Oxford University Press.

Gould, Jeffrey. 1998. *To Die in This Way: Nicaraguan Indians and the Myth of Mestizaje, 1880–1965*. Durham, NC: Duke University Press.

Grey, Devon. 2015. "Why Defend Obeah Rights, Rev. Dick?" *Jamaica Gleaner*, January 31. https://jamaica-gleaner.com/article/letters/20150131/why-defend-obeah-rights-rev-dick.

Gross, Paul R., and Norman Levitt. 1994. *Higher Superstition: The Academic Left and Its Quarrels with Science*. Baltimore: Johns Hopkins University Press.

Guerts, Kathryn. 2002. *Culture and the Senses: Bodily Ways of Knowing in an African Community*. Berkeley: University of California Press.

Guinee, William. 1992. "Suffering and Healing in Trinidadian Kali Worship." PhD diss., Indiana University.

Guinn, David E. 2011. "Religion, Law, and Violence." In *The Blackwell Companion to Religion and Violence*, edited by Andrew R. Murphy, 99–111. Malden, MA: Blackwell Publishing.

Hacking, Ian. 1983. *Representing and Intervening: Introductory Topics in the Philosophy of Natural Science*. New York: Cambridge University Press.

Hall, Catherine. 2002. *Civilizing Subjects: Metropole and Colony in the English Imagination, 1830–1867*. Chicago: University of Chicago Press.

Handler, Jerome S. 1996. "A Prone Burial from a Plantation Slave Cemetery in Barbados, West Indies: Possible Evidence for an African-Type Witch or Other Negatively Viewed Person." *Historical Archaeology* 30 (3): 76–86.

———. 2000. "Slave Medicine and Obeah in Barbados, circa 1650 to 1834." *New West Indian Guide* 74 (1–2): 57–90.

Handler, Jerome S., and F. W. Lange. 1978. *Plantation Slavery in Barbados: An Archaeological and Historical Investigation.* Cambridge, MA: Harvard University Press.

Handler, Jerome S., and Kenneth M. Bilby. 2001. "On the Early Use and Origin of the Term 'Obeah' in Barbados and the Anglophone Caribbean." *Slavery & Abolition* 22 (2): 87–100.

———. 2012. *Enacting Power: The Criminalization of Obeah in the Anglophone Caribbean, 1760–2012.* Kingston: University of the West Indies Press.

Hannerz, Ulf. 1987. "The World in Creolization." *Africa* 57 (4): 546–59.

———. 1996. *Transnational Connections: Culture, People, Places.* London: Routledge.

Haraway, Donna. 1991. *Simians, Cyborgs and Women: The Reinvention of Nature.* New York: Routledge.

Harding, Sandra. 2008. *Sciences from Below: Feminisms, Postcolonialities, and Modernities.* Durham, NC: Duke University Press.

———. 2015. *Objectivity and Diversity: Another Logic of Scientific Research.* Chicago: University of Chicago Press.

Harris, Sam. 2004. *The End of Faith: Religion, Terror, and the Future of Reason.* New York: W. W. Norton & Co.

———. 2007. *Letter to a Christian Nation.* New York: Alfred A. Knopf.

Harrison, Lawrence. 2010. "Haiti and the Voodoo Curse: The Cultural Roots of the Country's Endless Misery." *Wall Street Journal,* February 5.

Harrison, Lawrence, and Samuel Huntington, eds. 2000. *Culture Matters: How Values Shape Human Progress.* New York: Basic Books.

Hartigan, John. 2017. *Care of the Species: Races of Corn and the Science of Plant Biodiversity.* Minneapolis: University of Minnesota Press.

Hassanali, Shaliza. 2019. "PM Defends One Shot, One Kill." *Trinidad and Tobago Guardian,* January 12. https://www.guardian.co.tt/newspm-defends-one-shot-one-kill-6.2.754406.b771a2a041.

Hayes, Kelly. 2011. *Holy Harlots: Femininity, Sexuality, and Black Magic in Brazil.* Berkeley: University of California Press.

Hedstrom, Matt. 2007. "Review of Schmidt, Leigh Eric, *Restless Souls: The Making of American Spirituality from Emerson to Oprah.*" *H-Amstdy, H-Net Reviews,* September. https://networks.h-net.org/node/2602/reviews/2838/hedstrom-schmidt-restless-souls-making-american-spirituality-emerson.

Hegel, G. W. F. (1807) 1910. *The Phenomenology of Mind.* Vol. 2. London: Swan Sonnenschein and Co.

———. (1837) 1956. *The Philosophy of History.* Translated by J. Sibree. New York: Dover Publications.

Henry, Balford. 2013. "Senators Push for Decriminalisation of Obeah," *Jamaica Observer,* February 19.

———. 2018. *Religion, Magic, and the Origins of Science in Early Modern England.* London: Routledge.

Henry, Frances. 2003. *Reclaiming African Religions in Trinidad: The Socio-Political Legitimation of the Orisha and Spiritual Baptist Faiths.* Kingston: University of West Indies Press.

Henry, John. 1986. "Occult Qualities and the Experimental Philosophy: Active Principles in Pre-Newtonian Matter Theory." *History of Science* 24: 335–81.

Her Majesty the Queen v. J. Welsh, R. Pinnock, and E. Robinson. 2013. On Appeal from the Conviction Entered on Feb. 15 2008. Court of Appeal for Ontario. Heard Dec. 18–20 2018. Docket: C49268.

Her Majesty the Queen v. J. Welsh, E. Robinson, and R. Pinnock. 2007. Ruling Respecting Privileged Communications—Police Impersonating Alleged Religious Advisor. Ontario Superior Court of Justice, 8/23/2007. Court File No.: CRIMJ(P)1123/06.

Hernandez-Ramdwar, Camille. 2008. "Feteing as Cultural Resistance? The Soca Posse in the Caribbean Diaspora." *TOPIA* 20: 65–92.

Herskovits, Melville, and Frances S. Herskovits. 1947. *Trinidad Village*. New York: Alfred A. Knopf.

Hess, David J. 1991. *Spirits and Scientists: Ideology, Spiritism and Brazilian Culture*. State College, PA: Penn State University Press.

Hiltebeitel, Alf, ed. 1989. *Criminal Gods and Demon Devotees: Essays on the Guardians of Popular Hinduism*. Albany: State University of New York Press.

Hintzen, Percy. 2000. "Afro-Creole Nationalism as Elite Domination: The English-Speaking West Indies." In *Foreign Policy and the Black (Inter)National Interest*, edited by Charles P. Henry, 185–215. Albany: State University of New York Press.

Hirschkind, Charles. 2006. *The Ethical Soundscape: Cassette Sermons and Islamic Counter-Publics*. New York: Columbia University Press.

———. 2011. "Media, Mediation, Religion." *Social Anthropology* 19 (1): 97–102.

Hitchens, Christopher. 2007. *God Is Not Great: How Religion Poisons Everything*. New York: Hachette Book Group.

Hogg, D. W. 1961. "Magic and 'Science' in Jamaica." *Caribbean Studies* 1: 1–5.

Holbraad, Martin. 2012. *Truth in Motion: The Recursive Anthropology of Cuban Divination*. Chicago: University of Chicago Press.

Horton, Robin. 1967a. "African Traditional Thought and Western Science, Part I: From Tradition to Science." *Africa* 37 (1): 50–71.

———. 1967b. "African Traditional Thought and Western Science, Part II: The 'Closed' and 'Open' Predicaments." *Africa* 37 (2): 155–87.

Hossein, W. K. S. 2012. "It's Either Crime or Tough Action." *Trinidad Express*, July 1.

Houk, James T. 1993. "The Role of the Kabbalah in the Afro-American Religious Complex in Trinidad." *Caribbean Quarterly* 39 (3–4): 42–55.

———. 1995. *Spirit, Blood and Drums: The Orisha Religion in Trinidad*. Philadelphia: Temple University Press.

Houtman, D., and Meyer, B., eds. 2012. *Things: Religion and the Question of Materiality*. New York: Fordham University Press.

"How to Kill Obeah." 1891. *Jamaica Gleaner*, December 14.

Hucks, Tracey E. 2006. "I Smoothed the Way, I Opened Doors: Women in the Yoruba Orisha Tradition of Trinidad." In *Women and Religion in the African Diaspora: Knowledge, Power, and Performance*, edited by R. Marie Griffith and Barbara Dianne Savage, 19–36. Baltimore: Johns Hopkins University Press.

Humphreys, Adrian. 2008. "Lawyers Get Bad Vibes From Voodoo Sting." *National Post* (Brampton, ON), March 1.

Hurbon, Laënnec. 1995. "American Fantasy and Haitian Vodou." In *Sacred Arts of Haitian Vodou*, edited by Donald Consentino, 181–97. Los Angeles: UCLA Fowler Museum.

Hurston, Zora Neale. (1939) 2009. *Moses, Man of the Mountain*. New York: Harper Perennial Modern Classics.

Hutchison, Keith. 1982. "What Happened to Occult Qualities in the Scientific Revolution?" *Isis* 73 (2): 233–53.

"Items of News." 1909. *Port of Spain Gazette*, March 9.

James, Cyril Lionel Robert. (1938) 2001. *The Black Jacobins: Toussaint L'Ouverture and the San Domingo Revolution*. London: Penguin UK.

———. (1963) 2005. *Beyond a Boundary*. London: Yellow Jersey Press.

"James Was Unarmed: East Port of Spain Residents Dispute Cops' Story of Killing." 2018. *Trinidad and Tobago Guardian*, February 20.

Jameson, A. D. 2010. "What Is Experimental Art?" *Big Other*, March 12. https://bigother. com/2010/03/12/what-is-experimental-art/.

"January 2018 Is Bloodiest Month in T&T History." 2018. *Loop News*, January 31. http:// www.looptt.com/content/bloody-january-murder-count-60.

Johnson, Paul Christopher. 2007. *Diaspora Conversions: Black Carib Religion and the Recovery of Africa*. Berkeley: University of California Press.

———. 2011. "An Atlantic Genealogy of 'Spirit Possession.'" *Comparative Studies in Society and History* 53 (2): 393–425.

———. 2014a. "Introduction: Spirits and Things in the Making of the Afro-Atlantic World." In *Spirited Things: The Work of "Possession" in Afro-Atlantic Religions*, edited by Paul Christopher Johnson, 1–22. Chicago: University of Chicago Press.

———. 2014b. "Towards an Atlantic Genealogy of Spirit Possession." In *Spirited Things: The Work of "Possession" in Afro-Atlantic Religions*, edited by Paul Christopher Johnson, 23–46. Chicago: University of Chicago Press.

Johnson, Sylvester A. 2004. *The Myth of Ham in Nineteenth-Century American Christianity: Race, Heathens, and the People of God*. New York: Palgrave Macmillan.

Josephson-Storm, Jason Ānanda. 2017. *The Myth of Disenchantment: Magic, Modernity, and the Birth of the Human Sciences*. Chicago: University of Chicago Press.

———. 2018. "The Superstition, Secularism, and Religion Trinary: Or Re-Theorizing Secularism." *Method & Theory in the Study of Religion* 30 (1): 1–20.

Josiffe, Christophe. 2013. "Aleister Crowley, Marie de Miramar & the True Wanga." *Abraxas Journal* 1 (4): 29–42.

Jouili, Jeanette S. 2015. *Pious Practice and Secular Constraints: Women in the Islamic Revival in Europe*. Palo Alto, CA: Stanford University Press.

Kaden, Tom, and Thomas Schmidt-Lux. 2016. "Scientism and Atheism Then and Now: The Role of Science in the Monist and New Atheist Writings." *Culture and Religion: An Interdisciplinary Journal* 17 (1): 73–91.

Kamugisha, A. 2007. "The Coloniality of Citizenship in the Contemporary Anglophone Caribbean." *Race & Class* 49 (2): 20–40.

Kant, Immanuel. (1793) 1960. *Religion within the Limits of Reason Alone.* Translated by Theodore M. Greene and Hoyt H. Hudson. New York: Harper & Row.

Karp, Ivan, and Charles Bird, eds. 1987. *African Systems of Thought.* Washington, DC: Smithsonian Institution Press.

Keane, Webb. 2014a. "Affordances and Reflexivity in Ethical Life: An Ethnographic Stance." *Anthropological Theory* 14 (1): 3–26.

———. 2014b. "Rotting Bodies: The Clash of Stances toward Materiality and Its Ethical Affordances." *Current Anthropology* 55, no. S10: S312–S321.

———. 2016. *Ethical Life: Its Natural and Social Histories.* Princeton, NJ: Princeton University Press.

———. 2018. "Killing Animals: On the Violence of Sacrifice, the Hunt and the Butcher." *Anthropology of this Century* 22. http://aotcpress.com/articles/killing-animals-violence-sacrifice-hunt-butcher/.

Keel, Terence. 2018. *Divine Variations: How Christian Thought Became Racial Science.* Palo Alto, CA: Stanford University Press.

Keeney, Bradford, ed. 2002. *The Shakers of St. Vincent.* Philadelphia: Ringing Rocks Press.

Kelley, Robin D. G. 1999. "People in Me." *Utne Reader* 95: 79–81.

Kerrigan, Dylan. 2018. "Living under Militarisation and Insecurity: How Securitisation Discourse Wounds Trinidad." *Journal of Latin American and Caribbean Anthropology* 23 (3): 416–36. https://doi.org/10.1111/jlca.12341.

Khan, Aisha Karen. 2003. "Isms and Schisms: Interpreting Religion in the Americas." *Anthropological Quarterly* 76 (4): 761–74.

———. 2004a. *Callaloo Nation: Metaphors of Race and Religious Identity Among South Asians in Trinidad.* Durham, NC: Duke University Press.

———. 2004b. "Sacred Subversions? The Indo-Caribbean, Syncretic Creoles, and 'Culture's In-Between.'" *Radical History Review* 89: 165–84.

———. 2007. "Rites and Rights of Passage: Seeking a Diasporic Consciousness." *Cultural Dynamics* 19 (2–3): 141–64.

———. 2012. "Islam, Vodou, and the Making of the Afro-Atlantic." *New West Indian Guide* 86 (1–2): 29–54.

———. 2013. "Dark Arts and Diaspora." *Diaspora* 17 (1): 40–63.

Khatib, Sami. 2011. "Towards a Politics of 'Pure Means': Walter Benjamin and the Question of Violence." *Anthropological Materialism.* https://anthropologicalmaterialism.hypotheses.org/1040.

Klass, Morton. (1961) 1988. *East Indians in Trinidad: a Study of Cultural Persistence.* Prospect Heights, IL: Waveland Press.

Kripal, Jeffrey. 2007. *Esalen: America and the Religion of No Religion.* Chicago: University of Chicago Press.

Kuhn, Thomas S. (1962) 1996. *The Structure of Scientific Revolutions.* 3rd ed. Chicago: University of Chicago Press.

Kuklick, Henrika. 1996. "Islands in the Pacific: Darwinian Biogeography and British Anthropology." *American Ethnologist* 23 (3): 611–38.

Laidlaw, James. 2014. *The Subject of Virtue: An Anthropology of Ethics and Freedom.* Cambridge: Cambridge University Press.

Lakatos, Imre. 1970. "Falsification and the Methodology of Scientific Research Programmes." In *Criticism and the Growth of Knowledge*, edited by I. Lakatos and A. Musgrave, 91–196. Cambridge: Cambridge University Press.

———. 1978. "Science and Pseudoscience." In *The Methodology of Scientific Research Programmes: Volume 1*, 1–7. Cambridge: Cambridge University Press.

Lamb, David. 2011. *God Behaving Badly*. Downers Grove, IL: InterVarsity Press.

Lambek, Michael, ed. 2010. *Ordinary Ethics: Anthropology, Language, and Action*. New York: Fordham University Press.

———. 2012. "Facing Religion, from Anthropology." *Anthropology of this Century* 4. http://aotcpress.com/articles/facing-religion-anthropology/.

Latour, Bruno. 1993. *We Have Never Been Modern*. Cambridge, MA: Harvard University Press.

———. 2010. *On the Modern Cult of the Factish Gods*. Durham, NC: Duke University Press.

Laws of Trinidad and Tobago Vol. III. 1884. London: Waterlow and Sons.

Lazarus-Black, Mindie. 1994a. *Legitimate Acts and Illegal Encounters: Law and Society in Antigua and Barbuda*. Washington, DC: Smithsonian Institution Press.

———. 1994b. "Slaves, Masters, and Magistrates: Law and the Politics of Resistance in the British Caribbean, 1736–1834." In *Contested States: Law, Hegemony and Resistance*, edited by Mindie Lazarus-Black and Susan Hirsch, 252–81. New York: Routledge.

Lerche, Ian. 1997. *Geological Risk and Uncertainty in Oil Exploration*. San Diego, CA: Academic Press.

Lincoln, Bruce. 2006. *Holy Terrors: Thinking about Religion after September 11*. Chicago: University of Chicago Press.

Littlewood, Roland. 1993. *Pathology and Identity: The Work of Mother Earth in Trinidad*. Cambridge: Cambridge University Press.

Locke, John. (1689) 1796. *A Letter Concerning Toleration*. London: Huddersfield.

Long, Charles H. 1986. *Significations: Signs, Symbols, and Images in the Interpretation of Religion*. Aurora, CO: Fortress Press.

Lopez, Donald S., Jr. 2008. *Buddhism and Science: A Guide for the Perplexed*. Chicago: University of Chicago Press.

Lovejoy, Paul E. 1980. "Kola in the History of West Africa." *Cahiers d'études africaines* 20 (77–78): 97–134.

Lovelace, Earl. 2003. "Working Obeah." In *Growing in the Dark: Selected Essays*, edited by Funso Aiyejina, 216–26. San Juan, Trinidad and Tobago: Lexicon.

Lum, Kenneth Anthony. 2000. *Praising his Name in the Dance: Spirit Possession in the Spiritual Baptist Faith and Orisha Work in Trinidad, West Indies*. Amsterdam: Gordon and Breach.

Luto na Luta. 2018. "Ask the Supreme Federal Court of Brazil to Protect Afro-Brazilian Religious Freedom." https://www.change.org/p/supremo-tribunal-federal-ask-the-supreme-federal-court-of-brazil-to-protect-afro-brazilian-religious-freedom.

"Luto Na Luta! Fighting Violence against Afro-Brazilian Religious Traditions and Practitioners in Brazil." 2017. University of Texas Department of African and African Diaspora

Studies. https://calendar.utexas.edu/event/luto_na_luta_fighting_violence_against_afro-brazilian_religious_traditions_and_practitioners_in_brazil#.WwryA1Mvwvo.

MacGaffey, Wyatt. 1977. "Fetishism Revisited: Kongo 'Nkisi' in Sociological Perspective." *Africa* 47 (2): 172–84.

———. 2012. "African Traditional Religion." *Oxford Bibliographies*. http://oxfordindex.oup.com/view/10.1093/obo/9780199846733-0064.

Macedo, Eder. 1990. *Orixás, caboclos e guias: Deuses ou demônios?* Rio de Janeiro: Universal Produções.

MacIntyre, Alasdair. 1981. *After Virtue: A Study in Moral Theory*. London: Gerald Duckworth & Co.

Mahabir, Noorkumar, and Ashram Maharaj. 1989. "Hindu Elements in the Shango/Orisha Cult of Trinidad." In *Indenture and Exile: The Indo-Caribbean Experience*, edited by Frank Birbalsingh, 191–201. Toronto: TSAR.

Maharaj, Sat. 2006. "Casting Hinn Out." *Trinidad Guardian*, April 27.

Mahmood, Saba. 2003a. "Ethical Formation and Politics of Individual Autonomy in Contemporary Egypt." *Social Research: An International Quarterly* 70 (3): 837–66.

———. 2003b. "Questioning Liberalism, Too." *Boston Review* (April–May). http://bostonreview.net/archives/BR28.2/mahmood.html.

———. 2005. *Politics of Piety: The Islamic Revival and the Feminist Subject*. Princeton, NJ: Princeton University Press.

———. 2006. "Secularism, Hermeneutics, and Empire: The Politics of Islamic Reformation." *Public Culture* 18 (2): 323–47.

———. 2012. "Ethics and Piety." In *A Companion to Moral Anthropology*, edited by Didier Fassin, 223–41. West Sussex, UK: Wiley and Sons.

Maia, Suzana. 2012. *Transnational Desires: Brazilian Erotic Dancers in New York*. Nashville, TN: Vanderbilt University Press.

Mair, Lucy. 1974. *African Societies*. Cambridge: Cambridge University Press.

Malinowski, Bronislaw. (1925) 1954. *Magic, Science and Religion*. Garden City, NY: Doubleday and Co.

Marlon Rowe v. Her Majesty the Queen. 2006. Response to Application for Leave to Appeal. Supreme Court of Canada. Court File no. 31600.

Marriott, McKim. (1972) 1976. "Hindu Transactions: Diversity without Dualism." In *Transaction and Meaning: Directions in the Anthropology of Exchange and Symbolic Behavior*, edited by Bruce Kapferer, 109–42. Philadelphia: Institute for the Study of Human Issues.

Martínez, María Elena. 2008. *Genealogical Fictions: Limpieza de Sangre, Religion, and Gender in Colonial Mexico*. Palo Alto, CA: Stanford University Press.

Marx, Werner, and Lutz Bornmann. 2010. "How Accurately Does Thomas Kuhn's Model of Paradigm Change Describe the Transition from the Static View of the Universe to the Big Bang Theory in Cosmology? A Historical Reconstruction and Citation Analysis." *Scientometrics* 84: 441–64.

Masuzawa, Tomoko. 2005. *The Invention of World Religions, or, How European Universalism Was Preserved in the Language of Pluralism*. Chicago: University of Chicago Press.

Matory, J. Lorand. 2001. "The 'Cult of Nations' and the Ritualization of Their Purity." *South Atlantic Quarterly* 100 (1): 171–205.

———. 2005. *Black Atlantic Religion: Tradition, Transnationalism and Matriarchy in the Afro-Brazilian Candomblé*. Princeton, NJ: Princeton University Press.

———. 2009. "The Many Who Dance in Me: Afro-Atlantic Ontology and the Problem with 'Transnationalism.'" In *Transnational Transcendence*, edited by Thomas Csordas, 231–62. Berkeley: University of California Press.

Mayblin, Maya. 2017. "The Lapsed and the Laity: Discipline and Lenience in the Study of Religion." *Journal of the Royal Anthropological Institute* 23 (3): 503–22.

Mbembe, Achille. 2003. "Necropolitics." *Public Culture* 15 (1): 11–40.

McAlister, Elizabeth. 2002. *Rara! Vodou, Power, and Performance in Haiti and Its Diaspora*. Berkeley: University of California Press.

———. 2004. "The Jew in the Haitian Imagination: A Popular History of Anti-Judaism and Proto-Racism." In *Race and Nation in the Americas*, edited by Henry Goldschmidt and Elizabeth McAlister, 61–82. New York: Oxford University Press.

———. 2012. "From Slave Revolt to a Blood Pact with Satan: The Evangelical Rewriting of Haitian History." *Studies in Religion/Sciences Religieuses* 41 (2): 187–215.

———. 2014. "Possessing the Land for Jesus." In *Spirited Things: The Work of "Possession" in Afro-Atlantic Religions*, edited by Paul C. Johnson, 177–206. Chicago: University of Chicago Press.

McCloud, Sean. 2015. *American Possessions: Fighting Demons in the Contemporary United States*. New York: Oxford University Press.

McGovern, Mike. 2012. "Turning the Clock Back or Breaking with the Past? Charismatic Temporality and Elite Politics in Côte d'Ivoire and the United States." *Cultural Anthropology* 27 (2): 239–60.

McMahan, David L. 2004. "Modernity and the Early Discourse of Scientific Buddhism." *Journal of the American Academy of Religion* 72 (4): 897–933.

McNeal, Keith. 2011. *Trance and Modernity: African and Hindu Popular Religions in Trinidad and Tobago*. Gainesville: University Press of Florida.

———. 2012. "Religious Heterodoxy and the Orthodoxy of Death." Paper presented at the annual meeting of the Caribbean Studies Association, Guadeloupe, May 31.

Meeks, Brian. 1999. "NUFF at the Cusp of an Idea: Grassroots Guerrillas and the Politics of the 1970s in Trinidad and Tobago." *Social Identities* 5 (4): 415–39.

Mehta, Brinda. 2004. "Kali, Gangamai, and Dougla Consciousness in Moses Nagamootoo's *Hendree's Cure*." *Callaloo* 27 (2): 542–60.

Meudec, Marie. 2017. "Ordinary Ethics of Spiritual Work and Healing in St. Lucia, or Why Not to Use the Term *Obeah*." *Small Axe: A Caribbean Journal of Criticism* 21 (1, 52): 17–32.

Meyer, Birgit. 1999. *Translating the Devil: Religion and Modernity Among the Ewe in Ghana*. Edinburgh: Edinburgh University Press.

———. 2015. "How Pictures Matter: Religious Objects and Imagination in Ghana." In *Objects and Imagination: Perspectives on Materialization and Meaning*, edited by Øivind Fuglerud and Leon Wainwright, 160–86. New York: Berghahn.

Mintz, Sidney. 1966. "The Caribbean as a Socio-Cultural Area." *Cahiers d'histoire mondiale* 9: 912–37.

————. 1985. *Sweetness and Power: The Place of Sugar in Modern History*. New York: Penguin Books.

————. (1974) 1989. *Caribbean Transformations*. New York: Columbia University Press.

Mintz, Sidney, and Richard Price. (1976) 1992. *The Birth of African-American Culture: An Anthropological Perspective*. Boston: Beacon Press.

Mintz, Sidney, and Michel-Rolph Trouillot. 1995. "The Social History of Haitian Vodou." In *Sacred Arts of Haitian Vodou*, edited by Donald Consentino, 123–47. Los Angeles: UCLA Fowler Museum.

Mittermaier, Amira. 2010. *Dreams that Matter: Egyptian Landscapes of the Imagination*. Berkeley: University of California Press.

Mohammed, Patricia, dir. 2009. *Coolie Pink and Green*. Port of Spain: Trinidad and Tobago Film Co.

Morgan, David, ed. 2010. *Religion and Material Culture: The Matter of Belief*. New York: Routledge.

Morsi, Yassir. 2017. *Radical Skin, Moderate Masks: De-radicalising the Muslim and Racism in Post-racial Societies*. London: Rowman and Littlefield.

Mudimbe, V. Y. 1985. "African Gnosis Philosophy and the Order of Knowledge: An Introduction." *African Studies Review* 28 (2–3): 149–233.

Munasinghe, Viranjini. 1997. "Culture Creators and Culture Bearers: The Interface between Race and Ethnicity in Trinidad." *Transforming Anthropology* 6 (1–2): 72–86.

————. 2001. *Callaloo or Tossed Salad? East Indians and the Cultural Politics of Identity in Trinidad*. Ithaca, NY: Cornell University Press.

Murison, Justine. 2015. "Obeah and Its Others: Buffered Selves in the Era of Tropical Medicine." *Atlantic Studies* 12 (2): 144–59.

Naipaul, V. S. 1962. *The Middle Passage: The Caribbean Revisited*. New York: Macmillan.

Nelson, Diane M. 2003. "A Social Science Fiction of Fevers, Delirium and Discovery: the 'Calcutta Chromosome,' the Colonial Laboratory, and the Postcolonial New Human." *Science Fiction Studies* 30 (2): 246–66.

Niehoff, Arthur, and Juanita Niehoff. 1960. *East Indians in the West Indies*. Milwaukee, WI: Milwaukee Public Museum.

Noakes, Richard. 2019. *Physics and Psychics: The Occult and the Sciences in Modern Britain*. Cambridge: Cambridge University Press.

Numbers, Ronald L. 2010. Introduction to *Galileo Goes to Jail and Other Myths about Science and Religion*, edited by Ronald L. Numbers, 1–7. Cambridge, MA: Harvard University Press.

Nyman, Michael. 1999. *Experimental Music: Cage and Beyond*. Cambridge: Cambridge University Press.

Ochoa, Todd Ramón. 2010a. "Prendas-Ngangas-Enquisos: Turbulence and the Influence of the Dead in Cuban Kongo Material Culture." *Cultural Anthropology* 25 (3): 387–420.

————. 2010b. *Society of the Dead: Quita Manaquita and Palo Praise in Cuba*. Berkeley: University of California Press.

Ogunnaike, Ayodeji. 2013. "The Myth of Purity." *Harvard Divinity Bulletin* 41 (3–4). https://bulletin.hds.harvard.edu/articles/summerautumn2013/myth-purity.

Olmos, Margarite Fernández, and Lizabeth Paravisini-Gebert, eds. 2000. *Sacred Posses-*

298   REFERENCES

sions: *Vodou, Santería, Obeah, and the Caribbean.* 3rd ed. New Brunswick: Rutgers University Press.

———. 2011. *Creole Religions of the Caribbean: An Introduction from Vodou and Santería to Obeah and Espiritismo.* New York: New York University Press.

Olupona, Jacob K., and Sulayman S. Nyang, eds. 1993. *Religious Plurality in Africa: Essays in Honour of John S. Mbiti.* Berlin: DeGruyter.

O'Neill, Kevin. 2015. *Secure the Soul: Christian Piety and Gang Prevention in Guatemala.* Berkeley: University of California Press.

Ong, Aihwa. 2010. *Spirits of Resistance and Capitalist Discipline: Factory Women in Malaysia.* Albany: SUNY Press.

"Online Readers Outraged over Banfield's Death." 2016. *Trinidad Express, Multimedia Desk,* December 8. https://www.trinidadexpress.com/20161208/news/online-readers-outraged-over-banfields-death/.

Orsi, Robert. 2006. "Snakes Alive: Religious Studies Between Heaven and Earth." In *Between Heaven and Earth: The Religious Worlds People Make and the Scholars Who Study Them,* 177–239. Princeton, NJ: Princeton University Press.

Ortner, Sherry B. 2016. "Dark Anthropology and Its Others: Theory since the Eighties." *HAU: Journal of Ethnographic Theory* 6 (1): 47–73.

Otto, Bernd-Christian, and Michael Stausberg, eds. 2014. *Defining Magic: A Reader.* New York: Routledge.

Pagnucco, Ron. 1996. "A Comparison of the Political Behavior of Faith-Based and Secular Peace Groups" In *Disruptive Religion: The Force of Faith in Social Movement Activism,* edited by Christian Smith, 205–22. New York: Routledge.

Palmié, Stephan. 2002. *Wizards and Scientists Explorations in Afro-Cuban Modernity and Tradition.* Durham, NC: Duke University Press.

———. 2013. *The Cooking of History: How Not to Study Afro-Cuban Religion.* Chicago: University of Chicago Press.

Parés, Luis Nicolau, and Roger Sansi, eds. 2011. *Sorcery in the Black Atlantic.* Chicago: University of Chicago Press.

Parry, Jonathan. 2004. "Sacrificial Death and the Necrophagous Ascetic." In *Death, Mourning, and Burial: A Cross-Cultural Reader,* edited by Antonius Robben, 265–84. Oxford: Blackwell.

Paton, Diana. 2004. *No Bond but the Law: Punishment, Race, and Gender in Jamaican State Formation, 1780–1870.* Durham, NC: Duke University Press.

———. 2009. "Obeah Acts: Producing and Policing the Boundaries of Religion in the Caribbean." *Small Axe* 13 (1): 1–18.

———. 2012. "Witchcraft, Poison, Law, and Atlantic Slavery." *William and Mary Quarterly* 69 (2): 235–64.

———. 2015. *The Cultural Politics of Obeah.* Cambridge: Cambridge University Press.

Paton, Diana, and Maarit Forde. 2012. Introduction to *Obeah and Other Powers: The Politics of Caribbean Religion and Healing,* edited by Diana Paton and Maarit Forde, 1–44. Durham, NC: Duke University Press.

Pearse, Andrew. n.d. Andrew Pearse Collection. West Indiana Library, St. Augustine, Trinidad and Tobago.

Pérez, Elizabeth. 2016. *Religion in the Kitchen: Cooking, Talking, and the Making of Black Atlantic Traditions*. New York: New York University Press.

Phan, Peter C., and Douglas Irvin-Erickson, eds. 2016. *Violence, Religion, Peacemaking*. New York: Palgrave Macmillan.

"Police Involved in Witchcraft." 2018. *Daily Observer* (Antigua), May 15. https://antiguaobserver.com/police-involved-in-witchcraft/.

Poppi, Cesare. 2011. "The Hunted and the Haunted: Death, Exchange, and Spirits in Northwest Ghana." *L'Uomo* 1–2: 27–56.

Povinelli, Elizabeth. 2002. *The Cunning of Recognition: Indigenous Alterities and the Making of Australian Multiculturalism*. Durham, NC: Duke University Press.

———. 2006. *The Empire of Love: Toward a Theory of Intimacy, Genealogy, and Carnality*. Durham, NC: Duke University Press.

———. 2008. "The Child in the Broom Closet: States of Killing and Letting Die." *South Atlantic Quarterly* 107 (3): 509–30.

———. 2009. "Beyond Good and Evil, Whither Liberal Sacrificial Love?" *Public Culture* 21 (1): 77–100.

———. 2011. *Economies of Abandonment: Social Belonging and Endurance in Late Liberalism*. Durham, NC: Duke University Press.

———. 2016. *Geontologies: A Requiem to Late Liberalism*. Durham, NC: Duke University Press.

Prakash, Gyan. 1997. "The Modern Nation's Return in the Archaic." *Critical Inquiry* 23 (3): 536–56.

———. 1999. *Another Reason: Science and the Imagination of Modern India*. Princeton, NJ: Princeton University Press.

———. 2003. "Between Science and Superstition: Religion and the Modern Subject of the Nation in Colonial India." In *Magic and Modernity: Interfaces of Revelation and Concealment*, edited by Birgit Meyer and Peter Pels, 39–59. Stanford, CA: Stanford University Press.

Prashad, Vijay. 2001. *Everybody Was Kung-Fu Fighting: Afro-Asian Connections and the Myth of Cultural Purity*. Boston: Beacon Press.

Pravaz, Natasha. 2012. "Performing Mulata-ness: The Politics of Cultural Authenticity and Sexuality among Carioca Samba Dancers." *Latin American Perspectives* 39 (2): 113–33.

Puri, Shalini. 1997. "Race, Rape and Representation: Indo-Caribbean Women and Cultural Nationalism." *Cultural Critique* 36: 119–63.

———. 2004. *The Caribbean Postcolonial: Social Equality, Post-Nationalism, and Cultural Hybridity*. New York: Palgrave Macmillan.

Putnam, Hilary. 1990. "Realism with a Human Face." In *Realism with a Human Face*, edited by James Conant, 3–29. Cambridge, MA: Harvard University Press.

Putnam, Lara. 2012. "Rites of Power and Rumors of Race: The Circulation of Supernatural Knowledge in the Greater Caribbean, 1890–1940." In *Obeah and Other Powers: The Politics of Caribbean Religion and Healing*, edited by Diana Paton and Maarit Forde, 243–67. Durham, NC: Duke University Press.

———. 2013. *Radical Moves: Caribbean Migrants and the Politics of Race in the Jazz Age*. Chapel Hill: University of North Carolina Press.

Ramdass, Anna. 2018. "Bring Out the Soldiers." *Trinidad and Tobago Express*, May 22.

Rampersad, Sharlene. 2018. "Mom: Cop Was Trigger-Happy, Bipolar Man Shot Dead." *Trinidad and Tobago Newsday*, April 5.

Ramsaran, Dave. 2013. "The Myth of Development: The Case of Trinidad and Tobago." In *Caribbean Sovereignty, Development and Democracy in an Age of Globalization*, edited by Linden Lewis, 115–37. New York: Routledge.

Reddock, Rhoda. 1998. "Contestations over Culture, Class, Gender and Identity in Trinidad and Tobago: 'The Little Tradition.'" *Caribbean Quarterly* 44 (1–2): 62–80.

———. 1999. "Jahaji Bhai: The Emergence of a Dougla Poetics in Trinidad and Tobago." *Identities: Global Studies in Culture and Power* 5 (4): 569–601.

Report of the Lords of the Committee of the Council appointed for the consideration of all matters relating to Trade and Foreign Plantation, Part 3: Treatment of slaves in the West Indies, and all circumstances relating thereto, digested under certain heads, Part III. 1789. London. https://babel.hathitrust.org/cgi/pt?id=mdp.39015084394389;view=1up;seq=4.

Reynolds, Andrew. 2009. *Anglo-Saxon Deviant Burial Customs*. Oxford: Oxford University Press.

Ritchie, Susan J. 2002. "Contesting Secularism: Reflexive Methodology, Belief Studies, and Disciplined Knowledge." *Journal of American Folklore* 115: 443–56.

Robbins, Joel. 2004. *Becoming Sinners Christianity and Moral Torment in a Papua New Guinea Society*. Berkeley: University of California Press.

———. 2007. "Between Reproduction and Freedom: Morality, Value, and Radical Cultural Change. *Ethnos* 72 (3): 293–314.

———. 2013. "Beyond the Suffering Subject: Toward an Anthropology of the Good." *Journal of the Royal Anthropological Institute* 19 (3): 447–62.

Rocklin, Alexander. 2012. "Imagining Religions in a Trinidad Village: The Africanity of the Spiritual Baptist Movement and the Politics of Comparing Religions." *New West Indian Guide* 86 (1–2): 55–79.

———. 2013a. "Haunting Violence: Obeah and the Management of the Living and the Dead in Colonial Trinidad." *Religion and Culture Forum*, November 25. https://divinity.uchicago.edu/sites/default/files/imce/pdfs/webforum/112013/Rocklin%20Haunting%20Violence%20Final%202.pdf.

———. 2013b. "Obeah, Spirits, and the Politics of Religion's Making and Unmaking in Colonial Trinidad." Paper presented at the annual meeting of the Caribbean Studies Association, Grenada, June 5.

———. 2015. "Obeah and the Politics of Religion's Making and Unmaking in Colonial Trinidad." *Journal of the American Academy of Religion* 83 (3): 697–721.

———. 2016. "'A Hindu Is White Although He Is Black': Hindu Alterity and the Performativity of Religion and Race between the United States and the Caribbean." *Comparative Studies in Society and History* 58 (1): 181–210.

———. 2019. *The Regulation of Religion and the Making of Hinduism in Colonial Trinidad*. Chapel Hill: University of North Carolina Press.

———. Forthcoming. *Becoming Hindu: The Imposture of Religion and the Power of India in the Atlantic World*.

Roeder, Ellen. 2019. "Postponing Judgment Day: The Politics of Spiritual Warfare in Rio de Janeiro." MA thesis, Teresa Lozano Long Institute for Latin American Studies, University of Texas at Austin.

Romberg, Raquel. 2003. *Witchcraft and Welfare: Spiritual Capital and the Business of Magic in Modern Puerto Rico.* Austin: University of Texas Press.

Ryan, Selwyn. 1999. *The Jhandi and the Cross: The Clash of Cultures in Post-Creole Trinidad and Tobago.* St. Augustine, Trinidad and Tobago: Sir Arthur Lewis Institute of Social and Economic Research.

Samad, Ishmael. 2011. *"Oh Gord! Doh Shoot Meh Nah!" The Tragedy of Extrajudicial Killings in Trinidad and Tobago.* Bloomington, IN: AuthorHouse.

Sanderson, Stephen K. 2018. *Religious Evolution and the Axial Age: From Shamans to Priests to Prophets.* New York: Bloomsbury Publishing.

Sankeralli, Burton. 2008. *Of Obeah and Modernity.* Barataria, Trinidad: Philosophical Society of Trinidad and Tobago.

———. 2010. "Implementing Obeah." Studio 66, Barataria, Trinidad and Tobago. December 3.

Sarat, Austin, and Thomas R. Kearns, eds. 1993. *Law's Violence.* Ann Arbor: University of Michigan Press.

Schmidt, Leigh Eric. 2012. *Restless Souls: The Making of American Spirituality.* 2nd ed. Berkeley: University of California Press.

Schmitt, Carl. 1985. *Political Theology: Four Chapters on the Concept of Sovereignty.* Chicago: University of Chicago Press.

Schuppe, Jon. 2015. "George Zimmerman Blames Obama for Inciting Racial Tension." March 24. MSNBC. http://www.msnbc.com/msnbc/george-zimmerman-blames-obama-racial-tension.

Scott, David. 1991. "That Event, This Memory: Notes on the Anthropology of African Diasporas in the New World." *Diaspora* 1 (3): 261–84.

———. 1997. "The 'Culture of Violence' Fallacy." *Small Axe* 2: 140–47.

———. 1999. *Refashioning Futures: Criticism After Postcoloniality.* Princeton, NJ: Princeton University Press.

———. 2004. *Conscripts of Modernity: The Tragedy of Colonial Enlightenment.* Durham, NC: Duke University Press.

Scott, Garvin. 1986. *Scott Drug Report with all Names Called: Report of Commission of Enquiry into the Extent of the Problem of Drug Abuse in Trinidad and Tobago.* Pleasantville, Trinidad and Tobago: Unique Services.

Seaby, Graham. 1993. *Final Report for the Government of Trinidad and Tobago on Investigations Carried Out by the New Scotland Yard in Respect of Allegations Made by Rodwell Murray and Others About Corruption in the Trinidad and Tobago Police Service.* London: Metropolitan Police Office.

Seales, Chad E. 2013. *The Secular Spectacle: Performing Religion in a Southern Town.* New York: Oxford University Press.

Seelal, Nalinee. 2018a. "Bloodiest Month Ever—Murder Toll at 60." *Trinidad and Tobago Newsday,* January 31. https://newsday.co.tt/2018/01/31/bloodiest-month-ever-murder-toll-at-60/.

————. 2018b. "Sorry for Shooting You: Cop Regrets Gun Battle over Woman." *Trinidad and Tobago Newsday*, May 4. https://newsday.co.tt/2018/05/04/sorry-forshooting-you/.

Segal, Daniel. 1993. "'Race' and 'Colour' in Pre-Independence Trinidad and Tobago." In *Trinidad Ethnicity*, edited by Kevin Yelvington, 81–115. Knoxville: University of Tennessee Press.

Sehat, David. 2011. *The Myth of American Religious Freedom*. New York: Oxford University Press.

Seligman, Adam, Robert Weller, Michael Puett, and Bennet Simon. 2008. *Ritual and Its Consequences: An Essay on the Limits of Sincerity*. Oxford: Oxford University Press.

Seng-Guan, Yeoh. 2016. "Religious Praxis, Modernity and Non-modernity in Kuala Lumpur, Malaysia." In *Religion, Place and Modernity*, edited by Michael Dickhardt and Andrea Lauser, 184–204. Leiden: Brill.

Shapin, Steven. 1996. *The Scientific Revolution*. Chicago: University of Chicago Press.

Shapin, Steven, and Simon Schaffer. 1985. *Leviathan and the Air-Pump: Hobbes, Boyle, and the Experimental Life*. Princeton, NJ: Princeton University Press.

Shaw, Rosalind. 1990. "The Invention of 'African Traditional Religion.'" *Religion* 20 (4): 339–53.

————. 2007. "Displacing Violence: Making Pentecostal Memory in Postwar Sierra Leone." *Cultural Anthropology* 22 (1): 66–93.

Shaw, Rosalind, and Charles Stewart, eds. 1994. *Syncretism/Anti-Syncretism: The Politics of Religious Synthesis*. London: Routledge.

Shweder, Richard A. 2016. "Channeling the Super-Natural Aspects of the Ethical Life." *HAU: Journal of Ethnographic Theory* 6 (1): 477–83.

Sidnell, Jack, Marie Meudec, and Michael Lambek. 2019. "Introduction: Ethical Immanence." *Anthropological Theory* 19 (3): 303–22.

Silk, Mark. 1984. "Notes on the Judeo-Christian Tradition in America." *American Quarterly* 36 (1): 65–85.

Simpson, George Eaton. 1966. "Baptismal, 'Mourning,' and 'Building' Ceremonies of the Shouters in Trinidad." *Journal of American Folklore* 79 (314): 537–50.

————. 1970. *Religious Cults of the Caribbean: Trinidad, Jamaica, and Haiti*. Rio Piedras: Institute for Caribbean Studies, University of Puerto Rico.

Singh, Bhrigupati. 2012. "The Headless Horseman of Central India: Sovereignty at Varying Thresholds of Life." *Cultural Anthropology* 27 (2): 383–407.

Skurski, Julie. 2007. "Reviewed Work: *Wizards and Scientists: Explorations in Afro-Cuban Modernity and Tradition* by Stephan Palmié." *New West Indian Guide* 81 (1–2): 103–5.

Smidt, Wolbert. 2004. "Fetishists and Magicians—The Description of African Religions by Immanuel Kant (1724–1804)." In *European Traditions in the Study of Religion in Africa*, edited by Frieder Ludwig and Afe Adogame, 109–15. Wiesbaden: Otto Harrassowitz Verlag.

Smith, Christen A. 2016. *Afro-Paradise: Blackness, Violence, and Performance in Brazil*. Urbana: University of Illinois Press.

Smith, Jonathan Z. 1980. "The Bare Facts of Ritual." *History of Religions* 20 (1–2): 112–27.

————. 1993. *Map Is Not Territory: Studies in the History of Religions*. Chicago: University of Chicago Press.

Smith, Ted A. 2014. *Weird John Brown: Divine Violence and the Limits of Ethics*. Stanford, CA: Stanford University Press.

Smith, Theophus. 1994. *Conjuring Culture: Biblical Formations of Black America*. New York: Oxford University Press.

Sørensen, Jesper. 2014. "Magic Reconsidered: Towards a Scientifically Valid Concept of Magic." In *Defining Magic: A Reader*, edited by Bernd-Christian Otto and Michael Stausberg, 229–42. New York: Routledge.

Spencer, Paul. 1988. *The Maasai of Matapato: A Study of Rituals of Rebellion*. Manchester: Manchester University Press.

Spinoza, Baruch. (1677) 2001. *Theological-Political Treatise*. Translated by S. Shirley. Indianapolis, IN: Hackett Publishing.

Srinivas, M. N. (1952) 1965. *Religion and Society among the Coorgs of South India*. Bombay: Asia Publishing House.

Standem, Mekelu Kanta. 2013. *The Demonization of the Republic of Trinidad and Tobago — The Satanic Verses*. Bloomington, IN: iUniverse.

Starr, Bradley. 1999. "The Structure of Max Weber's Ethic of Responsibility." *Journal of Religious Ethics* 27 (3): 407–34.

Stasch, Rupert. 2009. *Society of Others: Kinship and Mourning in a West Papuan Place*. Berkeley: University of California Press.

Stengers, Isabelle. 2000. *The Invention of Modern Science*. Minneapolis: University of Minnesota Press.

————. 2012. "Reclaiming Animism." *e-flux* 36. https://www.e-flux.com/journal/36/61245/reclaiming-animism/.

Stephens, Patricia. 1999. *The Spiritual Baptist Faith: African New World Religious History, Identity, and Testimony*. London: Karnak House.

Stewart, Dianne. 2005. *Three Eyes for the Journey: African Dimensions of the Jamaican Religious Experience*. New York: Oxford University Press.

Stewart, Dianne, and Tracey E. Hucks. 2013. "Africana Religious Studies: Toward a Transdisciplinary Agenda in an Emerging Field." *Journal of Africana Religions* 1 (1): 28–77.

Stolow, Jeremy. 2008. "Salvation by Electricity." In *Religion: Beyond a Concept*, edited by Hent de Vries, 668–87. New York: Fordham University Press.

————. 2013. "The Spiritual Nervous System." In *Deus in Machina: Religion, Technology and the Things in Between*, edited by Jeremy Stolow, 83–116. New York: Fordham University Press.

Strathern, Marilyn. 2004. *Partial Connections*. 2nd ed. New York: AltaMira.

Stroumsa, Guy G. 2009. *The End of Sacrifice: Religious Transformations in Late Antiquity*. Chicago: University of Chicago Press.

Styers, Randall. 2004. *Making Magic: Religion, Magic, and Science in the Modern World*. Oxford: Oxford University Press.

Sulaiman, Mohammed. 2019. "Orientalism and Anti-Orientalism: Epistemological Approaches to Islam and Violence." In *Contesting the Theological Foundations of Islamism and Violent Extremism*, edited by Fethi Mansouri and Zulehya Keskin, 75–95. London: Palgrave Macmillan.

Sullivan, Kathleen M. 1992. "Religion and Liberal Democracy." *University of Chicago Law Review* 59: 195–223.

Sullivan, Winnifred. 2005. *The Impossibility of Religious Freedom*. Princeton, NJ: Princeton University Press.

Superville, Shane. 2018. "Obeah outside PoS Magistrates Court." *Trinidad and Tobago Newsday*, October 8.

Sutherland, Gail. 1991. *The Disguises of the Demon: The Development of the Yaksa in Hinduism and Buddhism*. Albany: State University of New York Press.

Szwed, John. 2006. *Crossovers: Essays on Race, Music, and American Culture*. Philadelphia: University of Pennsylvania Press.

Tagliabue, John. 2002. "Pope, at Ecumenical Meeting, Denounces Violence in Religion's Name." *New York Times*, January 25.

Tambiah, Stanley Jeyaraja. 1990. *Magic, Science, Religion, and the Scope of Rationality*. Cambridge: Cambridge University Press.

"T&T Police Appeal for Help as Country Records Bloodiest January in History." 2018. *Jamaica Observer*, January 30. http://www.jamaicaobserver.com/latestnews/T%26T_police_appeal_for_help_as_country_records_bloodiest_January_in_history?profile=1228.

Tanikella, Leela. 2003. "The Politics of Hybridity: Race, Gender, and Nationalism in Trinidad." *Cultural Dynamics* 15 (2): 153–81.

Taylor, Charles. 2007. *A Secular Age*. Cambridge, MA: Harvard University Press.

Téllez, Dora María. 1999. *¡Muera la gobierna! Colonización en Matagalpa y Jinotega, 1820–1890*. Managua: Universidad de las Regiones Autónomas de la Costa Caribe Nicaragüense.

Tepfer, Daniel. 2016. "Cops Arrest Santeria 'Priest' with Human Bones." *MySanAntonio (TX)*, February 3. https://www.mysanantonio.com/news/article/Cops-arrest-Santeria-priest-with-human-bones-6802798.php?cmpid=email-desktop.

Thomas, Deborah A. 2011. *Exceptional Violence: Embodied Citizenship in Transnational Jamaica*. Durham, NC: Duke University Press.

———. 2013. "Sovereignty/Intimacy: Political Openings in Contemporary Jamaica." In *Caribbean Sovereignty, Development and Democracy in an Age of Globalization*, edited by Linden Lewis, 165–88. New York: Routledge.

Thomas, Dexter. 2014. "Michael Brown Was Not a Boy, He Was a 'Demon.'" *Al Jazeera News*, November 26. https://www.aljazeera.com/indepth/opinion/2014/11/michael-brown-demon-ferguson-2014112672358760344.html.

Thornton, John. 1858. *A Gazetteer of the Territories under the Government of the East-India Company and of the Native States on the Continent of India*. London: W. H. Allen and Co.

Thorpe, Kimberly. 2009. "A Court Case Forced a Santeria Priest to Reveal Some of His Religion's Secrets: Its Ritual of Animal Sacrifice, He Revealed on His Own." *Dallas (TX) Observer*, October 22. http://www.dallasobserver.com/news/a-court-case-forced-a-santeria-priest-to-reveal-some-of-his-religions-secrets-its-ritual-of-animal-sacrifice-he-revealed-on-his-own-6406316.

"Three Cops Charged with Assault, Kidnapping." 2018. *Trinidad Guardian*, April 17.

Tremlin, Todd. 2010. *Minds and Gods: The Cognitive Foundations of Religion*. Oxford: Oxford University Press.

Trotman, David. 1986. *Crime in Trinidad: Conflict and Control in a Plantation Society, 1838–1900*. Knoxville, TN: University of Tennessee Press.

———. 1991. "The Image of Indians in Calypso: Trinidad, 1946–1986." In *Social and Occupational Stratification in Trinidad and Tobago*, edited by Selwyn Ryan, 385–98. St. Augustine, Trinidad: ISER.

———. 2007. "Reflections on the Children of Shango: An Essay on a History of Orisa Worship in Trinidad." *Slavery and Abolition* 28 (2): 211–34.

Trouillot, Michel-Rolph. 2002. "North Atlantic Universals: Analytical Fictions, 1942–1945." *South Atlantic Quarterly* 101 (4): 839–58.

———. 2003. *Global Transformations: Anthropology and the Modern World*. New York: Palgrave Macmillan.

Tsing, Anna. 2004. *Friction: An Ethnography of Global Connection*. Princeton, NJ: Princeton University Press.

———. 2015. *The Mushroom at the End of the World: On the Possibility of Life in Capitalist Ruins*. Princeton, NJ: Princeton University Press.

Turner, Victor. (1969) 2017. *The Ritual Process: Structure and Anti-Structure*. New York: Routledge.

———. 1974. "Liminal to Liminoid, in Play, Flow, and Ritual: An Essay in Comparative Symbology." *Rice Institute Pamphlet — Rice University Studies* 60 (3): 53–92. http://hdl.handle.net/1911/63159.

Tweed, Thomas A. 2006. *Crossing and Dwelling: A Theory of Religion*. Cambridge, MA: Harvard University Press.

Tylor, Edward Burnett. 1871. *Primitive Culture: Researches into the Development of Mythology, Philosophy, Religion, Art, and Custom*. London: J. Murray.

Ullucci, Daniel. 2011. *The Christian Rejection of Animal Sacrifice*. Oxford: Oxford University Press.

Umeh, John Anenechukwu. 1997. *After God Is Dibia: Igbo Cosmology, Divination and Sacred Science in Nigeria*. London: Karnak House.

United Nations. 2001. "Comments by the Government of Trinidad and Tobago on the Concluding Observations of the Human Rights Committee." U.N. Doc. CCPR/CO/70/TTO/Add.1.

Van Bladel, Kevin. 2009. *The Arabic Hermes: From Pagan Sage to Prophet of Science*. Oxford: Oxford University Press.

Van der Veer, Peter, and Steven Vertovec. 1991. "Brahmanism Abroad: On Caribbean Hinduism as an Ethnic Religion." *Ethnology* 30 (2): 149–66.

Van Woerkens, Martine. 2002. *The Strangled Traveler: Colonial Imaginings and the Thugs of India*. Chicago: University of Chicago Press.

Vásquez, Manuel. 2011. *More Than Belief: A Materialist Theory of Religion*. New York: Oxford Press.

Verran, Helen. 2001. *Science and an African Logic*. Chicago: University of Chicago Press.

Vertovec, Steven. 1993. "Hindu Mother Goddess Cults in the Caribbean." *Etnolog* 3 (54): 179–94.

———. 1998. "Ethnic Distance and Religious Convergence: Shango, Spiritual Baptist, and Kali Mai Traditions in Trinidad." *Social Compass* 45 (2): 247–63.

Vogler, Candace A., and Patchen Markell. 2003. "Introduction: Violence, Redemption, and the Liberal Imagination." *Public Culture* 15 (1): 1–10.

Walker, Daniel E. 2004. *No More, No More: Slavery and Cultural Resistance in Havana and New Orleans*. Minneapolis: University of Minnesota Press.

Warner-Lewis, Maureen. 1996. *Trinidad Yoruba: From Mother Tongue to Memory*. Tuscaloosa: University of Alabama Press.

Weber, Max. 1948. *From Max Weber*. Edited and translated by H. H. Gerth and C. Wright Mills. London: Routledge and Kegan Paul.

———. (1919) 2009. "Politics as a Vocation." In *From Max Weber: Essays in Sociology*, edited and translated by H. H. Gerth and C. Wright Mills, 77–128. New York: Routledge.

Weisenfeld, Judith. 2007. *Hollywood Be Thy Name: African American Religion in American Film, 1929–1949*. Oakland: University of California Press.

Welcome, Leniqueca. 2018. "Viewing Bodies: Violent Feeling to Un-Feel Violence within Trinidad." Paper presented at Caribbean Studies Association Meetings, Havana, Cuba.

West, Harry. 2005. *Kupilikula: Governance and the Invisible Realm in Mozambique*. Chicago: University of Chicago Press.

———. 2007. *Ethnographic Sorcery*. Chicago: University of Chicago Press.

Weszkalnys, Gisa. 2015. "Geology, Potentiality, Speculation: On the Indeterminacy of First Oil." *Cultural Anthropology* 30 (4): 611–39. https://doi.org/10.14506/ca30.4.08.

Williams, Eric. 1944. *Capitalism and Slavery*. Chapel Hill: University of North Carolina Press.

Williams, Joseph John. 1933. *Voodoos and Obeahs*. London: Allen & Unwin.

Williams, Raymond. 1973. *The Country and the City*. New York: Oxford University Press.

———. 1983. *Keywords: A Vocabulary of Culture and Society*. Rev. ed. New York: Oxford University Press.

Wilson, Peter. 1973. *Crab Antics: The Social Anthropology of English Speaking Negro Societies of the Caribbean*. New Haven, CT: Yale University Press.

Wilson, Sascha. 2018. "$250,000 Award for SoE arrest." *Trinidad and Tobago Guardian*, July 31. http://www.guardian.co.tt/news/2018-07-30/250000-award-soe-arrest.

Winch, Peter. 1964. "Understanding a Primitive Society." *American Philosophical Quarterly* 1: 307–24.

Winer, Lise, ed. 2009. *Dictionary of the English/Creole of Trinidad & Tobago: On Historical Principles*. Montreal: McGill-Queen's University Press.

Winslade, William J. 1971. "Adjudication and the Balancing Metaphor." *Logique et analyse* 14 (53–54): 403–7.

Wiredu, John. 1979. "How Not to Compare African Thought with Western Thought." In *African Philosophy*, edited by Richard A. Wright, 149–62. Washington, DC: University Press of America.

Wolf, Eric. 1982. *Europe and the People without History*. Berkeley: University of California Press.

Yates, Frances A. 1964. *Giordano Bruno and the Hermetic Tradition*. Chicago: University of Chicago Press.

———. (1972) 2013. *Rosicrucian Enlightenment*. New York: Routledge.

Yelle, Robert. 2010. "The Trouble with Transcendence: Carl Schmitt's 'Exception' as a Challenge for Religious Studies." *Method & Theory in the Study of Religion* 22 (2–3): 189–206.

Young, Robert. 1995. *Colonial Desire: Hybridity in Theory, Culture and Race*. London: Routledge.

Yousif, Adeeb. 2016. "Political Islam and the Darfur Conflict: Religious Violence and the Interreligious Potential for Peace in Sudan." In *Violence, Religion, Peacemaking*, edited by Douglas Irvin-Erickson and Peter C. Phan, 137–53. New York: Palgrave Macmillan.

Zane, Wallace. 1999. *Journeys to the Spiritual Lands: The Natural History of a West Indian Religion*. New York: Oxford University Press.

Ziarek, Ewa Płonowska. 1995. *The Rhetoric of Failure: Deconstruction of Skepticism, Reinvention of Modernism*. Albany: State University of New York Press.

INDEX

Entries with an asterisk denote pseudonyms to protect privacy.